T0281835

THE FIRST
CELEBRITIES

THE FIRST CELEBRITIES

FIVE REGENCY PORTRAITS

PETER JAMES BOWMAN

AMBERLEY

Jacket illustration: Front: Lady Charlotte Campbell. Oil on canvas by John Hoppner. By kind permission of the Duke of Argyll. Photograph by Nick McCann Associates. *Back:* 'Frontispiece to the Illustrations to Almack's'. Caricature by Henry Heath.

First published 2023

Amberley Publishing
The Hill, Stroud
Gloucestershire, GL5 4EP

www.amberley-books.com

British Library Cataloguing in Publication Data.
A catalogue record for this book is available from the British Library.

ISBN 978 1 4456 7789 7 (hardback)
ISBN 978 1 4456 7790 3 (ebook)

1 2 3 4 5 6 7 8 9 10

Typesetting by SJmagic DESIGN SERVICES, India.
Printed in the UK.

Contents

Acknowledgements

The 'Context' section of this book draws on studies of celebrity and its history for general questions and on primary and secondary biographical material for individual cases. Celebrity is a well-researched field, and the notes and bibliography should give an idea of the obligations I am under. The 'Portraits' section draws on three main types of sources: published diaries, letters and memoirs; manuscript letters and other documents; and newspapers. Access to the first was provided by the staff of the Cambridge University Library, and to the second by archivists in the UK, Germany and the USA. The tribulations of 2020 prevented me from consulting as much manuscript material for the chapter on Thomas Lawrence as I had wished, and I am all the more grateful to those archives that let me have copies that I could read at home.

The most important source is the third. Without digital archives of newspapers and their search facilities, this book would have been far harder to write. I mainly used the British Newspaper Archive, containing the British Library's newspaper collection. Two of my five celebrities have not been subjects of biographies, and even with the other three the ability to range easily over press coverage has made it possible to present new facets of their lives. References each time a newspaper is cited would have overburdened the notes, and I have omitted them since anyone wishing to follow up a citation can do so with a word, date and title search. It may also be worth mentioning that the journalistic practice two centuries ago of lifting chunks of text from other newspapers without attribution often makes it hard to know whether what is printed in one title found its way there from the columns of another. To avoid disfiguring the text, capitalised words in press articles are given in lower case.

Acknowledgements

My obligations in relation to images are set out in the captions. I would like particularly to thank Claude Piening for sending me a photograph of the portrait of Dorothea Lieven at the head of her chapter, sold by Sotheby's in 2004.

Non-standard spellings in quotes are neither corrected nor indicated.

CONTEXT

1

Celebrity Culture

A celebrity is a famous person. There is no denying the truth of this, but as a proposition it does not quite satisfy us. Of course celebrities are famous – we know their names, we talk about them – but are they really, properly famous? We would not call the most revered figures in a nation's history celebrities. Nor is it the case that celebrities are simply second-tier famous people. Rather they are different in kind; there is something about them, something a little tarnished perhaps, that may make us hesitate to admit being interested in them at all.

In trying to distinguish between celebrity and fame, let us start with the terms themselves. Meanings cannot be reduced to etymology, but origins are suggestive. The roots of 'celebrity' are the Latin *celebrare* ('to frequent'), *celeber* ('filled', 'crowded') *celebritas* ('a multitude') and *celebratio* ('a numerous assembly'), words that carry the extended sense of festivity, praise, proclamation. 'Fame' comes from *fama*, meaning 'talk' or 'what is said', and, referring to a person, 'repute' or 'standing'. Both derivations indicate a thing conferred by others rather than seized and owned by the individual. What is peculiar to celebrity is that the active participation of the crowd is required for it to exist at any given moment.

Turning to English usage, it is fair to say that as abstract nouns 'celebrity' and 'fame' have often been interchangeable. The first citation for 'celebrity' in the *Oxford English Dictionary* is from an article of 1751 by Samuel Johnson. In it he complains, 'I did not find myself yet enriched in proportion to my celebrity', and he could equally have written 'fame'. The same is true of the adjective 'celebrated', which is used in the titles of biographies written even earlier. Only in the first half of the nineteenth century, when 'celebrity' becomes a concrete noun, denoting something that one *is* rather than *has*, does any divergence occur. Since then it has become clear that celebrities enjoy one type of renown, but not the only one.

In seeking to define celebrity, cultural historians have contrasted it with a notion of fame that looks down from a plinth, toga-clad and wreathed in laurels. Fame is the reward for heroic deeds, courageous leadership, stoical self-sacrifice or transcendent genius in the service of a church, a monarch or a nation. It takes outstanding qualities, but once acquired it commands the homage of contemporaries and then secures immortality, a place in the pantheon. Later generations interpret it afresh, but this only renews its plenitude, never questions its validity. Celebrity, on the other hand, flares up in an instant, noisy and effulgent, its intensity heightened by the very ephemerality that condemns it to eternal silence and darkness once the excitement has died down. Its fuel is not greatness, but talent, glamour and novelty. And while fame wins reverence from passive spectators who accept it on its own terms, celebrity is subject to the 'multitude' who play a part in creating and then sustaining it.

Celebrity is, then, as its etymology suggests, transactional. It is shaped not just by an individual will, but also by the desires of the audience. The most engaged members of this audience are the 'fans', a term (derived from 'fanatic') that gained currency towards the end of the nineteenth century. Fans reel off facts and figures about the object of their admiration, engage with evaluations of her by others, spend time and money to enjoy her presence – or at least proximity – and make a public display of their devotion. But they are demanding too, wanting the celebrity to look and behave a certain way and provide inspiration. The celebrity is aware of fans' wishes and adjusts her demeanour in accordance with them, consciously and subconsciously, repeating the process later as these wishes evolve.

This interaction creates a focus on the celebrity as a person, to the point that this becomes more important than what she did to bring herself to notice in the first place. It is otherwise with a famous figure, who is esteemed for undertakings in the public sphere and whose private character is secondary. Celebrities are known for who they are, the famous for what they do or have done. But the strange thing about the audience's affective involvement with the celebrity is that they have next to no genuine contact with her. The relationship is indirect, mediated by the phalanx of managers, agents, publicists, photographers, personal assistants, make-up artists and so on who comprise what is called the celebrity industry. No celebrity can maintain a strong profile without these intermediaries, who supply the practical means for her to appear before an audience and ensure she does so in the most appealing way.

It is therefore a public face that fans experience, not a whole human being. But the aim of the celebrity industry, often very successfully prosecuted, is to make them feel that this is not the case. Fans enjoy the illusion that the celebrity is a real presence rather than a carefully contrived image, and that their relationship with her is a special, personal bond. Cosy autobiographies, carefully dosed revelations and records of private talk turn a stranger into a friend, almost an intimate. Opportunities to comment or orchestrate the comments of others on social media (or, more traditionally, to write fan letters) forge a further link, however tenuous it may appear to those who stand outside the relationship. Just as fans see in the celebrity what they wish to see, so their view of the footing they are on with her is based on what they wish to believe.

Fans conceive of their admiration for the celebrity as an act of interpretation, not a stance of meek wonderment. Odd behaviour, apparent character flaws or emotional struggles, supposedly candid photographs, and suspense as to what she will do or say next, all carefully deployed by the celebrity industry, prompt their urge to understand and sympathise with her. Often, individual fans will think they are the only ones sufficiently attentive and sensitive to fathom the hidden depths beneath the surface. The inescapable fact of the celebrity's physical inaccessibility only adds to this interpretative impulse. That someone who seems so near, saturating the fans' consciousness, is tantalisingly just out of reach, only sharpens their desire to know her better, to be the best readers of the story of her life. Making fans feel superior to other fans is part of the work of the celebrity industry.

The need to be close to the celebrity, to sense some degree of ownership of her, makes fans susceptible to the astute techniques by which she is promoted, especially the presentation of advertising as news, of publicity as independent journalism. Because the agents, managers and publicists responsible for the celebrity's public persona also control access to her, they have a strong leverage over the media, which publish what these controlling figures want and in the way they want it. Journalists selected for celebrity interviews may themselves have been interviewed to make sure they will be deferential, and editors submit copy for approval before it is printed. Light 'fluffy' pieces of gossip may even be collaborations between journalist and publicist. Similarly, talk-show interviews on television, billed as frank and revelatory, are choreographed image-control.

The celebrity industry is only successful if it stays behind the scenes. One way it conceals its operations is by giving all the credit for her success to the celebrity herself. The prominence she has gained is seen either as the result of unique gifts that inevitably propel her into the limelight, or as the prize of tireless endeavour and indomitable self-belief. Popular biographies present their subjects as having a magical aura and claim we will never see their like again, or make them heroes of morality tales of victory against naysayers and adverse circumstances. Such narratives are readily adopted by celebrities themselves, whose vanity they flatter, and by fans, who wish to justify an enthusiasm others might find puerile or demeaning. This is not to say that charisma or star quality, let alone single-mindedness, are fabrications, merely that the celebrity industry exaggerates their efficacy.

The objective of this industry is profit, and the celebrity is deployed to make as much as possible for as long as possible. Fans buy tickets for performances or sporting events and merchandise bearing the celebrity's name, from cheap trinkets to costly clothes and perfumes. TV companies, publishers and other print and online media make offerings of various sorts. To encourage fans to part with their money the physical divide between them and the celebrity is temporarily breached by staged encounters, which are memorable occasions for them but generic experiences for her. The most avid fans own a collection of texts and objects connected with the celebrity, and this deepens their sense of having a privileged comprehension of her, even though as mass-produced items they symbolise the distance they are designed to overcome.

Fans are thus consumers, and the celebrity, or rather her public face, is a good to be bought and sold. And, like articles associated with luxury or superior lifestyle, the celebrity is marketed as a brand. Because branded goods are often not essential to the basic comfort of consumers, they are turned into objects of desire. Consumers must be made to want to possess them as a way of flattering themselves, and they will only keep spending if they keep forming new desires. Goods are therefore tweaked, repackaged and newly marketed, and this brand innovation applies to the celebrity image too. Moreover, the value of the celebrity brand can be harnessed for the sale of other things. Celebrities endorse food, clothing and toiletries, make guest appearances on television shows, and grace the openings of entertainment and leisure venues. Actors are under contract to promote films they appear in by giving interviews and attending premieres, activities that also enhance their own visibility.

A portion of the profit from this work naturally accrues to the celebrity herself and constitutes an incentive for achieving public recognition in the first place. Even for minor and short-lived stars the financial rewards can be considerable, and for those of humble origins and few qualifications these dwarf the sums they might otherwise earn. The celebrity may additionally acquire influence in a particular field, giving her the gratification of being a role model or mentor to others. What is more, the currency of celebrity is convertible. As one career runs its course or grows too physically demanding, another opens up. Athletes become presenters and actors become politicians, transferring their skills of self-presentation and working an audience from one setting to another.

More compelling even than these attractions is a psychological need. Would-be celebrities experience the normal human desire for recognition and praise with such force that they are willing to live before the public in order to expand the number of people capable of appreciating them. They wish to be valued not just for what they have accomplished, but for themselves. Whereas traditional fame is incidental to greatness, the crown of an illustrious life, celebrity can be directly sought, and the activity that enables it is thus a means to an end. Indeed, those with the slenderest outward achievements may gain the greatest self-fulfilment from popularity since their innate worth seems to be confirmed by admiration they receive in their own right. Leaving behind lives of mundane obscurity, they both realise and transcend themselves; they escape from the crowd by winning the crowd's plaudits. And the fact that what is celebrated is a constructed image does not spoil their pleasure, for this image appears, at least initially, simply to be the best version of themselves.

There is, then, plenty for the celebrity to enjoy, and she can enjoy it for a long period if she conducts herself wisely and is well directed by her handlers, whose interests are of course served by her continuing appeal. Nonetheless, even the most level-headed celebrity benefiting from the best promotional strategy must pay a price for the sweets of success. Most obviously, she must sacrifice the comfort of keeping her private life completely private. With adroit management she may be able to maintain some sort of existence outside the public domain, but it will be confined and precarious. Nor is this merely an inconvenience to the celebrity and those closest to her. It can, in some cases, cause her very identity to become unstable because of a blurring of outward and private self. This process must be described if we are to understand fully how celebrity works.

What the audience respond to, as we have said, is the public image of the celebrity. This is a construct that derives substance from the real person yet differs from her. It is a simplified version, with contradictions and awkward inadequacies elided and other features accentuated so as to present a psychologically and socially coherent entity. The contours of this image are drawn by the celebrity and the celebrity industry, but no less by the gaze of the audience. While wishing to engage with her as an authentic, self-created person, the audience inevitably shape her through their desires and expectations. We all unwittingly see other people as fairly rounded and defined, granting confused open-endedness only to ourselves, and in the case of the celebrity this reductive view has a radical constitutive effect on her public persona.

Of course, much of the audience want to admire the celebrity and be inspired by her, but their fascination makes them eager to know her better and better. Once intrigued by an aspect of her life, they become assertive, even aggressive, in trying to find out more about it, and so she and those working with her have to feed them information that may not be the whole truth but cannot be entirely false either. This establishes a pattern of mutual manipulation. And although theories of celebrity culture sometimes treat audience and fan as interchangeable terms, many people follow the fortunes of a celebrity without being fans, just as many people follow individual sports without having a favourite player. Neutral or hostile audiences are even more likely to force the celebrity into justifications of herself, until her image gleams with the armour it needs to fend off criticism.

On first perceiving its emergence, the celebrity's attitude to her public image varies. With a degree of intellectual detachment she may cope quite well and play up to it with ease and even amusement. However, having sought celebrity as a form of self-validation, as a way of being cherished for her personal qualities, she may be disconcerted to find that what others see in her does not match what she sees herself. If she has opinions or values she wishes to advocate she will be frustrated to find the audience, partly primed by the industry, more interested in trivial details of her daily life, her family relationships or her taste in clothes. Worse, these questions encroach ever further into the territory usually designated as private. As time goes by, she may feel less and less like her public image, but also that the real self into which she can retreat dwindles. Meanwhile, to keep the show on the road, she must follow the script created for her.

As the literary historian Tom Mole puts it, 'The celebrity *individual* enters a feedback loop in which being a celebrity affects his or her self-understanding, so that neither self nor celebrity can be conceptually quarantined from the other.'[1] This presents a risk to the celebrity's psychological wellbeing. She finds it hard to be 'normal' with her family and friends, and cases of behavioural problems, addiction and even mental breakdown are well documented. It is almost as if self-alienation is a punishment for her ambition. Having coveted celebrity status as a means of transcendence, replacing an unfulfilling self with a brighter one that is closer to her idea of who she really is, she sees this improved version change into a caricature that slowly undermines the foundations of stable identity. Liberation becomes entrapment, and the public face turns round and begins to gnaw at the real person behind it.

Turning from the celebrity to the society she lives in, we find another mixed picture: on the one hand, celebrity culture brings advantages or is an indicator of desirable conditions; on the other, it distorts human emotions and degrades the social fabric. There has been a tendency among commentators of various political stripes in various forums to concentrate on the negative impact of this culture, to deplore its shallowness and insincerity. Academic teaching and research in the humanities have implicitly and sometimes explicitly defined themselves as a bulwark against it, as champions of a literary and artistic canon against the popular dross of the moment, turning the distinction between fame and celebrity into a hierarchy of artefacts. It is therefore salutary to begin a consideration of the social aspect of celebrity culture by looking on the bright side.

First, modern mass media can launch people of ordinary backgrounds to prominence, whereas in many societies for much of history the avenues to fame, especially political and military, have only been open to those of 'high' birth. Whatever else it is, celebrity culture is the enemy of entrenched privilege. Moreover, the success of a celebrity who is 'one of us' may inspire in others a hope to equal it, whereas the honours won by those of high rank seem impossibly remote. Indeed, the desire for the older form of fame, a place in a national pantheon, can now seem anachronistic. 'In the twenty-first century, the immortality of traditional fame has taken a back seat to the incandescence of celebrity,' as Joseph A. Boone and Nancy J. Vickers put it.[2] Even if it is a meretricious distinctiveness that brings a celebrity to the fore, the democratic openness of the system and the diversity of those it advances are welcome.

The drive to emulate is still more positive if the celebrity has done something noteworthy in the first place, which, despite the cavillers, she often has. Also beneficial is the fact that we can discuss her and her tilt at stardom with one another. Although personally inaccessible, she has a widespread familiarity that makes her a test case for various attitudes and actions, for the social codes that govern the lives of all citizens. Even when celebrities divide opinion, they provide a topic of conversation or 'gossip' that brings people together and acts as a whetstone on which moral awareness is sharpened. As the cultural theorist Graeme Turner observes, such gossip is 'a way of sharing social judgements and of processing social behaviour' and 'one of the fundamental processes employed as a means of social and cultural identity formation'.[3]

At an individual level, too, the bond with a celebrity can be useful, supplying a sense of wholeness through emotional identification. Such attachments are a solace to those who feel alienated by modern patterns of life and employment and by the erosion of traditional community structures. The sociologist Chris Rojek explains the value of such 'para-social interaction':

> It is as if the celebrity provides a path into a genuine meaningful experience, and the routine order of domesticity and work is the domain of inauthenticity. [...] This is a form of second-order intimacy, since it derives from representations of the person rather than actual physical contact. None the less, in societies in which as many as 50 per cent of the population confess to sub-clinical feelings of isolation and loneliness, para-social interaction is a significant aspect of the search for recognition and belonging.[4]

Better still, this interaction can bring people interested in the same celebrity together, leading to communal activity, online or otherwise, that fosters real friendships.

Alongside these benefits, the audience gain a feeling of power from the role they play in constituting celebrity. Although guided by the industry, their responses to the object of their attention retain a large degree of autonomy. The celebrity is a person, but also the story of a person, and the audience can claim to be the main storytellers. They admire her struggle against adversity, enjoy her panache in the first flush of success, pity her when she meets with reverses, judge her if she sins, forgive her if she makes amends, and condemn her finally if she trespasses too far or repents too little. The audience, including even fans, mete out praise and censure, raise the celebrity up and bring her down. Her failings remind them that she is no better than they, and her shame makes them feel better about the setbacks and humiliations of their own lives.

Expressed like this, the audience's use of their control over the celebrity appears ungenerous, and this brings us to the first of the damaging effects of celebrity culture on society. The melodrama of human greed, carnality and deception so vigorously enacted in the mass media arouses the baser instincts of the population, promoting a desire to punish errant individuals in the public eye. The audience's antagonism towards particular stars can combine with resentment at their own addiction to looking into the firmament that contains them. As the pioneering historian of celebrity Leo Braudy said, there is a 'need to admire and to find a scapegoat for that need'.[5] Whether the resulting vindictiveness then infects face-to-face relationships is hard to know, but it can manifestly partake of misogyny and other prejudices the circulation of which is to be regretted.

In puncturing the self-importance of celebrities or berating them for misdemeanours, the media make drastic incursions into their private realm. This invites censure, though it has been observed that those who inveigh against such incursions are often happy to consume the information they yield. And while it may be argued that the risk of such treatment is part of what celebrities sign up for, punitive displays of their dirty linen not only harm them and create an ugly spectacle, but introduce a prurient, judgemental tone to the public arena and strike at cherished notions of the sanctity of the domestic sphere. This joins a number of other trends, including the growth of commercial databases, the manipulation of social media and the intrusiveness of the state, to smudge the boundary between private and public and make people lose hope that privacy can be meaningfully upheld.

Celebrity degradation has a long history. More recent is the spread of voyeuristic interest in pseudo-celebrities, who take the shift in emphasis from attainment to personality that divides celebrity from traditional fame to a new extreme. People of no discernible talent are thrust into the public gaze, for example in reality TV shows, to see how they fare under testing circumstances. The fact that they usually know the score and go ahead anyway for financial gain or a moment in the spotlight only partly mitigates the unwholesomeness of the experiment. The sight of such people achieving recognition kindles the desire for similar excitement in others, causing wave upon wave of brash attention-seeking. And we should spare a thought for the many unknown casualties of celebrity culture: those who, whatever their natural claims to notice, never step out of obscurity. Their yearning is so strong, their goal so near, that failure is oppressive.

There are further ills to record among the audience. While it is too easy to decry the emotional investment in celebrities as spurious, as a symptom of the hollowing out of society, the part played by the celebrity industry and its profit motive does corrode the human value of the celebrity-audience bond. Facile morality tales about stars and fake experiences for their fans abound. And when secondary relationships with celebrities supplant primary ones with friends and family, being preferred as less challenging or more glamorous, the resulting social and personal impoverishment is palpable. Another risk is that interest in a celebrity can become obsessive, causing jealousy and rage, fostering strange delusions and, in exceptional cases, leading to aberrant behaviour like stalking. A small number of celebrities have been murdered by possessive fans.

***

So far this discussion has stayed on a general plane, and we must acknowledge its limitations and glibness. The contrast between fame and celebrity we began with is only as useful as such things ever are. It offers a way of describing how reputations are created and sustained, but many periods of history reveal fame and celebrity side by side, their outward forms hard to tell apart. Often the aspirations of individuals cannot be neatly labelled: some want instant celebrity, some lasting fame, some both. Their right to recognition is a matter of perception too: we can emphasise either their special qualities and attainments or the role of media, markets and facilitators in their rise. Moreover, a celebrity, as we shall see, can become famous, and the famous can be celebrities. Indeed, once the culture of celebrity is established it almost inevitably penetrates the old model of fame. Winston Churchill was the greatest Briton of his generation, and at the same time he was a celebrity.

The distinction between doing and being also holds little water. It is safe to say that William Shakespeare is famous for what he did and that reality TV stars are fêted for their looks and antics rather than any durable legacy. But what of the hypnotic actor, the inspirational religious leader or the charismatic politician, whose often lasting impact derives from the force of their personalities? Many celebrities do something special to win acclaim in the first instance, like the aviator Charles Lindbergh, who made the first nonstop solo flight across the Atlantic. Conversely, some enduringly famous people achieve little. Princess Alexandrina Victoria of Kent did nothing to become Queen of the United Kingdom and nothing very remarkable during the sixty-three years of her reign, yet she is one of the most notable figures in British history.

Having said all this, the fame–celebrity dichotomy is worth retaining, less to classify the nature and conduct of particular people than as a model of renown in broad social and economic terms. It is the 'apparatus' of celebrity culture, the meshing of three agencies – individual, audience, industry – that is distinctive and modern.[6] Once we understand this apparatus, we know that depictions of celebrity as simply the reward for personal excellence, the unhealthy mania of fans, or the vehicle for third-party enrichment are inadequate. None of the three agencies is dominant. Each has the capacity to surprise and frustrate the others, but when the collaboration works smoothly, everyone wins: the individual attains prominence and wealth; the audience enjoy the private and social pleasures of fandom; and the industry provides jobs and income to those it employs.

So when did it all begin?

2

The Birth of Celebrity Culture

Unlike people and animals, social constructs such as celebrity culture are not born at a particular time. In fact they are not born at all. Instead they slowly take shape until a point is reached where they recognisably, though still incompletely, fit a term coined at a later date. It is an odd way to think about the past, but history is inevitably a looking back from the perspective of today. So does celebrity culture emerge at a steady pace, moving towards its current complexity and pervasiveness, or is there an onward rush, perhaps precipitated by a breakthrough like newspapers, photography, film or television, that allows us to speak, in everyday terms, of its 'birth'?

If there is, scholars disagree about when it happened. Some see celebrities existing in ancient times, some as emerging during the nineteenth century or after the turn of the twentieth, with the advent of moving pictures a favoured moment.[1] All the same, something that could tentatively be called a consensus places the genesis of celebrity culture in the second half of the eighteenth century, or, slightly later, in the Romantic era, with London generally given as its birthplace.[2] Supporting this view is the earliest use of the word 'celebrity' for a person rather than a quality. We would typically expect this to occur after the appearance of what it describes, so that men and women now identifiable as celebrities should have been active a few decades in advance of the label being applied to anyone. The *Oxford English Dictionary* shows the first instance of the word to denote a person in the public eye in 1849, but there are examples from the 1830s.[3]

If celebrity arrived as a new sort of fame towards the end of the eighteenth century, what ushered it in? Historians agree that in that century Great Britain, with its stock market, complex systems of credit and global trade, was the first truly capitalist economy. Better farming methods improved yields, while steam power and other forward leaps in technology made mining and manufacturing on a large scale possible. Meanwhile, due to a geographically concentrated domestic market and an excellent network of roads and canals, the revolutions in agriculture and industry were matched by a consumer revolution. The increasing demand for goods that enhanced comfort, beauty and luxury in the home and status outside it was readily met by makers of furniture, textiles, tableware and so on. Advertising attained a new sophistication, creating desires where none had existed before and the conviction that satisfying them would bring lasting happiness – the essence of consumerism.

Economic progress brought about changes in demography and outlook. The population grew rapidly and waves of migration took place from the countryside to towns. The burgeoning political awareness of the artisanal and particularly the middle class led to a relative decline in the authority of the monarchy and the landed elite. Young minds were flooded with an ambition to fulfil innate potential rather than class destiny. Slowly, and in the main quietly, ideas of democracy and meritocracy gained ground. In line with this, the formation of taste shifted to theatres, debating societies, literary clubs and coffee houses in London and elsewhere, which generated more intellectual and cultural energy than the seats of the aristocracy or the stolid court of George III. And as the expanding bourgeoisie had ever more time and money for leisure pursuits, new industries sprung up to cater for the hobbies and amusements it indulged in.

Accompanying these social developments was a rise in literacy that made the printed word accessible to half of Britain's population by 1750 and created a large new readership for newspapers, journals, books and pamphlets. This swelled further at the turn of the nineteenth century owing to advances in the production of printed matter. First came the paper-making machine of Henry and Sealy Fourdrinier, patented in 1806, which automated the manufacture of paper from rags and produced continuous rolls that could be cut to various sizes. From 1800, wooden, hand-operated presses were replaced by the cast-iron press developed by the third Earl Stanhope, employing a system of levers to intensify the force of the screw and reducing by nine tenths the effort required to print a sheet. The Stanhope press was itself superseded by technology Friedrich Koenig perfected during the first two decades of the new century, using steam and replacing flatbeds with cylinders in rotary motion.

Newspapers, produced under strict time constraints in a highly competitive market, got a huge boost from cheap, efficient printing.

Even before these technical improvements they had prospered. In 1702 there was one daily newspaper in London; in 1793 there were sixteen.[4] During the same period the provincial press blossomed from almost nothing to the point where every sizeable town had at least one title providing local and national news. In the early nineteenth century circulation expanded further and methods of gathering news became speedier and more sophisticated. Alongside the dailies were the weeklies, giving an overview of recent events, and middlebrow monthly magazines, offering a mixture of politics, reviews, articles of general interest, and curious or amusing anecdotes.

One of the most striking features of the press at this time is the amount of personal information it contained. The American diplomat Richard Rush, writing in 1818, was astounded at the way British newspapers made private matters public:

> Every thing goes into the newspapers. In other countries, matter of a public nature may be seen in them; here, in addition, you see perpetually the concerns of individuals. Does a private gentleman come to town? you hear it in the newspapers; does he build a house, or buy an estate? they give the information; does he entertain his friends? you have all their names next day in type; is the drapery of a lady's drawing-room changed from red damask and gold to white satin and silver? the fact is publicly announced. So of a thousand other things. The first burst of it all upon Madame de Stael, led her to remark that the English had realized the fable of living with a window in their bosoms.[5]

Most of this reporting was respectful, the more so as its very triviality suggested that almost any detail about a particular person's life was worth knowing. The servility of 'fashionable movements' columns and reports of high-society parties was such that even those being fawned over must at times have felt a little queasy.

The other side of the coin glints just as hard in lengthy accounts of divorce proceedings and in the poisonous denigration and innuendo directed at well-known persons not in favour with a newspaper's editor. A story of dubious veracity could be presented as a reader's letter and later disowned, and to prevent the editor's motives being impugned salacious items were reported in a moralising tone. In any case libel laws were weak, and if journalists pretended to conceal their victims' identities by giving only the first and last letters of their names they could write what they liked. The poet Samuel Taylor Coleridge expressed his disgust in an essay of 1810:

> There are men, who trading in the silliest anecdotes, in unprovoked abuse and senseless eulogy, think themselves nevertheless employed both worthily and honourably, if only all this be done '*in good set terms*,' and from the Press, and of *public* Characters: a class which has encreased so rapidly of late, that it becomes difficult to consider what Characters are to be considered as private.[6]

The demand of newspaper readers for gossip was 'as voracious and universal as the appetite of a shark', according to the diarist Charles Greville, with the 'grossest and most disgusting' matter devoured the soonest.[7] Journalists did anything to satisfy this appetite, and paying disaffected servants for juicy titbits was common practice. Blackmail and bribery were rife. At the extreme end of the scale a brazen extortionist like John Williams, writing under the pen name Anthony Pasquin, would blacken every name until he was paid off. More commonly, an editor took a small consideration from those who had been mauled in his paper and wished to be let alone or from those who wished to see an enemy belaboured.[8] Conversely, public figures or their proxies could cross his palm for glowing notices of their social activities or charitable giving, a secretive but widespread custom that has not been fully studied. No one spoke of 'self-advertisement', but if the term did not exist the thing certainly did.

In his memoirs the radical politician Henry Hunt tells an amusing anecdote about this aspect of the press:

> Mr Clifford had brought me acquainted with all the tricks, frauds, and deceptions of the public press; and, to convince me that almost the whole of the public press of that day was venal and corrupt, he proved to a demonstration, by some *practical experiments*, that for a *few pounds*, any thing, however absurd, might be universally promulgated; particularly if the absurdity was in favour of the ruling powers. For instance, he wrote a paragraph, the greatest hoax that ever was, in praise of the mild and amiable manners, the courtesy, and the humanity of Harry Dundas. Now, said he, to show you how this will be promulgated by the venal press, and how it will be swallowed by John Bull, give me *five shillings*, and I will put it into the hands of one of the runners for collecting information for the papers, and you shall see it in all the newspapers, both in London and the country. I produced the crown-piece immediately, and out it came, in one of the morning

papers, the next day; and as he had predicted, it was copied into all the London and country papers. Thus the humanity and suavity of one of the most unfeeling and impudent Scotchmen that ever crossed the Tweed, was cried up to the skies, and he was eulogised by some of them as the very cream of the milk of human kindness![9]

A curious supplement to the diet of truth and falsehood newspapers fed to the public about their idols and villains were the period's *romans à clef*, or novels with a key. These gave thinly disguised depictions of living people and real, usually scandalous incidents, stimulating an urge in readers to recognise people of note or perhaps themselves. Pioneered in France a hundred years earlier, this type of fiction was popularised in Britain in the second half of the eighteenth century, among others by Georgiana, Duchess of Devonshire, who skewered a number of worldlings in *The Sylph* (1778). The genre had its fullest flowering in some of the Silver Fork novels of high society churned out from the late 1820s to the early 1840s. Marianne Spencer Stanhope's *Almack's* (1826) created such a stir that a key to its characters was published by popular demand.

If the print media and topical fiction turned people figuratively into objects of the public gaze, images did so literally. The London art market flourished in the late eighteenth century, thanks in part to the founding of the Royal Academy of Arts in 1768 and the growth of art criticism in newspapers. The Royal Academy's annual exhibitions were very popular, especially after their removal in 1780 to Somerset House. Between a third and a half of the pictures on display were portraits, which seems remarkable until one considers how they gratified the sitter's vanity and the viewer's curiosity. Other art societies held smaller exhibitions, and some portraitists had their own shows, so that those who commissioned their work had to allow a fee-paying public to enjoy it before it adorned their walls. The desire to see portraits was further satisfied by auctions and by visits to country houses, now accessible in return for tips to servants, an early form of visitor charge.

The range of people commissioning portraits widened, with the prosperous middle class as keen as the nobility to own a collection of family pictures. A pleasure to possess, they were also status symbols for those aspiring to rise in society and for those who had risen. A likeness by an eminent artist like Thomas Gainsborough, Sir Joshua Reynolds, George Romney, John Hoppner or Sir Thomas Lawrence was a promotional tool. One of Hoppner's sitters gained materially from his skilful brushwork, as *Rambler's Magazine* noted in 1775: 'Miss Bailey, whose picture, painted by Hoppner, was so much the admiration of the town, at the last exhibition, has just been married to a young gentleman of considerable fortune in the country. That lady, though of a genteel family, was quite unknown in the polite world, till her charms were exhibited on canvas.'[10]

Paid a fixed rate according to size of canvas, portraitists treated their subjects equally. Reynolds took no less care with the Pacific Islander, the Chinese page or the Cherokee warrior who sat for him than with the greatest peers in the land. An artist could make a celebrity too. Romney made an MP's lowly-born mistress his muse, setting Amy Lyon on the path to becoming Emma, Lady Hamilton and one of the most beguiling figures of the age.

The sight of beautiful portraits, perhaps recalled to memory by an exhibition catalogue, sparked in many a wish to possess such images themselves, and so engravers set to work to produce copies. New engraving methods, such as the use of steel rather than copper plates, made reproduction cheaper, and customers had a choice of prices based on the size of prints and whether they were plain or coloured. Such was the demand for engraved portraits that they sometimes went on sale before the original work had been exhibited. Their wide dissemination made actresses and society belles in particular easy to recognise, exposing them to being mobbed as they emerged from shops or walked in other public places. The collecting impulse took hold among buyers of prints, who put together albums or indulged in 'grangerising', the pasting of images as illustrations into books.

Not all images of prominent persons made them look good. Satirical prints, often called caricatures, which had their golden age in the final decades of the eighteenth century, boisterously ridiculed those they portrayed, reducing them to extreme physical types and showing them in undignified postures. Distinguishing features and mannerisms were mercilessly exaggerated, be it the mobile, bushy black eyebrows of Charles James Fox or the obese, trussed-up figure of the Prince of Wales, later George IV. This graphic satire had political significance, robbing established authority of its mystique and allowing the powerless to laugh at the powerful and gloat over their tribulations. The mercenary flattery of portraitists and the demotic mockery of caricaturists made for an uneasy balance in the representation of people in the public eye.

Other images proliferated too. The illustrated catalogues of Josiah Wedgwood, whose technical innovations and clever marketing transformed the manufacture of ceramics, included large numbers of portrait medallions and figurines of well-known people, offered at prices many could afford. And for three decades after her arrival from France in 1802 Marie Tussaud toured the British Isles with her waxworks, using a rare promotional genius to draw larger and larger crowds to see her astoundingly lifelike figures. Her collection grew, with French and British royalty sharing space with military heroes, popular actors and notorious criminals, some based on casts taken from life and dressed in clothes that had belonged to the originals. In 1835 Madame Tussaud and her waxworks put down roots in Baker Street, London. Her last model, fittingly, was of herself.

The economic, social and cultural changes of this period, along with developments in the print and visual media, caused an explosion of public renown. Existing paths to success opened to a larger segment of the population and new ones appeared. Following these paths was a generation better educated than any before it. Schooling was a patchwork of institutions run by churches, charities and private individuals, but it provided instruction to the hungry minds of even the poorest children. Modest beginnings did not stop Michael Faraday, John Dalton, Humphry Davy and George Stephenson from reaching the summits of science and engineering. Other self-made strivers won esteem in a myriad of occupations: artists, explorers, inventors, physicians, singers, prize-fighters and chefs, while rough-hewn campaigning politicians rubbed shoulders with the gentry and nobility outside and occasionally inside parliament.

The highest repute was still reserved for the military commanders and statesmen who embodied traditional fame, almost all well born. The Duke of Wellington and Earl Grey maintained this type of profile with dignity for decades. Alongside them were those at the pinnacles of the arts and sciences. In a lecture of 1818 the critic William Hazlitt distinguished their status from what he called 'popularity': 'Fame is not popularity, the shout of the multitude, the idle buzz of fashion, the venal puff, the soothing flattery of favour or of friendship; but it is the spirit of a man surviving himself in the minds and thoughts of other men, undying and imperishable.'[11] But how many people had a realistic chance of fame, even in fields open to them, and why labour for laurels that might be won after long years or posthumously when the public applauded those who cut an immediate dash? The slow dismantling of social barriers fostered self-esteem in all conditions of women and men – and the desire to have it validated by others.

The cynosure of those seeking this validation was the capital, as Pierce Egan explained in his rollicking *Life in London* (1821), which relates the 'sprees' of Corinthian Tom, Jerry Hawthorn and Bob Logic:

To acquire 'excellence' in the Metropolis is a circumstance so 'devoutly to be wished,' that it is the genuine passport throughout all the provinces in England; nay more, it is wafted across the briny deep, and this sort of 'greatness' is acknowledged, admired, and sought after in all parts of the world.

LONDON is the looking-glass for TALENT – it is the faithful emporium of the enterprising, the bold, the timid, and the bashful individual, and where all can view themselves at full length, affording innumerable opportunities either to push forward, to retreat, to improve, or to decide. In no other place can FORTUNE be so successfully wooed as in London; and in no other place does she distribute her favours with so liberal a hand.

So liberal, in fact, that some reached their goals without doing anything of real note or even disclosing much talent. The media, avid for novelty and sensation, created evanescent stars, the votaries of what Egan called 'notoriety':

NOTORIETY here is everything, and the various modes to obtain it are so numerous that the eye is fatigued with the contrast of the *elegant* and *ridiculous* forms which so rapidly assail it: and, after all, it is of so fleeting a nature in London, that very few persons can flatter themselves on having NOTORIETY long in their possession.[12]

The term used for such persons was 'lions', which survives in the verb 'to lionise'. The life of a lion was brief but intense. 'The good people of England are notorious for their love of what is frequently called "a lion" – while their attachment lasts it is always at fever-heat,' observed the travel writer Lord Albemarle.[13] To the fore among these beasts were the dandies, who cultivated eccentricities to garner attention: Joseph Haynes always wore a green coat and earned the sobriquet 'Pea-green Haynes', while Robert 'Romeo' Coates paid theatre managers to let him perform in major roles, had a curricle in the shape of a scallop, and wore furs in the height of summer.

The prince of the dandies was George Bryan 'Beau' Brummell, who rose from obscure origins by dint of chaste elegance, cutting jibes and an affectation of boredom. Like many denizens of the new world of celebrity, he was borne along by audacity and self-belief, as the political hostess Lady Hester Stanhope discovered:

I recollect his once saying to me, in Bond Street, riding with his bridle between his forefinger and thumb, as if he held a pinch of snuff, 'Dear creature! Who *is* that man you were talking to just now?' – 'Why,' I answered, 'that is Colonel—.' – 'Colonel what?' said he, in his peculiar manner; 'who ever heard of his father?' – So I replied, 'And who ever heard of George B.'s father?' – 'Ah! Lady Hester,' he rejoined, half-seriously, 'who, indeed, ever heard of George B.'s father, and who would have heard of George B. himself, if he had been anything but what he is? But you know, my dear Lady Hester, it is my folly that is the making of me. If I did not impertinently stare duchesses out of countenance, and nod over my shoulder to a prince, I should be forgotten in a week: and, if the world is so silly as to admire my absurdities, you and I may know better, but what does that signify?'[14]

How astonished Brummell would be, by the way, to know that he achieved real fame after all. Known for what he was rather than what he did, holding no office, producing nothing and gaining no honours, he could surely only be a celebrity. To his peers his reputation must have seemed the flimsiest gossamer, for what claim on posterity did a man have who passed his time in dressing himself, attending high-society parties, and gambling for high stakes? Yet his name lives on because historians of dress credit him with founding a masculine sartorial tradition that survives, at least in formal wear, to this day. His insistence on cleanliness, simplicity of cut and plain colours was a reaction to the gaudy extravagance of earlier male fashions, and since his day men have worn dull, uniform colours, with the only possible distinction being in the quality of tailoring, and yielded all that is bright, elaborate and ornate to the female sex. If this was his doing, and to a degree it was, he is entitled to his fame.

Brummell is the exception that proves the rule, though, and other dandies of his era, like lions in general, achieved nothing more than being talked of while they lived. When the theologian John Henry Newman stated in 1848 that 'notoriety, or the making a noise in the world, has come to be considered a great good in itself,' there had been generations of this exhibitionism, made possible, as Newman said, by ceaseless news reporting. Some exhibitors dazzled for years, some glimmered for weeks or months, some tried and failed to shine. One such half-celebrity was Ann Hatton, a member of the Kemble stage dynasty who would not let lameness and smallpox scars keep her down. She lectured at the morally dubious Temple of Health in Pall Mall, faked her own suicide in Westminster Abbey, wrote novels, poetry and a libretto, and tried to sell an account of the lives of her better-known relatives. 'For Hatton,' writes the literary historian Judith Pascoe, 'fame was an end in its own right; every foray into theatrical and literary realms was fuelled by a desire to be celebrated by the public at large.'[15]

Even such small fry attracted interest, while bigger fish in the celebrity pond had a substantial following and sometimes dedicated fans. While they lacked the imposing stature of great leaders and heroes, they offered apparent proximity instead. Celebrities were tangible to their audience, representative of them, directly inspiring to them, susceptible of emulation by them. They proved that anyone of any background could make a name for himself or herself. They also helped people to surmount the feelings of dispersion and atomisation caused by rapid demographic change, in particular rural-urban migration. In *The Great Metropolis* (1836–1837), James Grant says nowhere has a more shifting population than London, which he calls 'a great vortex, drawing persons from all parts of the world into it'.[16] In this isolating, socially fragmented environment celebrities offered reassurance by seeming all of a piece.

An example of this reassurance is James Boswell's relationship with Samuel Johnson. Boswell was a failed fame-seeker, a deracinated Scot in London, a married libertine, a hard-drinking gambler prone to depression. After a mixed career of little distinction he amazed the world with a biography of a brilliant, crotchety, domineering essayist and lexicographer. *The Life of Samuel Johnson* (1791) is a masterpiece for its recreation of an intellectual world and its affectionate but frank account of a flesh-and-blood human being, with details of his daily life and passages of verbatim conversation. The author is not an omniscient recorder, but an intimate friend of his hero who strives to understand him. By writing himself into Johnson's life Boswell overcame his inadequacies and his fractured self became whole. Within two generations the *Life* was better known than Johnson's writings, and now it is considered to be the finest biography in the English language – an extreme case of a fan appropriating a celebrity.

Boswell acted alone and knew his subject well, but anonymous audiences had a measure of control over celebrities too. The Polish philosopher Krystyn Lach-Szyrma, who sojourned in London in the early 1820s, perceived that British politicians, long before universal suffrage, belonged through the print media to the general population: 'The distinguished people of Britain are easy to recognise because, having been entrusted with state affairs, their lives are public rather than private and their thoughts and deeds are the subject of conversation throughout the country. By articles in the newspapers and other journals they become common property.' Similarly, the actor Joe Cowell saw that 'the mob must ever have their idol, whether in religion, politics, or the drama, upon familiar terms.'[17] The outlines of the constitutive role of the audience, an essential feature of celebrity culture, were already discernible.

Knowing they were beholden to an audience with some access to their private sphere, celebrities courted 'public opinion', as it was already called. Some even fed newspapers with information, possibly in the form of press releases.[18] They authorised biographies and wrote autobiographies. In a crowded field of competitors, they kept their image fresh with 'performances' of their own celebrity. Lady Hester Stanhope, who left Britain for good in 1810, later recalled the case of an unnamed duchess in her youth.

> She sometimes would employ her own people to puff her off. You would see a man in a shop in Bond Street say to people of the shop – 'Whose fine carriage is that yonder?' – [']That's the Duchess of **********'s, sir,' the shopman would reply. Then another man, pretending to be a stranger to the first, would cry out, 'Good God! – the Duchess of **********! do let me look: I would give more to get a sight of her grace than I would of the king. – Pray, excuse me: I shall be back in a moment;' – and off he would run.[19]

And celebrities could ensure a final flash of interest when they died by leaving the necessary materials for newspaper obituaries. From being monuments of the great presented as chronicles, obituaries developed at this time into miniature exercises in real biographical writing, with characterisation and incident to the fore.

It happened, of course, that celebrities made missteps or were roughly handled by the press. Then they learnt the invidiousness of their role, according to the artist James Northcote:

> A man in a conspicuous position must stand a strict examination; every fault if his own, or even of his family, will be raked up, and, if possible, brought against him; the world will not let him enjoy his distinction for nothing, for it is looked upon by them as an infringement of their common rights. You must pay for notoriety, as you pay for everything else.

Others were less gloomy. After all, bad publicity was often less bad than it seemed, and better than no publicity. As the Prussian Prince Hermann von Pückler-Muskau noted while in London in 1826, 'A newspaper article that would drive a Continental into hiding for three months will only provoke a glimmer of schadenfreude here and within twenty-four hours be forgotten.' Richard Rush recorded an evening in 1818 at the home of George Canning, the most charismatic politician of his generation (and incidentally a man of middle-class stock). After dinner some of the guests leafed through Canning's collection of political caricatures, bound in large volumes, and Rush was surprised to find their host, himself targeted in some of the images, standing by to explain their meaning. As a public man, he knew such attacks solidified his renown, while their uniform crudity blunted the audience response and thus their power to harm him.[20]

* * *

A capitalist economy, democratic ideas, urbanisation, increased opportunities to come to notice, ready promotion of those who did so, the centrality of personality to renown, techniques of image control, a rumbustious free press, and the role of the public in creating and sustaining reputations – all these allow us to speak of a celebrity culture arising in the late eighteenth and early nineteenth centuries. Celebrities operated in many areas, but similarities in the mechanisms that generated and supported them suggest a pattern. Some features of Regency celebrity culture seem modern. Autograph hunting became a craze, and letters were bought and sold for good prices. In 1788 the first British book of facsimiles by famous hands appeared, and in 1819 Sotheby's held its first sale exclusively of autographs. The celebrity endorsement was common too. Beau Brummell's tailors made sure his custom was known, and 'the first celebrity chef' Antonin Carême, who designed the modern chef's hat, suggested the best place to buy one.[21]

All the same, we must beware of what the historian Stella Tillyard calls 'the delight at recognising ourselves in the mirror that the past seems to hold up'. The differences are huge. Photography, recorded sound, film, television and the internet have extended the reach and appeal of celebrities. Early stars had no agents, managers or publicists to assist them. Data-driven marketing of celebrity-related products lay in the distant future. And while people who were 'famous for being famous' already existed, there were no instant celebrities created by talent shows or accidental celebrities thrust into the spotlight despite themselves; nor was anyone groomed for a turn in the sun by the entertainment industry.[22] But is today's celebrity different in kind or merely in degree from what it was at its 'birth'? The best way of looking into this question is to examine the two fields of endeavour in which celebrities throve best during the Regency: writing and acting.

3

Byron and Other Poets

George Gordon, Lord Byron. Postcard after Richard Westall.

Advances in the technologies of print and paper-making that changed Britain's newspapers also benefited the publishers of books, while demographic and economic expansion and the spread of education created a new market for them. At the turn of the eighteenth century literary writers rarely earned much from sales of their works. Instead, they had patrons, published by subscription, received sinecures and pensions, enjoyed a private income, or a combination of these. Print runs were small and books expensive; copies were precious objects to be enjoyed within communities of appreciative readers. By the close of the Romantic period all this had altered. Authorship was a profession serving a socially and geographically diverse market. Publishers advertised extensively and used improved distribution networks to sell their wares, now much cheaper, to individual customers and lending libraries throughout the land.

More readers reading more books sounds like progress, as does the ability of writers to support themselves. However, concerns arose that the commercialisation of authorship and the replacement of small, cultured audiences with mass reading had lowered standards. In a study of 1833 the novelist Edward Bulwer-Lytton admitted this had happened, but did not blame writers:

> It is natural that writers should be ambitious of creating a sensation: a sensation is produced by gaining the ear, not of the few, but the many; it is natural, therefore, that they should address the many; the style pleasing to the many becomes, of course, the style most frequently aimed at: hence the profusion of amusing, familiar, and superficial writings. People complain of it, as if it were a proof of degeneracy in the knowledge of authors – it is a proof of the increased number of readers.[1]

Others saw readers as the sufferers, groaning under the weight of new books or, to change the metaphor, drowning in a flood of printed dross. In her essay 'The Age of Books' the poet and critic Maria Jane Jewsbury took a humorous look at the literary scene of the 1820s. She supposed that if its writers were all swept away the country would be as depopulated as after a five years' war; that one's least intelligent friend and youngest daughter might well be published, and one's washerwoman and barber were probably rising authors too. These were 'glorious days for the rag-gatherer and the paper-maker', Jewsbury continued, but 'the public rather resembles a spoiled child, that is crammed with trash from morning till night, and then upbraided with its unhealthy appetite'.[2]

Whether readers were content to feed on trash and just wanted the tastiest sort, or whether they desired real nourishment from works of higher merit, they needed some means of choosing among the countless titles advertised in newspapers and stocked by booksellers. In the old days of coterie literature there had been a compact between writer and reader: they might know each other personally, and even if they did not, they shared a well-defined taste culture. When this limited circle of reception was superseded by a large body of anonymous readers, writers had to make judgements about what was likely to please the greatest number. And, as their books jockeyed for position, so too did the authors themselves, courting an audience who were aware of their power to confer or withdraw favour. This led to the rise of the author as personality.

An early example was Samuel Johnson, whose unpolished manners, slovenly dress and virile combativeness were elements of an artfully cultivated image as an unpretentious man who had made his own way and thought the only sensible reason for writing was to make money. His inspired, aggressive conversational style won many admirers and caused many quarrels, but always placed him at the centre of attention. Frances Burney, who achieved overnight fame with her first novel *Evelina* (1778) and followed it with further successes, was outwardly the opposite of Johnson: decorously timid, self-doubting, deeply respectful of her elders and fearful of publicity. But behind this façade Burney sedulously kept herself before her public, mixing in literary society, inviting the protection of influential men, and prompting chivalrous solicitude with her notoriously tiny appetite and delicate health.[3]

By the start of the nineteenth century it was accepted that the profile of authors comprehended their life as well as their writing. They took their place in published memoirs, diaries and collections of letters and in the mushrooming genre of the biographical dictionary. Portraits of them were engraved for single sale or as frontispieces for their works. As with other celebrities, people gossiped about them and newspapers recorded their doings. By attending literary salons and giving courses of lectures, authors circulated almost as much as their books. In 1822 the lawyer John Whishaw regretted he had seen little of the Irish novelist Maria Edgeworth and her family while they were in London: 'Their time was engrossed by visits and sights, and their friendship was expanded like leaf gold over a prodigious surface. A popular author, however, must be considered in some degree as a public character.'[4]

Further emphasis was put on authors' personalities by the monthly and quarterly periodicals that flourished before and after 1800.

The function of *Blackwood's Edinburgh Magazine*, the *Monthly Review*, the *Critical Review* and their rivals was to guide readers through the thickets of books all around them. They also set aesthetic standards, once the preserve of patrons and a cultured, tight-knit audience but thrown into disarray by mass publishing and the amorphous reading public. Periodicals were at the heart of literary culture, and the adherence of their anonymous contributors to an editorial line gave each organ an imposingly institutional feel. As early as 1767 the satirist Archibald Campbell remarked that people would not look at a new book 'till they have consulted their monthly Oracles, a Magazine, a Museum, or a Review'; and William Jerdan, the long-standing editor of the *Literary Gazette*, founded in 1817, recalled that it was 'the court of appeal for all the literature of the period'.[5]

Like writers, periodical editors had to judge how to address readers despite having no direct knowledge of their likes and dislikes. A safe assumption, given the nature of newspaper and wider celebrity culture, was that a biographical approach would go down well. Book reviews in the *European Magazine* and the *London Review* closed with a note on authors, and many periodicals printed their memoirs, records of their conversations and series of biographical sketches with titles like 'Portraits of Authors', 'Contemporary Authors' and 'Sketches of Living Poets'.[6] The best-known series was the 'Gallery of Illustrious Literary Characters' in *Fraser's Magazine* from 1830 to 1838, evaluating writers in a chatty tone and regarding their output as an expression of their characters. The periodical's reviews were just as personal: favourable ones praised the taste and morals and unfavourable ones condemned the ignorance and folly of the author.

The importance of the person holding the pen was also understood by publishers and reflected in their promotional strategies. Along with advertisements proper, which gave basic details of a title, often with quotes from reviews, they planted 'news' about authors and books in friendly newspapers. Such coverage allowed the contours of an author's character to take shape, creating a brand that was used in subsequent advertising, sometimes with the suggestion that his or her latest work was eagerly awaited – 'hyping' as it was later called. In a few cases a name acquired a cognomen: Ann Yearsley, who had been a milkmaid, was called 'Lactilla' or the 'Milkmaid Poet'; James Woodhouse was 'the Shoemaker Poet' or 'the Poetical Shoemaker'; and John Clare, a farm labourer's son who shot to fame when his *Poems Descriptive of Rural Life and Scenery* came out in 1820, was the 'Northamptonshire Peasant Poet'. Such labels ensured visibility in the teeming literary marketplace.

So writers were turned into celebrities by an apparatus made up of journalists, lexicographers, engravers, printers, reviewers and publishers, all with pecuniary motives and none in overall control. Most writers went along with it willingly, for the waning of patronage made them reliant on book sales and they knew that without name recognition their earnings would be small. Pierce Egan was probably not far wrong in claiming that all writers were fame-seekers:

> It will, perhaps, scarcely be denied, that few, if any, writers, out of the great mass of living scribblers [...] who possess 'souls above buttons,' can be so insensibly *frigid* as to be careless *about* the pleasing, grateful, inspiring, nay, golden advantages resulting from the smiles of that supreme goddess of the gods, FAME!'[7]

Readers were responsive to the efforts of authors and the nascent celebrity industry to fascinate them: they wrote fan letters; they collected autographs and engraved portraits; most of all, they bought books in unprecedented numbers. As the decay of the coterie system ended real contact between readers and writers, a virtual intimacy replaced it. Literary publishing in the early nineteenth century is thus an example of how celebrity works to overcome the alienation felt by consumers when cultural goods join the market economy.

With poetry in particular, the light trained on the writer as a person was strengthened by illumination from another source: Romanticism. Impatient with the dry rationalism of Enlightenment philosophy and the balance and restraint of Classical literature, Romantics asserted the primacy of imagination and self-expression. What counted for them, exclusively, was the human heart. The true poet was endowed with the rare gift of articulating the stirrings of his heart, whose uniqueness guaranteed the originality of his work. There was a political aspect to this too, a frustration with quotidian reality and the limitations imposed by custom and hierarchy. The cosmic desire to realise the inner self against all such obstacles inspired awe and devotion in readers, who felt the same frustration and sensed that for all his individuality the poet gave voice to their longings as well.

This picture of the unworldly genius, inspired and defiant, bears no resemblance to the portrait we have painted of the celebrity writer: the self-promoting professional aware of being caught up in a web of relationships essential to his success. Indeed, as we shall see, the lofty idealism of Romantic aesthetics sometimes defined itself against the workaday pragmatism of commercialised literature. Nonetheless, the Romantic movement and the culture of celebrity in literature did have things in common. They shared an origin in the decline of patronage and of the settled community of taste that guided writers in selecting their style and subject matter. As writers became more autonomous in social and commercial terms, so too creatively they had to find their own way and do so without being quite sure of the sentiments of an inchoate readership.

Also like celebrities, Romantic poets wished to fascinate others and be treated according to their estimation of their own worth, regardless of social background. And because claims to poetic genius were founded on self-revelation, private character was at the centre of interest. Readers studied the habits and collected anecdotes of their favourite poets, revelled in their eccentricity, even made long journeys to see their homes or places associated with them. The upsurge in biographies and autobiographies in this period, with their focus on private life and revealing anecdote, is attributed as much to Romanticism as to celebrity culture. Finally, true poets must have an inner nature that is singular but universal, making them a transcendent version of the common man, just as celebrities resonate most if they seem special but at the same time represent the ambitions and values of their public.

Enter Lord Byron, the most Romantic celebrity and celebrated Romantic. His breakthrough came with the publication in 1812 of the first two cantos of *Childe Harold's Pilgrimage*, which made him the talk of the town. 'He continues to be the greatest attraction at all parties and suppers,' observed Elizabeth, Duchess of Devonshire. *Childe Harold*, she wrote, 'is on every table, and himself courted, visited, flattered, and praised whenever he appears'. The physician Henry Holland, who saw Byron at this period, agreed: 'His presence at this time made the fortune of any dinner or drawing-room party for which it could be obtained.'[8] *The Giaour* and *The Bride of Abydos*, both of 1813, added further glory, and in the next year *The Corsair* sold 10,000 copies on its first day in print. Much more was to come, including the masterpiece *Don Juan*, begun in 1819 and unfinished when Byron died aged thirty-six in 1824. The furore his work created was unprecedented.

Several elements combined in Byron's poetical tales to enchant his readers: the foreign, sometimes exotic settings, which tantalised a generation cut off from the Continent by war; the theme of striving for freedom from the shackles of social convention and political oppression; the scatterings of contemporary references, many of them invigoratingly controversial; the explicit portrayal of the morbid thoughts of those who toil in despair or despondency; and a refusal to stick to the etiquette of poetic diction and avoid subjects traditionally deemed unfit for poetic treatment. Readers thrilled to a writer who did not portentously reveal a truth or point a moral but spoke directly to their hearts. The immediacy and emotional potency of his verse made it seem almost a direct transcript of his feelings.

Byron's heroes, the vehicles for the affective force of his poems, are aristocratic rebels with a heady mix of self-assertion and world-weariness, titans who hold aloof from the crowd and strain to fulfil a majestic destiny. They have an aura of impiety, violence, eroticism and grandeur, and with it the suggestion of some dark secret, some past crime. Or perhaps their innate nobility has been warped by an unjust fate. Not all Byron's works contain protagonists like this, but many do, and it was the family resemblance of these portraits, as well as their spirited composition and rich emotional colouring, which led readers to think they must be disguised versions of the author. In Walter Scott's words, 'You cannot for your soul avoid concluding that the author, as he gives an account of his own travels, is also doing so in his own character.' The politician Lord Dudley made the same point in more critical terms: 'His finest fruits savour of the parent crab, or rather the noxious Upas of his pride and malevolence.'[9]

Byron's identification with his heroes made the urge to know him overwhelming. Readers tried to satisfy this urge in two ways: they collected all available information on him from printed sources and oral transmission; and they combed through his poems for clues about his life. On both counts, Byron ensured that the evidence was fragmentary and unclear. Turning to the poems first, there are what appear to be confessional moments, as when the hero of *Manfred* is tormented by his obscurely illicit love for Astarte, which was read as alluding to the poet's relationship with his half-sister Augusta Leigh. Such intimations are more compelling for the enigmatic melancholy of Byron's alter-egos. Consider the eponymous hero of *Lara*:

> In him inexplicably mix'd appear'd
> Much to be loved and hated, sought and fear'd.
> Opinion varying o'er his hidden lot,
> In praise of railing ne'er his name forgot;
> His silence form'd a theme for others' prate;
> They guess'd – they gaz'd – they fain would know his fate.

What had he been? what was he, thus unknown,
Who walk'd their world, his lineage only known?
A hater of his kind? yet some would say,
With them he could seem gay amidst the gay;
But own'd that smile, if oft observ'd and near,
Wan'd in its mirth and wither'd to a sneer;
That smile might reach his lip but pass'd not by,
None e're could trace its laughter to his eye.[10]

As for Byron the man, his allure was based on his good looks, rank and political radicalism, and above all on hints of unfathomed depths and debaucheries beneath the gleaming surface. He maintained a bitterly cynical attitude to the world around him; he behaved sullenly and distantly at entertainments; at Newstead Abbey, his country seat, he reportedly drank from a skull; and he refused to deny rumours of sexual impropriety. In other words, Byron seemed rather like his heroes. When his jilted mistress Lady Caroline Lamb depicted him as a heartless seducer in *Glenarvon* (1816), his publisher John Murray correctly predicted the novel would do him no harm. A vital part of the celebrity economy, as opposed to the economy of traditional fame, is personality, which makes a figure in the public eye tangible. Notoriety, being known for something bad, has advantages – within limits – because it is absorbing in itself and because it shows the celebrated individual to be made of flesh and blood.

In fact, Byron may not have been as Byronic as he gave himself out to be. The equation between the man and his creations was made before the former was very familiar, and it is possible he adapted his conduct to align with the poetry and boost his renown. Some said he was a well-adjusted man who only pretended to be 'mad – bad – and dangerous to know', in Lady Caroline Lamb's famous phrase. Charles Greville believed Byron knowingly inhabited a character that did not belong to him and tried to appear worse than he was, 'a species of perverted vanity the most disgusting'. According to Walter Scott he exaggerated his vices, spoke of non-existent duels, and 'loved to be thought awful mysterious and gloomy'. And Byron's estranged wife Annabella Milbanke contended that he 'wished to be thought partially deranged, or on the brink of it' and spoke of 'his acted insanity'.[11]

This means that Byronic heroes after *Childe Harold* were not just reiterations of a successful formula, but restatements of his own public image. The man promoted the poetry and the poetry the man, and the two became inseparable in people's perceptions. For this to work well Byron knew he must look the part. He went on drastic diets and sported a debonair but casual style, with an open neckline and wide trousers, the latter to hide his club foot, and he made the most of his curling dark hair and muscular physique. In images he liked his face shown in profile or three-quarter view, judging these to flatter him most. He was not an easy sitter for artists – a volatile, quickly bored man who nonetheless always wanted to look heroic, sublime and melancholy and fussed over details of their work. Portraits of him tend to look dramatic but rather staged, not least the one by Thomas Phillips of him in traditional Albanian costume. In appearance too, Byron became Byronic.[12]

In typical celebrity mode his life became a story. The twists and turns of his theatrical liaison with Lady Caroline Lamb and anecdotes of women fainting in his presence or of ravished chambermaids were components of a narrative widely related. He made sure to keep this narrative moving and played his part with panache in a sequence of adventures and stunts designed to bring him forward in the brightest of lights. To the novelist Lady Blessington he avowed he was a role-player without a real character of his own, itself an attention-seeking confession but probably with some truth in it. He also contrived to exude mystery, as the painter Benjamin Robert Haydon recalled on his death: 'Byron is a great loss to the Literature of the Age. He kept it always in excitement, with all the prerogatives of a man of genius – what is he about! – what has he done! – what is he going to do [...] With all his faults he was a fine creature.'[13]

A 'fine creature' is just what he seemed to adoring readers, who quoted him more than any other author in their commonplace books and sent him streams of letters. His mainly female correspondents seized at the implied invitation to read his life through his work and gained an access to him that felt real, and because the poetic heroes he lurked behind were so attractive, his fans' gaze was filled with desire. In their letters, some addressing him as 'Corsair' or 'Childe Harold', they recalled favourite passages, offered their own poems, and used charged, even erotic language to describe their responses to his verse. They said they knew him and felt his passion, despair and rejection of the world, and the vision of an intrinsically good man distorted into bitterness inspired a yearning to reform him and make him happy. The cult of the moody outsider was born.[14]

Despite his mask of self-sufficiency, Byron enjoyed being popular and was sceptical about poets who wanted immortal fame instead. In *Don Juan* he mocks the writer who 'reserves his laurels for posterity' and suggests he has 'generally no great crop to spare it'; in any case, he contends, posterity is a feeble support for the poet in his present endeavours. His own approach is different: 'I shall adapt my own poesy, please God! to the fashion of the time, and, in as far as I possess the power, to the taste of my readers of the present generation; if it survives me, *tanto meglio*, if not, I shall have ceased to care about it.'[15] With friends he frankly relished his success in the here and now. To Lady Melbourne he exulted when *The Corsair* made a splash; and to Thomas Medwin he admitted that he was proud of the fat fees Murray paid him, that he sought to appeal to female readers ('Who does not write to please the women?'), and that he luxuriated in the high-society accolades won by *Childe Harold*.[16]

Some of his contemporaries were conscious of this attitude, and it made them doubt the sincerity of his poetry. As Annabella Milbanke put it, 'He is the absolute monarch of words, and uses them, as Bonaparte did lives, for conquest, without more regard to their intrinsic value.' Others, with fewer personal reasons to dislike him, were of the same view. The politician John Philpot Curran alleged that 'my Lord weeps for the press, and wipes his eyes with the public.' Lady Blessington, reflecting on his decision to fight for Greek independence, judged, 'The end and aim of his life is to render himself celebrated: hitherto his pen has been the instrument to cut his road to renown, and it has traced a brilliant path; this, he thinks, has lost some of its point, and he is about to change it for the sword.' Later, Thackeray declared that Byron '*never* wrote from his heart. He got up his rapture and enthusiasm with an eye to the public.'[17]

In forging his reputation Byron did not act alone. Together with portraitists and the engravers who copied their works, his helpers included eager booksellers and the friendly and unfriendly reviewers whose heated contention kept him fresh in people's minds. Robert Charles Dallas acted as his literary mentor, offered the manuscript of *Childe Harold* to John Murray, and then edited it with him. Murray's canny advertising launched the work and, with it, the phenomenon of 'Byromania'. Subsequent titles benefited from Murray's marketing skill: giving presentation copies to people of note, priming reviewers, ordering prints of Byron as frontispieces or for general sale, using his famous bookseller dinners to promote him, and sealing letters with a signet ring bearing his image.[18] When Dallas fell from grace the role of unpaid assistant was filled by John Cam Hobhouse, who devoted years to travelling with Byron, helping him with composition and sorting out his literary, financial and personal affairs.

Hobhouse and other devotees ascribed Byron's colossal success solely to his poetic genius, his utterance of sentiments that touched his readers' hearts, and his honesty in tackling difficult subjects. In fact, it was, as well, the product of the celebrity apparatus, in which the individual, industry and audience all played their part and all stood to gain. Each work, with its characteristic hero, setting and style, was a repackaging of a well-liked product. Each was different from its forerunners, offering something new, but at the same time readily recognisable, a comfortable and familiar presence in the busy marketplace of literature. The brand known as Byronism, embracing the poet and his poems, was both popular and profitable, so the only concern was to keep it going.

This was the view of his publisher and readers, but Byron himself came to feel trapped in a commercial logic that stood in the way of creative innovation. He wished to try new genres and felt he could not compose any more poetical tales without stagnating. He was also alive to the inevitable criticism that his work was getting repetitive. John Murray tried, with varying success, to keep his leading author's shoulder to the tried and tested wheel. Many readers and reviewers wanted more of the same and were disappointed when he gave them historical dramas instead, considering these not to be authentic productions of his pen. He found the weight of expectations ever more burdensome, and in moments of disillusionment he declared he would not be the creature of others' appetites, and specifically that he was sick of writing for women as this only made them want more.

Byron's readers constrained him in another way. Having been invited to read his poems to know him, they insisted their knowledge be respected and he behave accordingly. It was said he reduced them to a state of vassalage, but the image may be reversed. Through his works, readers saw him as a rebel, a hero, a lover, a misanthrope, and at first he liked playing to the gallery. In time, though, he grew tired of roles better suited to a fictional than a real being and felt the self-alienation that bedevils the celebrity experience. Yet he could not act out of character or stop writing Byronic poems, for, like other celebrities, he was addicted to his audience. Charles Greville grasped this: 'That he very sincerely entertained a bad opinion of mankind may be easily believed; but so far from his pride and haughtiness raising him above the influence of the opinion of those whom he so despised, he was the veriest slave to them that ever breathed.'[19]

Others made hay while his sun shone. Journalists followed his fortunes and publishers spewed out pirated editions of his work, sub-Byronic material by other hands, and parodies of his style. Inferior copies of portraits appeared, and these spawned more likenesses in various formats, including satirical prints and, later, chinaware and busts. Slowly his visual image was degraded and turned into an assemblage of traits: the curled forelock, square jaw, open-necked shirt and flared trousers.[20] Young men like Edward Bulwer-Lytton and Benjamin Disraeli aped his manner and turned it to their own purposes. Byron had culled Byronism from various sources, including Milton's *Paradise Lost*, Goethe's *Faust* and the Gothic novels of Ann Radcliffe; what he never counted on was that others would continue the process of defining it. Operating outside his and his publisher's control, this appropriation of the brand simplified and coarsened it, and made it feel even more of a straightjacket to Byron himself.

In January 1815 he and Miss Milbanke married. Twelve months later she left him and began proceedings to obtain a legal separation. Earlier his fast lifestyle had added to his glamour, but the infamy he acquired after a year of marital infelicity was another matter. Having stoked speculation about his private life, Byron now watched as it was stoked by his enemies, foremost among them his wife's lawyer Stephen Lushington. Stories of incest, sodomy and cruelty began to swirl around him. The whiff of transgression became the stench of depravity, the outsider an outcast. He left England in April 1816, never to return. During his final years his name was blackened further by *Don Juan*, which was deemed so licentious as to be unreadable by women. He was chastised for polluting the minds of the public and sales declined. Those who had disliked him all along for promoting immorality and exciting hysteria had the upper hand.

The critic John Gibson Lockhart argued after Byron's death in 1824 that readers bore some blame for his aberrations. 'We [...] insisted upon saddling Byron, himself personally, with every attribute, however dark and repulsive, with which he had chosen to invest a certain fictitious personage, the hero of a romance.' This blending of Byron with his protagonists prompted the author to do likewise, making him brood on negative feelings, dissect his blackest thoughts, and take perverse pleasure in what others would shrink from:

> We tempt him to indulge in these dangerous exercises, until they obviously acquire the power of leading him to the very brink of phrenzy – we tempt him to find, and to see in this perilous vocation, the staple of his existence, the food of his ambition, the very essence of his glory – and the moment that, by habits of our own creating, at least of our own encouraging and confirming, he is carried one single step beyond what we happen to approve

of, we turn round with all the bitterness of spleen, and reproach him with the unmanliness of entertaining the public with his feelings in regard to his separation from his wife. This was truly the conduct of a fair and liberal public!

The cycle of creation, celebration and degradation of the celebrity by the audience, first seen in full with Byron, became commonplace after him. Henry Holland, recalling his case in 1872, saw a pattern: 'It was one of those whimsical spectacles, periodically occurring, where an idol is suddenly set up by hands which afterwards help assiduously to take it down. [...] I have seen many of these epidemic impulses of fashion in London society, but none more marked than this.'[21]

Even in his own day, Byron was not the only writer to discover that celebrity was enjoyed at the audience's sufferance, and that with the shrewdest calculations of writer and publisher this audience still remained a volatile part of the equation. The anonymity, diversity and sheer number of readers were exciting but disconcerting; it was hard to know what they would think, how they would respond. In addition, writers sensed that consumer approbation and good sales were no proof of literary quality, indeed that they might point to a superficiality that would before long consign a work to oblivion – a disquieting thought for those who took pride in their craft. Related to this was the sense of estrangement when the public valued their work for qualities other than those they themselves thought salient.

Also unpalatable was the power of critics. Good reviews were a boon, but in an age of strong political and literary partisanship there were many bad and some violent ones, showing the consequence of attention to person as well as output in a celebrity-soaked world. A notorious case of hostile reviewing was the *ad hominem* assault on the 'Cockney School' of writers (John Keats, James Leigh Hunt, William Hazlitt) in *Blackwood's Edinburgh Magazine* from 1817 to 1819. A few years later John Wilson, as 'Christopher North', the principal writer for *Blackwood's*, said he found the idea of reviewing without hard comments about authors unthinkable. Looking back in old age to the second decade of the century, Leigh Hunt wrote:

Readers in these kindlier days of criticism have no conception of the extent to which personal hostility allowed itself to be transported, in the periodicals of those times. Personal habits, appearances, connections, domesticities, nothing was safe from misrepresentations, begun, perhaps, in the gaiety of saturnalian licence, but gradually carried to an excess which would have been ludicrous, had it not sometimes produced tragical consequences. It threatened a great many more, and scattered, meantime, a great deal of wretchedness among unoffending as well as offending persons.[22]

The curiosity of readers about authors as people, the eagerness of reviewers to cater to it, and the way some authors actively sought media exposure diminished respect for their right to privacy. It could also make them personally accessible in inconvenient ways. The didactic poet Felicia Hemans had unannounced visitors to her Lakeland cottage: 'Think of my being found out by American tourists in Dove's Nest! The young ladies, as I feared, brought an album concealed in their shawls, and it was levelled at me like a pocket pistol before all was over.'[23] Admirers of the nature poet John Clare flocked to his humble cottage, and if this was at first flattering it soon became irksome, leading him to sigh that he had become a peep show. Such voyeurism was a debasement of the illusion of intimacy on which celebrity status depends.

A strong public persona like this suited publishers, who saw writers as an asset from which present and future revenue could be drawn. They therefore enjoined them to behave and write in the approved style, in other words to imitate themselves. It is a curious twist that publishers exploited the Romantic notion of unique individuality and originality, which fuelled interest in authors' private lives, to turn them into commodities. Byron is an example of this, of course, and so is Clare, whose growing desire to be seen as a poet rather than a peasant poet faced stiff resistance. In emancipating themselves from patrons, writers found that they had merely exchanged one species of bondage for another. To the poet Thomas Moore, publishers were 'bibliopolists'.[24] Little wonder success soured on many writers, and that some experienced feelings of confusion about their identity.

Publishers were unscrupulous not just in how they treated authors but in their marketing too, especially the already-mentioned use of advertising masquerading as news. At its simplest this might be a sentence or two in the miscellaneous columns of a newspaper about the stir a book was causing, and the unsuspicious saw nothing amiss. Such 'puffing', as all indirect publicising was known, does not seem so terrible, but the scale of its use slowly corroded trust. The essayist Abraham Hayward stated that the only sectors more reliant on it than the book trade were quack medicine and auctioneering, and even this was doubtful.[25] The most vigorous puffer, Henry Colburn, boasted that with an advertising budget of £200–£300 he could make the public buy any book, however mediocre. He also made it plain to editors of newspapers he advertised in heavily that he did not wish to see any negative coverage of his authors.

Worse was the corruption of criticism. To boost their incomes many authors wrote for periodicals, and here they found the temptation to jettison objectivity strong: friends leaned on them and strangers bribed them for a good write-up; their publishers wanted a helping hand for other writers in the same stable; or they stooped so far as to review themselves. When John Wilson saw a lukewarm draft criticism of a book of his for *Blackwood's Edinburgh Magazine* he got the editor's permission to find his own reviewer. He gave the task to John Gibson Lockhart, who provided a glowing piece. Two years later Lockhart wanted Wilson to return the favour, but as Wilson was busy Lockhart wrote his own review instead and was paid for doing so.[26] Even the upright Walter Scott noticed his own *Tales of My Landlord*, while Henry Colburn bought periodicals and expected his authors to review one another in them. Such self-trumpeting and cronyism, like fake advertising, was often called 'puffing' or 'puffery'.

Naturally there were calls for reform. In his mock epic *The Puffiad* (1828) Robert Montgomery denounced the practice, and six decades earlier another poet, Thomas Chatterton, claimed in his satire *The Art of Puffing* (1770) that it gave shallow works the most exposure, while writers of merit were ignored. Others argued that the corollary of trash doing well by dint of puffery was that works of quality could not succeed without it. Coleridge contemplated a lampoon on the reviewing system entitled 'Puff and Slander' (though he was not above commending his own writing using the device of a bogus letter in his *Biographia Literaria*). Malpractice and the protest it elicited should not make us overlook the existence of ethical reviewing, but by the end of the Regency period gross venality in the promotion of books had badly damaged the credit of authorship and publishing.

Obliged to court publicity, hawked about by publishers, puffed in dishonest reviews, and consumed by an anonymous public for whom reading was an act of possession, writers must sometimes have felt like prostitutes. John Clare makes this analogy in his *Don Juan*, calling the two professions 'the luckless twins of shame'.[27] Many felt at least that literature was engaged in a silent struggle with commerce for its soul. William Hazlitt, the most significant theorist of fame in the early nineteenth century, blamed Byron for being willing to slake his audience's thirst for sensation. Such conduct was all too common and made writers forget the higher goal of enduring fame: 'A modern author may (without much imputation to his wisdom) declare for a short life and a merry one. Literary immortality is now let on short leases, and he must be contented to succeed by rotation.'[28]

In Maria Jane Jewsbury's comic sketch 'The Young Author' the title figure trains as a literary celebrity by adopting every passing fad and cant phrase. He drops quotes from other writers, keeps his study '*dis*arranged for effect', says he works at night because the day is full of domestic noise, and lives off dry biscuits, wine and coffee. At parties he is seen in an amethyst-coloured waistcoat or with his arm in a sling, and he cultivates a pale, languid look and a dry cough so people think he is ill. Mothers worry his genius will kill him, and their daughters pronounce him most interesting. He tries to appear intellectual by finding fault with others' writing but is not above stealing ideas from half-forgotten essayists. Aside from the inevitable love poetry, he writes theatre criticism for a newspaper and verse for magazines (using *Walker's Rhyming Dictionary*) and labours at a tragedy to be called *The Burning of Rome* or *The Siege of Gibraltar*. His career falters, much to his indignation, and he gets into debt.[29]

Star after star rose and fell. In *Don Juan* Byron imagined a London literary reception for the eighty greatest living poets, while Keats mocked 'the commonplace crowd of the little-famous – who are each individually lost in a throng made up of themselves'. Like other minor celebrities, these figures were known as 'lions', and like lions in a circus they had to perform. Most of all, they had to shine at parties, as Thomas Moore records the wit Sydney Smith observing: 'His description of the *dining* process, by which people in London extract all they can from new literary lions, was irresistibly comic. "Here's a new man of genius arrived – put on the stew-pan – fry away – we'll soon get it all out of him."'[30] The lions' antics created the expectation that all authors would make a public show of themselves, although many had no bent for it and found it draining.

A reaction was bound to set in against these excesses, and it took the form of a renewed emphasis on the value of posterity. The Romantic poets William Wordsworth, Samuel Taylor Coleridge, Percy Bysshe Shelley and John Keats all declared for it, as did the critic William Hazlitt.[31] The principle is easily stated: the poet, knowing that real fame is awarded by the future to the past, not by the present to itself, tries to produce works of lasting worth rather than instant appeal, and their survival after his death redeems a life spent in relative or complete neglect. Though this posture entails obvious sacrifices, not least pecuniary ones, it is liberating. Instead of seeing mass readership as a worry and a challenge, instead of trying to ascertain and satisfy its preferences, the poet looks to the ideal public of tomorrow.

This is not disengagement, for the poet encourages readers to attain a higher level of discrimination so they can comprehend his wisdom. In Wordsworth's view poetic genius is necessarily ahead of its time, and one of its tasks is to create a taste. The barrister Henry Crabb Robinson put it to him that some readers were unable to appreciate his verse: 'Wordsworth seemed to tolerate this class, and to allow that his admirers should undergo a sort of education to his works.'[32] Hazlitt takes a similar but distinct position by giving the better type of critic a vital role in forming the canon. The rank of a literary work is determined not by initial popularity, he says, but by the judgement, exercised over time, of those with cultural authority. Universal suffrage may be good for electing parliaments, but in matters of taste only those of refined understanding should decide. Whether aesthetic judges are poets or critics, the elitism of this vision is the same.

Regarding his own poetry, Wordsworth's forward gaze was steady. He endured bafflement, contempt, even ridicule before its quality was recognised, but self-belief saved him from mortification at seeing lesser men preferred. Robinson noted 'the just feeling of confidence which a sense of his own excellence gives him', and when the poet Zillah Watts said she thought Milton's 'Lycidas' the greatest elegy in English, Wordsworth replied that it stood beside his own 'Laodamia' as one of the twin immortals. He was so disenchanted with readers of his day that he professed reluctance to see his work in print. 'My own feelings urge me to state, in sincerity, that I naturally shrink from solicitation of public notice,' he told the artist Haydon. 'I never publish anything without great violence to my own disposition.' To another he dismissed the lack of contemporary praise for his poems:

> Trouble not yourself upon their present reception; of what moment is that compared with what I trust is their destiny, to console the afflicted, to add sunshine to daylight by making the happy happier, to teach the young and gracious of every age, to see, to think and feel, and therefore to become more actively and securely virtuous; this is their office, which I trust they will

faithfully perform long after we (that is, all that is mortal of us) are mouldered in our graves.[33]

Wordsworth abhorred the cult of personality and the use of the writer's image to sell books. He took a dim view of literary biography, which he thought pandered to idle curiosity and trivialised a life that ought to be represented by publications. With these his only epitaph, the writer kept his dignity; in a biographer's hands he was reduced to an assemblage of anecdotes and quirks. Furthermore, this personal approach coarsened the public mind and violated the sanctity of the domestic space.[34] These ideas, which reflect Wordsworth's obsession with having sole authority to shape his life story, are probably the more acute for being penned at a time of Byron's separation scandal. The spectacle of Byron's rapid shift from adulation to revulsion was a warning against setting up and then losing control of a celebrity image. For Wordsworth he offered a morality tale, an unedifying narrative of splendour and misery, of vanity and folly.

The risk of overt resistance to celebrity culture is that it re-enacts a process that has already occurred. As we have said, the Romantic notion of original genius and unique subjectivity assisted the development of the quite different phenomenon of literary celebrity by focusing on the writer's personality, which became a marketable image. Disliking this connection, some poets rejected celebrity and its commercial logic but still cleaved to the Romantic ideology of artistic creation, and they did so by refusing to seek applause and taking up a position outside the whirlpool of renown. However, this stern purity itself became a public image, especially if it was insistently asserted.[35] And this image, like any other, lent itself to promotion in the literary marketplace. Its appeal was to those – vocal in any age – who thought cultural production had become rubbishy and yearned for something more elevated.

The case of Wordsworth shows how celebrity culture embraces the anti-celebrity stance. His decision to live in a remote Westmorland home, there to ruminate on man and nature as a philosopher-poet, fascinated critics and was, to his horror, central to their discussion of him. Were his plain, wholesome habits and separation from the society of his intellectual equals sublime independence or unsociable churlishness? Would this lifestyle yield majestic, uncluttered poetry or lead to self-indulgent sterility? Would his genius atrophy among rustics, or would it prosper behind a shield raised against the enervating influence of the metropolis? These were questions explored by commentators of the stature of John Wilson, William Hazlitt and Francis Jeffrey; the point, for us, is not who had the best answers, but that Wordsworth's very disavowal of celebrity made him a celebrity. The lone genius is a powerful brand.

* * *

Where does all this leave Byron, who welcomed immediate success and sneered at those who fixed their gaze on the distant horizon of posterity? It seems he was genuinely pessimistic about his poetry's longevity, yet was, or professed himself to be, content. His friend John Cam Hobhouse recorded his thoughts:

> He says himself that his poems are of that sort, which will, like everything of the kind in these days, pass away, and give place to the ancient reading, but that he esteems himself fortunate in getting all that can now be got by such passing reputation, for which there are so many competitors.

Elsewhere Byron said he had enjoyed renown as a poet between the ages of twenty and thirty but had no idea whether it would last.[36] To be sure, his prolific and certainly uneven output seemed to range him among serial petitioners for public approval rather than candidates for immortal laurels.

Some of Byron's most discerning contemporaries thought more of his verse than he did. Shelley was among the Romantic poets who accepted the split between passing celebrity and true fame, but his 'Adonais' implies that with Byron the first is a precursor of the second. Of the same mind was John Murray, who said he had created a 'ferment' that would 'subside into lasting fame'.[37] It is noteworthy that those who condemned Byronism often deemed his verse to be of the highest order, and all the more dangerous for that. In the decades after his death he did suffer a partial eclipse. To the Victorians he appeared brilliant but insincere, a degenerate poseur who aped his far-fetched characters and embodied the vacuity of the Regency. In this view he also demonstrated the damage celebrity culture could do, denaturing a fine talent and turning it to unworthy goals.

Yet Byron's standing did not decline anything like as much as some assumed it would, and today he is a canonical writer whose works are laboriously edited and published as classics. He is immortalised in statues and stained glass and the subject of fat biographies.

'Byronic' is still a term to conjure with, and its eponym continues to fascinate us as a flamboyant, invigorating rebel who blurred sexual and social boundaries. Nonetheless, this is not a simple tale of the celebrity jinx overcome, because while Byron remains famous, and has a much stronger visual presence in people's minds than Wordsworth, Coleridge, Keats, or Shelley, their work is more read than his. The Byronic persona, which at first seemed a flashy way of promoting his poems, is his most enduring achievement. His greatest creation was himself.

4

Actors and Actresses

Portrait of Elizabeth Farren by Sir Thomas Lawrence.
Metropolitan Museum of Art.

Aside from writers, the biggest celebrities of the Regency were the leading men and women of the stage. Very naturally too, since the element of performance required to maintain celebrity status could hardly be better mastered than by people who earned their living with role-playing and audience interaction. Indeed, the emotionally vivid, accessible type of renown that was supplanting the older model of fame at his time was both symbolised and influenced by actors' ability to communicate feelings and create public intimacy.

It would be hard to overstate the popularity of theatregoing in the late Georgian period. James Grant's survey of London life describes theatres as 'the principal source of amusement' for all social strata: 'The highest and the lowest, the most intellectual and most illiterate, evince an equal partiality to them.'[1] Most towns of any size had a playhouse and there was a galaxy of travelling companies. In London only Covent Garden and the Theatre Royal, Drury Lane were licensed to perform serious plays, but smaller theatres provided a mixed fare of pantomimes and melodramas (lightweight pieces with music). Audiences were not the decorous body of later times, but rowdy and raucous, and easily distracted from what was happening on stage by disturbances in the auditorium. Nonetheless, they were passionate about plays and performance, and much of their clamour expressed approval or disapproval of the entertainment they had paid to see.

This enthusiasm existed despite the lack of first-rate plays written in the eighteenth century and the limited repertoire by the end of it. But if the drama stagnated, acting did not. The most signal advance in the histrionic arts was made by David Garrick, who replaced the static, declamatory manner of his day with a more natural technique using simple gestures and facial expressions drawn from his study of physiognomy. This approach allowed Garrick to take almost any role with ease. Under his influence actors, rather than rhetorically produce a character, inhabited it and conveyed its essence visually as well as orally. This gave an emotional immediacy in tune with the cult of sensibility that flourished in the latter part of the century. Garrick's style was carried further by the tragic actress Sarah Siddons, who added a gripping energy of gesture and movement and invested familiar lines with new nuances of meaning and intensity.

The displacement of playwrights by actors was clear from the theatre criticism that filled ever more newspaper column inches. The play's structure and language often seemed hardly worth discussing, particularly if it was an old warhorse, a derivative patchwork or a hurried adaptation of a foreign work, and so attention moved to the stage presence of actors and their revelation of character. Dramatic criticism was only slightly less corrupt than literary criticism, and the better-known actors could ingratiate themselves with the gentlemen of the press. Leigh Hunt recalls:

> It was the custom at that time for editors to be intimate with actors and dramatists. They were often proprietors, as well as editors; and, in that case, it was not expected that they should escape the usual intercourse, or wish to do so. It was thought a feather in the cap of all the parties; and with these feathers they tickled one another. The newspaper man had consequence in the green-room, and plenty of tickets for his friends; and he dined at amusing tables. The dramatist secured a good-natured critique in his journal, sometimes got it written himself, or [...] was even himself the author of it. The actor, if he was of any evidence, stood upon the same ground of reciprocity.[2]

These were piping times for the stars of the stage. In the absence of the modern director they were free to interpret roles as they wished. Their obligation to rehearse was minimal, in part because the rest of the cast were expected to work around them. Their salaries dwarfed those of other members of the same companies, supplemented by benefit nights on which they took all the receipts. They went on lucrative provincial tours, playing with local performers as they moved about. Such status and remuneration were in stark contrast with the circumstances into which many of them were born. Their rise from indigence to wealth, from obscurity to the margins of the fashionable world, reflected the social mobility that celebrity made possible. This in turn reinforced the shift in attitudes that enabled those without inherited status or wealth to seek and win popular esteem. Finally, it raised a profession long associated with vagrancy, immorality and unruliness to a new respectability.

As with other celebrities, so with actors what they did and who they were became one. A performance that elicited tears or laughter from an audience made them want to know more of the player who had so moved them. Great interest was aroused by displays of physical attractions, as occurred when women played male or 'breeches' parts that revealed their stockinged calves. This interest was teased into a sense of intimacy by prologues and epilogues written for particular company members, which they delivered 'as themselves' but which contained witticisms that blended them with their roles. Most actors were less versatile than Garrick, appearing repeatedly as rogues, great ladies, hoydens or whatever, and they had roles written for them as such. This typecasting, having presumably drawn on their real nature, then informed the way they were seen as private people, to the point that their best parts were used as nicknames for them.

Painted portraits underscored the high status of popular actors and the conflation of actor and role. Because these portraits were usually exhibited and engraved for general sale before being delivered to the purchaser, they made the features of sitters familiar even to those who had not seen them on stage. Some depicted actors in famous roles, some acting in a generic way, some in private life, showing that they were celebrities on and off the stage. Artists were glad to paint stage idols, whose likenesses would add to the appeal of exhibitions and yield a good sale of prints. They made good subjects in another way too, for they treated posing for a portrait as a performance, a coherent projection of personality. Artists were forced to share the financial rewards of their work when it was reproduced on playing cards, figurines, fans and other knick-knacks, but at least actors could be pleased that their faces were everywhere.

Meanwhile, newspapers informed their readers of actors' activities in and out of the theatre, as did the pot-boiling pamphlets that flowed from the presses. The growth of popular biography from the latter decades of the eighteenth century was particularly strong in this field, and many notable thespians gave their own version of events in memoirs. Both genres bolstered the standing of stage celebrities by plotting their lives as a sequence of problems overcome and victories won, with the contributions of others downplayed. As well as burnish careers, these books showed actors as private people and provided a myriad of behind-the-scenes anecdotes. Despite their usually genial tone they were meant as serious testaments to their subjects, though few were as tendentious, or as long, as Anne Mathews' four-volume celebration of her husband Charles, a much-loved comedian.

Actors were survived by their biographies, autobiographies and portraits, but in an era before recorded sound and film they faced the prospect that their art, unlike that of painters or writers, would die with them. Sometimes it died well before that, as in the case of the child actor William Betty, known as 'The Young Roscius'. After creating a sensation in Ireland Betty appeared at the age of thirteen at Covent Garden and Drury Lane in 1804. The frenzy to see him was such that people queued for hours to get tickets, invaded private boxes, and jostled for seats. After repeated scenes of mayhem theatre managers took to hiring guards to control audiences.[3] When Betty appeared in Shakespearian roles people swooned and wept, and they hardly had time to dry their eyes before a merchandising campaign sprang up to offer them medallions, snuff boxes, coffee cups and other trinkets, all adorned with the comely youth's image.

The craze continued and Betty pocketed vast sums before taking a break from the stage in 1808 to attend Cambridge University. On his return in 1812 he fell flat, and later comebacks fizzled out. The artist Haydon recalled his strange career:

> His fame, when a boy, was certainly never exceeded by any one; not even Buonaparte had ever a greater share of public attention for the time. Columns of the public journals criticised and lauded him. The prince, the nobility, the ladies doated on him. I remember, when he was confined with a cold, a 'bulletin' was obliged to be put up in the windows of his house to satisfy the eager enquiries of the world. Poor fellow! When grown to man's estate, without feeling, or capacity, or sense, he attempted again to excite the applause of the world. But alas! the novelty was over; faults were no longer pardoned, because youth was no longer the excuse for them. He was now criticised as a man, and he sank like an exhalation of the evening, never to rise again.[4]

Even in his glory days Betty's acting had not been wonderful, as adult performers well knew. It was merely very good for a child, and this touched the heartstrings in the same way as modern talent shows that exhibit promise rather than finished skill. Spectators gape as someone attains stardom in a flash and thereby holds out the promise that they – or perhaps their children – might do likewise. By adopting a juvenile star, Betty's fans also made themselves part of an unfolding story, but sadly the extraordinary boy grew into an ordinary man, as has happened with many child stars since.[5]

The nickname 'The Young Roscius' alluded to the exemplary Roman actor Quintus Roscius Gallus, but the immediate reference was to David Garrick, often hailed as 'The English Roscius'. This was canny marketing since it connected the boy with the finest actor in living memory, someone who, unlike Betty, went a long way by his various attainments to overcome the evanescence of the actor's art.[6] A self-made man who had left his trade as a vintner to tread the boards, Garrick not only brought a new suppleness and emotional range to acting, but used his personal example to give it a new dignity. He lived as a gentleman, with his country house, his reputation as a connoisseur, his collection of early dramas in manuscript, and his relaxed mingling with lords and ladies. Furthermore, he had a very productive career as a theatre manager, writing and adapting plays, bringing in higher levels of professionalism, notably in ensemble acting, and making improvements in decoration and lighting.

For all his apparent seigneurial ease, Garrick was a tireless self-promoter. His vigilance about dramatic criticism spawned the well-known story that when Edmund Kean complained to Garrick's widow that critics did not appreciate his acting, she replied that he ought to write his own reviews as her husband had. He was accused of treating social occasions as exercises in networking, of acting his own gentility, and of endlessly soliciting applause from his acquaintance. The novelist Oliver Goldsmith joked:

> On the stage he was natural, simple, affecting;
> 'Twas only that when he was off he was acting.[7]

Aware of the impact of visual images, Garrick sat to William Hogarth, Johann Zoffany, Sir Joshua Reynolds and others, often commissioning portraits himself. He was painted as a family man, in his best roles, and as an emblematic actor, notably in Reynolds's *David Garrick Between Tragedy and Comedy*, in which two muses fight over him. Images in other formats proliferated. Though he lived just before the celebrity apparatus of individual, industry and audience was fully formed, Garrick's self-fashioning had celebrity characteristics.[8] His death prompted a flood of tributes and he was given a public funeral, with a cortege of fifty vehicles processing to Westminster Abbey, where he was interred in Poets' Corner.

The decades after Garrick's death in 1779 were the era of John Philip Kemble, Charles Mayne Young, Edmund Kean and William Macready, but more actresses than actors became household names. This reflects the depth of female talent. 'The progress of refinement has thrown the stage open to a competition of the two sexes, and often inscribed a female name in the highest rank of theatrical merit,' wrote the theatre historian James Boaden in 1827.[9] In addition, the physical allure of women was more potent. Beauty could be their undoing, of course, and a few generations before actresses had been stigmatised as harlots. The move towards respectability in the theatre during the eighteenth century and the influence of positive role models, along with improved remuneration, allowed actresses to exploit their looks without having to tolerate lewd advances or listen to offers of protection they could not afford to refuse.

The admiration of fêted actresses as creative artists and as women was ardent, and their images appeared on cups, tiles, screens and every other conceivable surface. This gave them a strong presence in the public imagination that they could channel to their advantage. As well as enthralling men, actresses inspired women and sparked new modes. When Mary 'Becky' Wells played the part of Cowslip in John O'Keeffe's *Agreeable Surprise*, her Cowslip hats and gowns became the rage. Wells herself was referred to as Cowslip, one of many instances of a part sticking to a player. Another trendsetter was Frances Abington, whose headdress for the part of Kitty in James Townley's *High Life Below Stairs* started appearing in milliners' shop windows and became known as the 'Abington Cap'. According to a biographical dictionary of actors, 'Everything she did or said was remarked, especially by women where clothes were concerned.'[10]

As sartorial innovators, actresses came into contact with the regular leaders of fashion, aristocratic ladies, who befriended them and discussed aspects of dress with them. There were cases of actresses giving stage costumes to peeresses and receiving their cast-off gowns to wear on stage or in society. Through such connections they had access to the best addresses, where in return for hospitality they gave a dash to entertainments.[11] Sometimes they were called in to superintend the amateur theatricals that had become a fixture in upper-class households. With their talent for emulation, they used these experiences to acquire superior manners and diction, which polished their playing of well-born characters and further boosted their credentials to mix in the first circles. The wealthiest imitated ladies of quality by giving alms and subscribing to charities, always making sure that their gifts were reported in the newspapers.

These two groups of women were linked by portraits and their reproduction. On account of the keener interest in the 'fair sex', actresses were painted more than actors. Artists knew how insatiable was the appetite for pictures of female theatre stars, and in executing them their fee might be less important than a share of the profits from engravings and the publicity gained from exhibiting canvases. Given such incentives, it is not surprising that many of these portraits were not commissioned at all, but undertaken at their own risk by painters. The sitters gained equally. Some were shown in the attitudes and costume associated with their most famous roles; others struck relaxed poses in elegant contemporary attire with the smartest accessories. Either way, these works were advertisements for future performances and emphatic statements of celebrity status, material success and social acceptance.[12]

A comparison between these grand-manner portraits and those of society belles reveals no patterns of difference, not even subtle ones. Like actresses, aristocrats were depicted in their own clothes, but sometimes in historical or theatrical costume, and even as goddesses or allegorical figures, giving them the thrill of adopting a fantasy identity. In pose, expression, dress, physical setting and artistic treatment, the two categories of sitter were handled alike. As the historical novelist Katherine Thomson memorably put it, all of Sir Joshua Reynolds's female subjects looked like ladies and all of Sir Thomas Lawrence's like 'demireps', meaning women of ill repute.[13] Nor is there any record that this equality of representation was found objectionable, which is itself good evidence of the levelling effect of celebrity.

One of the most dazzling portraits of an actress was Lawrence's of Elizabeth Farren, dressed in a diaphanous white muslin dress and fur-trimmed pelisse and carrying a huge fur muff. When it was painted Farren was a leading light of the London stage, in demand for Shakespearean heroines but above all for comedy parts, which she played with grace and vivacity. Despite her background in the rough-and-ready world of strolling players, she was noted for the taste of her performances and her seemingly innate ladylike bearing, accentuated by a tall, slender figure. She was also known for her strict sexual propriety, and when the unhappily married Earl of Derby offered her an arrangement he was made to realise he had misjudged her badly. For a while he ate humble pie, but finally she agreed to see him in company and later accepted his proposal of marriage in the event of his wife's death.

This engagement lasted eighteen years, and during it they only met with a third person present, usually Farren's mother. The public were gripped by this spectacle of platonic devotion and caricaturists had their fun, not least as Lord Derby's short, portly figure contrasted unhappily with his beloved's. But whatever darts of satire flew at them, Farren's virtue could never be a target. Because of her spotless character and refinement Lord Derby's family welcomed her, his first wife having abandoned him, and other ladies of rank met her on terms of respect and friendship. Her association with the nobility was strengthened when she was invited to oversee amateur theatre at the London residence of the Duke of Richmond. In 1797 the earl's wife died, and after a final performance in her signature role of Lady Teazle in Richard Brinsley Sheridan's *School for Scandal*, Farren became his countess. 'She retired from simulated to real dignity,' wrote the theatre biographer John Adolphus, and the transition was seamless.[14] It was a happy marriage and produced three children.

The fairy tale of Elizabeth Farren underscores how theatrical celebrity was a more female than male phenomenon. Not only were more actresses than actors widely known, but their opportunities for social advancement were greater because they could marry well and gain handles to their names. Another example of this is Eliza O'Neill, a favourite in comedy and tragedy who wed an Irish MP in 1819 and became Lady Wrixon Becher. By contrast David Garrick, for all his gentility, was not even knighted. The position of a top-billing actress was even more striking when compared with that of other women: she rose from simple beginnings to an extent unthinkable by almost any other means; she occupied the sole public forum where a woman's speaking voice could be heard; her artistic freedom gave her a strong cultural identity and real cultural influence; she escaped the logic of separate spheres, whereby the man was active outside and the woman inside the home; and she gained a financial autonomy unmatched by all but heiresses and rich widows.

Of course, this is a one-sided picture. The upward mobility and independence of actresses presented a challenge to the existing order that caused unease in some quarters and would not go unmet. A long-established, still formidable social hierarchy that made a fetish of titles and antecedents could not simply be batted aside by low-born thespians who made heaps of money, kept their own carriage, and had a household of servants. Just as bad, actresses' careers implied a disregard for the norms of feminine reticence. To be ambitious for professional success and achieve it by means of public display was to reject the constraints other women abided by. Pamphlets and articles on these questions made uncomfortable reading for actresses, who were also subjected to endless newspaper chatter and satirical prints about their vanity, greed and their quarrels with one another, topics that were much less covered in relation to male performers.

Nor is it entirely true that actresses had sloughed off the old association with mercenary sexual laxity. The notion that a woman willing to exhibit herself on stage for payment must be personally available to the right bidder was a tenacious one. It was kept alive by the institution of the green room, in which privileged patrons could mingle with the cast and wealthy, dissolute men sought out female players. Some women fell into the old practice of allowing themselves to be maintained by an admirer or living in concubinage with a man who could not or would not marry them. For every Elizabeth Farren there was one Dorothea Jordan, the long-time mistress of the Duke of Clarence, later William IV. The press was fascinated by the private lives of actresses, assumed the worst about them, and fed its readers with titillating, innuendo-filled reports on the subject.

Along with money and romance, extramarital affairs gave an actress increased public profile. Some could not resist courting notoriety and drew the male gaze with intimations of potential or actual licence. But an actress who let herself be seen as a sex symbol and sought to turn the ardour she aroused to her advantage played a risky game. An example of its dangers is provided by the story of Mary Robinson, known as 'Perdita' because she excelled in this role in Shakespeare's comedy *The Winter's Tale*. In 1779 the Prince of Wales saw her in this play and grew so enamoured that he offered her £20,000 to be his mistress. Their affair ended after little more than a year, and as the prince was less generous than he had promised to be Robinson sought to parlay her time as a royal paramour into a more durable status as an arbiter of style and object of desire.

While still with the prince she had won plaudits for introducing the 'Perdita', a flowing muslin gown that imitated the lines of Greek statuary. After this her wardrobe choices were closely watched and lavishly praised. She never stood still. Now she was spotted in a stylised peasant costume, now as a society lady parading in Hyde Park, now in a daringly androgynous riding habit. 'My fashions in dress were followed with flattering avidity,' she recollected in her *Memoirs*.[15] The newspapers dilated on her clothes, her equipages and the luxury goods she indulged in, no doubt with the full consent of those who furnished her with these items. Her appearances in public places were circumstantially described, and soon she garnered more attention for her performances outside than inside the theatre. A series of affairs with eminent men, possibly including the Whig leader Charles James Fox, added piquancy to her renown.

Robinson sharpened her profile with portraits by Gainsborough, Reynolds and Romney. These were so widely disseminated as prints that Pierce Egan imagined her face was familiar in the frozen wastes of Russia. Actress, socialite, courtesan and conspicuous consumer, she tirelessly renewed herself and kept her male and female fans agog. Her *Memoirs* reveal that she loved attention as much as money. On a benefit night in the theatre she 'looked forward with delight both to celebrity and to fortune', and when she quitted the stage it was 'the most gratifying testimonies of public approbation' that she would miss most.[16] She turned to composing love poetry, and here too she was front and centre, often in the pose of a bereaved woman in need of solace. In the 1790s she wrote novels that were promoted using the scandal surrounding her and the promise of more revelations. In fiction and verse, she offered a simulacrum of herself, an erotically charged illusion of intimacy.

Despite this careful self-projection Robinson knew from the outset that control of her image could be wrested from her, and that the path she had taken left her open to attack. Her pert replies to detractors did not deter them, and in the *Memoirs* she recalled being 'assailed by pamphlets, by paragraphs, and caricatures, and all the artillery of slander'. Crude, even obscene prints were published at the time of her affair with the Prince of Wales, and later James Gillray drew a series of caricatures of her and her lovers. In the anonymous *Memoirs of Perdita* (1784) she was pilloried as a seductress who affected innocence while being more expert in the sexual arts than the great whores of antiquity. She also, uniquely, featured twice in the *Tête-à-Tête* series about prominent liaisons in the *Town and Country Magazine*.[17] Frustratingly for her, every time she was abused someone made money out of her image.

Such relentless scrutiny, positive and negative, fanned the flames of Robinson's celebrity, and everyone wanted a good look at her:

> Whenever I appeared in public, I was overwhelmed by the gazing of the multitude. I was frequently obliged to quit Ranelagh, owing to the crowd which staring curiosity had assembled round my box; and, even in the streets of the metropolis, I scarcely ventured to enter a shop without experiencing the greatest inconvenience. Many hours have I waited till the crowd dispersed, which surrounded my carriage, in expectation of my quitting the shop.[18]

She might profess to find such scenes wearisome, but she knew she was complicit in them and gratified by them. More worrying was the fact that while portraits and literary texts, in their different ways, presented her in the most winsome form, it grew harder for the real woman to sustain the role of fantasy object. Ageing and a debilitating illness robbed her of her magnetism, and it was in the nature of the reputation she had built that after the flight of youth it would crumble. Absences from view that may initially have been calculated to stoke curiosity became an escape from a burdensome public image, and when she died she was an isolated figure.

In terms of sexual morality, no one was further removed from Mary Robinson than Sarah Siddons, who married aged eighteen and persevered in her joyless union for over thirty years, bearing seven children, before she and her husband separated in 1804. In addition, Siddons stood far above Robinson as an actress; indeed, she towered over her era. She was born into a theatrical family, and her brother John Philip Kemble was one of the best actors of his generation. After years in the provinces and one false start in London, she made a furore at Drury Lane in 1782. With fine classical features, a tall, lithe figure and natural grace, Siddons had a strong onstage presence. Her total immersion in her roles and the majestic intensity of her performances made audiences sob and shriek. Even those who kept their wits about them never forgot the experience of her acting.

Her reign as the queen of tragedy lasted decades, and so thoroughly did she enrapture her fans that appearances while heavily pregnant and in later years with a bloated body racked by rheumatism did little to lessen her power over them. They remained captive as her stage manner evolved so that it relied less on physicality and vigour and more on imposing bearing and clever use of costume. Though she played a multitude of roles, her staples were those associated with stoicism, grandeur, passion and devotion. She was supremely dignified as Queen Katherine in Shakespeare's *Henry VIII* and as Volumnia in his *Coriolanus*. Above all, Siddons made Lady Macbeth her own, playing the bloody heroine as a wife and mother rather than as a power-hungry monster, and turning the sleepwalking scene into a mesmerising study in mental derangement.

She was so associated with these characters that theatregoers only wanted to see her in them. But just as she inhabited her roles, so they inhabited her, and her queenly bearing in private life was often remarked upon. In any case, the fusion in people's minds between actor and part predisposed them to discern gravitas in Siddons, and especially in her earnest but by no means exceptional devotion to her duties as a wife and mother. In dress she aimed for a simple harmony that bespoke modesty and restraint, for too ornate or modish a style would have detracted from her poise and the awe it inspired. She is known to have given sartorial advice to women in fashionable circles, in which she was not only made welcome, but treated as an acquisition. According to her first biographer,

> Mrs Siddons became the glass 'in which our noble youth did dress themselves'; and those who frequented her exhibitions became related to her look, to her deportment and her utterance; the lowest point of imitation, that of dress, was early, and wisely too, adopted; for it was at all times the praise of Mrs Siddons to be exquisitely chaste and dignified in her exterior.[19]

Siddons was painted many times, and she understood the power of visual images. In Gainsborough's portrait she is elegant and self-assured, emphatically a gentlewoman. She was not a gentlewoman by birth, and her striped silk gown, fox-fur muff and beaver hat trimmed with feathers were the rewards of her own industry. In wearing them, and looking just like Gainsborough's titled beauties, she was playing a part as much as when in historical costume on stage.[20] An equally famous portrait by Reynolds depicts her as the tragic muse. Siddons claimed to have directed how this was to be painted in detail, and although her account is disputed it shows her determination to appear as she saw fit. She also dissuaded Reynolds from using his usual engraver in favour of one she thought would produce a more flattering copy. She even took lessons from the sculptor Anne Damer so that she could make a bust of herself.

Like Robinson, Siddons wrote her memoirs; unlike her, she did so from a position of strength, with her professional and personal credit intact. Rather than dwell on joys and sorrows or justify her conduct to others so as to win sympathy, as Robinson had done, she concentrated on highlights of her career and reflected on her major roles, above all Lady Macbeth. These writings were not published in her lifetime; rather they were incorporated in Thomas Campbell's authorised biography that came out a few years after she died.[21] Siddons fashioned another memorial by nominating a successor in the form of her niece Fanny Kemble, a star of the Victorian stage. This moment of dynastic inheritance is captured in a double portrait by Henry Perronet Briggs that shows a pensive Kemble with her hand tenderly placed on her venerable aunt's arm. On Siddons's lap is an open book, probably a Shakespeare play.

Siddons was respected and popular throughout her career, and her moulding of her image was largely successful. But even she had to learn that audiences could not always be subjected, and that a public persona could be reshaped by unfriendly hands. A misunderstanding about a benefit performance in Dublin led to accusations of avarice, turning the financial gains of her hard work against her, and satirical prints showed her hoarding sacks of money. She faced down critics and triumphed, but her reminiscences record bewilderment and misery at the sudden withdrawal of audiences' affection. She was also lampooned for overblown acting and, in later years, for her excessive weight. 'Alas! What an empty bubble is public favour!' she remarked in 1810, and the man of letters Alexander Dyce recorded a similar reflection: 'Mrs Siddons used to say that the public had a sort of pleasure in mortifying their old favourites by setting up new idols.'[22]

Perhaps it was feelings of vulnerability that made Siddons grow more and more regal. The translator Robert Pearse Gillies spoke of 'that sustained dignity or solemnity of which Mrs Siddons could not, upon any occasion, not even in ordinary life, divest herself', while the writer and actress Elizabeth Inchbald called her a tragedy queen who acted a part among members of her own family. The novelist Frances Burney found a woman trapped by her renown:

> Mrs Siddons manners, quiet and stiff, in voice, deep and dragging; and in conversation formal, sententious, calm and dry. I expected her to have been all that is interesting [...]. But I was very much mistaken. Whether fame and success have spoiled her, or whether she only possesses the skill of representing and embellishing materials with which she is furnished by others, I know not, but I still remain disappointed.[23]

This stiffness was occasioned by discomfiture at the expectations people brought to a meeting with her. Having a character to maintain as the incarnation of tragedy and as a cultural authority could freeze anyone's conversational powers.

On stage she was a victim of her own celebrity in another way: she went on too long, confirming Leo Braudy's maxim that 'the glow of being observed and appreciated by others cannot be given up.' Admirers rued her refusal to retire, which gave young theatregoers a false impression of her abilities. In 1811 Henry Crabb Robinson, a fervent fan, wrote that her waning stagecraft gave him 'real pain', and a year later, for the first time, he saw her 'without any pleasure'.[24] After finally bowing out she made appearances for charity and gave public readings, but otherwise she was at a loss during these years and felt empty and sad. She complained to Samuel Rogers of this and told him that in the evenings, as she sat alone moping, she would recall the nervous excitement she had always felt as she prepared herself in her dressing room to meet a crowded house. Fanny Kemble felt chastened at the spectacle of the old lady's despondency:

> What a price she has paid for her great celebrity! – weariness, vacuity, and utter deadness of spirit. The cup has been so highly flavoured that life is absolutely without savour or sweetness to her now, nothing but tasteless insipidity. She has stood on a pinnacle till all things have come to look flat and dreary; mere shapeless, colourless, level monotony to her. Poor woman![25]

Nothing is harder for celebrities, or calls for more courage, than to step out of their own story.

* * *

The lives of Regency poets and actors illustrate a culture of celebrity that is recognisable today. Moreover, parallels between its workings for these two groups show it to have been a larger phenomenon, not something that arose separately for each. Extending our survey to music and sport would duplicate the pattern: spheres of activity with their own structures and vocabulary hosting the same mechanism for the production of famous names. Over the next two centuries the power of this mechanism expanded, but the basic moving parts were already in place. It may not have been fully understood then, as it is now, that renown is a commodity; but the role of personality in shaping it, the print and visual media in driving it, and the public in sustaining it, were evident. Also evident was a hunger for personal validation that existed independently of any ambition for lasting achievement, though the two often merged. Celebrity desire was as strong then as it has been since.

PORTRAITS

1

The Parvenue Duchess

Harriot, Duchess of St Albans

Harriot Mellon, Duchess of St Albans by Sir William
Beechey. National Portrait Gallery.

In replying to Sir Walter Scott's congratulations on her marriage to the 9th Duke of St Albans in June 1827, the new duchess proposed a subject for his next book:

> What a strange, eventful life has mine been, from a poor little player child with just food and clothes enough to cover me, dependent on a very precarious profession, without talent or a friend in the world! 'to have seen what I have seen, seeing what I see'! Is it not wonderful? Is it true? Can I believe it? First the wife of the best, the most perfect, being that ever breathed, his love and unbounded confidence in me, his immense fortune, so honourably acquired by his own industry, all at my command, – and now the wife of a Duke!
>
> You must write my Life. 'The History of Tom Thumb,' 'Jack the Giant Killer,' and 'Goody Two Shoes' will sink compared with my true history written by the Author of *Waverley*; and that you may do it well, I have sent you an inkstand. Pray, give it a place on your table in kind remembrance of Your affectionate Friend.[1]

The duchess had ten years more to live, and, while her proposal to Walter Scott was made in jest, she did resolve to have a biography written by a well-disposed author. Her urge to have the last word, or at least direct it, was natural. People were always writing about her, and the intensity of both eulogy and detraction was exceptional. The duchess's character and conduct, the implications of her steep social ascent, even basic facts about her life were argued over so much that media coverage was a welter of discord. The voice missing from all this was her own, for she had decided, partly on the advice of friends, not to enter the fray. Instead she looked about for her biographer.

The person she selected was Louisa Sheridan, a contributor of verses to illustrated annuals. During long interviews she told her the story of her life, and when she died in 1837 she left Louisa an annuity of £50. However, Miss Sheridan abandoned the task, and it devolved on the poet and biographer Margaret Cornwell Baron-Wilson, who was approached by the publisher Henry Colburn. Mrs Baron-Wilson had not known the deceased personally, but her *Memoirs of Harriot, Duchess of St Albans*, published in two volumes in 1839, could not have been more obliging. In the opening chapter she portrays the duchess's 'frequently misrepresented' character with the capitalised themes of *religion, charity, truth, generosity, cheerfulness* and *wit*, and the whole book is punctuated and then terminated with unctuous, sentimental reflections on the subject's virtues.

Alongside this tone the voice of the duchess is ever-present because of the author's reliance on Louisa Sheridan's notes, passed to her by Colburn and forming 'the groundwork of these volumes'. Portions of text are in the duchess's own words, sometimes with remembered dialogue, and other passages without quotation marks are clearly her table-talk. Indeed, Mrs Baron-Wilson refers to her own 'editorship' and calls herself 'the compiler of these volumes'.[2] The voices of the two women combine in a duet of honeyed piety and genial vigour from which the duchess emerges as a pattern of excellence. The lack of objectivity provokes scepticism, but for many episodes of her life there is no source but this book. Press articles, pamphlets, obituaries and memoirs offer alternative views on the duchess as a public figure; but for the early phase we are as reliant on Mrs Baron-Wilson as she was on her subject, who, for information on her very first years, was reliant on her very unreliable mother.

* * *

No independent evidence exists of when or where the girl who became Duchess of St Albans was born or who her father was. Her mother Sarah, whose maiden name is also unknown, was a stage-struck milliner's assistant from County Cork. Sarah joined a company of strolling players as wardrobe keeper and money taker, travelling with them to Wales, but after a while the troupe was disbanded and she made her way back to Cork, where she had an affair that resulted in a pregnancy. By her account the man in question was Mathew Mellon, a lieutenant in a regiment raised by the East India Company who was on sick leave and staying in Ireland for his health. They married secretly in 1777 and moved to London, where Harriot was born. Before she drew her first breath Lieutenant Mellon had sailed for India, never to be seen again, and his wife learnt that he had died of consumption during the passage.

No record survives of the marriage, or of Mellon himself, and it is unlikely Harriot was born in wedlock. But Sarah had her story and she stuck to it. She insisted that her 'husband' had been a man of good family, and whenever her daughter misbehaved she was told not to disgrace the 'high blood' in her veins. Harriot always believed the story of her origins in general outline, but laughed off the notion of superior ancestry. What is certain is that when she was born her mother was alone and without means of subsistence. Fortunately, Mr Kena's travelling company, for which she had worked previously, was resurrected and took her on in her old role. It was a precarious

existence, but full of variety and incident. While touring in Lancashire
Sarah married the company's fiddler Thomas Entwisle (or Entwhistle).
He was an affectionate stepfather to the five-year-old Harriot, but out
of respect for the memory of Lieutenant Mellon she did not take his
name.

The Entwisles left Mr Kena to join Thomas Bibby's company, which
for a long while was based in Ulverston, Lancashire. Harriot's home
life was at times tempestuous. Entwisle was an easy-going, idle man,
fairly well educated but fond of drink and low company. He deferred
to his beautiful, hot-tempered wife yet could not avoid her flashes of
irascibility. Nor could Harriot, whose childish pranks and games with
children apparently of her own class fell foul of her mother's notion of
her gentility and resolve to make a fine lady of her. When Mrs Entwisle
flew into a rage she could be brutal, but Harriot did not rebel, partly
from fear and partly from awareness of her mother's devotion and
the sacrifices she made to pay for her schooling and dress her smartly.
Indeed, in later years her unceasing though sorely tried loyalty to her
mother was considered a proof of her sterling character. Meanwhile
Mrs Entwisle had the gratification of seeing her clever, spirited girl
taken up by some of the town's better families.

In 1787 Harriot made her stage debut in Ulverston's theatre, a barn
belonging to an inn. Her part was Little Pickle in *The Spoiled Child*,
which required not much more than romping about in a laurel-green
tunic made by her mother. Audiences greeted the child warmly, and
Bibby gave her other 'hoyden' parts in similarly unsophisticated plays.
This was the beginning of what Mrs Entwisle was determined would
be a notable career. She knew that the theatre was the best means of
raising Harriot to a better station in life, and that this could, with care,
be achieved without taint to her respectability. She watched over her
like a hawk, making sure she minded her manners, wore clean clothes,
and kept out of trouble. She learned to speak correct, unaccented
English at a private day school run by Miss Calvert, who took a shine
to her and introduced her to poetry out of school hours. She was also
taught to sing and dance gracefully.

The next change of scene takes us, probably in 1789, to Stafford,
where the Entwisles joined Samuel Stanton's company. Here, while
continuing her schooling, Harriot gained proficiency as a player and
won plaudits across the Staffordshire circuit plied by the company.
Stanton stood higher than Bibby, and the rising actress was exposed
to a better standard of performances. Just as importantly, a sizeable
county town offered more scope for her mother's pushiness and her
own likeability to propel her upwards in society. Her greatest conquest

was the family of Mr Wright the banker, whose daughters vied to lend her gowns, gloves and shoes. As the Entwisle household descended into acrimony and, in the husband's case, drunkenness, the well-to-do families of the town, and the towns the company visited, took pity on the pretty, bright-eyed but demure girl. She had an open invitation to their homes and at last spent most of her days and even nights there.

The narrative of Harriot Mellon's childhood and youth in the Baron-Wilson biography is full of colourful episodes related in later years to Louisa Sheridan. These episodes tend to show the Entwisles' narrow, insecure circumstances, the gaiety and variety of their itinerant life, Harriot's irrepressible sense of fun and quick-wittedness, the desire of everyone she met to treat her kindly, and her devotion to her mother despite being roughly treated by her. These lively, sometimes slightly cloying anecdotes body forth the story of a girl whose positive outlook, allied to friendliness and fundamental decency, won all hearts. It is a pleasing story, probably with a large element of truth, but it has a single, highly subjective source in the memories of a woman in late middle age who had gained great wealth and status – not by birth or endeavour, but by the charm of her person.

Before long Harriot would be swept higher than the circles she had already entered, but first she went through a time of trial. It began with an apparent stroke of luck. In October 1794 Richard Brinsley Sheridan, the playwright and manager of the Drury Lane Theatre who also represented Stafford in Parliament, paid the town a visit. While there he went to the theatre and saw Harriot, now sixteen or seventeen, in *The Belle's Stratagem* and *The Romp*, and declared himself pleased with her acting. Taking this breezy compliment seriously, Mr Wright and her other supporters pressed him to engage her for Drury Lane. The affable Sheridan, having no wish to disoblige his constituents, made positive noises that they construed as a promise. Then months passed without a word from the London manager, who seemed to have forgotten his undertaking. However, Mrs Entwisle, thinking just one final push would launch her daughter in the metropolis, took her there and found lodgings near the Strand.

They had a long wait. One day Harriot called on Sheridan, who struggled to remember who she was, then renewed his compliments and said he would keep her in mind. She saw how little it meant and went back in tears to her mother, who made her own assault on the playwright but came away equally dejected. At this point they might have gone home, in which case Harriot's star would never have been born. Instead they moved to a cheap cottage in Southwark and bided their time. As the weeks went drearily by and their money ran short they appealed to the faithful Stafford banker, who sent the manager a strong letter. Harriot was invited to call a second time, and when she did so Sheridan asked her to read scenes from his play *The Rivals*. Her reply, very clever or very naïve, was that she dare not, but would he do her the honour of reading them himself? He read almost the whole play to his rapt auditor, who was inspired to join in and take two of the parts. He so enjoyed the experience that he engaged her at once.

Young Harriot started on 30 shillings a week, from which various deductions were made. Her debut, as Lydia Languish in *The Rivals*, took place in September 1795, but she was too nervous to do herself justice. Because the theatre was well stocked with first-rate talents, including Sarah Siddons, Dorothea Jordan and Elizabeth Farren, she was mainly cast in minor roles. There is little point in enumerating forgotten characters in forgotten plays, but during her first seasons she filled any gap, tackling interpolated songs as well as dialogue. She took the parts of leading actresses if they were unable to perform and acquitted herself creditably in them. During these early London years she made a study of Mrs Jordan, the first comic actress of the day, and imitated her technique closely. Gradually she was given better parts, and in 1797–1798 her salary went up to £2 a week.

Compared with what top-billing players received this was modest, but the prestige of being in the Drury Lane company allowed her to earn far more in places that lured London actors when their theatres closed for the summer. For several years she had engagements at the Theatre Royal, Liverpool, where she played the major roles she had understudied in London. Once Sarah Siddons was there at the same time, according to Mrs Baron-Wilson, and electrified the green room by grandly introducing her to the company as her friend and as a woman of the utmost propriety of conduct.[3] Whether materially aided by this endorsement or not, Harriot became a firm favourite in Liverpool and was given her own benefit nights. In the summer of 1798 she cleared £269, over twice as much as she earned in a year at Drury Lane.[4] In 1801 she accepted an invitation to Southampton, where, if the receipts did not match those of Liverpool, the warmth of the audiences did.

Harriot's earnings enabled her and her parents to leave Southwark for rooms in what is now Russell Street, Covent Garden, and over time they took over the whole house. Here she gave parties for the theatrical set. On one occasion she had the floor coloured blue by the Drury Lane scene painters to create a novel effect. Anne Mathews, wife of the actor Charles Mathews, recalled these gatherings: 'At the entrance of the room appeared the hostess, radiant with smiles and genuine hospitality, to welcome her willing guests, having then, perhaps, more happiness in her heart than when after splendour enriched and better taste adorned the scene.' This is our first sight of her in her finest role, that of creative party-giver. We also hear for the first time a refrain in her own and others' accounts of her: that she was happiest before she had riches. Mrs Baron-Wilson relates that the duchess visited her old Russell Street abode every year, 'shedding tears of pleasure at contemplating the miserable little building'.[5]

As a young woman our heroine looked forward, not back, and her hopes were fixed on the stage. She was gaining in the estimation of critics, and by the turn of the century she had won a firm place in audiences' affections. Her field was decidedly comedy, and she drew on an innate sense of humour and a talent for mimicry to represent pert chambermaids, loquacious schemers and sprightly hoydens. Her acting was enhanced by a sweet, fairly low voice, full of sunshine and laughter, and by a radiant appearance, which an unnamed actor quoted by Mrs Baron-Wilson delineates: 'Miss Mellon was a remarkably handsome brunette, but did not look a bit like an actress. She was more like one of the genuine beauties of a quiet village two hundred miles from town. [...] [She was] blooming in complexion, with a very tall fine figure, raven locks, ivory teeth, a cheek like a peach, and coral lips.' Other pen-portraits add sparkling black eyes, a pretty nose and mouth, and a slim but buxom form. Again and again the healthy, rural quality of her beauty is stressed. 'One would deem her the inhabitant of some happy meadow, where sorrow and London smoke were alike unknown,' wrote the actor and theatre writer William Oxberry.[6]

To an extent Harriot's face was her fortune. Her looks led her to be chosen for some parts, and her success in them was a little too easily won. Assured of popularity in her favourite roles, she did not try to extend herself. Conveying deep emotion, especially woe and despair, overtaxed her, and in any case audiences used to her flirtatious vivacity and good humour were loath to accept such exhibitions. 'She should never attempt seriously to cry,' wrote a reviewer after she had done so in a play called *The Wheel of Fortune*. 'The audience, accustomed to her merry face, thought she was jesting, and hailed her tears with laughter.'[7] It was also said her homespun air made her unsuited to play ladies of quality, as Elizabeth Farren did so well. Her education and the patronage of Stafford's best families had given her a deportment far above her mother's, but with her rustic beauty went a certain rusticity of manner, and she was never 'ladylike'.

Newspaper critics placed her in the second tier of performers, and the verdict of writers on the theatre was mixed. For Lord William

Pitt Lennox she was 'almost a second Mrs Jordan', James Boaden found her 'certainly above mediocrity' but lacking the will to achieve greatness, and William Oxberry saw no 'high finish' in her work.[8] She succeeded, said Oxberry, less by what she did than what she was:

> When in spirits, she was more fascinating than excellent, and pleased the senses more than the mind. She played to all our sensibilities, not to our thought; and the applause she excited, was too frequently given to the witchery of the woman, rather than the powers of the actress.[9]

Her *Gentleman's Magazine* obituarist concurs: 'Her acting was not at all calculated to bear the analysis of minute criticism, yet it was such as to disarm adverse opinion, and to win by its witchery what it failed to secure by its excellence.' She was most effective in roles she could invest with her own character, and the actress Frances Abington thought she basically played herself.[10] Best of all was the animation with which she recited addresses written specifically for her. During summer tours it was even plainer than at Drury Lane that her appeal was her personality, not her histrionic skill: 'It seems to be a singular fact, that wherever she performed in the provinces, although not a first-rate actress, she always secured the largest benefits. There was a general feeling in her favour, from her unaffected good-nature, cheerfulness, industry, and the probity of her nature, which seemed to lead the inhabitants of each place to give their best support.'[11]

If theatregoers liked the woman in the actress, those who knew the woman personally liked her no less. Fellow players found her diligent, friendly and down-to-earth, and she was kind to those in need of help, financial or otherwise. She bought winter cloaks for hard-up colleagues and pots of porter for workmen rebuilding Drury Lane after the fire of 1809. Outside the theatre, too, her charity was expressed. She gave Christmas dinners and gifts to prisoners confined for small debts; let out the ground floor of her house for a nominal rent to a needy widow; and made articles of baby linen for poor mothers.[12] She never forgot an obligation. She stayed in contact with the Wrights of Stafford all her life and sent regular parcels of tea, sugar and clothing to her widowed landlady there. And when her Ulverston landlord saw her in Liverpool and sought to avoid what he feared might be an awkward encounter for her, she approached him cordially and introduced him to the party of ladies she was with.

As Harriot reaches her mid-twenties we expect to hear something of romance. However, aside from a disappointing episode with an unworthy suitor named Mr Barry, there is nothing to report. She had grown up listening to her mother's lectures about the evil of amorous folly and inestimable value of chastity, and in their Southwark years Mrs Entwisle had escorted her the three miles to Drury Lane for each rehearsal and performance, waited for her, and escorted her home. More than this, Harriot was too naturally prudent for her peace of mind to be easily disturbed. Nor did her beauty inflame others. She chose to delight rather than enslave, and her object was everyone she met, not a chosen swain. It is as if her loveliness was wholesome in its effect as well as in itself. Whether it was winning the hearts of tradespeople so that they wanted to oblige her rather than just take her money, or moving a coachman to relinquish his fare when he realised she could not pay it, she brought out the best in people.[13]

This portrait is too flattering to be a perfect likeness, but it is not simply the concoction of Mrs Baron-Wilson and her subject; there are other testimonies. Anne Mathews recalled Harriot's visits to the cottage she and her husband rented in Colney Hatch, just north of London. 'A youthful, slim and beautiful creature' and 'all joy and simplicity', she joined the couple in their capers round the village and saw the funny side of everything, even when she fell in a pond: 'How many other drolleries have I seen her enact at various periods.' The artist Benjamin Robert Haydon had a similar impression: 'It is my honest conviction there was nothing in Harriet Mellon but a girlish, romping, full-hearted, rich enjoyment at seeing every man, woman and child about her as happy as herself.' Oxberry's account also emphasised her kindness and exuberance. As Mathews put it, 'a more popular person never existed'.[14]

These are strong, disinterested commendations. All the same, the picture of Harriot Mellon during these years, like the picture of her girlhood, is largely the one she drew herself. In the anecdotes she relates she often has a misadventure, but either her winsomeness makes others come to her aid or she is reconciled by her sense of fun and indomitable spirit to what has occurred. These anecdotes are too plentiful even to summarise, and one must do duty for them all:

> When I was a poor girl, working very hard for my thirty shillings a week, I went down to Liverpool during the holidays, where I was always kindly received, and derived the greatest advantage from all my benefits. I was to perform in a new piece [...] and in my character I represented a friendless, orphan girl, reduced to the most wretched poverty. A heartless tradesman persecutes the sad heroine for a heavy debt owing to him by her family, and

insists on putting her in prison, unless some one will be bail for her. The girl replies, 'Then I have no hope – I have not a friend in the world.' 'What! will no one go bail for you to save you from prison?' asks the stern creditor. 'I have told you I have not a friend on earth,' was my reply. But just as I was uttering the words, my eyes were attracted by the movements of a sailor in the upper gallery, who, springing over the railing, was letting himself down from one tier to another, until finally reaching the pit he bounded clear over the orchestra and foot-lights, and placed himself beside me in a moment, before I could believe the evidence of my senses.

'Yes, you shall have one friend at least, my poor young woman,' said he, with the greatest expression of feeling in his honest, sun-burnt countenance. 'I will go bail for you to any amount. And as for you (turning to the frightened actor), if you don't bear a-hand and shift your moorings, you lubber, it will be the worse for you, when I come athwart your bows.'

Every creature in the house rose; the uproar was perfectly indescribable; peals of laughter, screams of terror, cheers from his tawny mess-mates in the gallery, preparatory scraping of violins from the orchestra; and amidst the universal din, there stood the unconscious cause of it, sheltering me, 'poor, distressed, young woman,' and breathing defiance and destruction against my mimic persecutor. It was impossible to resume the play, so the orchestra played 'God save the King,' while the curtain dropped over the scene, including my chivalric sailor. He was only persuaded to relinquish his care of me by the illusion being still maintained behind the scenes; the manager pretending to be an old friend of mine, unexpectedly arrived to rescue me from all difficulties, with a profusion of theatrical bank-notes. To these the generous sailor would fain have added from his own hardly-earned gains; which being gratefully declined by such a newly-made heiress as myself, he made his best sea-bow to all on the stage, shook hands heartily with me and the manager, and then quietly went home, under care of some of the party.[15]

When this took place Harriot was not yet a celebrity, but the passage shows how actors, simply by practising their craft, create the public intimacy associated with celebrity. In performing a role they (often) perform their own nature, the nature that led them to be cast in the first place. On that memorable night in Liverpool Harriot played a sweet, ingenuous girl who inspired protectiveness in others – rather like Harriot herself. But how much of this persona was the real woman, how much fabricated image? We cannot know, but in the light of her subsequent life the anecdote seems a carefully crafted autobiographical parable, revealing in miniature, even down to her mock enrichment at the close, how a woman triumphed because she inspired noble emotions in all who knew her.

The opening years of the new century were uneventful. At Drury Lane her value was undisputed, and every summer she prospered in the provinces. She achieved something of a breakthrough in January 1805 when she created the role of Volante in John Tobin's acclaimed comedy *The Honey Moon*, Dorothea Jordan having rejected it. The reviews were gratifying, the play held the boards for several seasons, and Sir William Beechey's portrait of Harriot as Volante was published as a coloured engraving and sold well. By this time two other pictures of her were in circulation, and her public image was taking shape. She was advancing socially too, having cultivated influential friends ever since her arrival in London and volunteered to coach aristocratic amateurs in private theatricals. 'There never was such a stupid task as drilling fine people,' she groaned, but she decided it was worth the effort.[16]

The first tangible fruit of her upward trajectory was obtaining from a crony of the Prince of Wales the office of postmaster at Cheltenham for her stepfather. Thomas Entwisle had been a member of the Drury Lane orchestra but in 1804 was dismissed for perpetual drunkenness. He was elated with his new position and untroubled by his complete lack of relevant experience. To spend time with her parents Harriot devoted part of the summer of 1805 to appearances at Cheltenham, and in the first flush of the celebrity that *The Honey Moon* had brought her she decided to have a benefit night. Among the visitors at the fashionable spa town was Thomas Coutts, reputedly the richest man in London. A letter soliciting his patronage was rewarded with a gift of five guineas for a box in the theatre, and before it arrived Harriot met the elderly banker while out walking and renewed a slight acquaintance from the Drury Lane green room.

At this time Thomas Coutts was just shy of his seventieth birthday, four decades older than Miss Mellon. Born in Edinburgh, he had long headed the banking house that bore his name and raised it to great distinction, making it the bank of choice for the royal family and the nobility. He was rather reserved but kind-hearted and cultured, a munificent patron of the arts who counted writers and actors among his friends. The only unconventional act of his life had been to wed a maidservant of his brother's, by whom he had three daughters:

Frances, who married the first Marquess of Bute; Susan, who married the third Earl of Guilford; and Sophia, who married Sir Francis Burdett. By 1805 Coutts had for forty-two years been a loyal spouse to a woman who could not be an intellectual companion for him, and latterly she had succumbed to mental illness and was no companion at all. The sad, lonely man was in Cheltenham to refresh his worn-out constitution, and Harriot, with her sunny amiability, proved just the tonic he needed. Back in London their friendship became close.

The age gap and Coutts's wealth caused the obvious surmise to be made. Journalists sniggered that acting was now Harriot's ostensible rather than real profession, and they assumed a necklace of paste brilliants she wore in the theatre was a gift of real diamonds from the smitten old banker. Snide jokes were made about a certain actress making a slip near a prominent banking house or a certain plutocrat acquiring a relish for melon and paying a high price for it. However, many who knew the pair were persuaded that their connection was chaste.[17] They were never together without the companion she had taken when her parents moved to Cheltenham or her successor. His three daughters, dignified matrons with grown-up children, would have shunned her if they had thought she was his mistress, but they met her in the theatre and visited her at home. Coutts's continuing devotion to his wife, whose care he could easily have entrusted to others, and Mrs Entwisle's obsession with her daughter's virtue also argued against an adulterous attachment.

Coutts's letters confirm that the friendship of banker and actress was not illicit.[18] He wrote to her with sadness of his wife, with pride of his daughters, and with joy of herself. Money was another topic. Harriot already had savings and investments, and he praised her management of these and her interest in bank accounts, annuities and stock. Even when he began to send what may be called love letters he harped on her spotless virtue, which would be odd in a private correspondence had she been his mistress. What these letters also reveal, though, is that he paid her an allowance and gave her gifts. To account for her improved circumstances, manifest in the carriage she now kept, they claimed a lucky lottery ticket had won her £5,000 or £10,000, a flimsy blind that elicited a good deal of mirth. He must have given her the funds to purchase Holly Lodge, Highgate, a leasehold villa set in fine grounds, as well as a house in Worthing, farms in Essex, and land and cottages in Cheltenham.

Uncertainty in the public mind about the nature of the relationship made it an engrossing topic, and the question of whether Harriot would carry on acting added a further layer of speculation. She did, and while some said this was a façade of respectability she remained popular for the decade after her success as Volante and earned more than before. All the same, it is fair to say her career stagnated during this time: she had a run of bad luck with characters in new plays; her figure acquired a fullness that made her less suited to girlish parts; and she faced a rival in Maria Rebecca Duncan, a younger, possibly more skilful actress. Reviewers thought Harriot showed a lack of artistic development and an increasingly workaday approach. She had more and more coverage in the press, but mainly in connection with her personal rather than her working life, a natural progression for an emerging celebrity. Much of it was impertinent banter, a plague from which she would never again be free.

In January 1815 the sufferings of Mrs Coutts came to an end. In February Harriot left the company she had joined two decades earlier; her heart was no longer in acting, and she gave it up without regret. After a botched, secretive ceremony that was declared invalid she and Thomas Coutts were legally united in April. He was seventy-nine, she thirty-seven years old. The press was respectful in the main, but some people suspected she was leading him by the nose and many more that she must have taken the low road to the altar. Craufurd Bruce, another banker, wrote that Coutts had 'made a most dreadful exemplification of himself, in getting quit of the Cook Maid and going to the Stew of the Green Room [...] Since his Marriage he has had a fit, not like the Giant refreshed, but from attempting I suppose what his powers were not equal to.'[19] More generous was an epigram that did the rounds in several versions:

> An apple we know was old Adam's disgrace.
> Who from Paradise quickly was driven;
> But yours, my dear Tom, is a happier case,
> For a Mellon transports you to Heaven!

The old man's case was happy indeed, and so it remained in the seven years left to him. His notes and letters to Harriot, sometimes written when they were under the same roof, pour out his gratitude:

(1816) You are a most extraordinarily good and intelligent person; intuitive knowledge from Heaven and perfect goodness graces every action of your Life. *The gift of Heaven!* In every station of life your goodness has always been seen by those capable of judging or appreciating it, and there has never been anything wrong in you, or anything in your heart or conduct but virtuous goodness, most truly and sincerely dear to me and making me the happiest of men. My life would, indeed, have been most miserable and not worth preserving without you.

(1819) I can truly say I have every day been more and more convinced of your goodness, purity and unbounded kindness to me, and to all belonging to me or connected with me, and of your truth, fidelity, and honourable and virtuous attention and love to me.

(1821) Be assured, my lovely Harriot, I shall, while on earth, never have a wish beyond the happiness of your being preserved to me in health and happiness, and that the obligations I am under to you, were there nothing else, will ever induce me to act steadily and with the purest love and affection to you without deviation to the end.[20]

She rejoiced in him just as much: 'A more happy couple does not, nor ever did exist,' she wrote. Acquaintances remarked on the unlikely mutuality of their devotion, among them Lord Erskine, the Lord Chancellor, who congratulated Coutts on finding a wife who presided admirably at his table, dispensed pleasure to all around her, and paid him such ceaseless attention. A homely tableau is provided by Mary Nollekens, whose husband Joseph made a bust of Coutts in 1816. Harriot came to the sculptor's studio every day that Coutts was there, she recalled, bringing in soups and other delicacies and heating them herself over the fire: 'I believe it did me as much good to see old Mr Coutts enjoy every spoonful of it as it would have done had it passed through my own mouth.'[21]

The newly-weds lived in Southampton Street, Covent Garden and at Holly Lodge, while Coutts's daughter Lady Guilford occupied his main house on the corner of Stratton Street and Piccadilly. Harriot had to find her feet as a hostess. Two weeks into her marriage she received the Duke of York, and soon after it was the turn of the prince regent. She told Thomas she worried what great folks would think of her, but he replied that if she was simply herself everyone would approve. All the same, she knew that as the wife of London's foremost banker she had to temper her effervescence and assume a statelier air. She made the adjustment, though not without an occasional look over her shoulder, as Haydon noticed when he called about a loan:

A look from her at once told me all was altered. [...] All went on with gravity and decorum till we came to a bust of Mr Coutts by Nollekens. Nolly was a character. Harriet Mellon's love of humour made her forget Mrs Coutts' sense of dignity. She went off like a rocket and mimicked Nolly's manner to perfection. But times were altered; she was the great banker's wife, – I his suppliant for cash; – freedoms must be over. Mr Coutts gave her a look which iced her. In a minute or two she curtsied low to me, and swept out of the room; but she could not help turning that eye of hers as she went. A glance was enough to convince me she was Harriet Mellon still.[22]

Others judged her adaptation to her role to be far from complete, and if they had known Coutts's advice simply to be herself they might have said she followed it too well. The physician Charles Meryon thought her speech commonplace and ignorant, and he transcribed her garblings of foreign expressions. He also frowned on her habit of appealing to her servants for corroboration of what she said and repeating their anecdotes. Unlike Haydon, Meryon thought she had total authority over her spouse. The lawyer Lord Glenbervie rather despised Mrs Coutts too. 'It is surprising,' he wrote, 'in what a sensible, quiet, gentleman-like manner Mr Coutts does the honours of his house, his table, his cellar, and of his good-natured, burly, vulgar, frank, hospitable housekeeper-like wife.' Glenbervie saw them again and warmed a little more to his hostess on account of her constant attention to her elderly husband.[23]

The couple must have guessed that some of those they invited into their home would pick holes in them, and they had the strength to rise above it. A greater test of their equanimity were their respective families. When the Entwisles had moved to Cheltenham, ten years prior to Harriot's marriage, she had been relieved to see them go, for her mother's interference and her stepfather's fecklessness had grown worse. Nonetheless, she remained a dutiful daughter, calling to mind all they had done for her as a child. Thomas Entwisle was a predictably hopeless postmaster, and when the town's exasperated residents petitioned for his removal, only Coutts's intercession with powerful friends kept him in post. Once his wife started brewing her own ale and matched his intake of alcohol the downward path was set, and for the remainder of their lives Harriot was pained by their peevish, grasping, embarrassing behaviour. Sarah Entwisle died a month after her daughter's marriage, and after four more unruly years her husband followed her in May 1819.

Worse still was the conduct of Coutts's daughters, especially Lady Guilford and Lady Burdett. They had smiled on Harriot during her ten-year friendship with him, perhaps through gritted teeth, but the marriage, which seemed to point to her having been his mistress, outraged their sense of decorum. It also touched off a snobbery that was keener for the fact that their mother had been a servant. Thirdly, they felt that Harriot was taking advantage of their father, and even his evident love for her could not reconcile them to her being his wife. The tale of family recriminations, ructions and reconciliations is too tedious to narrate. Harriot stayed outwardly calm and emollient, but Thomas, whose adoration of her never diminished, was slowly estranged from his daughters, with whom he had been on excellent terms. A decision took shape in his mind for which he is better known than for any other act in his long life.

In consequence of the family feud Lady Guilford moved out of the Stratton Street house and the Coutts's moved in. Harriot redecorated it with swagged damask curtains, silk wall hangings, chandeliers, mirrors, marble busts and other specimens of Regency flamboyance. The scene was set for lavish dinner parties, and waiting to attend them were the Royal Dukes of York, Clarence, Kent and Sussex and a host of other domestic and foreign notables. Even more splendid afternoon entertainments, known as breakfasts or *fêtes champêtres*, took place at Holly Lodge once the couple had embellished the house and its grounds. In both places guests were regaled with vocal and instrumental music and even ballet. Journalists reporting these occasions needed all their descriptive powers to capture the richness of the banquets, the glittering guest lists and the beauty of the décor. Not everybody was impressed, and many agreed with the diarist Thomas Creevey that such extravagance was in poor taste.[24]

Vying with her parties for the attention of the press was Mrs Coutts's philanthropy. Her first efforts were ill judged, most of all her distribution of food, clothing and money on a vast scale at Holly Lodge. Vagrants camped at the gates in large numbers and she was accused of playing the Lady Bountiful, the more so as the parish withdrew relief from those who received her charity, so that the real beneficiaries were ratepayers. Finding too much greed and cavilling and too little gratitude, she ceased her Holly Lodge benefactions in 1818. Other gifts continued: for almshouses and infirmaries; for the poor living near her Essex properties; for the payment of Bow Street Runners, the precursors of the Metropolitan Police; and for the relief of poverty in Ireland, her mother's native country. Her munificence to debtors in the Staffordshire county gaol must have made their experience of incarceration unique. The newspapers applauded, and phrases like 'with her accustomed liberality' kept recurring.

The names of Thomas and Harriot Coutts were in society columns when they arrived in or left London, drove round Hyde Park 'in a chariot and four', attended the theatre and 'expressed the greatest satisfaction', or went into the country to 'enjoy rural retirement'. In Brighton a hotel brazenly overcharged them (£491 for thirteen days), and Thomas said that despite being well off he could not afford to stay there again. A dispute with a Highgate neighbour prompted the couple to erect a high wall at the boundary of their property and then pull it down when they had made their point. Not all stories were so anodyne. Their personal physician was conjectured to be Harriot's lover, a smear his own wife believed. At first the Coutts's ignored the gossip, but it became so persistent the doctor's appointment had to be terminated. His replacement was a depressive hypochondriac whose bizarre conduct led to his being pensioned off, and when he committed suicide cries of cruelty were directed at the couple.

Most hurtful was the charge that Harriot was a greedy adventuress. An anecdote about the retail jeweller Thomas Hamlet was known to many:

> One day after the coronation of George IV, Hamlet made his appearance at the house of Mr Coutts, in Piccadilly, the corner of Stratton Street. It was during dinner; but, owing no doubt to a previous arrangement, he was at once admitted, when he placed before the rich banker a magnificent diamond cross, which had been worn the previous day by the Duke of York. It at once attracted the admiration of Mrs Coutts, who loudly exclaimed, 'How happy I should be with such a splendid specimen of jewellery.' 'What is it worth?' immediately exclaimed Mr Coutts. 'I could not allow it to pass out of my possession for less than £15,000,' said the wary tradesman. 'Bring me a pen and ink,' was the only answer made by the doting husband; and he at once drew a cheque for that amount upon the bank in the Strand, and with much delight the worthy old gentleman placed the jewel upon the fair bosom of the lady.

Naturally, people wished to know if great wealth and an eminent husband had implanted self-importance in a woman previously loved for her unaffected humility. Stories of high-handedness and tantrums caused sage heads to nod, and even Harriot's friend Anne Mathews felt she had grown 'inordinately self-endeared'.[25] On the other hand, no one doubted her devotion to Thomas, which was unremitting. Acquaintances gave her credit for this, as did the press. She was, said the *Morning Post*, 'exemplary in her attentions to him; she is never absent from him – all pleasures are cheerfully resigned, but such as he can partake of.'

Aside from newspapers, there is little to document the latter years of the Coutts marriage. Thomas and Harriot were seldom apart and wrote few letters. Their journeys became shorter and stays away from home briefer, but they still entertained and made charitable donations. Thomas continued to correspond with clients of the bank and write dinner invitations, but towards the end of 1821 he grew weak. Harriot nursed him assiduously, prolonging his days and filling them with as much pleasure as his sufferings permitted him to feel. His death in February 1822 at the age of eighty-six was followed by an elaborate funeral befitting his position in society. Of his long life the last seven years had been the best, and in her bereavement Harriot would have known this. His old friend Lord Erskine thanked her for her 'most exemplary conduct' towards him and for 'giving him a new and happy existence when most men cease to exist, and without which he must long ago have left us'.[26]

No sooner had Thomas Coutts died than tongues started to wag about his will. Had he left £900,000, or was it as much as £3,000,000? It was reported that he had left it all, including his preponderating share in Coutts & Co., to his wife. Was he punishing his daughters for snubbing her by cutting them out, or did he trust her to support them? Was he bequeathing everything to Harriot so as to avoid legacy duty? Would her name now be printed on the bank's cheques? After these questions had been bandied about for a few days the *Morning Post* stated in early March that 'all that has been said in some of the Papers relative to the property of the late Mr Coutts is without foundation.' Three days later, however, *Saunders's News-Letter* announced that Harriot was now the richest woman in the kingdom, if not in Europe. Some were appalled, but there was a palpable sense of wonder at the old man's trust in her, and articles appeared praising her for bringing so much joy to his twilight years.

After the funeral Mrs Coutts withdrew from society to grieve. In the next eighteen months she toured the West Country and the North of England, dispensing charity but keeping herself to herself and providing little matter for the newspapers, some of which printed stories of her acting days for want of anything better. During this period she began the practices of devotion to her husband's memory that lasted to the end of her life. His statue always stood in the state room at Stratton Street and his portrait in her boudoir. She took the pillow on which he had died and a casket of his letters wherever she went in her travelling carriage. The five guineas he had given for her Cheltenham benefit she never spent, but kept as 'luck-money'. In her Book of Common Prayer she wrote an account of a dream in which he exhorted her not to despond, and on each anniversary of their wedding she kissed his desk at the bank. This veneration was well known, and formed a shield against her detractors.

The rumour was right: Harriot was her husband's sole legatee. His will was valued for probate at £900,000, but this excluded freehold property and the real amount was far larger. Even more amazingly, he made her the senior partner at the bank, entrusting her with complex business of which she had no experience. As the courtier Lord Rivers wrote, 'He could not have taken a more effectual method of proving her worth, of justifying his choice of her.' Soon she was on good terms with the other partners. She left day-to-day decisions to them but checked figures they sent her, once finding a discrepancy of £10, and intervened now and again to approve a loan they would have refused. In 1831 she wrote to Edward Marjoribanks, who was to succeed her as senior partner, 'I do flatter myself that all my kind dear friends in the old Shop are well pleased with me and convinced how dear to my heart is the prosperity of our splendid House.'[27] Aided by them, she left it in even better shape than she had found it.

With absolute control of her late husband's estate, Mrs Coutts had to decide what to do about his daughters. Thomas had vacillated on the question, sometimes saying they should get nothing, but she took a mild view and granted them almost £10,000 a year each. She also looked among their children for an heir, wanting Coutts money to stay in the family and in any case having no near relations of her own. Her first choice was Lady Bute's son Lord Dudley Coutts Stuart. She gave him a position at the bank and groomed him as her successor: 'God bless you my dear Dudley. May your life be prosperous honourable and happy – that you may inherit all the Virtues of your blessed matchless Grandfather is my fervent wish.'[28] He blotted his copybook by gambling heavily and marrying a daughter of Napoleon's brother Lucien, despite Harriot's dislike of the French in general and the Bonapartes in particular. She gave him £2,000 a year, but his chances of inheriting his grandfather's fortune were gone.

In November 1823 several newspapers stated that 'Mrs Coutts, after nearly two years mourning for the death of her husband, has returned to the circles of fashion, and mingles again in society.' That winter she gave a few parties, but remained fairly quiet. It was not until a large dinner at Stratton Street and a Holly Lodge fête for 700 people in the summer of 1824 that she was fully back in the public eye. The press feasted on both occasions: the sumptuous settings, the distinguished guests, the exquisite dinners, the superb music and so on. Another preoccupation of the papers was to find her a second husband. In February 1824 the *Oxford Journal* reported whisperings that she would marry Robert William Elliston, the roguish, hard-drinking lessee of the Drury Lane Theatre, and the *Yorkshire Gazette* stirred the same pot in July. Or she might prefer the Duke of York, a widower and, like all George IV's brothers, short of funds.

In August 1824 Harriot set off for Scotland with a sizeable retinue, including outriders. 'The appearance of this cavalcade on the road will fill the hearts of innkeepers with delight,' remarked the *Morning Post*. Everywhere she went she was treated as a high dignitary. In Edinburgh the Lord Provost acted as her host and received a silver vase for his trouble. She then visited noblemen and gentlemen at their seats, including Sir Walter Scott at Abbotsford, before heading south in October. The *Fife Herald* disliked the coverage of her tour:

> Now that Mrs Coutts had again returned to London, our brethren of the Scottish press will have time to breathe and to recollect themselves after so much bustle and excitement. Mrs Coutts arrives here! – Mrs Coutts is observed there! – Mrs Coutts intends to breakfast, to dine, or to sup, in a third, fourth, and fifth place, and the prying eye of Fame is at her carriage door, and Mrs Coutts cannot even *intend*, much less *perform*, any thing, without giving rise to a paragraph! We are sure that this very charitable – and so far as we have any business to know – very well conducted lady, is quite sick and tired of all this trumpeting and blustering.

Whether this supposition was correct only time would tell, but letters she wrote after returning to London reveal different memories of Scotland: seeing the first house her 'dear Tom' had dwelt in and the room in which he had been born; and visiting the bank premises 'where his playful sweet youthful days were spent'.[29]

Whatever Harriot thought of the fuss made of her in Scotland, it was more agreeable than the other side of the coin, which was persistent censure and slander. Old chestnuts were reheated, chiefly the claim she had been Coutts's mistress before becoming his wife. Of the jokes directed at her, some were clumsily boorish, some deeply malicious. Mrs Baron-Wilson asserts that the fount of calumny was not the press itself, but 'satirical contributions'.[30] At least four of these had appeared during the previous decade for private or public sale (dates of publication are estimates):

> *The Golden Nuptials, An Epithalamium on the Marriage of T. C—tts, Esq. and Miss H. M—ll—n.* (1815)
>
> *Fine Acting; or, a Sketch of the Life of Miss H. M— of Drury Lane Theatre, and of T. Coutts, Esq., Banker.* (1815)
>
> *Mr Percy Wyndham's Strictures on an Imposter, and Old Actress, formerly Bet the Pot-Girl, alias the Banker's Sham Widow, with Particulars of her Appearance at the Bar of Bow-Street, of the Child Manufactory at Highgate, and Madam's Sleeping at the Horns at Kennington.* (1822)
>
> *Secret Memoirs of Harriot Pumpkin, Or the Birth, Parentage and Education of an Actress. In which are Developed a Variety of Interesting and Amusing Anecdotes; Her Private Acquaintance for many Years; the Vicissitudes to Which She was Exposed; and Her Extraordinary Marriage with Old Croesus!! To Which is Added the Art of making an Ostentatious Shew-Off under the Color of Charity, the Whole Pourtraying Her Never-Forgiving and Malicious Disposition.* (1825)[31]

Such anonymous pamphlets were common, but few people were put on the rack as Harriot Coutts was. All four titles are scurrilous, but the last outdoes the rest for inventive malignancy mixed with just enough truth to inflict pain. 'Miss Pumpkin' is a talentless actress of low birth who cajoles susceptible men into advancing her career. One day the fabulously rich Mr Croesus makes her a dishonourable proposition and is thrilled when she accedes to it: 'So enchanted was this old dotard at the glorious news, that he threw up his wig to the ceiling and danced a Strathspey round it.' They spend a night at a tavern, giving her a chance to admire his 'beauteous wrinkles'. The fable of the winning lottery ticket conceals what has really been purchased, and Miss Pumpkin settles in a suburban cottage so that old Croesus can visit her undetected. She gives money to the poor and gains a name for benevolence, but spends as much on publicising her charities as on the charities themselves.

Miss Pumpkin gains complete ascendancy over her lover, and once he is a widower she bundles him into marriage before his first wife is even in her grave. Mother Pumpkin Croesus, as she now is, screws ever more money out of the 'imbecile misled gentleman' and uses it to set herself up as a rival to well-born ladies who just months before would not have deigned to look upon her. She revels in the flattery of her guests, who in truth despise her and laugh into their sleeves at her 'upstart consequence'. Her basest act is to inveigle Mr Croesus into casting off his own children and committing 'indisputably an act of second childhood' by leaving her his whole fortune. When he dies she affects a grief she does not feel and pays a 'hungry *Pamphleteer*' to produce a memoir of him. At the end she stands triumphant, 'the fat, greasy, voluptuous Mother Pumpkin Croesus devoid of every principle which could dignify the human heart.'

The hungry pamphleteer here alluded to is the author of the *Life of the Late Thomas Coutts* (1822), which takes a diametrically opposed view.[32] After a few pages on the banker and his first wife he turns to Harriot, whom he represents as a cruelly traduced woman. He leaves open the question of whether she was pure before entering into matrimony, but otherwise he extols her without stint: her beauty and grace, her generosity to her parents, and her dignity in the face of the 'envenomed shafts' of her enemies. The story that Coutts allowed her an unlimited draft on the bank is dismissed, and their hurried union is justified by the first Mrs Coutts having 'morally ceased to exist a long time before her decease'. The rest of the pamphlet enlarges on her detractors' villainy and on her merits and fascinations, her boundless charities, and her husband's adoration of her. George IV himself is called as a witness: 'The first gentleman of the empire has pronounced her a well-bred woman.'

Harriot is not known to have commissioned the *Life of the Late Thomas Coutts*. Indeed, the equivocation about her chastity and the statement that Thomas bought Holly Lodge for her, which contradict her story, make it appear more likely that it was written, like the screeds against her, to make money from a subject that engrossed the public. Interestingly, this text mentions motives beyond journalistic opportunism for the volume and toxicity of the attacks on her. It points the finger at Sally Stephenson, her first companion, who had had to leave her service when she 'displayed certain symptoms that were calculated to awaken suspicions that she was no longer a vestal'. It further asserts that Harriot's wealth excited envy in those who had known her before she acquired it. Mrs Baron-Wilson agrees with the second point, explaining that Mrs Coutts had dropped some early acquaintances at her husband's behest and that they channelled their gall into the pens of unprincipled scribblers.[33]

Mrs Baron-Wilson also states that some of Harriot's old theatre colleagues made applications for financial help tinged with threats to besmirch her reputation if she refused.[34] Alongside these desperate initiatives, and perhaps murkily entwined with them, were plans to write libellous texts and then offer to suppress them. At almost the same time the courtesan Harriette Wilson, or rather her publisher John Joseph Stockdale, was offering her former clients, including the

Duke of Wellington, the chance to buy their way out of a mention in her *Memoirs*. Oxberry, writing during the widowhood of Mrs Coutts, gives instances of her summary responses to those who solicited payment for their silence, in one case snatching a man's manuscript and thrusting it in the fire.[35] Whether these episodes were linked to the titles cited above is unclear, but Harriot's defiance before such provocation became part of the legend of her life, just as Wellington's retort of 'Publish and be damned' to Stockdale became part of his.

Some newspapers adopted the tone of the abusive pamphleteers. None did so more than *John Bull*, a Tory weekly edited by Theodore Hook, of which the diarist Creevey wrote that 'its personal scurrility exceeds by miles anything ever written before.' Among Harriot's outings in *John Bull* was an innuendo-filled squib of 1824 about her accidentally sitting on a glass vase, followed up with commentary presenting her as overweight, bossy and self-regarding. Many found jibes against an unprotected widow distasteful, and the periodical editor Cyrus Redding reproached Hook in person for his 'unmanly attacks on Mrs Coutts'. Hook took no notice, and his strongest vilification of her lay ahead. Many copied him. The claim in her *Gentleman's Magazine* obituary that 'no woman in any age or any country was ever assailed with half so much acrimony' stretched the truth only a little.[36]

Worse was to come, but it was during and after her first marriage that Harriot was most upset by such malevolence. Later she said she had 'outlived all sense of annoyance', and that the days when it could injure her 'peace and health' were over.[37] At some point in her five-year widowhood she wanted to hit back. She approached two jurists, James Scarlett (later Lord Abinger) and Henry Brougham (later Lord Brougham and Vaux), and they summoned the Marquess of Bristol and the Earl of Lauderdale, friends of the Coutts's, and Sir Edmund Antrobus and Sir Coutts Trotter, partners at the bank. Harriot passed a mass of letters to these men proving her estimable character and asked them to determine how she should act. They advised her that while they entertained no doubts of her propriety she should avoid prosecution, which would bring much trouble with little reward, and instead treat defamation as beneath her notice. Her feelings rebelled against this judgement, but she felt bound to abide by it.

On balance, she fared better in the pages of fiction. A character in Pierce Egan's *Life in London* (1821) identifies her, without naming her, as 'one of the most amiable and worthy of her sex'. Her ability as an actress, devotion to her elderly husband, and concern for the relief of the poor make her, he says, 'a real ornament to her sex'.

Charles Molloy Westmacott ushers her, also anonymously, into *The English Spy* (1825–1826) with a damning biographical sketch and then has his characters engage in a flippant exchange about her. One speaks of her '*high* character', with a footnote explaining that 'high' is used as of game to mean no longer fresh. The most memorable portrait is Mrs Million in Benjamin Disraeli's *Vivian Grey* (1826). So imperious that even as a guest she dominates an aristocratic household, she is nonetheless won over by the clever young hero when he tells her that control of a princely fortune is the highest calling he can imagine.[38]

As with many episodes in her life, the official version of Harriot's first meeting with William Aubrey De Vere Beauclerk, 9th Duke of St Albans, is picturesque but uncorroborated. It took place, Mrs Baron-Wilson says, at a dinner party at which he, then Earl of Burford, was meant to advance his interest with another heiress. Instead he talked to Harriot all evening, their love of Shakespeare forming the topic of conversation.[39] No date is provided, but Lord Burford was present at two dinners Harriot gave in December 1824, when he was twenty-three years old and she probably forty-seven. Soon he was following her everywhere. Better grist for journalists was hard to imagine, and reports of a forthcoming marriage alternated with gleeful derision. *John Bull* did its worst with a fake advertisement: 'Wanted, by a widow, at the head of a long-established Banking-house in the metropolis, a Beau Clerk [...] Should he be approved on trial, he will probably be admitted as a sleeping partner.'[40]

For the next two years this question was picked over, the more so as the earl was notorious for trying to replenish his family's coffers by securing a wealthy bride. He had failed with the Liverpool heiress Fanny Gascoyne and with Lady Elizabeth Conyngham, daughter of the king's mistress, earning some ridicule on the way. The general view was that he was good-looking and good-natured but somehow mentally deficient – 'a fool and a booby', an 'imbecile', 'nearly an idiot' are among the labels applied to him – yet his letters, while banal, do not indicate a limited intellect.[41] Rather, Burford was a simple man whose passion for the stage and need to marry money drew him to the portly banker's widow who had once been a player. The icing on the cake for observers of this odd courtship was that the mother of the first Duke of St Albans had been an actress: Nell Gwyn, the mistress of Charles II. Would a second actress now rescue the family from its financial difficulties?

Harriot carried on giving 'superb fêtes' and 'elegant entertainments' for top-notch people. She was listed among guests elsewhere, though not remotely often enough to constitute a fair return for her tireless hospitality. At home and away, Burford's name appeared alongside hers, rather demeaningly as part of her 'suite' in some reports. 'The sun and air of St Albans' was being transplanted to 'some extensive Melon beds at Highgate', quipped *John Bull*. In the summer of 1825 Lady Guilford at last condescended to present her stepmother at one of the king's receptions, known as drawing rooms, and she had the pleasure of reading a description of her dress in the aristocratic *Morning Post*. Her charitable activity was undiminished, and wherever she and her 'vast retinue' went in search of amusement the local papers dwelt gratefully on the satisfaction of shopkeepers.

In July 1825 Burford's father died. 'The Duke of St Albans is dead so now Mrs Coutts may be a D[uche]ss, if she thinks it worth while,' gossiped the political hostess Lady Cowper.[42] Newspapers printed denials, supposedly from the lady herself, but if she planted these to smother speculation she fanned it again in the autumn by making a second tour of Scotland with the new duke and one of his sisters. During this journey there were more reports of impending or even completed nuptials, followed by the usual puerile banter. Harriot made a second visit to Abbotsford to see Sir Walter Scott, who was amused by the duke's pursuit of her and by the 'lively brisk and jolly' widow herself:

> It is the fashion to attend Mrs Coutts' parties and to abuse her. I have always found her a kind friendly woman without either affectation or insolence in the display of her wealth and most willing to do good if the means be shewn to her. She can be very entertaining too as she speaks without scruple of her stage life. So much wealth can hardly be enjoyd without some ostentation but what then? If the Duke marries her he ensures an immense fortune. If she marries him she has the first rank. If he marries a woman older than himself by twenty years She marries a man younger in wit by twenty degrees. I do not think he will dilapidate her fortune – he seems quiet and gentle. I do not think she will abuse his softness – of disposition or shall I say of heart – The disparity of ages concerns no one but themselves – So they have my consent to marry if they can get each other's.

Scott liked Harriot, but he had his fun with her. When she told him about Dudley Coutts Stuart he enjoyed the 'tragi-comic distress of my good friend on the marriage of her presumptive heir with a daughter of Lucien Bonaparte'.[43] It seems the transition from charming young woman to middle-aged 'character' was complete.

The London press hailed the return of Mrs Coutts to the capital, and for the next two years she (with or without the duke) could not give or attend a party, move from London to Brighton and back, or even take an airing in her carriage without it being recorded. She gave a dinner 'in a style of Eastern splendour'; she made 'the most liberal gratuities' to good causes; she attended the opening of parliament 'attended by the Duke of St Albans and the Earl of Lauderdale'; she was spotted at her front parlour window in a white satin dress, 'a sight well worth the attention of the curious'. For the *London Magazine* it was too much: 'One cannot take up a newspaper without seeing where Mrs Coutts is; it is the only point on which all the journals are always perfectly well informed.' The main subject of interest was the duke's courtship, and for a long time it seemed not to be prospering. Jokes were made about Mrs Coutts's 'Lord in waiting' and his desire to pluck a large, ripe melon.

Harriot temporised because she wanted to be sure that her suitor, who proposed formally in the spring of 1826, knew his own mind. Finding him steadfast, and liking his amiable, upright character, she yielded at last, and in June 1827 a small, private wedding took place at Stratton Street. The Whig hostess Elizabeth, Lady Holland must have heard of it from friends:

> Mrs Coutts is finally married. The ceremony went off very decorously. The Duke in returning thanks at the health of the D. and Duchess being drunk spoke very properly, better than he could have done de son chef; so it must have been prepared. The King, in reply to all Mrs C.'s communications upon the subject of the marriage, wrote a civil reply, which was read at breakfast. Before the ceremony Mrs C.'s servants wore the Coutts livery; immediately after, they appeared in the St Albans yellow & black stockings.[44]

Beside neutral press notices there were some unkind comments on the age gap between the parties, how much money the bridegroom had received and what he was expected to do for it, and whether the bride, who was hard upon fifty, would give him a 'pledge of love', in other words a child. The *Pottery Gazette*, mindful of the golden opinions she had won in Staffordshire decades before, was disgusted by this tone: 'If private worth be the test of merit, then this lady, whether as Miss Mellon, Mrs Coutts, or the Duchess of St Albans, is as kind and as good a creature as ever was formed in the female character.' Private reactions were varied. John Cam Hobhouse found the duke's choice of wife foolish and base, but at the Weimar Court the reigning duchess said his marrying an actress who had preserved her reputation was a noble deed.[45]

A few months after the wedding a laudatory poem by John Taylor appeared in the *Gentleman's Magazine*.

> Lady, I knew thy blooming youth,
> Admir'd thy sense and open heart,
> Defended thee, with zealous truth,
> When malice aim'd her venom'd dart.
>
> I knew thee in domestic life,
> As daughter, dutiful and kind,
> I knew thee as a tender wife,
> To ev'ry gentle care inclin'd.
>
> I knew thee in thy widow'd state,
> When Fortune had her favours pour'd,
> With charity, not pride elate,
> Spreading around thy plenteous board.
>
> Now to high rank I see thee rise,
> A rank thy merits well may claim,
> Not proudly scorning former ties,
> But all those merits still the same.
>
> And thou, in person and in mind,
> Art qualified that rank to grace;
> In both we Nature's bounty find,
> On both we fair pretentions trace.
>
> Oh! may'st thou long thy rank possess
> And health attend thy mortal day,
> Thy consort and thyself to bless, –
> So ends my Muse her simple lay.[46]

Of course Harriot wanted her husband's title and he her money. However, her gifts of £30,000 in cash and an Essex estate worth £25,000, while handsome enough, were less than a hardened fortune hunter would have expected, and the Coutts fortune stayed under her control. In general, the couple gave an impression of mutual regard. The duchess was the dominant partner, and Lady Morgan heard of her scolding the duke 'like a naughty schoolboy', but he rebelled if she was too overbearing and once made off from Portsmouth to London alone, forcing her to follow him and effect a reconciliation. Rumour had it that she flounced into the Pittville Pump Room in Cheltenham while he was declaiming the part of Brutus in *Julius Caesar* and said he must desist for he knew no more of acting than a goose. However, according to the Prussian tourist Prince Pückler-Muskau she coached him in lovers' parts so they could amuse friends with dialogues from well-known dramas.[47]

Harriot's ten years as a duchess were the long climax of her fairy tale. They were also a remarkably static period. She engaged in the same pursuits continually, with some development and variation but few major events that might give shape to a chronological narrative. It seems best to take a thematic view, considering the main facets of her life in turn and relating them to her phenomenal celebrity. The main source is the press, which devoted itself to her with greater intensity than when she had been the wife and widow of Thomas Coutts, though many had found that to be excessive. The *Western Times* mused in 1831 that 'the Duchess of St Alban's has been for many a year as good as a war or an insurrection to the columns of some of the journals.' As Anne Mathews put it, 'She could not stir abroad, but like a shining comet she was wondered at.'[48]

The greatest publicity she gained was for her parties. Many were held at Stratton Street, redecorated several times during these years and christened St Albans House after the duke sold his own town residence in 1829. The size of the property permitted dining, dancing and concerts for hundreds of guests, with opera singers and other musicians brought in for fat fees. Rooms were lined with shrubs or small trees, flowers were wreathed round triumphal arches, and no end of plate and statuary was on display. Actors performed scenes from plays or presented *tableaux vivants*, and profusions of symbolic décor commemorated historical events like the end of the Wars of the Roses. Even more extravagant than the parties themselves were their write-ups, particularly in the *Morning Post*. An article of 1828 is typical of scores of others:

Her Grace the Duchess of St Albans yesterday entertained a very numerous company of the highest distinction to dinner and supper, at her residence in Piccadilly. On this occasion the saloons of that elegant mansion were brilliantly illuminated, and the decorations, which were of the most costly and splendid description, vied only with the magnificence displayed in the antichambers, which presented a collection of the most rare and odoriferous exotics. The tables were supplied with the choicest delicacies of the season [...]. The extensive assortment of rare and choice fruits, together with the great variety of refreshments prepared for the dessert on this occasion, surpassed anything of the description ever before witnessed. In fact, Lucullus himself, when in the zenith of his glory, and with all the luxuries of ancient Rome, could not surpass the splendid entertainments given by her grace on this most tasteful and sumptuous occasion.

These articles often ended with a list of the peers, in descending order of rank, who had entered the 'sparkling vortex' of a party at St Albans House.

The same magniloquence described the *fêtes champêtres* at Holly Lodge. These were on a still grander scale, with the ground floor of the villa and the gardens transformed into a fairy-tale scene. Tents and small temples were erected, lamps were hung from trees, and on one occasion tropical birds were hired. A small orchestra would play and there might be turns by well-known vocalists and actors, the Adelphi Theatre's corps de ballet, a band of the Grenadier Guards, or groups of touring artistes like Tyrolese minstrels, Bavarian gypsy dancers and Chinese acrobats. Guests could take part in May Day games or archery competitions. At one fête a Swiss herdsman's melody was sung and a girl in Alpine costume milked two cows garlanded with flowers. The fresh milk was then used to prepare a syllabub that the duchess herself handed round. The food and drink were superlatively good and the expense astronomical. The *Standard* reported that an event in 1831 cost between £1,500 and £2,000.

The duchess certainly liked showing off, but she did not keep up an exhausting round of festivities year upon year just to feed her vanity. She relished giving parties, and the genius for hospitality friends had perceived in her Russell Street days found its full flowering in the dazzling world of fantasy she created for her guests. It was pure theatre, produced by a woman whose years acting in other people's shows had prepared her to stage her own. She loved to see people happy and did the honours of her house kindly, putting new guests at their ease and making introductions, while the duke danced with young ladies who had been overlooked by other men. The contrast was great between this and the chilly formality of most society gatherings. 'Her fêtes,' wrote Pückler-Muskau, 'combine the greatest opulence with variety and originality, whereas it would be difficult to conceive anything more monotonous, tedious and indeed fatuous than the English balls and routs of the Season.'[49]

Next to her entertainments, Harriot's philanthropy brought her the most attention. Having learnt a lesson from the chaotic scenes at the Holly Lodge gates and from plausible impostors who had preyed on her, she was now discriminating with her bounty. But she was still eager to be generous. She ordered winter clothing for the needy in the vicinity of Redbourne Hall, her husband's Lincolnshire seat, and had cottages put up for his tenants' labourers. She was a patroness of charitable balls, contributed to the building of schools, and donated to hospitals, dispensaries and benevolent institutions. Mrs Baron-Wilson and others relate many kindnesses to individuals. One day she learned of a poor widow living with her little boy in a wretched hovel, so when she was out Harriot filled it with furniture and provisions, employed glaziers to replace broken windows, and dressed the boy in a pretty new costume. On her return the widow was so astonished at the metamorphosis that she fainted away.[50]

Unlike other actresses who married up, Harriot never lost her zest for the theatre and wished to give back to the profession that had served her so well. As Mrs Coutts and as Duchess of St Albans she opened her purse for theatrical funds all over the country, causing public toasts to be drunk to her, and often bought tickets for benefit nights. She paid a quarterly allowance to her former dresser and one-off amounts to actors in financial trouble. Her open-handedness was recalled in memoirs, communicated to her biographer, and reported in the press. It would appear she supported Edmund Kean, though information is hazy. She also interested herself in musical artists, donating to the Choral Fund, making a gift to the Drury Lane singer Ann Wilson, and becoming a benefactress to the mezzo-soprano Maria Malibran. If she heard a band play somewhere she requested a particular piece and then rewarded each member in turn.

Harriot's third well-known activity was travel. For months at a time she and the duke meandered through the kingdom, a long line of carriages bearing them, their physician, Harriot's companion Eleanor Goddard, an array of servants, and such Beauclerk and Coutts relations as wished to accompany them. They stopped for days or weeks in one place. Cheltenham saw a good deal of them, as did the Isle of Wight and the seaside towns of Kent and Sussex. Provincial newspapers traced the movements of 'these noble personages', and reports of their doings reached levels of triviality normally reserved for members of the royal family: they dined and then repaired to an assembly room; went for a walk with their carriage following; expressed delight with a local beauty spot; or visited a theatre and enjoyed the performance. Journalists announced that their localities were on the ducal pair's itinerary, but sometimes, like the writer in the *Hull Packet*, had to admit to uncertainty on this important point:

> The Duke and Duchess of St Albans have been expected in this town for some days past; up to last evening, however, they had not arrived. On Sunday and yesterday much curiosity prevailed upon the subject, and numbers of expectants were on the look out, anxious to behold the elevated individuals who have latterly engrossed so large a share of public conversation.

Crowds really did gather for a glimpse of them, often alerted to their approach by a merry peal of bells from the local church. The residents of Leamington evinced 'a great curiosity to obtain a view of the Noble Visitants', and at the Ascot Races Harriot was 'surrounded by an immense throng'. In theatres cheers were raised for them, which they graciously acknowledged. On their first journey to Redbourne Hall in 1828 thousands lined the streets of Louth to watch them pass, women pursued the duchess from shop to shop, and men stood on each other's shoulders to look into the rooms they took at the King's Head. When the duke and duchess made an excursion to Brigg to open a new bridge a large portion of the town's residents met them on the road. Their cavalcade then took a circuitous route through the town, which was decked with flags in their honour. 'Their graces appeared highly gratified by the respectful attention paid them,' noted the *Stamford Mercury*.

This adulation was a tribute to Harriot's celebrity, but no less to her generosity, which won gratitude while adding to her renown. Everywhere she went she sought out good causes to support and laid out money in shops. At short notice she would order flowers from a nursery, arrange a dinner for the officers of a local regiment, or act as the patroness of a charity ball. In place after place she left alms for the needy or issued them with tickets for provisions chargeable to herself. In Weymouth she bought up all she could from the grocers of nearby villages and distributed her harvest among the town's poor. Her presence was a form of economic stimulus for a small community. In Ryde in the Isle of Wight she was hailed for 'giving life and spirit to this town', and elsewhere we read of gladdened hearts and votes of thanks. The *Edinburgh Weekly Journal* described a Scottish journey of 1835 as 'one continued series of benefactions'.

More time still was filled with sojourns in Brighton. The duchess developed a settled dislike of Redbourne, so when the couple wished to be away from London and Highgate, especially in the colder months, they went to the fashionable Sussex resort where she had passed happy days before her second marriage. First they lived at an address on Kings Road, but as this could not accommodate their entire household they took a mansion in Regency Square, which soon, like their London residence, acquired the name St Albans House. Each winter the duchess gave a cluster of parties almost as grand as those in the capital. The *Morning Post* had a Brighton correspondent to do them justice in the approved flowery style, as well as spotting her at the theatre or driving in the streets. According to Mrs Baron-Wilson, 'St Albans House became the head quarters of social gaiety, and seemed the centre around which all the fashion, wit, and pleasure of the place revolved.'[51]

Even more than the *Morning Post*, the Brighton press followed the couple's every step: the joyful news of their imminent arrival; the hope that they would make a good long stay; the regret on learning of their plans to leave; and sadness on the day of their departure. What might look like servility was recognition of the good Harriot did. 'The liberality and benevolence of the Duchess makes her presence at all times desired by all classes,' explained the *Brighton Gazette*. She supported shops and the theatre, and in winter the indigent received needful items from her. She liked to be spontaneous and spring surprises, such as the gift of a gold necklace round her neck to a bride about to be married or a parcel containing £300 left behind after an anonymous visit to an impoverished gentlewoman. 'Her generosity and kindness to the poor have become proverbial,' stated the *Brighton Patriot*. 'Her hand is always open to relieve their distress; to allay the sufferings of the widow, the orphan, or the wretched.'

Be it her social life, her largesse or her travels, newspapers could not get enough of her. Not all readers felt the same, and both gushing adulation and court-circular banality raised the hackles of those not disposed to admire her. They did not want descriptions of her clothes and jewellery when she went to the theatre, constant updates on her health when she was unwell, heraldic jargon about the coat of arms emblazoned on her equipages, or streams of anecdotes about her earlier life. The *Globe* turned the subject to ridicule by imparting the 'important piece of information' that she had danced with Sir George Warrender at a party. The *Western Times*, not having heard anything of her or the duke for six days, asked if they had fallen into a trance. More earnest was the disapproval of the *Poor Man's Guardian* at long press reports of Lucullan parties thrown by a plundering capitalist who did nothing to warrant her vast income.

Irritation at the duchess's constant media presence was increased by the suspicion that she was paying for it. Was she, as some said, a serial self-publicist with a budget for 'puff paragraphs'? How, without her or her proxies' help, could journalists disgorge so much detail about her parties? They had runners to gather news who may have spoken to servants, but would this have sufficed for the long, luminous articles they wrote? And what of events described before they had taken place, like one in Brighton that would be 'upon a scale of magnificence entirely unknown, even in the Palace of the Kremlin'? Party-givers did send guest lists to the papers, as the reminiscences of the travel writer Charles MacFarlane make clear.[52] Perhaps they went further and produced what we would now call press releases. It was in no one's interest for the precise mechanism to be known, and it is veiled in mystery. Whatever Harriot did, she was only following the practice of every other hostess in London.

It is less likely that she had a direct hand in the reporting of her charities, but she never objected to her name being attached to them. James Boaden, misquoting Alexander Pope, said she did not 'plan secret good, and *blush* to find it fame'. Anne Mathews thought she sometimes wished to act without it being known, but that her love of scenic effects and surprises gave publicity to her initiatives and led to the charge of self-display. According to Mrs Baron-Wilson, she had no desire for attention and often gave anonymously, but although her household had instructions to keep quiet on this topic the deeds of someone so famous were bound to be broadcast. The *Gentleman's Magazine* said she was not a philanthropist from love of fame, while Oxberry, writing before her second marriage, mentions previously unknown cases of theatre people receiving gifts from her.[53]

Whatever Harriot did to shape her public image, she was not alone responsible for it – no celebrity ever is. It was the media that sustained interest in her, as the *Atlas* perceived:

> It is very singular that the press should be angry about her Grace's publicity; for, after all, who is it that gives her publicity but the press itself? – and yet this very press is the first to turn round and calumniate her for that into which it has forced her. No doubt her Grace may be fond of exhibition – she may have all the silliness of rank and idleness; but if the press would let her alone, she could have no publicity. We will answer, that if the press permit her, the Duchess of St Alban's would, in six months, be as little known to the great body of the public, no matter how she struggled for fame, as the quiet portress at her Grace's gates.

Moreover, as with any celebrity, her visibility was used by others for their own purposes. Whereas she could have no pecuniary motive for deploying her image, those with something to sell exploited it, mainly in hidden advertising. An instance of this is the *Courier* announcing that while in Brighton she and the duke 'honoured the Steyne House Confectionary with a visit'. Or this in the *Bury & Norwich Post*:

> We understand that during her late visit to this city [Bury St Edmunds], the Duchess of St Alban's purchased of Mr Blakely several shawls, manufactured by Messrs Shickle, Towler, and Co. and her Grace was pleased to express her admiration of the beauty of the fabric, and her desire to promote the trade of this city.

A geranium was named after her, as was a steamboat plying the River Witham between Lincoln and Boston, and a newly composed set of quadrilles was dedicated to her. Finally, the duke was the first of four providers of testimonials in the *Dorset County Chronicle* to the skills of the magician Signor Blitz, who was about to appear in Dorchester.

Harriot's detractors fed off her celebrity too. Indeed, the journalists who railed against her prominence would have pulled long faces if she had disappeared off the face of the earth. Long after she married the duke they kept up their tasteless jokes about her being 'in that state that married ladies should be' or 'in the way ladies wish to be who love their lords', in other words pregnant. Her looks were the target of merciless raillery. Few traces remained of her beauty; the once slim figure was very bulky and she had a powdering of facial hair. Hostile newspapers remarked on her need to pause for breath as she walked to her seat at a public event or jested that the stomacher was the most bejewelled part of her gown because the most important. She was 'our fat friend' or 'Whiskeranda', and there were charges, made half-implicitly to heighten their effect, that she was not just a glutton, but a drinker too.

Theodore Hook's *John Bull* treated the Duchess of St Albans as it had Mrs Coutts, and even the unworldly artist William Etty, spotting her in Brighton in 1834, knew she was its favourite target.[54] Hook's misogynistic pleasure in pummelling a well-known woman was aped in the sporting title *Bell's Life in London*. Neither, however, sank to the depths of the *Age*, a scandal-sheet edited from 1827 by Charles Molloy Westmacott, who had torn Harriot to pieces in his novel *The English Spy*. Like *John Bull*, the *Age* held to the narrow view that only those utterly loyal to the monarchy, the established church and the peerage were patriots. It saw an enriched and ennobled ex-actress as a threat to the social order, and for all its populism it objected to press fawning on her in the name of exclusiveness, not equality. But Westmacott's main aim as editor was not to propagate his politics, but to libel people so viciously that they paid for his silence.

The *Age* threw old brickbats with new violence. It claimed the duchess forced herself on public notice by paying for positive reports and never gave a shilling to charity without advertising it. On her looks it was as insolent as could be, even calling her a 'whapper' (whopper); it had fun with the Holly Lodge breakfast parties, not least certain unscripted actions of the dairy cows; and the insinuations about her past as Miss Mellon may be imagined. The *Age* also hated obsequious writing about her in other papers, and its parodies of this are funnier than the heavy jokes about the lady herself. The papers in question hit back by condemning the *Age* for trespassing against the chivalry due to a woman and the common humanity due to anyone. An unknown author composed a long poem in her defence entitled *Epistle to Harriet, Duchess of St Albans; or, The First Lash of Nemesis* (1828). The lash of the title is applied to Westmacott, and quite as thoroughly as scores of his victims no doubt wished it to be.

Neither Westmacott nor Hook would be silenced, and their sarcasm was imitated by lesser hacks. Most of these did not care about Harriot one way or the other, but shared the savage joy of blasting a celebrity. Mrs Baron-Wilson quotes the words of one of them:

> Her sudden elevation has made her name familiar to every class of our readers, and the public are more amused with a matter affixed to her name than to one of which they have never heard. Some papers began by attacking her perhaps from mercenary motives, with the hope of being 'bought up;' and we continue it for the fun of the thing.

The biographer further observes that constant, strident repetition of falsehoods made many readers who at first dismissed them finally believe them (a lesson many propagandists have digested and made use of since), and she claims that 'no lady of her own times ever suffered more from the envy and malignity of others.'[55]

Denigration gained visual force in the satirical prints that began to appear when she was Mrs Coutts and proliferated after her second marriage. She is instantly recognisable: fat and mustachioed, smug and overdressed, accoutred with bags of coins, melons and a ducal coronet, her character as a self-important arriviste underlined by the wooden humour of the speech balloons. A fair specimen of the genre is Robert Cruikshank's 'Sketch of St Albans; or, Shaving the New Maid Dutchess' (1827). It shows her, cheque book in hand, being shaved by the duke, while the duke's uncle counts money on a table and Thomas Coutts in the form of a wig stand looks on and says, 'When I bought that *Melon* I never intended any one to taste it but myself.' These images must have been very familiar. In 1835 the *Evening Chronicle* reported that a barber accused of begging, under the magistrate's questioning, made the courtroom laugh by saying, 'I've been engaged in my official capacity with the Duchess of St Albans.'

It is hard to know how our heroine felt about her celebrity. She was so disgusted at being mobbed in Louth in 1828 that she vowed never to go there again, yet when crowds stared at her as she ate in her carriage at the Ascot Races the same year the *Berkshire Chronicle* noted 'the ease and nonchalance with which the Duchess viewed the gaze of her unasked visitors; and the marked good-humour she displayed'. As for ill-treatment in the media, the statement quoted earlier suggests she grew inured to it, and pillories in word and image did not deter her from travelling in state, giving lavish parties, and showering money on good causes. On the other hand, a note of 1828 to one of the six men who had advised her suggests she was still upset: 'God bless you dear Lord Bristol for your letter of comfort,' she wrote. 'I will attend strictly to all your most excellent advice.' He was evidently still against the idea of actions for libel, and his counsel was echoed in the *Literary Gazette*:

> True dignity or sterling worth can always look down upon and despise malignant attacks and falsehood: at all events, though every person of sense in the country who gives the matter a thought at all, must condemn the silly or mischievous clamour kept up about the Duchess of St Albans, it is clear that to answer the assailants is to play their game, and descend to an arena the very appearance in which bespeaks weakness of character or injudiciousness of conduct.[56]

The only public defence of the duchess came from the duke. A month after their wedding the *New Times* printed his praise for her disposition, heart and temper, which perfectly qualified her to make a man happy. A year later, at a function in Lincoln, he again spoke up for her: 'I am proud of my wife, and I love her. [...] I take this public opportunity, Mr Mayor, to say that the Duchess and myself despise the miscreants who affect to doubt her virtue.' These interventions reflect well on a man dismissed as a simpleton, the more so as he had his own crosses to bear as a celebrity's spouse. In graphic satire he was depicted as a slight, timid boy, led about by his wife, and in the press he was presented as a sidekick or ignored altogether. If he did get a few lines of print, they might not be pleasant reading. A report of his birthday celebrations of 1830 in the *Age* is typical: 'The Duke made a most sensible speech of about two minutes and a half, during which he expressed all his ideas on the Corn Question, Currency, Affairs of Greece and Portugal, Reduction of Taxation, East India Monopoly, the East Retford Affairs, Reform in Parliament, &c. &c.'

The duke only came to notice on his own account as Hereditary Grand Falconer of England. This was a pure sinecure until he had the idea of actually acquiring hawks and reviving the long-dead sport of falconry. A first attempt was made at Redbourne Hall in 1828. The hawks duly swooped down on the partridges let loose for them, and afterwards spectators had music, fireworks and good fare. Exhibitions were held in many more places, directed by the duke in his ceremonial costume, and attracted friendly notices. Inevitably, though, things went wrong: at one display the hawks refused to perform on being given pigeons instead of partridges as quarry; on another a hawk absconded and was shot by a fowler miles away; and a Sussex farmer billed the duke £10 for damage done to his land. Newspapers made merry with these mishaps, and the *Examiner* scoffed that as he rode about in his green jacket, golden girdle, trimmed gauntlets, turned-up hat with a large white feather, and buskins with gold spurs, the duke was lucky to escape being hooted at or pelted by small boys.

Just once the couple took revenge on their tormentors in the press. In the summer of 1828 news spread that they would settle in France because of the abuse they received at home. Consternation set in. Would they really spend all their money abroad? They sailed in early August, and the *Globe*, among many others, was gloomy:

The Duke and Duchess of St Albans are gone to reside (it is said, but we hope untruly) permanently in France, her Grace being, it is rumoured, much dissatisfied with the ingratitude of the English. We do not know what is meant by this statement, but as the departure of her Grace is said to have been attended with the discharge of nearly forty servants, we cannot but regret that any thing should have occurred to disgust her Grace and render destitute so many individuals, to say nothing of the injury inflicted upon her tradesmen by the expenditure of her fortune in a foreign country.

The papers cheered up when it became known that the Parisians, apprised of the couple's riches, were fleecing them mercilessly, while the city's *haute volée* ignored them. Harriot disliked the French no less for seeing them on their own soil, and in September she and the duke made the return crossing. They had probably never intended to stay for more than a few weeks, but had started a hare to unsettle those who had offended them.

Behind the praise and dispraise, rumour and counter-rumour, it is hard to discern the real woman. What was she like as a friend, relative or employer? She had a hasty temper, as even Mrs Baron-Wilson concedes, and in the agitation of her anger she could say strong things. A wilfulness some had observed during her first union grew more pronounced during her second. It was encouraged by the habits of command that wealth gave her, but must have been in her nature, inherited from her far more arbitrary and despotic mother.[57] Her letters to Dudley Coutts Stuart, though friendly, show her trying to prod him into becoming a suitable heir, which he no doubt found irksome. On the other hand, she was said to be a fair mistress of her household, and attentive to the needs of her servants in and out of health. They spoke well of her, which is a moral litmus test for anyone situated as she was at this period.[58]

Those who knew Harriot personally almost all liked her: theatre people John Bannister, Walter Donaldson, Robert William Elliston, Michael Kelly, Fanny Kemble, Anne Mathews, William Oxberry and Frederick Reynolds; the men of letters Lord Albemarle, Lord William Pitt Lennox, Prince Pückler-Muskau, Sir Walter Scott, Cyrus Redding and George Augustus Sala; the artist Benjamin Robert Haydon and the sculptor's wife Mary Nollekens.[59] The woman who rises from the pages of their memoirs was kind, cheerful and loyal. Her munificence, misguided or not, sprang from real sympathy, and the poor loved her. She had the frailty of wanting gratitude and recognition, yet there are instances of her giving covertly and taking the secret to the grave. Her probity in money matters and in the general transactions of life was absolute. Her tastes in art, music and literature were straightforward, with a strong bias in favour of what was British, and she delighted in the beauties of nature, flowers above all.

Though sensible and down-to-earth in everyday matters, she was credulous, believing in the prophetic power of dreams, keeping horseshoes to ward off evil, and having a terror of being in a group of thirteen. She had more superstition than religion, and Mrs Baron-Wilson never lays the paint on so thick, or distorts her portrait more, than when she claims a strong Christian faith for the duchess.

As a companion she was cheerful and lively, and she had a prompt, boisterous sense of humour. Fanny Kemble relates that after seeing an unnamed play one evening with her husband's sisters she took them behind the scenes and introduced them to the actor who played Charles II: 'There, my dears; there's your ancestor.'[60] She had a great love of anecdotes, which she enjoyed no less if she heard them than if she told them herself. Many found their way into Mrs Baron-Wilson's book and give authenticity, however one-sided, to its picture of her.

It is an enigma why a woman of Harriot's intelligence and spirit should make it her goal, long and tenaciously pursued, to move in exclusive circles. She liked giving parties and loved her husband, but she also saw both as vehicles to raise her up in the world. It was an unworthy enterprise, and the limits of its success were painfully obvious. She was invited to court and received the royal dukes at home (though it was whispered they came because they had debts with her bank) but gaining admittance to the empyrean of London society was another matter. Her lowly birth and the suspicion she had been a married man's mistress counted against her. Moreover, while her manners and diction were good, she was never a refined woman, and in middle age she had a bustling vulgarity about her. Finally, the fact that her entertainments outdid those of the real leaders of fashion caused resentment. For all these reasons she ran into an invisible barrier that no thoroughgoing parvenu could pass.

The view of female guardians of gentility is well documented. The Duke of Wellington's friend Mrs Arbuthnot disliked Harriot's use of profuse expenditure to lure people to her parties and thought George IV let himself down by admitting her at court. Lady Hardy, the wife of Nelson's Hardy, went to one of Harriot's fêtes but 'was not anxious for any great intimacy there' and did not stay long. The Whig hostess Lady Holland regretted having to dine with her in Brighton, though she disliked seeing her openly snubbed at a diplomatic banquet.[61] Some ladies would not attend her parties, let alone invite her to theirs, and the duke's unmarried sisters were censured for living under her roof. Most tellingly, Harriot never gained a voucher for the holy of holies, the weekly balls in Almack's Assembly Rooms in St James's, which were policed by six or seven high-society patronesses. Newspapers were divided in their verdicts on such slights, but their being public knowledge was humiliating in itself.

One wonders why the aloofness of the fashionable world did not revolt Harriot from the outset, and how she could be so weak as to keep renewing her attempts to gain entry to it. If anything qualified her defeat, it was that she had tried to scale the summit of society on her own terms. The desire for acceptance did not extend to the snobbery of gliding away from her origins and career. Indeed, she referred to her early struggles candidly and without affectation, and of her theatre memories she spoke with pleasure and, for some tastes, rather too much. There was a kind of defiance in this, a will to penetrate the elite while remaining a professed outsider, and if this made her task harder at least it mitigated the shame of failure. As Duchess of St Albans she was stranded, rejected by the class to which her title and fortune aligned her, but removed by those advantages from the genial company of her old comrades of the stage.

Undaunted, or apparently so, Harriot carried on her glittering life in the public eye. The attention of newspapers to her parties, the duke's falconry shows and their other activities did not abate. At the same time, the world around them was changing. The heyday of Regency hedonism was receding as sterner ideas of duty and virtue took hold, as middle-class values encroached on aristocratic culture and slowly ushered in Victorianism. This was palpable at court, where after George IV's death in 1830 the tone was set, not by the rackety, volatile Duke of Clarence, now William IV, but by his consort Queen Adelaide. She was a soft-hearted woman and would not have wished to hurt anyone's feelings, but she set her face against receiving women with a 'past', whatever their rank. As the Duchess of St Albans had been admitted to George IV's drawing rooms, the new court did likewise, but royal parties and state balls were a different matter.

Harriot felt the chill of the new climate in early 1831 while she and her husband were in Brighton. The king and queen gave a ball at the Royal Pavilion, to which they invited him but not her. The duke, to his credit, did not go. The press was all over the story, and Creevey chuckled that 'old Mother St. Albans' had been absent from the ball but 830 people then residing in Brighton had attended it. The queen's friend Lady Howe justified the exclusion: 'Does a coronet necessarily bring with it complete oblivion of the past? Does vice become virtue under a rim of strawberry leaves? The brand remains on the brow though diamonds of countless value sparkle above it.'[62] The duchess sought to overcome this rejection by going to court more gorgeously attired than ever. At the coronation later in 1831 she was bedecked in jewels and gold embroidery, outshining the other peeresses, but suffered the indignity of being cold-shouldered by them all.

The queen's frostiness (the king was as friendly as he dared be) stoked tensions between the duchess and her Beauclerk and Coutts relations, who were welcomed at court. After some wrangling the duke's sisters went to a ball given by the queen, also in 1831; Harriot saw this as treachery and ejected them from St Albans House. There were bad passages with Lady Guilford about drawing rooms, and with Sir Francis Burdett about money. Things were always patched up after a fashion, and members of both families joined the duchess's 'suite' on her travels. 'The most perfect cordiality exists between all branches of the St Albans family, notwithstanding insidious reports to the contrary,' announced the *Court Journal* in 1834, which sounds like a paid insertion to counter hints of a more fractious reality. Harriot continued to pay large allowances to the Coutts's, and when Lady Guilford was ill in 1836 she and her husband accompanied her from place to place as she sought the best air for her recovery.

For the duchess, loyalty to her first husband's family was loyalty to him. 'The name of Coutts – and a right good one it is – is, and ever will be, dear to my heart,' she told Sir Walter Scott after her remarriage. She still intended to leave her fortune in his family, not to the Beauclerks, and wanted a single successor. Who should it be? The question was the weightier for the fact that the bank was flourishing, and by 1830 her income from this source alone was £80,000. Her choice, after much deliberation, fell on Angela Burdett, the youngest daughter of Sir Francis and Sophia, Lady Burdett. Born in 1814, she was a tall, thin, earnest girl. In Harriot's last years she became a regular companion, staying with her in London and joining her on her travels round the country. As a boy the journalist George Augustus Sala often saw them together: 'To me, the Duchess comes back stately, benignant, in black velvet and diamonds.'[63] It is the last contemporary recollection of her, and it is a kind one.

By the mid-1830s she had serious rivals in the art of entertaining, but she exerted herself to maintain her primacy and the newspapers were still full of her hospitality. In 1836 balls and fêtes succeeded each other at a bewildering pace, and one day she hired a steamboat to take 'a numerous party of fashionables' to Richmond. A tour of the West Country in the autumn created the usual fanfare, and she won praise for the 'judicious distribution of part of her immense wealth'. As before bell-ringers merrily proclaimed her approach, and for the last time she saw glad faces in town after town. She wintered in Brighton, giving alms to hundreds of its poor and a large donation to the Sussex County Hospital, while the duke regaled crowds with the agility of his hawks. In January they gave a large party at which he appeared as a Scottish clan chief and delivered a comic recitation, 'which afforded considerable amusement'.

In February 1837, still in Brighton, a St Valentine's Day ball was enlivened by a little boy appearing as Cupid and shooting love arrows among the dancing pairs. Harriot moved to London for the Season, but in late March an inflammation of the chest laid her low. By May she was very ill. She pressed on with plans for Holly Lodge fêtes, but a 'low nervous fever' forced her to abandon them. She had to be lifted in and out of her carriage for rides in the grounds, with their flowers and the view of London. At last even this exercise was too much, and in June she moved to Stratton Street, where she spent two months in the great dining room, comforted by her husband and subsisting on arrowroot soaked in brandy. Her illness, which may have been cancer, baffled her medical attendants. When she felt the end was close she asked to be carried up to the room where Thomas Coutts had died. There, clutching his pillow, she followed him on 6 August. She was about sixty years old.

The surge of newspaper print that greets the death of a celebrity lasted for weeks. Details of her final days alternated with anecdotes of her life and accounts of the funeral procession that took her coffin to Redbourne Hall for burial among the duke's family. Obituaries long and short appeared and reappeared. The *Morning Post* paid her a dignified tribute but asked if she might have done better not to become a duchess. The *Morning Chronicle* was respectful, though it believed she had been the mistress of Thomas Coutts before she was his wife. The *Gentleman's Magazine* assumed their relationship was platonic and praised her for bravely bearing with calumny and being a friend to the poor. The *Morning Herald*, too, hailed her charities, which had begun at a time when she hardly had money to spare. The *Age's* negative verdict was allied with an uneasy vindication of its conduct towards her.

As Harriot took her last breath, she knew her final performance lay ahead. Her will was calculated to cause a sensation, the more so as the capital of Coutts & Co. had doubled during the fifteen years in which she was the senior partner. She left her husband £10,000 a year and the use of Holly Lodge and a London house, all to revert to the estate when he died. Otherwise, aside from a legacy to Lady Burdett and smaller bequests, her fortune, some £1,800,000, went to Angela Burdett, who was required to add the name Coutts to her own. However, Angela could neither touch the capital nor influence the running of the bank, and her income was to be paid by trustees. Comments and questions were endless. The main one was whether she had been wrong to leave her husband only a life interest and cut out other relations in favour of a single person. It was said the duke might challenge the will, though he denied it.

Thomas Coutts would have been proud of the way she had handled and disposed of her inheritance. His granddaughter, later created

Baroness Burdett-Coutts, had his clear judgement and diligence and Harriot's desire to alleviate distress, and the combination yielded the foremost philanthropist of the Victorian era. Hers was a wise munificence, avoiding publicity and carefully discriminating between deserving and undeserving causes. There was a rumour she might marry the widowed duke, but she did not, being wedded instead to the obligations her wealth imposed on her. He, meanwhile, seduced a servant girl and then married Elizabeth Gubbins, an Irishwoman of some fortune who bore him a son and a daughter. The fashion for falconry had died with the first duchess, as did the interest the newspapers took in the duke. He spent most of his time living quietly at Redbourne and died in 1849, aged forty-eight, of an epileptic fit.

The gentlemen of the press who had estimated Harriot's career so variously returned to her one last time when Mrs Baron-Wilson's *Memoirs* came out in 1839. Some deplored the book's hagiographical tone; others found it a useful corrective to the slander previously heaped upon its subject. To survey all the reviews in newspapers and periodicals would detain us too long. Suffice to say the biography attracted as wide a range of opinions as the woman it portrayed had done during her life. Sales were good, and Colburn published an enlarged edition in 1840. In its preface Mrs Baron-Wilson strenuously denied having been bribed to praise the duchess and insisted the book was a normal commercial undertaking, the publisher having supplied the material and paid her for her work. This, it would seem, was true.

Without her biographer's rose-tinted filter, Harriot appears as a benevolent woman who enjoyed staging her benevolence. She spread happiness and then stepped back to admire her handiwork. Thus she lived on the border between reality and imagination, private self and public persona. Her celebrity brought her joy and vexation, and when the latter was strong she recalled the dream in which Thomas Coutts had urged her never to lose her spirits. His trusting love, more yet than her ascent to wealth and status, was the basis of her self-worth, and she would have been glad that the *Globe* saw in her experiences 'proof of how fortune may be created and secured by conduct which engenders esteem and excites attachment throughout all circumstances in life'. Her wish to present her story as an illustration of this heart-warming notion captures the mixture of complacency and goodness in the woman, but mainly the goodness, and merits an affectionate remembrance for Harriot, Duchess of St Albans.

2

The Tsar's Intriguer

Princess Dorothea Lieven

Dorothea von Lieven by an unknown artist.

In his *Vanity Fair*, published as a book in 1848 but set in the years before and after Waterloo, Thackeray describes women who, like the Duchess of St Albans, impress the uninitiated as being in the pink of fashion but are nothing of the sort:

> While simple folks who are out of the world, or country people with a taste for the genteel, behold these ladies in their seeming glory in public places, or envy them from afar off, persons who are better instructed could inform them that these envied ladies have no more chance of establishing themselves in 'society,' than the benighted squire's wife in Somersetshire, who reads of their doings in the *Morning Post*. Men living about London are aware of these awful truths. You hear how pitilessly many ladies of seeming rank and wealth are excluded from this 'society'. The frantic efforts which they make to enter this circle, the meannesses to which they submit, the insults which they undergo, are matters of wonder to those who take human or woman kind for a study.[1]

Contrasting with these strivers, and keeping them forever at bay, are the great ladies who direct the great world. And of these none was more severely exclusive than Countess, later Princess Lieven.

She was born Dorothea (Daria) von Benckendorff in Riga on 28 December 1785, a member of the Baltic German nobility who enjoyed large privileges in return for service to the Romanov tsars. Her father was military governor of Riga and her mother a lady-in-waiting at the St Petersburg court. Dorothea and her siblings Maria, Alexander and Constantine spent part of their childhood in the turreted grandeur of Riga Castle, their father's official residence. Their mother died when Dorothea was eleven years old, and the Empress Maria Feodorovna, who had regarded Baroness Benckendorff as a close friend, took the two girls under her wing and placed them in the Smolny Institute, an aristocratic convent school in St Petersburg. In later years the princess was mocked for her scanty education, but if the convent did not stock her mind with much information it gave her a perfect poise, a familiarity with court etiquette, a fluency in French, German and Russian, and the ability to converse pleasingly. She also developed a lasting love for music and learnt to play the piano with finesse.

In the summer of 1799, when Dorothea was thirteen, the empress removed her from school and appointed her a lady-in-waiting. At the same time she introduced her to the husband she had selected for her. Count Christopher Lieven was twelve years older than Dorothea, from the same Baltic German background, and like her a Lutheran.

Although not a man of exceptional ability, his sober, punctilious character and the interest of an influential family had secured him a very rapid rise through the ranks of the army, and he was already a major general and minister of war. Marriages among titled families in Russia were arranged and dynastic, and brides as young as possible. Both parties entered wedlock willingly enough in February 1800, but Dorothea's later recollection is poignant:

> How joyfully I left my convent, how delighted I was with my beautiful clothes, how well my wedding dress suited me, how pleased I was with my success when the Empress put some of her diamonds on me and took me in to the Emperor Paul, and he led me into his drawing-room to show me to his Court! I should have liked to get married every day, and I thought about everything, except that I was taking a husband.

Nonetheless the couple's life together began well. Dorothea wrote to her brother Alexander that she was happier than she could express, and that only someone who knew her husband could comprehend how deeply she loved him.[2]

In March 1801 the arbitrary, cruel and possibly deranged Tsar Paul I was assassinated. Under his son Alexander I the Lievens' favour continued and the count was a member of the young monarch's inner military circle. During the next few years he was often away from St Petersburg on active service and other missions, and even at home he had so much business that his wife saw little of him. She bore him a daughter who died in infancy and three sons, Alexander, Paul and Constantine, but neither motherhood nor her court duties satisfied her or filled up her time, and she grew bored and restless. She also became aware of her husband's shortcomings. Behind his polished exterior he was rather a dour, strait-laced man, cold in temperament and ponderous in manner. He was a considerate guide and protector to her, and she still loved him and craved his company, but when he was away she indulged in flirtations with other men.

The countess was her husband's antithesis. She had a lively mind, a sharp sense of humour, volatile emotions, and a love of excitement. The conversational skills that so captivated people at the apogee of her influence were maturing. She was precise and succinct, often penetrating, though in a playful rather than forceful way, graceful, light-hearted, irreverent, but never improper. The colleagues Count Lieven invited home were much taken with her witty talk. And she cultivated another engaging trait in the company of these important, busy men, who felt in need of sympathy and understanding: she became an intelligent listener. She enjoyed her success, but she gradually realised that her roles as high-society wife and marionette in the intricate rituals of the imperial court did not fulfil her. She needed mental stimulation, and she needed a field in which she could nurture her talents and achieve something on her own account.

Lieven resigned from the army early in 1808 to join the foreign ministry, and two years later he was gazetted ambassador to Prussia. It was a frustrating appointment. Russia had made peace with the all-conquering French and consented to the dismemberment of Prussia, its former ally, so a tsar's representative met with little warmth in that country. Moreover, Berlin was a social and cultural desert, and Dorothea wrote home that her only pleasures were eating, sleeping and walking in the park with her children. Lieven's recall in late 1811, occasioned by Napoleon's preparations to invade Russia, came as a relief. All the same, the countess did not look forward to resuming her tedious round at the St Petersburg court, so she rejoiced to learn in September 1812 that her husband had been chosen as the new ambassador to the Court of St James's. He was just as happy: 'I have been given the most brilliant, important and pleasant post I could have hoped for.'[3]

The circumstances of their arrival in London in December 1812 could not have been more auspicious. A Russian ambassador was a novelty, there not having been one since the now defunct Treaty of Tilsit of 1807 had established peace between Napoleon and the tsar. Indeed, the French grip on the Continent in the preceding years had been such that only four countries had a diplomatic presence in Britain. The Lievens' prestige was enhanced by the crushing defeat his country was just then inflicting on the *Grande Armée*, and they were hailed with shouts of 'Russia forever'. They had a generous allowance and could entertain on a large scale at the embassy in Harley Street and at Streatham Park, the villa they took just south of the capital. 'Half a diplomat's success hinges on his hospitality and his grand manners,' the countess wrote later. 'You dominate where you please, and you do not truly please unless you know how to spend.'[4]

Count Lieven looked the part. He was a well-made man, fairly tall and slim, with curling dark hair, blue eyes and regular features. His solemn dignity and reserve kept people at a distance but without causing offence. In the execution of his duties his unruffled style concealed, at least initially, his mediocre intellect. 'He is very busy, and, I think, is doing well. He is esteemed and liked,' Dorothea told her brother Alexander. She herself, just twenty-seven when she arrived in Britain, made her mark with a tall, erect figure, stylish demeanour and perfect French. The diarist Lady Shelley thought the way she held herself was 'perfection', and many were as curious as the society hostess Lady Jersey, who climbed on a chair at a ball to get a view of her. 'I am everywhere received as no other foreigner has been, and I flatter myself that I have been a success,' she told her brother. According to Elizabeth Craven, Margravine of Ansbach, she was treated 'as if she was a princess'.[5]

The newspapers noted her social activities and court appearances in fulsome language. The *Courier* observed that at a ball given by the prince regent in February 1813 his mother Queen Charlotte 'conversed with this Lady during the greater part of the evening, and was highly pleased with her fascinating manners'. Whether the queen really was pleased is questionable given the account of the countess's behaviour on the same day by Lady Elizabeth Feilding:

> Her manners are extremely polished, and she is much shocked at the abruptness and want of grace of the English ladies. She sat very demurely by the Queen, and spoke very little, for I suppose she had nothing to say. She was horrified at the crowding and squeezing at Court, and says that these things are 'mieux arrangés at St. Petersburg.' Mrs. Fielding was rather shocked at her giving her opinion of everything here with so much *sincerity*.

Dorothea was indeed disappointed by London society and by the regent's court, neither having the stateliness to which she had been accustomed. She forgot how arid she had found the Russian capital when she had lived in it and, out of her element and a little homesick, she criticised her new environment in letters home. England was wealthy and full of fine scenery and splendid houses, she said, but it was not the land of emotion or imagination and seemed monotonous even in its beauty. Her most persistent criticism was that the British, however well born, were gauche. Elegance of form, self-possession and refined conviviality were all absent.[6]

Some of her new acquaintance shared her views. Despite the long war with France British aristocrats were cosmopolitan, often liking foreign culture, fashions and food better than their native equivalents. And what could encapsulate Continental sophistication better than Dorothea's seemingly effortless superiority? Her error, as Lady Elizabeth Feilding noted, was not to hide her disdain, and this was resented. 'I don't admire the Countess,' remarked the Irish beauty Frances Calvert. 'She looks very haughty, as if she despised us all.' The regent's daughter Princess Charlotte found her ill tempered, as did the diplomat Sir George Jackson: 'People were prepared to be most civil to her, and there is no distinction that has not been heaped on her. But all would not do, and she is now very unpopular.' Report of her undiplomatic hauteur reached Russia, and in the spring of 1814 the country's foreign minister Count Nesselrode noted that 'Lieven continues to succeed as well as his wife continues to fail.'[7]

Much of Lieven's early business in London concerned plans for the restoration of the Bourbons in France after the anticipated defeat of Napoleon. In 1814, following his abdication, a delicate task fell to the count and countess together. That summer a host of European dignitaries were in Britain to celebrate the Allied victory, among them Tsar Alexander I and his sister Grand Duchess Catherine. The latter came first, and her tactlessness kept the Russian embassy in constant agony. She told the regent how to treat his daughter, curtly dismissed offers of marriage from two of his brothers, and had it in mind to visit his estranged wife. Averting the last threat and removing people obnoxious to the court from the grand duchess's dinner party guest lists required deftness. It was required again when the tsar offended his host by snubbing his mistress Lady Hertford and consorting with members of the Whig opposition.

Dorothea's adroit management of recalcitrant royalty helped her overcome the insecurity in a new setting that her supercilious air had in part been worn to conceal. During the festivities she gave superb balls and receptions at the Russian embassy and thoroughly enjoyed herself. Observing the missteps of the tsar and his sister in London, she decided to improve her own image. She learned the art of flattery, praising people's houses, saying she would miss someone when they parted, approving of their tastes. 'Mme de Lieven [...] is become famous for civility and *empressements* to everybody,' wrote Lady Granville in 1816. 'Her manner is much softened.' Two years later the American envoy Richard Rush noted her 'dignity, intelligence and grace', but also her 'kindness'.[8] This wish to please removed the one obstacle to an appreciation of her qualifications as a leader of society. It was now apparent that these qualifications were of a high order.

Physical attributes were the smallest part of her charm. She was reckoned to have a pretty face, with bright grey eyes, glossy dark tresses and sensual lips, but she was far too lean and had large ears, a red, pointed nose and a very long neck. Countervailing these defects was an expert dress sense. Sometimes she chose historical costumes, as on an evening in 1813 when she was admired in a high-necked, long-sleeved black velvet gown with a ruff and a single chain of large diamonds but no other ornamentation, her hair dressed flat on top in the manner of Mary Queen of Scots.[9] In general, her style had an imposing, austere quality that accorded well with her height and perfect carriage. The Duke of Wellington told her he had suggested another woman take her as a model: 'I advised her to beg you for a list of your wardrobe and to try to adopt some of your grand air, and above all to develop the habit of holding herself as if there were no means in the human form of bending either the neck or the back!'[10]

Newspapers show Countess Lieven to have been a trendsetter throughout her twenty-two years in Britain. Often her clothes were described at length and their originality emphasised. In 1816 the *Morning Post* was impressed by a black velvet headdress decorated with diamonds in spiral form and the *Observer* by a white satin dress with a border and drapery of silver netting; and so it continued year upon year. A description in the *Morning Post* of a gown she wore for a celebration of George IV's birthday in 1822 must stand for dozens:

> A magnificent dress of silver lama, the arrangement of these quite novel: the front, or apron, beautifully drawn to represent a bouquet of flowers, composed of bright and frosted silver, round the bottom of which, being the same pattern, and so the whole being so massive and costly, as to be oppressively heavy to her Ladyship. Head-dress, feather and diamonds.

Not for the first or last time, the desire to be conspicuous in attire involved a degree of physical discomfort.

More striking still was her conversation, which the Whig statesman Lord Holland called 'extremely brilliant, her observations neat and pointed' (it is curious to think she spoke French and her British acquaintance could savour what she said). Many specimens of her quirky wit are recorded. Finding her host the Duke of Devonshire in a testy mood, she said to the other ladies, 'We're driving him to despair. I've never seen a man so disconsolate at having women in his house. We'd better leave. He can't stand it much longer.' She was an able exponent of charades and other means of enlivening country house parties, and one hostess found her 'for a whole week invariably gay and brilliantly agreeable'. A fine pianist, she once even led the hired band from the instrument at the residence of the Austrian ambassador Prince Esterházy. At Stratfield Saye, the Duke of Wellington's, she tried her hand at the harpsichord, to the relief of the duke, who had run out of ideas for entertaining his guests.[11]

She was a prankster too. At one country house party the young Earl of Clanwilliam, through the seeming good offices of another guest, was given an assignation by a heavily veiled girl seen walking in the vicinity. Later, as he was in a room dashing off a note to her to finalise the arrangements, in came the girl on Countess Lieven's arm, walked up to him, and raised her veil to expose the face of the countess's son Paul.[12] Another victim was the timid Spanish ambassador the Duke of Frías. During an overnight party at the Lievens' villa someone said a murder had once taken place there, and when the duke asked in which room the hostess's embarrassment made him think it must be his. Fearing a ghost, he consulted his valet, footman and groom, who advised him to barricade his door, but he decided to keep it open so the ghost could get out. He made two servants sleep in his room with the third just outside and kept it well lit all night. The other guests laughed heartily at him, but he was too terrified to take offence.[13]

The hero of another story was the regent's oafish brother the Duke of Clarence. One night in late 1814, at a dinner at the Royal Pavilion in Brighton, he took a fancy to the ambassadress. When she left the party to return to her nearby lodgings, Clarence insisted on handing her into her carriage, then pushed the footman aside as he was raising the step and got in next to her. She takes up the narrative:

All this was done so quickly that I had no time to stop it, but I felt very ill at ease. Hardly was he in the carriage than he said:

'Are you cold, Madame?'
'No, Monseigneur.'
Are you warm, Madame?'
'No, Monseigneur.'

(His conversation always began like that.)

'Permit me to take your hand.' (This was an extra.)
'It is needless, Monseigneur!' But this did not prevent him from taking my hand. Fear seized me, for he was evidently very drunk. With the other hand I hastened to lower the carriage window as a precautionary measure. As I did not wish to use it, I soon racked my brains for something to distract his attention. I have said that he was very stupid, very ignorant of everything. He took no interest in anything, great affairs preoccupied him not at all. He had only one fixed idea in politics – Hanover. For him everything was concentrated in that.

This came to my mind and I said to him at once:

MADAME LIEVEN: Do you know, Monseigneur, that my husband has had a courier from Vienna to-day?

CLARENCE: What has the Congress to do with me?

MADAME LIEVEN: Wait a minute, it is something that they have decided the question of Hanover.

CLARENCE: What! Hanover? You don't mean that.

He had let go my hand for a moment. It was good, but he had to be distracted for four or five minutes.

MADAME LIEVEN: The necessary moment has come and, well, Hanover is given to Prussia. (He leaped out of his seat.) Yes, to Prussia, but they are indemnifying you on the side of Westphalia and of Saxony.

CLARENCE: G(od) D(amn)! Does my brother know this?

MADAME LIEVEN: I don't think so yet, and I beg you, Monseigneur, not to tell him. It is a secret which I tell you now.

CLARENCE: But we shall never allow that. Impossible! Castlereagh will be attacked in the Commons.

And he swore and got carried away, and forgot me very completely amid a torrent of great words. At this moment the carriage came to my door, I got down slowly, planted my Prince in it, and said 'Good evening' to him.

The next day she told all to the regent, who roared with laughter and kept the joke going with his brother as long as he could.[14]

These anecdotes did the rounds and made the countess a hit with a leisured class that was forever seeking amusement. They also placed her in an intricate web of gossip: spinning stories and being spun into the stories of others. Her letters brim with comic characters and spirited sketches, and she appears, as either narrator or heroine, in the amusing tales of diarists and letter-writers. Initially this renown was circumscribed, not penetrating far beyond her aristocratic peer group. Like other grandees, she was often in the newspapers, but in a benign way, with her presence at dinners, gyrations in ballrooms, and interaction with royalty respectfully tracked. Later, though, she would be prodded, poked and passed about in the press, and would learn the price of celebrity, especially for a person whose indiscretion and love of ridiculing others were notorious.

For now, Dorothea exulted in her fame. 'I am literally fought for,' she told Alexander in 1816. 'It is not fashionable where I am not, and I have even arrived at amusing the English and amusing myself at the same time.' The same year she bragged that her parties and Lady Jersey's were 'the most agreeable and the most brilliant'.[15] The Russian's evenings, known of course as *soirées*, were on Sundays during the Season. She might give a dinner, ball or large reception on Saturdays too, so that each week newspapers chronicled at least one 'elegant assembly', 'select party of fashionables', 'magnificent entertainment' or similar, often with the standard panegyrics about food and décor. Occasionally she helped others' parties along. As well as tinkling the ivories for Prince Esterházy and the Duke of Wellington she in 1817 'condescended with her usual goodness and amiability to do the honours of the evening at the Spanish Ambassador's Fete', in the words of the *Morning Post*.

No less exalted than her role as diplomatic hostess was her position as one of the six, sometimes seven patronesses of the balls held each Wednesday in the Season at Almack's Assembly Rooms in King Street, St James's. The patronesses' strictness in matters of dress and defence of the upper stratum against the incursions of new money were formidable. In afternoon conclaves they mulled over each application for a voucher and then sorted the rejected aspirants into two groups: those who might try again and those who need not. For such as entered the hallowed precincts after a campaign of toadying and scratching around for testimonials, the joy was intense. The physician Henry Holland was 'often witness of the effects of this dominating passion, having seen more than one case defying medicine, cured by a ticket for Almack's opportunely obtained'.[16] By all accounts the balls themselves were nothing special; it was being there that mattered.

The countess was invited to become a patroness about a year after settling in England. While the other names kept changing, hers was constant for two decades. She and Princess Esterházy, who joined the 'high mightinesses' a couple of years later, had special responsibility for assessing applications from foreign visitors. The Russian was reputed to be the most exigent of the ladies, and the memoirist Rees Howell Gronow found her 'haughty and exclusive'.[17] Her place on the Almack's committee multiplied her appearances in society columns, with her execution of her duties and tasteful attire being commended. There is no clear source for the oft-repeated story that she introduced the waltz to London by whirling round the Almack's dance floor with the young secretary at war Viscount Palmerston, but such legends are the stuff of celebrity lives. What is certain is that she was an excellent dancer, and in accounts of balls in the press she is often in the leading pair.

Once she had found her place in British society Dorothea began liking it, and her letters home were full of pleasures enjoyed and the expectation of more. While her hosts were still gauche, they made up for it by having 'so great a fund of good-nature, cordiality, and good sense'.[18] She made a few close friends during these years. One was Harriet Granville, daughter of the glamorous Georgiana, Duchess of Devonshire and wife of the politician and diplomat Viscount, later Earl Granville. Her letters, already cited, reveal her as a mordantly witty woman, observant and sharp-tongued but warm and loyal. Another was Emily Cowper, née Lamb, married to the wealthy fifth Earl Cowper and sister to the future prime minister Lord Melbourne. She, too, was perceptive and amusing, but her temperament was softer and more equable. Both women were as clever and vivacious as the Russian, and this created their bond with her.

If the social round was more fun than the countess had foreseen, so were other aspects of life. While autocratic Russia was intellectually barren, liberal Britain was a ferment of ideas. In particular politics could be freely discussed in the press and society, while the power of parliament in a constitutional monarchy allowed the higher classes, restricted in Russia to acting as functionaries or courtiers, to have a real say in the governance of their country. The countess heard the great topics of the day talked over at parties and dinners – impossible in St Petersburg for fear of government spies. Her curiosity was piqued. *Saunders's News-Letter* noticed her at a parliamentary debate on Catholic emancipation in 1814, and four years later the same organ saw her on a viewing stand during the Westminster hustings at which the radical Henry Hunt gave a speech. Slowly politics filled more space in her letters and she acquired what Harriet Granville called a 'piercing, unbounded understanding' of the subject.[19]

Her husband's position gave her a particular interest in questions with an international aspect. Because Lieven's written French was imperfect she had been in the habit of correcting or even rewriting his dispatches since their time in Berlin; now she paid more heed to their contents. She also found she could help him collect information. Etiquette forbade his presence, but not hers, at gatherings of leading Whigs, so she went alone to Holland House and other places where the opposition met. Her social status gave her access to great men in public life, and they came to realise that her ready apprehension of complex topics made her a rewarding interlocutor, one to whom they all too easily divulged confidential information. She grew ever more knowledgeable, and the seeds of her role as an unofficial diplomatic operator were sown. Gone were the days when she could comment laconically that her husband was busy and seemed to be doing well.

Governments across Europe were making the adjustment from war to peace. In Britain the Tory prime minister Lord Liverpool, a man of solid worth rather than surpassing ability, was content to take a managerial approach to his cabinet. Its leading light was the foreign secretary Lord Castlereagh, who piloted the coalition that defeated France in 1814. Napoleon then subjected Europe to a further burst of his destructive energy before being finally subdued in 1815, and again it was Castlereagh who orchestrated the allies' efforts. Along with Austria's Prince Metternich and Tsar Alexander I, he was the architect of the international order that kept the peace until the middle of the century. The structure they created was not static but required constant renewal through dialogue between the powers. An early task was creating the conditions for France's return to what was called the Concert of Europe. To this end, a congress was held in Aachen in 1818, and the tsar instructed the Lievens to attend it.

By this time cracks in their marriage were visible. Count Lieven had tacitly conceded his wife's greater talents by letting her help with his official correspondence, but now, as she slowly gained a profile of her own, their differing capacities became clear to everyone. The count's grave and dignified mien only went so far, and when politicians and diplomats discovered his limitations they did not refrain from commenting on them. People joked that the ambassadress was the real ambassador, and he was given the nickname 'Vraiment' after the half-surprised ejaculation that was always on his lips. 'A good sort of man, but very dull' was the view of the novelist Lady Charlotte Bury. The countess tried to shore him up by deferring to him in public, but a tincture of artifice belied these demonstrations. The Comtesse de Boigne, who was in London at this time, recalled: 'He was totally eclipsed by his wife's undisputed superiority, but she made a show of attention to him and appeared both submissive and devoted. She was all but never seen without him: walking or driving, in town, in the country, in society – everywhere they were to be found together. And yet no one believed this harmony was real.'[20]

Indeed, rumours of Dorothea's infidelity persisted all through her time in England. Early on there was talk of an affair with Earl Gower, later

Duke of Sutherland. Harriet Granville happened upon them together early in 1816, and in the same year Princess Charlotte spoke of her equivocal reputation.[21] It was probably no more than a heavy flirtation, but the count was jealous and picked quarrels with his wife about which parties she could attend alone and what time she should come home to bed. They had many fallings-out and makings-up, their growing incompatibility offset by habits of long union and devotion to their sons. Dorothea's frustration with her partner's inferiority and pettiness was exacerbated by the society of men whose minds struck sparks in hers, and it was only a matter of time before she fell in love with one of them. When the moment came, everything happened very fast.

The Congress of Aachen, if not as merry as the 'Dancing Congress' of Vienna four years before, had balls, dinners, concerts and excursions to leaven the negotiations about war indemnities and the withdrawal of the army of occupation from France. Among the women Dorothea reigned 'with absolute sway', according to Castlereagh.[22] Among the men the dominating figure, even above the British foreign secretary, was Metternich, aged forty-five and at the height of his power. Although happily married, the Austrian chancellor was a philanderer. Soon his Olympian demeanour, witty talk and shrewd flattery won the countess over, as her scintillating cleverness enraptured him, and they became lovers. After the congress closed and they parted their relationship was cemented by an intense secret correspondence. His letters dilate on his life, his achievements, his philosophy and their love; of hers only extracts survive, mainly about her experiences and impressions of Britain. The more personal passages she suppressed.

The countess and the prince were united by politics as well as love. They shared a conservative outlook and saw their countries as anti-democratic bulwarks. She gave him insights into Russian and British attitudes to international questions and information about British political culture that he found invaluable. She thereby strengthened the alliance of Austria and Russia, and it was pleasant to be valued by the Coachman of Europe. Castlereagh, who shared their reactionary perspective more than he could avow to his colleagues, used her as an unofficial conduit to him. Wellington, likewise a minister and in the same ideological camp, showed her letters he wished Metternich to see but dare not show Esterházy without cabinet approval. Her ties through her husband with Russia's foreign minister Nesselrode, in whose estimation she grew fast, made her a sort of intermediary, connecting and urging on like-minded actors on different stages.

The epistolary romance with Metternich was the final phase of Dorothea's political apprenticeship. The acuity of her perception, the charm she exerted on statesmen, and her importance as a channel of communication between them are apparent in her letters, which also exhibit her skill in painting people and scenes in words. Metternich did not stint in his praise: 'I much prefer your letters to all the dispatches in the world [...] You are among the small number of people who see things as they are, who seize the heart of everything.'[23] Only twice were they able to renew their passion: the British monarch's visit to Hanover in 1821 and the Congress of Verona in 1822. However, the affair and the correspondence that sustained it were no secret in fashionable and diplomatic circles in Britain, and an uneasy suspicion arose that the ambassadress was feeding unscrupulously obtained information to Vienna.

She was indeed, and her principal source was none other than the regent, who became king on his father's death in 1820. Dorothea took no pleasure in his overheated rooms, overpowering perfumes, over-rich food and overflowing alcohol, or in watching him pursue his weary revels with his new pea-brained favourite Lady Conyngham. But she was a courtier to her fingertips and assiduously cultivated him. He grew fond of her and stood godfather to her fourth son, who was named after him. This created no tension with Lady Conyngham, who had the matronly shape the king preferred and regarded the thin Russian with complacency. Too fickle and selfish to have real friends, George IV was lonely and found in the countess a sympathetic listener. He told her of his detestation of Tory and Whig politicians and disgust with the policies of his ministers, and she recorded it all in letters to Metternich, sometimes verbatim.

The amount of time Dorothea spent at court, usually without her husband, did not go unremarked. Lady Granville noted her 'high favour' and Lady Cowper said she 'never saw anything like her favour'. These were friends, who took a relaxed view of her activities, but others shuddered to think of the king opening his mind to one who was sure to pass it all on to her lover. In 1822 she settled a spat between Lady Castlereagh and Lady Conyngham that briefly drove a wedge between the foreign secretary and his sovereign. Castlereagh, who liked Dorothea and found relief from the strains of office in talking to her, was grateful for the intervention but pained that a foreigner had won him the right to see his wife decently treated at court. His brother Lord Stewart was struck by the Russian's leverage. 'I congratulate you,' he told her, 'you must be proud of yourself. You have made the king obey you on every point.'[24]

While cosying up to the king, the countess did not neglect his brothers. The Dukes of Clarence and York were regular visitors to the Russian embassy, the latter often speaking almost non-stop for hours and then thanking her for the pleasure she had given him. She also won over the Duke of Wellington, who, like Castlereagh, saw more in her than a means of clandestine communication with Metternich. Harriet Arbuthnot, the duke's Egeria, or special female counsellor and friend, tried to keep him from her, but a shared love of gossip brought the warrior and the diplomat's wife together. This, the countess told her brother, was of great utility:

Wellington is the only one who laughs at everything, and, above all, talks of everything. He is charming, agreeable, and accommodating in the highest degree; he is a most excellent resource for us, and is quite happy if one will pet him. The truth is that London bores him, and that he is never so much at ease as in our house.

To give balance to her political connections and enrich her dispatches to Metternich and her husband's to Nesselrode, Dorothea began a flirtatious correspondence with the Whig leader Earl Grey. In 1823 she informed Metternich that she was dividing her efforts between Wellington and Grey, and that the latter had grown 'very attentive'.[25]

The countess's footing with great men of the realm raised her social prestige even higher. In 1823 the Russian embassy moved to Ashburnham House, Dover Street, in the Hay Hill area of Mayfair, 'one of the finest edifices in London', according to the *Morning Post*. Her receptions swelled in size and luxury, and she took to giving concerts and *soirées de danse*. Hostess or guest, she was the life and soul of the party. Lady Granville said one event would have been dull without her 'gaiety and cleverness' and that a second was flat until her arrival brought 'an immense improvement'.[26] In less cheerful moods she was peevish, freezing the tedious with a sardonic rejoinder or putting the vulgar in their place. By now she was proficient in English, while still preferring French. Whether in or out of spirits, and whichever language she used, her droll, pungent speech was famous, as was her taste. In the memoirs of the day her sayings and doings, her clothes and parties elicited ever more comment.

Newspapers devoted increasing space to her movements at home and abroad, attendance at royal functions, visits to the theatre and opera, influence as an Almack's patroness, innovations in dress, and, above all, her entertainments. Here is the *Morning Post* in May 1825:

The Countess Lieven, the Lady of the Russian Ambassador, gave a *Fete* of almost unexampled splendour, on Thursday night, on Hay-hill.

The Front-hall, resembled a forest of flowering shrubs: the Inner-hall, the Great Stair-case, the Corridor, and the five magnificent apartments, together with the *Boudoir*, were similarly decorated. Some of the rooms resembled an amphitheatre of flowers; in others they were disposed in every recess, and had a magical effect, from the manner in which the lights were placed. At eleven o'clock the dancing commenced, which was led off with great animation. The Quadrilles were new, but they were eclipsed by the Polish dances. There was a regular increase of company till two o'clock, at which hour the muster exceeded 500.

It was three o'clock before the supper was announced in the Saloon and Library below. This was a regular set-down supper, with one hundred and fifty covers; and the tables were several times replenished. The viands and the wines were all above praise; many did not quit the pleasures of the table till five o'clock, and it was not till half-past six that the music had ceased.

As with any fully fledged celebrity, nothing was too small to note. The *Morning Post* reported that after an assembly at the Austrian embassy in 1821 she was caught in a scramble for waiting carriages and had her dress torn. When she passed through Dover later that year on her way to Russia the *Globe* gave particulars of her arrival there, the company of soldiers that welcomed her, the gun salute from the Western Heights, and the ladies and Russian officers in her suite. The count had accompanied her only as far as Gravesend, where he had embarked for Russia on his own 'to save travelling through France'.

Dorothea never referred in her letters to this coverage, perhaps deeming it beneath her notice, but she knew how high she stood in her own set. She also knew that, while she was sought after, many women disliked her – those who had been put in the shade while she dazzled, had been her supplicants for entry to Almack's, or had felt the rasp of her abrasive tongue. Bores and fools of both sexes did not enjoy being treated as such, and many more quailed at what Lady Granville called her 'dry and conclusive' way of speaking. And if she belittled absent acquaintance the kink of human nature that finds pleasure in telling people the unkind things others have said about them ensured that her sallies reached their ears. The dandy Thomas Raikes saw that she had 'not failed to make many enemies'; the Comtesse de Boigne thought she was 'little liked, but much feared in London'; and Harriet Arbuthnot believed her to be 'not popular, notwithstanding her talents & cleverness'.[27]

Some hoped a rival would appear. The only one she acknowledged was the already-mentioned Sarah Sophia, Countess of Jersey, known as Queen Sarah because she seemed to reign over society. An arcane dispute between them about precedence, whether a woman's rank or her husband's job weighed more in determining who should escort her into dinner, provided entertainment; otherwise they treated each other warily. With the French and Prussian ambassadresses making little impact, Dorothea's only competitor in the diplomatic corps was her fellow Almack's patroness Princess Esterházy. Mrs Arbuthnot was eager to see them spar at Stratfield Saye in 1826: 'They hate each other like poison, with all the affectation of great fondness.' There was not much in it, though, for the Austrian was a frank, kind-hearted woman, lively enough among friends but no match for the Russian. 'A mediocre person,' the latter called her.[28]

With her political star rising and her social star at its zenith, Dorothea had cause to be satisfied. Life, she told Alexander in 1823, was 'too grandly delightful here not to be unbearable anywhere else'. She was not always content, for flaws in her temperament prevented her from being so. The greatest of these was extreme susceptibility to boredom. 'I find boredom so frightful that I prefer any other form of suffering,' she told Metternich.[29] She hated solitude, felt little interest in books or art, and, like other great ladies, had little to do with household management or the care of her children. If left to her own devices she grew panicky. She begged correspondents for news and shamelessly copied or showed letters from others to get a good return. On her travels, in the terror of loneliness, she forgot herself so far as to engage social inferiors in conversation, and was obliged to rebuff the poor souls if they sought to renew the acquaintance later.

Her incessant need for stimulation aroused mirth, not least when it manifested itself in the displays of inquisitiveness to which she owed her nickname 'The Snipe'. When the diarist Charles Greville was handed a letter in her presence she could hardly contain herself, 'and she was very angry that I would not let her see the whole of it'. At the Congress of Verona Lady Londonderry had the same experience:

> The other day I received a note from the Emperor during dinner and her curiosity was so excited that, after repeatedly asking who it was from, she put out her thin red paw to snap at it. But Metternich, who was sitting between us, interposed [...]. She was not to be pacified and, as I took care she should not see the note, turned sulky.[30]

It did not take much to irritate her, and her moods oscillated wildly. Like other highly strung people, she fretted about her health. She was afraid of draughts, complained of fevers and a weak chest, and made sure her wraps were carefully arranged over her. She closed windows or stopped them being opened, and lit fires wherever she could. Journeys were bound to make her ill, as did the late hours of the Season, and London's fogs were surely going to kill her.

These anxieties were accompanied by fits of lassitude that made social status and diplomatic designs suddenly appear pointless. Then she would quit London for the villa on Richmond Hill that after a few changes she and the count had fixed on as their country residence. It was her idyll: 'What a delicious spot! The loveliest in all this lovely England.'[31] Here, while her husband worked in London, she passed days with her sons, striding through fields or being rowed on the river, until the three eldest departed to complete their education in Russia. Another favourite place to relax was Brighton, where she stayed in a series of rented properties, usually with the count. She took a handful of holidays abroad and undertook the long journey to Russia a few times, but most years she did not leave England. Usually, a brief period away from London was enough to make her want to hurry back to the social and political excitement it offered.

In the winter of 1823–1824 Dorothea left this scene for longer, but with other pleasures in prospect. Her doctors had advised her to spend the cold months in Italy, and with her husband tied to his desk in London it seemed she had every chance of a blissful reunion with Metternich, who was to accompany the Austrian emperor south of the Alps. On reaching Milan after an arduous journey she learned that the chancellor's plans had changed. She was furious: 'I have left all my comforts, all the interests of my life, all my intellectual habits, for the sake of an alien sky which draws my body but leaves my mind utterly vacant.'[32] She faced the realisation that the relationship with Metternich, sustained for years mainly by letter, was on the wane. He was losing interest, and so was she. Indeed, had he been anyone but the Coachman of Europe would she have been satisfied with his wordy, self-absorbed epistles for so long?

Recent moves on the diplomatic chessboard drove them apart too. Austria and Russia, hitherto so close, took divergent views of Greece's fight for independence from Ottoman rule. Austria objected on principle to revolt against established authority, but for Orthodox Russia a wish to help its co-religionists coincided with the lure of establishing a dependent ally and wresting control of the Bosporus and Dardanelles from Turkey. Without alignment of their countries on this pressing topic, Dorothea's very political affair with Metternich lost much of its meaning. Word from Vienna that his amorous eye was roving merely hastened the inevitable end. She wrote to him in a desultory way until late 1826, but she found his determination to keep the 1815 settlement blinkered and her admiration for him dwindled. When she learnt a year later that, his first wife having died, he had taken a bride more than thirty years his junior and beneath him socially, contempt was the only emotion she had left.

In moving out of Metternich's orbit the countess reasserted her nationality. Their alliance had served the legitimist cause both their countries championed, but Russians at the Congress of Verona had shunned her, assuming her loyalties to be Austrian. The trust of Nesselrode and the tsar could only be conditional, and to shore it up she henceforth worked exclusively for Russia, regardless of whether its foreign policy looked conservative or liberal. She also knew she would have no part to play at all unless she remained in a functional marriage with a senior diplomat. The affair with Metternich, she now saw, could easily have scuttled her. In any case, she was still fond of her husband. She missed him while travelling alone and hated having to arrange where to dine and sleep herself. In general he was a comforting presence in her life: 'Although my husband's company does not really suit my cast of mind or my heart, all the same he is a creature who loves me, to whom I belong, who is concerned about me. It is intimacy, habit, domesticity, all so sweet and indispensable to a woman!'[33] In the absence of his testimony at this time it is hard to know how Lieven felt about his wife or how much he knew about her and Metternich. When the marriage reached its crisis the cause was not her infidelity, but her usurpation of his diplomatic role.

In the latter part of her Metternich period the countess had joined a cabal against the British foreign secretary. This was no longer Lord Castlereagh, who had committed suicide in August 1822 while under severe mental strain. His successor in office and as leading figure in the government was the liberal Tory George Canning. His cocksure handling of parliament, direct appeals to the nation, support for nationalist uprisings abroad, and scorn for Castlereagh's reactionary alliances irked George IV, who liked foreign autocracy better than British constitutionalism. Canning's methods also annoyed some in his party, who in any case despised his obscure birth. This enmity gave rise to the 'Cottage Coterie', of which the aims were to frustrate his policies and, if possible, eject him from his post. Named after the Royal Cottage, Windsor, where the conspirators met, it comprised the king, the Duke of York, the Duke of Wellington (to an extent), the Austrian, Russian and Hanoverian envoys – and our heroine.

One point of contention between Canning and his antagonists was his disapproval of France's intervention of 1823 in Spain to help the absolutist Ferdinand VII put down a liberal revolt. A second was his support for Spain's self-governing American colonies in their quest to become sovereign states. The coterie needed to inform Vienna and St Petersburg of his designs and of domestic efforts to thwart them, while at the same time gauging the assistance it was likely to receive from the reactionary powers. This was possible thanks to Dorothea's secret correspondences with Metternich and Nesselrode. The latter began in 1823 when she used her flair for concise elucidation to summarise a lengthy dispatch of her husband's, and the foreign minister was so pleased he asked her for similar compositions by each post. He sent letters in return, founding an exchange that launched her as an independent agent in her government's service.

When Canning found out what was going on he hit back hard. He told the king he intended to recognise the South American states and made a veiled threat to expose the coterie's workings. To a friend he confided, 'If, after such a denunciation and the debates which would have followed it, the L[ievens] and Esterházy did not find London too hot for them, I know nothing of the present temper of the English nation.'[34] The king was cowed and surrendered. It was a defeat for Dorothea too, but she turned it into a victory by changing tack. The skill and force with which Canning had bested the plotters aroused her admiration, as did his eloquence and intellect. This was a man to work with, not against, and the occasion came when Russia and Austria differed on the Greek question. High Tories under Wellington were pro-Austrian and pro-Turkish. Canning was neither, and she now wished to enlist his help in forwarding Russian aims. Long Metternich's willing instrument, she was now his adversary.

Her idea was to bring Russia, with British support, to the point of facing down Turkey to secure autonomy for Greece. In the summer of 1825 she travelled to St Petersburg and had two audiences with Alexander I, who, having been under Metternich's spell himself, was in an agony of uncertainty whether to break with him. Dorothea urged him to do so and reassured him that Canning was not a Jacobin, as he had heard, but a potential partner in advancing a pro-Greek policy. The tsar pondered what she said and was convinced. She had been like a revelation, he told Nesselrode, who instructed her orally to make overtures to Britain and handed her a note for Count Lieven: 'Believe all the bearer tells you.' After reaching London as a 'living dispatch', she went with her husband to Brighton, where the foreign secretary was resting, and sought his assurance that Britain would not oppose a belligerent Russian stance towards Turkey. Canning, keen to support Greece and outflank Metternich, reacted favourably.

He was happy to fall in with the ideas of a woman who had been cajoling him for a while, quite overcoming his previous dislike. After her return from Russia their friendship really blossomed and he took to paying her weekly calls to discuss current affairs. They both had a sense of the ridiculous, and at social gatherings their eyes would meet in shared amusement. She made no secret of her esteem, and Mrs Arbuthnot commented sourly on their 'courting' and her gushing praise.[35] Unrest in Portugal provided a chance to cement the alliance between their countries, which upheld the constitutionalist cause while Austria promoted an absolutist counter-revolution. What really mattered was Greece. The death of Alexander I in November 1825 might have upset the new diplomatic alignment, but his successor Nicholas I maintained it. The result was the St Petersburg Protocol of April 1826, demanding that Turkey accept an autonomous Greece under nominal Ottoman control.

The rapprochement between Russia and Britain was a delicate matter. It started from a point of deep distrust, and a false move by either side could have made the other pull back. Success would have been impossible without the countess's clear objectives and ability to insinuate herself. What she helped bring about was no less than a new footing for Anglo-Russian relations and a smoothing of the path to Greek independence. Tsar Alexander, after speaking to her in 1825, called her a stateswoman.[36] Tsar Nicholas, on his coronation in 1826, raised Lieven to the rank of prince and awarded him the Grand Cross of the Order of St Andrew. His wife, long treated in London like a princess, now was one. These marks of favour were blazoned in the British press, and Dorothea lost no time in ordering new stationery engraved with a coronet. In letters to her brother she poured out her patriotism and worship of the imperial house.

She was now at the apex of her power, though not yet of her public visibility, as a political operator in Britain. But how could a foreigner with no formal position gain influence over such men as Castlereagh, Wellington, Grey and Canning? Why were they, and many others, so eager to talk to her; why did they put such faith in her; and why were they so easily drawn into indiscretions by her? Part of the answer lies in the highly personal nature of international politics. Ministers and envoys served their countries faithfully, but the conditions in which they did so were cloistered and intimate. Decision-makers in Europe were a tiny knot of people with no bureaucracies to prop them up. They wrote letters in their own hand and took decisions with little consultation. Slow communications obliged ambassadors to proclaim their nation's stance on developing situations and even sign treaties themselves. In this context the private feelings of men and the trust that subsisted between them were of great importance.

The first basis of trust was class solidarity. One reason Dorothea had trouble getting the tsar to put his faith in Canning, and Canning had trouble getting his fellow Tories to back him, was the perception that he was not quite a gentleman. The second basis was familiarity. Government ministers and diplomats were generally in post for long periods, and this gave them a chance to assess the risk of accepting each other's professions of goodwill. The salience of personal credit made it vital for an ambassador to forge relationships through social contact with major political figures of his host country. This gave him a sense of their thinking that he passed on to his own government, which often had no other source for this information. Far from home, needing to inspire trust and know where to bestow it, and carrying a great weight of responsibility, diplomats not surprisingly developed what the countess termed 'a sort of freemasonry'. They were, she said, 'a kind of race apart, formed out of all nations'.[37]

The mistress of Ashburnham House was an honorary member of this group through her role as a hostess. Her skill in making a party go and her engaging curiosity about current affairs placed her head and shoulders above other diplomatic wives. Statesmen knew of no more congenial drawing room then hers, and some of her smaller gatherings took on the character of a political salon, a place 'where business and amusement, and flirtations and political intrigue could be simultaneously carried on', as her *Morning Chronicle* obituary put it. While British hostesses in this field were always Whig or Tory, she welcomed members of the government and opposition alike without compromising herself or them. Party spirit was entrenched, so the neutrality of the princess's salon offered a rare chance to reach across the divide. In this setting she made the discovery that led her to assume a special and significant role, one for which being a woman was not a hindrance, but an essential qualification.

She discovered that British politicians inhabited a drab, hidebound masculine world, and that because many women felt they must not speak of politics these men lacked female companions with whom they could speak of the stresses of public life. The experience of unburdening themselves to a charming, bright-eyed woman who listened attentively, grasped what they said, and made perceptive, funny replies turned their heads. 'A man who feels he is understood immediately becomes well disposed towards the person who understands him,' she observed. Caressing the self-regard of important men was easy and rewarding. One day the diarist Creevey watched her work on the leading Whig

Edward Ellice, exploiting his vanity to turn him into a sieve and find out everything he knew. In saying vanity made Ellice so garrulous, Creevey asked rhetorically who was free of it. Dorothea's answer: 'Heavens, they are made of it – the clever man, the fool, every man has his share.'[38]

Ellice was in good company. The Duke of Wellington frequently said things that should not have reached the ears of anyone outside the inner core of the government.

> He tells me things like this simply in the course of conversation. I make no comment; I do not look surprised, so that I never give him cause to think it would be better for his own interests not to confide in me. He regards me as a perfectly convenient and safe audience. He feels the need to talk, and he thinks there is nothing more natural than to tell me everything.[39]

This understates her deftness in prising Wellington open, for he was no fool. Nesselrode declared that her ability to inspire confidence in prominent men was hitherto unknown in the annals of England. Her obituarist in *John Bull* wrote, 'Her skill in worming out political secrets is represented as truly wonderful – she knew everything.' An unnamed statesman of her acquaintance said she leafed through men as one might leaf through a book.[40] Everything she gleaned was relayed to St Petersburg in her bulletins to Nesselrode, the weekly budgets of British news and gossip she was now sending to the Empress-Mother Maria, and letters to her brother Alexander, who in 1826 became the director of the Russian secret police.

Chiefly motivated by love of her country, the princess also took great pleasure in her 'profession', as she called it.[41] Exploiting the personal nature of diplomacy to serve Russia, she gained something personal in return that became like a drug: not status, not money, but power as an end in itself. She joked about her inability to live without politics, but the deprivation, when she felt it, was real. This was apparent to those around her and is clear from her correspondence. In her letters to Alexander from 1812 to 1834 social matters and chatter about individuals are gradually edged out by questions of state and the part she played in them. Dependence on the thrill of the diplomatic game made her a natural risk-taker: 'I detest cautious people,' she told Metternich. And it turned her into a cynic: 'I am delighted that there should be a general confusion in Europe; it helps me pass the time more pleasantly,' she wrote to Lady Cowper.[42]

Since she mixed friendship with politics, Dorothea was accused of cultivating people and then dropping them if they ceased to be useful.

Many shared Harriet Arbuthnot's view that she was an 'abominably false' woman always acting a part. Others countered that diplomats made expedient ties of amity as a matter of course, with no taint of baseness, and that as an unofficial member of the same corps she should have equal latitude. In any case she did have true friendships: those with Emily Cowper and Harriet Granville endured, as did her bond with the Duchess of Cumberland, the unpopular wife of George IV's most unpopular brother. Among men her attachments with Lords Grey and Aberdeen transcended considerations of political benefit, and she corresponded with both long after her departure from England. 'She is always true & constant to her friends,' judged Lord William Russell after having known her a long time.[43]

A woman stepping with assurance into the man's world of politics caused mixed feelings. Metternich said she knew men so well she could do much of their work, and Tsar Alexander I thought it a pity she wore skirts as she would make a fine diplomat. The writer Ralph Sneyd said she joined a masculine mind with feminine grace, and a letter to *The Times* after her death stated that 'she had the clearness and virility of man's intellect with the tact of woman's.' Others were less pleased. 'It is curious enough,' wrote Mrs Arbuthnot, 'that the loves & intrigues of *une femme galante* sh^d have such influence over the affairs of Europe.' The subtly misogynistic word 'intrigue' was often used against her. 'She had the reputation of being very much an intriguer,' recalled the Comtesse de Boigne. 'The greatest *intrigante* possible' was the politician Lord Malmesbury's verdict. Even Lady Holland, who had a soft spot for her, saw her as a schemer and mischief-maker.[44]

Dorothea believed her approach was feminine: 'I am a woman and very much of a woman. I want things passionately and I believe them readily.' On the other hand, she knew she was any man's equal and told Grey she could do her husband's job. Her letters pulsate with contempt for purely decorative women like Lady Conyngham: 'Not an idea in her head; not a word to say for herself; nothing but a hand to accept pearls and diamonds with, and an enormous balcony to wear them on.' She respected the unpretending domesticity of those like her sister Maria, but she told Metternich she did not wish to be hedged in by such conventions herself.[45] She was not alone in this. Aristocratic women, though neither electors nor elected, were active in British politics as salon hostesses, unofficial canvassers, letter writers and counsellors of their menfolk. Families that controlled the electoral interest in a parliamentary seat vested this authority in a woman in the absence of an effective male head.

All the same, it was felt that limits should be set on women for the good of public life and of themselves. Male and female commentators claimed women lacked the stamina, powers of concentration and emotional restraint needed for more direct involvement. Some found the field already open to 'petticoat politicians' too large. They were guilty of 'unfeminine and Amazonian habits' (*Chester Chronicle*, 1816), of 'forgetting the reserve and decorum which ought to belong to the female character' (*Bell's Weekly Messenger*, 1819). Their conduct ill became 'the chaste and honourable dames of Britain' (*John Bull*, 1823), and they should not speak 'where delicacy and decorum ought to impose silence' (*Dublin Morning Register*, 1831). Indeed, political females should be thrown in the Thames (*Bell's New Weekly Messenger*, 1832) or at least 'exposed and held up to the indignation of society' (*Globe*, 1833). The time when Dorothea would be singled out for criticism on this head was not far off.

Following the St Petersburg Protocol she cried George Canning up unreservedly. In February 1827 Lord Liverpool suffered a stroke, and it was clear he would be replaced by Wellington at the head of the traditionalist 'High Tories' or by Canning with liberal Tories and moderate Whigs. Dorothea urged the king, now reconciled with Canning, to appoint him. He did so, and the new prime minister made a government from men of both parties. In forming his cabinet he consulted his Russian friend, who persuaded him to make Lord Dudley foreign secretary on the understanding that he would be a mouthpiece for Canning himself. In July the ministry formalised the St Petersburg Protocol as the Treaty of London, signed by Russia, Britain and France. A month later Canning, aged only fifty-seven, was dead. His hybrid government limped on in a slightly altered shape under the hapless Lord Goderich and collapsed in January 1828. Princess Lieven's influence on British policy collapsed with it.

Goderich's successor was Wellington, leading a High Tory administration. He and Dorothea had been on such good terms that he had consented to be godfather to her fifth son, born in 1825 and named Arthur after him. This was the final act of their friendship, for her wooing of Canning was necessarily at the expense of her ties with the duke, who treated her with the frostiness of a slighted man. 'He neither considers her as a friend nor as a politician,' Mrs Arbuthnot was glad to find.[46] The princess, for her part, could not see why he had expected her to subscribe to his ideas on European affairs rather than those that forwarded her country's interests. She now feared he would reverse her gains for the tsar. She was right to worry: British foreign policy would now be favourable to the ideas of Metternich, place the ancient alliance with the Turks above new enthusiasm for the Greeks, and treat Russian aims in the Balkans with suspicion.

Relations between the erstwhile friends never broke down fully, and in response to her appeal he went to some trouble to secure the return of her letters to Metternich. Despite this good turn, she so resented being excluded from his councils and so disliked his Eastern policy that she used all possible means against him: she rallied the Canningite wing of the Tory Party, which existed for several years after Canning's death; she intensified her friendship with Lord Grey, urging him to believe he could head a Whig-Canningite ministry; she plotted with extreme conservatives who abused Wellington for yielding to the demand for Catholic emancipation; she used her visits to court to sow discontent with the premier in the king's mind; and she painted the new government in the darkest colours in her letters to St Petersburg. 'Out of hatred to the Duke, [she] would do anything to contribute to his overthrow,' wrote Charles Greville.[47]

Although Wellington knew of these machinations, he remained calm and polite. Now and again the princess attempted to restore their old intimacy, but she got nowhere. She even tried to soften up Mrs Arbuthnot, who wanted to 'laugh in her face' at such a brazen change from her recent behaviour, which was 'as cold as possible'. She had more luck with the Earl of Aberdeen, Wellington's foreign secretary. At first she thought him timid and inept, nothing more than the prime minister's chief clerk at the foreign office, and she sought to beguile him purely as a matter of policy. In time she would perceive wit and acuity behind his shy exterior, and they became friends and political allies. He was charmed by her straight away, despite their opposing views on Turkey and Greece, and Lord Grey was shocked at his disclosing confidential information to her: 'You surely must have fascinated Aberdeen to make him talk in such a manner.'[48]

When Turkey, backed by Austria, flouted the terms of the Treaty of London, war with Russia was inevitable. Wellington, partial to Turkey but bound by the treaty, was awkwardly placed. In May 1828 the tsar's army invaded Ottoman lands, and after a poor start its commander Count Diebitsch took Adrianople (Edirne) and dictated a treaty there in September 1829 that annexed territory and created an independent Greece. Sidney Herbert, later war secretary, believed Wellington would have resisted the Russian advance on Adrianople, but because Canningites and Whigs, inspired by the Greek cause, were plotting with Princess Lieven to topple him, he held back.[49] If true this shows her influence even when on bad terms with the prime minister of the day. She certainly made Aberdeen nervous. 'The Representatives of Russia in this country are engaged in every intrigue which can possibly be set on foot to shake the King's Ministers,' he wrote a few months after the end of hostilities.[50]

Rumours of this friction filled newspapers while the war was still going on. In May 1829 several London titles carried the story of a row in which the princess used menace and womanly wiles to induce the duke to follow a pro-Russian line, but he was impervious to it all. The *Globe* rubbished this claim and regretted that gossipmongers put out such nonsense. The *Morning Chronicle* was more inclined to trust this report and added that the 'fair diplomatist' took the failure of her powers of persuasion so ill that she intended to leave the country. Other papers spoke of her imminent departure, and it was deemed significant that she quitted Devonshire House one evening before the prime minister arrived. On the other hand, she attended a party given by the Duke and Duchess of Wellington, which scotched the idea that she was avoiding him. At last, it was discovered that the Lievens would stay, ending a two-week welter of speculation.

Russia's victory put Dorothea in tearing spirits. She related to Grey a 'very droll' dialogue with Aberdeen in which he feebly lamented that Britain had been duped by Russia into standing aside while Turkey was dismembered. Grey replied that this would have amused him had he not felt mortified as an Englishman. 'Madame de Lieven talks immensely big,' Harriet Granville observed. Both women were at Chatsworth with their husbands when news came that Russia had opened negotiations with Turkey. Charles Greville was with them:

Our Russians were of course triumphant, and the Princess's good humour was elevated to rapture by a very pretty compliment which was paid to her in the shape of a charade, admirably got up as a *pièce de circonstance* and which has since made some noise in the world. The word was Constantinople, which was acted [...]. The whole represented the Divan, the arrival of Diebitsch's Ambassadors, a battle between the Turks and Russians, the victory of the latter, and ended by Morpeth as Diebitsch laying a crown of laurel at Mme. de Lieven's feet. She was enchanted, and of course wrote off an account of it to the Empress.

This did indeed make a noise. 'Base toadying' Mrs Arbuthnot called it, and when she told the duke he was 'much nettled'. Others, too, recoiled from Dorothea's jubilation. 'I only like her in adversity; she is too violent in prosperity,' the fourth Lord Holland said later.[51]

With the Greek question settled, at least in broad terms, Dorothea's relations with Wellington thawed a little and he resumed his visits to the Russian embassy. There was no real reconciliation, though, and he still distrusted her. With good reason too, for although she was a useful go-between during the long process of drawing Greece's borders and finding a king that the major powers could all accept she was still caballing. In particular she was trying to effect a junction of Canningites and Whigs, now with Lord Palmerston, the lover of her friend Lady Cowper, in the frame as prime minister. The *Age* thought she was soliciting the king in Palmerston's favour:

> It is fact – positive fact – Lord Palmerston thinks he ought to be Prime Minister [...] And powerful interest has been made for him in a high quarter. Now, what we are going to tell is a great secret, but true withal.
>
> The highest quarter has been assailed to gratify Lord P. in this his rational desire, by no less a person than Princess Rustyfusty herself. We mean the real Russian Ambassador, the Princess Lieven, wife of our old friend, the veteran and steady stager of Ashburnham House; who, out of respect, we presume, to the memory of the Empress Catherine, submits respectfully to female government. What influence Palmerston possesses over her, or how he acquired it, we do not know.

This was a warning, but she did not heed it. Lord Ellenborough, the Lord Privy Seal, believed she so hated Wellington that she could not refrain from intriguing even at risk of overreaching herself. Charles Greville also thought her judgement was clouded: 'Mme de Lieven with all her cleverness exhibits very little wisdom in making herself a hot partisan against the Duke.'[52]

She was sailing close to the wind. Mrs Arbuthnot said her insolence was 'beyond all bearing' and urged her friend to have the Lievens recalled. He thought it over, and talk of him sending her away reached Dorothea's ears. In December 1829 she told Grey he might already have contacted St Petersburg about this, and in January 1830 she said she had information that he had done so.[53] Her friend Lady Cowper heard of it, too: 'I cannot bear to think of such a possibility,' she wrote. In the end he decided against the measure, believing it could cause ructions with Russia and not wishing to look petty. Instead, he opened a new channel of communication to the Russian court through the British ambassador Lord Heytesbury so as to bypass the Lievens. It was not enough for Mrs Arbuthnot, who would have bundled

Dorothea onto the next steam packet for Calais: 'The Duke is a great deal too forebearing with the Russians,' she sighed.[54]

Whether he would have remained so is another matter, and the ambassadress could count herself lucky that the Wellington ministry fell in November 1830. However, the main reason for its fall – social unrest caused by economic hardship and the premier's refusal to countenance a fairer system of parliamentary representation – made her conservative heart palpitate. Across the Channel a revolution overthrew Charles X in July, and the European ruling class to which she belonged looked vulnerable. But she kept her focus on the immediate interests of Russia, and which type of British government would best serve them. When William IV, who had succeeded to the throne in June, asked Lord Grey to form a Whig ministry, it seemed the old cordiality with St Petersburg would return. Her masters in Russia, who knew only autocracy, wondered how they would get on with such a progressive government, but she allayed their concerns.

The advent of the Whigs also boosted Dorothea's role as a political agent in London, for Grey was her soul mate. Stylish, commanding and, despite his liberal views, highly aristocratic, he felt, as she did, that public life was depressingly full of ill-bred dullards. Their correspondence, though mainly about current affairs, had a romantic aroma, and it was said Grey spent the first part of each day writing to the princess and perfuming his letter with musk. There were flashes of irritation between them, but the general tone was trusting and flirtatious, with a flow of well-turned compliments. Whether they had a sexual relationship, as some have suggested, cannot be known. At any rate, by the time he entered Downing Street she was his Egeria, and when in London he visited Ashburnham House or the Richmond villa very often, sometimes daily. She told him she was neither Whig nor Tory: 'I only display one colour – that is, yours. I am *Grey*.'[55]

As her admirer settled into office, Dorothea told him he ought to 'assume a certain pomposity' and 'show himself proud', advice he scarcely needed.[56] She counselled him too on the composition of his cabinet, suggesting he bolster his position by conciliating moderate Tories. Her most significant intervention was in favour of her *protégé* Palmerston, still a Canningite Tory rather than a Whig at this stage. She later wrote an entertaining memorandum on the process that led to him becoming foreign secretary, and if it is to be believed she more or less carried him to his desk. The reality was probably different, but Grey did consult her and she did press him to appoint the former war minister, whom Russia would find more palatable than a full-blown liberal and who had assured her of his goodwill to her country.

It certainly looked to others that she had launched him. 'Well, after all, it was Madame de Lieven who made Palmerston,' reminisced the later Lord Chancellor Lord Chelmsford.[57]

With the death of King George she lost her privilege of pouring honey and gall into the royal ear. William IV, who as Duke of Clarence had made a buffoonish attempt to seduce her, was friendly and invited her to the famously dull receptions he and Queen Adelaide gave at Windsor and Brighton. But he was wary of her, and he told Esterházy why: 'She'll try to get about me & talk smoothly; but, if she catches me, I'll be d[amne]d.' The change of monarch was thus a setback, but a minor one, for the crown's influence on government was in decline. A more important pillar of Dorothea's political power was her social prestige, and this was solid. Indeed, from 1826, the year of her rise in rank, her standing was at its highest. Long service made her effectively the head patroness of Almack's, and her Wednesdays counted for even more than her earlier Sundays. She was, said Lady Cowper, 'Queen of Wednesdays'.[58]

No one could give nine balls before Easter, as she did in 1830, without sometimes feeling jaded. 'I am looking forward much to the repose of the recess,' she wrote to Lord Grey just then. 'You cannot imagine how tiresome society is to me.' But if she was ever tempted to reduce her entertaining, she remembered its value to the political profile that really mattered to her. Similarly, though she wearied of the vapidity of her fellow Almack's patronesses, she did not think of resigning. Nor did she cease to mark herself out with the elegance of her dress. People who knew her in these years were in no doubt of her position. Thomas Raikes believed no foreigner had ever attained such influence in British society. Prince Pückler-Muskau called her the sun and the rain of London society, the 'non plus ultra of fashion', and, in English slang, 'the thing'. The reason for this, he explained, was that she was 'the absolute beacon of refined womanhood'.[59]

Those who wanted her to face stiffer competition were in hopes when a second Dorothea entered the scene. In 1830 France's 'Citizen King' Louis Philippe chose Prince Talleyrand to be his ambassador in London, and with him, on what precise terms no one knew, came his nephew's estranged wife, the Duchess of Dino. A stylish, attractive woman, she acted as Talleyrand's hostess and showed great conversational skills. At last it seemed the imperious Russian had a rival in the diplomatic sorority. Creevey watched eagerly at a country house party: 'The female Lieven and the Dino were the people for sport. They are both professional talkers – artists quite, in that department, and the Dino jealous to a degree of the other. We had them both quite at their ease, and perpetually at work with each other; but the Lieven for my money! She has more dignity and the other more grimace.' However, those expecting a regular exchange of scratches were in for a disappointment, for soon the two francophone Baltic Germans got on well. In her memoirs the duchess described the princess as the most feared, courted and respected woman in London, her house as the most select, and her political authority as beyond question.[60]

From 1826 Dorothea bulked larger than ever in the press, with the standard topics of her parties, social activity, court attendance, travel and clothes predominating. Triviality reached new heights. She went to see Brighton's suspension bridge with 'her blooming progeny'. She and her husband found a linchpin missing from their carriage on the way from Windsor to London: 'The deficiency, however, was soon supplied, and the Prince and Princess continued their journey.' She fainted at the coronation in 1831 and was taken to the queen's robing room, 'where every attention was paid to her'. Now and again a note of facetiousness crept in. After a degree ceremony at Oxford the men dined in a college and the ladies had to eat at the Angel Inn: 'The fair troop, headed by Princess Lieven, has determined, we hear, to petition the King for a charter for an University of their own.' The new institution would not, the writer goes on, offer bachelor degrees.

'Despite hiding herself from the public gaze, she had become a celebrity,' wrote the fourth Lady Holland, daughter-in-law of the Whig hostess.[61] It is true the princess did not court fame, hankering only after power in her own world. Yet her renown placed her within the celebrity apparatus, and people derived entertainment or profit from an image no longer under her control. Several likenesses were produced, two of them referring to her supposed introduction of the waltz to London. In 1813 George Cruikshank depicted her in his satirical drawing 'Longitude & Latitude of St Petersburgh', of which the humour is in her being tall and thin while her dancing partner, usually identified as the diplomat Prince Pyotr Kozlovsky, is short and fat. The theme was taken up in the anonymous 'Sketch of a Ball at Almack's' used as the frontispiece of the second volume of Gronow's *Reminiscences and Recollections*. Seen from behind, she is recognisable from her elongated neck.

Dorothea was better served by high art. She sat to the painters John Lucas and George Henry Harlow and the sculptor Thomas Campbell. Most widely known were the portraits by Sir Thomas Lawrence, one in oil and one in pencil. Pückler-Muskau saw an engraving of the latter by William Bromley and found it made her look prettier than she was.[62] When the Royal Academy exhibited Bromley's work in 1823 praise rang out, some of it doubtless hidden advertising. For the *Examiner* his version captured the charm of Lawrence's study and was 'to the life in its fleshy tones'. The *Literary Gazette* found it united 'the utmost grace of composition with the greatest skill of execution'. The *Morning Post* printed an honest advertisement with prices (£1 11s. 6d. for artist's proofs; 15s. for prints) as well as a notice extolling Bromley for his 'exquisite work of art', Lawrence for the 'feminine delicacy and grace' of his pencil, and their subject as 'one of the most distinguished beauties of the fashionable world'.

She fares less well in two Silver Fork novels. In Charles White's *Almack's Revisited* of 1828 she is Princess Nasowitch, who chooses friends and footmen according to the shape of their legs. A character says no one who knows her well can like her, and it is implied she has a lover. But her balls are highly fashionable and no manoeuvres left untried to gain admission to them. Two years later Lady Charlotte Bury portrayed her as Comtesse Leinsengen in *The Exclusives*. She has a polished air, a cynical outlook on life, a studied style of dress, a fear of the damp and a red nose. She speaks abruptly in a mixture of French and English, pretends not to care for politics, is easily bored, and treats most people snootily. Her role in the plot is as a member of a small knot of ladies who seek to make high society more exclusive than it already is. Dorothea also featured without disguise in some verses Lady Shelley recorded in her diary for 1826:

> Un air d'ennui et de mépris
> D'une reine de théâtre, la dignité factice;
> Des broderies, des bouderies
> Des garnitures – comme quatre –
> Voilà l'ambassadrice à la façon de Barbarie.[63]

The princess's name was variously used in marketing. She was a dedicatee in advertisements for piano scores by Joseph Mazzinghi in the *Morning Chronicle* and for Russian melodies with vocal and piano parts by John Barnett in the *Globe*. A 'musical notice' about J. Weippert's Almack's Waltzes in the *Public Ledger* was advertisement presented as news, and one of the pieces, 'arranged for the piano-forte in a very pleasing manner', was named for the princess. She appeared in longer puffs of 1832 for the newly opened Beulah Spa, near Norwood in Surrey. The *Morning Chronicle* dilated on her admiration for the resort, while the *Morning Post* showed that its precious style could be adapted for outdoor scenes:

[Beulah Spa] was so crowded that the Princess Lieven, who graced the fête with her presence, was obliged to tread her way through the avenue of carriages which thronged the entrance. The Princess, whose exquisite taste in the charming scenery of nature is so justly appreciated, expressed herself delighted at this lovely specimen of English landscape; nor did her Highness regret the inconvenience she suffered to view this picturesque spot. The sun shone with effulgence; indeed the weather was an Indian summer, which gave additional beauty to the tinted foliage of the oaks.

Dorothea was also the vehicle of indirect advertising in *Morning Post* write-ups of her parties. For a ball in 1824 Mr Stevens decorated the rooms with flowers and plants and Colinet exhibited new flourishes on his flageolet. For a fête a year later Mr Jenkins of the Regent's Park nursery grounds supplied the flora. The surnames are in upper case, and it would be interesting to know what was paid for such insertions. Nurserymen, musicians, and also caterers like Gunter's of Berkeley Square, must have had a budget for this purpose.

With Lord Grey in office, Dorothea's political influence seemed even stronger than during Canning's short premiership. But how much weight did she really have? Her letters to the earl were adulatory, and in his company she kept the incense burning. Charles Greville was fascinated: 'Grey who is always under the influence of female flattery was attacked by Madame de Lieven the other day, who told him he was naturally all that is right-minded and good, but was supposed to be influenced against his own better judgement by those around him.' But Greville's surmise that these tactics answered her purpose underestimated the statesman, who cherished the princess, perhaps loved her a little, but knew of what clay she was formed. Talleyrand, an excellent judge of human nature, thought she spared no coquetry in trying to influence him and succeeded 'to a certain extent'.[64] Two tricky questions soon tested her: Belgium and Poland.

The Congress of Vienna had granted Belgium to Holland to create the United Kingdom of the Netherlands, ruled from The Hague by the Protestant House of Orange. The Catholic Belgians, aggrieved on the score of taxation as well as of religion, revolted in August 1830. The Dutch king received support from Russia, which had much to fear from national uprisings, and from the other conservative powers Austria and Prussia, while the liberal French government, hoping to make Belgium a satellite, threw its weight behind the rebels. It was plain the Belgians would not again submit to Dutch rule, so the question became who should be the new state's king. Princess Lieven sought to keep Britain and Russia in concord despite Palmerston's tendency to lean towards France. She did so by expounding each side's concerns to the other and urging both to see the threat posed by an expansion of French power. As Talleyrand perceived, 'Lord Grey's particular friend' was an obstacle to France's designs.[65]

Russia's fears of insurrectionary contagion were realised by a revolt of its Polish subjects in November. While the tsar set about crushing it, Dorothea tried to prevent sympathy for the Poles in Britain from hardening into an official position. She asked Grey to curb criticism of Russia in the *Courier*, to which he retorted that governments could not muzzle the press: 'I really thought that you had been long enough in England to understand this matter.' He agreed to alter an allusion to Poland in the king's speech so that what was a war sounded like a disturbance, but she failed to dampen the pro-Polish views he shared with Palmerston or steer them away from seeking constitutional protections for Poland. Russia defeated the uprising on its own terms in October 1831, and Lady Holland (the Whig hostess) was relieved not to meet the princess at this time: 'Perhaps she might have given us pain by her exaltation about the Poles.'[66] Her tendency to gloat, already seen after Russia's victory over the Ottomans, was notorious.

The flame of freedom was extinguished, but Dorothea's Polish problem was not. She could not stop Britons expressing horror at Russian brutality or dissuade Lord Grey from privately receiving the exiled Polish leader Prince Czartoryski. The *Sun* upbraided her for wishing to dictate whom the premier might invite to his home and revealed that his wife had had words with her: 'We are glad to find that the Countess Grey took so dignified a course with the meddling she-diplomatist.' Czartoryski was the lion of the day and invited everywhere, raising the prospect of an explosive encounter with the princess. Thomas Moore heard two Whig ladies discuss whether the Pole should stay away from parties the Russian might attend or whether hosts were responsible for keeping them apart. He thought Czartoryski should go where he liked because he represented a great cause and should not shrink from meeting an 'instrument (for she is a very zealous one) of the oppressor of his country'.[67]

Lord Grey and Princess Lieven could not stay angry with each other for long, and after tetchy passages over Poland the playful tone of their letters returned. With the Belgian problem resolved by the installation of Leopold of Saxe-Coburg as king, both of the immediate sources of tension between Russia and Britain were gone. However, the two powers were still far apart on questions of governance and the aspirations of stateless nations, and there was every chance they would quarrel again. As for Dorothea, she was beginning to lose the dexterity and patience that were crucial in her branch of diplomacy. Instead, she displayed sullen obstinacy and a short fuse. Lady Cowper saw this: '[She] is a dear good soul, but very like a Spoilt Child, cannot bear contradiction and has not temper to stand things turning out differently from her wishes.'[68] Whatever looked like resistance to Russia met with a fury that contrasted with the pragmatic, long-term approach of her earlier years.

She further forgot that even the large diplomatic field she occupied had boundaries. Any appearance of encroaching on internal affairs of her host nation would damage her, yet she ignored the risk. 'English domestic politics excite my curiosity and interest to the utmost,' she told Grey, and the pleasure of swimming in these bracing waters, combined with the aim of serving Russia, made her plunge in again and again. This was first manifested in her plots during Wellington's government. Harriet Arbuthnot fulminated against this 'uncalled for interference in our internal concerns' and was pleased when George IV, late in his reign, called her to order. The duke agreed with his friend, saying the Lievens had 'played an English party game instead of doing the business of their sovereign' while he was in office. Even Grey, whose path to power she was smoothing, more than once gently warned her away from this area.[69]

The press was less gentle. It had decried her schemes against Wellington, and it more strongly resented her perceived hostility to electoral reform, the centrepiece of Grey's legislative programme. The *Morning Advertiser* muttered darkly of a mission to Brighton to liaise with the queen, a known anti-Reformer. Several papers stated Dorothea was in the same camp, and two years after the Representation of the People Act was passed in 1832 *Tait's Edinburgh Magazine* recalled her efforts to thwart it. Certainly, the measure offended her aristocratic notions by extending the middle-class franchise, but no firm evidence exists that she tried to stand in its way, and she denied the charge.[70] But the impression that she liked to poke her nose into British affairs gave credence to the story. An article printed in several papers in 1833 said she was an example of the typically Russian phenomenon of female influence on politics.

As her political deftness deserted her, so did the supremely refined manners to which she owed her lofty perch in society. Her avidity for political tidings became tediously obsessive, her frank style of speech degenerated from vivacity to forcefulness, and her crushing of bores grew more insolent and less amusing. She was sharper, haughtier, sulkier.[71] Those she had nettled gladly passed on hearsay about her marriage, which was in deep trouble. Even if he was still blind to her amours, the prince knew he was seen as a makeweight. 'Princess Lieven is the Ambassador: Prince Lieven is absolutely a nonentity,' wrote the American envoy James Gallatin. He was the moon to her earth, said Pückler-Muskau.[72] The smallest spark ignited rows between them, after which Dorothea usually apologised. This was no secret in their circle, and press reports of her extensive socialising without him allowed the wider public to draw their own conclusions.

A celebrity who had not sought renown, the princess had too much, and it was turning sour. She needed to improve her image, and a few scraps of newspaper evidence suggest she tried to do so. At the nadir of her relations with Wellington in 1829 the *Morning Post* announced that the Lievens had gone to a party at his house, an odd insistence on just two of many guests. During a bad patch with Grey in 1832 several papers stated that 'The Princess Lieven and Countess Grey are almost inseparable. There scarcely passes a day that they do not meet.' The same year brought reports of great warmth at court: 'The Princess Lieven is a great favourite with the Queen' (*Court Journal*); 'Prince and Princess Lieven are constant guests at the Pavilion' (*Spectator*). Were these paid insertions? If so, they could not mask a decline of her power apparent from a sentence in the *Windsor and Eton Express*, also in 1832: 'At one time there was hardly a Lord or Commoner who was proof against the sneers of the Princess Lieven.'

As the sands shifted, her ties with Grey and Palmerston changed in different ways. During the last administration both men had relished the discomfiture she caused the Iron Duke, but the sight of her oar being thrust into British political waters was not soon forgotten, and when she looked to be repeating the manoeuvre under their watch they were ready. Hence her relative lack of leverage with them in relation to Belgium and Poland, which took her by surprise. Grey kept up his sentimental attachment and still confided in her. In early 1834 she told her brother he had just spoken to her about British relations with Russia, the unsettled condition of Spain, Louis Philippe's fortunes in France, the current state of Belgium, and a commercial treaty with Prussia.[73] Not so Palmerston: although his mistress and later wife was one of Dorothea's best friends, and he had to some degree benefited from her patronage, he found her meddling intolerable and resolved to put an end to it.

In 1833 British unease at maritime concessions Russia had gained by treaty from Turkey caused more friction. The princess got up a whispering campaign against the foreign secretary, and he took the opportunity for revenge presented by the tsar's refusal to accept Sir Stratford Canning as Lord Heytesbury's successor at the embassy in St Petersburg. When he would not withdraw the nomination Dorothea was furious. She urged Nesselrode to stand firm, abused Palmerston for his rudeness, and tried to set him at odds with Grey's ambitious son-in-law Lord Durham. Emily Cowper tried to restore the peace, but feelings ran too high and the consequence was a strain on the women's friendship. Slowly it dawned on the princess that if the British offered no alternative to Canning and the post remained unfilled, the tsar, to keep parity, would have to recall her husband. The spectre of leaving the political hive of London rose up before her.

What ensued was a slow-motion nightmare. Dorothea appealed to Palmerston directly to break the deadlock: 'I frankly admit that all my dignity leaves me when I only think of the possibility of having to leave this country [...] It would utterly upset my life, destroy all my pleasures.' He considered relenting and began a diplomatic dance with Grey, Canning, Nesselrode and the tsar as they sought a solution to a contrived problem. The princess made the voyage alone to speak with Nicholas I, who sailed to meet her in the Gulf of Finland. It availed nothing: neither side could back down without losing face. In any case, Palmerston felt the Russian court needed to be taken down a peg, and that removing the Lievens would achieve that end. This stance accorded with a growing British repugnance for Russian policy. To Charles Greville the princess spoke bitterly of the language of newspapers and parliamentarians and said the British blamed all untoward developments across Europe on Russia.[74]

The press was mostly respectful toward the Lievens during the last scene of their British drama, but *The Times* landed a blow at Dorothea's most vulnerable moment, just after news in May 1834 of the tsar's decision to withdraw his ambassador:

The recall of Prince Lieven, or, rather, of Madame la Princesse, is an 'event.' We cannot say of her Serene Highness that the 'petit nez *retroussé*' has occasioned much mischief, whatever her organs of speech or her implements of writing may have done; nor indeed is it quite credible that the cause commonly assigned to this earthquake in the diplomatic world should be the true one – viz. Her Highness's appetite for meddling in politics, and assuming the direction of every cabinet in Europe, because any time for almost these 20 years she has given abundant provocation of that kind. There never figured on the Courtly stage a female intriguer more restless, more arrogant, more mischievous, more (politically, and therefore we mean it not offensively) odious and insufferable than this supercilious Ambassadress.

For most people, this went too far. The *Morning Post* called it 'brutal' and said no man worthy of the name could have written it. The *Globe* too thought it unmanly and defended the princess for acting in her country's interests. For her the *The Times*'s closeness to ministers made its diatribe hard to bear. She poured her heart out to the Duchess of Dino, who was sympathetic to her feelings and appalled by the article that had wounded them.

Her misery was plain. Lord William Russell tried to offer comfort but found her distress 'not to be alleviated'. To Charles Greville she seemed 'inconsolable' and to Lady Holland 'more wretched than can well be imagined'.[75] She loved the idea of Russia, its might and glory, but the thought of returning to its stilted court and harsh climate was shattering. The concentration of power in one man's hands would give her no scope for political activity, not even the satisfaction of tracking the twists and turns of a public political culture. The future seemed bleak. The kindness of friends was a solace, and Lord Grey touched her heart with his sincere sorrow. Others regretted that one of society's brightest stars, after shining for twenty years, was about to vanish. The Duchess of Dino felt most people would miss her and she would leave a big gap, while Lady Holland thought the recall 'the event of the day' and said it seemed 'to afflict most people'.[76]

It only remained to depart with her head held high. Her final weeks in London were filled with valedictory visits and farewell dinners. The prince received kind tributes from colleagues and an honorary degree from Oxford. At a dinner for resident diplomats the princess looked her best in the sumptuous new national dress the Russian court had decreed should be worn on such occasions. She was placed next to the foreign secretary, who was ill at ease. Everyone knew he had engineered her removal. 'Palmerston has got rid of her because he is afraid of her, & he is right but that does not diminish our loss,' wrote Lord William Russell.[77] On her last day she was presented with a bracelet that a group of friends had bought by subscription. It had a large pearl with a rosette of diamonds and bore the text 'Testimony of regard, regret and affection presented to Princess Lieven on her departure by some English ladies of her particular acquaintance'. She sobbed on receiving it.

Since speculation had begun the previous year about their future in London, the Lievens had been in the press more than ever. In their final weeks the attention was constant. What Dorothea wore at every court and social function was described, as was an auction of some of the couple's effects. The bracelet aroused much curiosity: its value and appearance, the jewellers who made it, and rumours that thirty ladies had contributed to its purchase but seventy more had refused. The main theme was the huge role the princess had played in the pleasures of the metropolis, and how keenly her absence would be felt. The *Globe* observed that she had 'held a station in English society which, perhaps, no other foreigner ever attained', and that she owed this not to her position as ambassadress, but to her 'distinguished qualities of mind and character'. She was not replaced as an Almack's patroness, and their number went from seven to six.

In early August 1834 the Lievens left Ashburnham House for the Woolwich Dockyard, where they boarded a vessel provided by the Admiralty and sailed for Hamburg. A month later they reached St Petersburg, where the prince took up his new appointment as governor of the tsar's son and the princess resumed her dormant one as a lady-in-waiting. Despite the marked favour of the imperial family, she felt bored and lonely. She had little to do, few friends, and no mental stimulation. As her mind froze, so did her body, unused to the rigours of the climate, and when autumn turned to winter chest pains tied her to her bed. Then her youngest sons George and Arthur died in quick succession of scarlet fever, and this calamity made the urge to get away irresistible. In the spring of 1835, her husband accompanied her as far as Berlin, and from there she went alone to Baden-Baden for the summer. In September she moved to Paris.

In this, the worst year of her life, the princess sent piteous letters to her British friends and begged them to distract her with news. She missed the country painfully. 'Was I not right to shed tears of blood when I left England?' she wrote to Lady Cowper from Berlin. 'Did I not realize that to leave England was death?'[78] Lady Granville, now British ambassadress in France, found her depressed on her arrival in Paris, but she decided to make her home in the city and start afresh. She set up as a political hostess, giving small evening receptions and once again offering neutral ground to statesmen whose public jousts precluded private intercourse. Major figures in the Chamber of Deputies and resident diplomats became her intimates, basking in her ability to bring out the best in everyone. She was practising her old trade in a new setting, and, with intervals of sorrow and weariness, she began to enjoy herself.

A shadow over her life in Paris was the further deterioration of her relations with Prince Lieven. Uppermost in his loyal mind was his responsibility to the tsarevich, which he could exercise without her help, and after their parting in Berlin he wrote little and coldly. When the tsar frowned at Dorothea's residence in liberal France, Lieven told her to come home. She parried, citing her weak health. He next offered to meet her while he was in Germany taking the waters, but she really was ill this time and unable to make the journey, while the tsar's prohibition kept him from going to Paris. Since she persisted in staying there despite imperial disapproval, he threatened to cut off her allowance, and even did so for a while. He was so angry that when their son Constantine died in 1838 he did not inform her, leaving her to find out later when her letters to him were returned. In 1839 Lieven himself died without a reconciliation having taken place. Her sorrow for her husband of nearly four decades was brief.

In Russia, people said the princess had been unwilling to leave Paris because of a new love affair. They were right. François Guizot was the minister of public instruction and leader of the moderate, as opposed to advanced, liberals in France. Austere, priggish, bourgeois, a scholar as well as a public man, he was not an obvious match for her. Politics brought them together, and so did empathy with each other's moods of grief and despair, for Guizot was a double widower and buried a teenaged son early in their friendship. He marvelled at her polish and charm, she at the breadth and power of his mind. For the first time she had a lover who knew her thoroughly and could enter into all her thoughts. In 1837 they pledged themselves to an informal but eternal union. The passion of this middle-aged pair, evident to us from their letters and to their acquaintance from their unconcealed devotion, caused a good deal of mirth, but they did not care.

Dorothea's Paris salon, open each evening, was as important as its London forerunner. Everyone went, and the hostess was liked, respected and a little feared. She was now a private person rather than an ambassadress, and the slight official basis for the diplomatic operations in which she had excelled was gone. Instead, she did her best to make Guizot great. She encouraged him to extend his interests from domestic administration to foreign policy and imparted as much high-society etiquette, urbanity and self-possession as he could well assimilate. Some of her letters to him are those of a tutor. She also taught him all she knew of the diplomatic arts and of political life in Britain, a country he admired and had studied as a historian. In the years from 1840 to 1848 he was foreign minister and then prime minister of France, and her friendships with Lord Aberdeen and by now also with Sir Robert Peel created bonds that served him well.

In making Guizot her project, she embraced the cause of France. To Russia, once her fiery love and pride, the tsar's severity had made her indifferent. She told Lady Cowper she owed 'no gratitude to anyone in that cold country'. With this change of allegiance came a change of temper. No one could accuse her of mischief, for she was working to keep France and Britain on good terms. This was needed because the two nations were at odds in a succession of crises that could have escalated without relations of trust between the protagonists. In person, too, the princess was different: warmer, kinder, more serene. Charles Greville knew her well during these years:

> Nothing could exceed the charm of her conversation or her grace, ease, and tact in society. She had a nice and accurate judgement, and an exquisite taste in the choice of her associates and friends; but though taking an ardent pleasure in agreeableness, and peculiarly susceptible of being bored, she was not fastidious, full of politeness and good breeding, and possessed the faculty of turning every one to account, and eliciting something either of entertainment or information from the least important of her acquaintance.

Though she mellowed, she lost none of her sparkle. Harriet Granville received 'the most perfect letters' from her, 'more interesting and amusing and agreeable than I can say'.[79]

Dorothea visited England several times in the 1830s and 1840s and kept abreast of British politics by corresponding with friends and reading newspapers. Her letters recalled happy memories of the country, which, to judge from continuing press attention to her life in France, had not forgotten her either. In 1848 she and Guizot were flushed across the Channel by the deluge of revolution in Europe. She spent time with old friends while he busied himself writing a book about King Charles I. The following year it was safe to return to Paris, where Guizot, his political career over, devoted himself to historical research and the princess reopened her salon. The Crimean War of 1854–1856, which pitted her two adoptive countries against the land of her birth, forced her into exile again, but only briefly, for the French authorities took pity on the sickly old lady and winked at her return to Paris from Brussels despite her nationality.

She suffered intestinal and pulmonary complaints in her final years but was happy in her marriage, as it was in all but name. In late 1856 an attack of bronchitis turned to pneumonia, and when the lifelong hypochondriac came face to face with death, she showed fortitude.

During her last night an old friend, just arrived in Paris, came to her. 'I thought I would die this evening,' she told him, 'but it didn't come off.' The next day, 27 January 1857, Guizot, her son Paul and a nephew were with her. She told them she was ready, and when she felt the end coming she asked to be left alone. An hour later she died, and a note was placed in Guizot's hand: 'Thank you for twenty years of affection and happiness. Do not forget me. Farewell, farewell. Do not refuse my carriage tonight.'[80] She left him her carriage, against which his asceticism had always rebelled, and an annuity of eight thousand francs. Her remains were transported to Courland and buried in the Lieven family chapel beside her two youngest sons.

The princess's illness and death were reported in Britain and rumours aired about her will, relationship with Guizot, and a possible autobiography. Obituaries, all in all, were ungenerous. The *Morning Post* recalled her accomplishments but held her to have been a troublemaker and an instrument of the 'exclusively Russian system' of employing women in affairs of state. The *Manchester Guardian* thought she had great opportunities to do good but left few records of having done any. The *Court Journal* and *John Bull* were broadly respectful but depicted her as a wily schemer. The *Morning Chronicle* mentioned her 'powers of conversation and intrigue', the *Atlas* her 'life of struggle, of turmoil and intrigue'. On the other hand, a correspondent of *The Times*, which had once vilified her, called her a brilliant woman and a force for conciliation in the world. In the wake of the Crimean War anti-Russian sentiment was palpable, and the charge of intriguing was routinely coupled with her nationality.

Private verdicts of those who had known her in London also show more admiration than liking. This would have troubled her but little, for she had wished to win minds, not hearts. The political career she carved out was unique, and it was for this that she was remembered. Yet the road to politics would have been closed had it not been for her triumph in society, which in the short term brought her as much fame as the vocation it enabled. The *Caledonian Mercury* wrote that she 'exercised greater influence in the world of fashion than any foreign lady we ever saw or heard of'; Lord Malmesbury thought her 'one of the most fashionable ladies in society'; and Talleyrand noted the 'indisputable power that Madame de Lieven exerted over English society'. The basis of this was refinement and personal distinction, a subtle perfume not easy to distil in words. Charles Greville, Thomas Raikes, the fourth Lady Holland and the Austrian diplomat Joseph Hübner all used the same phrase: she was a great lady.[81]

3

The Last Grandee

Richard Grenville, Duke of Buckingham and Chandos

'A View of a Temple near Buckingham'. Etching by
Robert Dighton. National Portrait Gallery, London.

In July 1810 the former prime minister Lord Grenville was installed as chancellor of the University of Oxford. It was a major event in the social calendar, and a fashionable audience of both sexes filled the wooden benches of the Sheldonian Theatre. For five hours they were regaled with Latin speeches, a sermon in English, verses in both languages, and musical performances. The new chancellor conferred honorary doctorates in civil law on twenty men, including his elder brother the Marquis of Buckingham and his nephew Earl Temple. Several other members of the Grenville family were present. When Lord Buckingham received his degree the audience hissed, and when his son Temple received his they hissed even more. In response the young earl was heard to say, 'Populus me sibilat, at mihi plaudo; Ipse domi simul ac nummos contemplar in arca.' The words are Horace's: 'The public hiss at me, but I applaud myself in my own house as I contemplate the money in my chest.' The scion of an enormously rich and powerful dynasty, he felt no need to court popularity.[1]

The rise of the Grenvilles is a story of lucrative marriages, accumulation of land, establishment of local patronage, growing political importance, and steady progress through the ranks of the nobility. It began with the union of Richard Grenville and Hester Temple in 1710 that brought together two Buckinghamshire gentry families, the Grenvilles of Wotton and the Temples of Stowe. The bride's brother turned the distinction he earned as a soldier, diplomat and politician to financial advantage and was awarded the title Viscount Cobham. He married well but had no children, and on his death he was succeeded by his sister's eldest son, who consolidated the two estates he inherited and made a splendid alliance of his own, as well as gaining a step in the peerage as Earl Temple. Like his uncle, Lord Temple died childless, but his brother George, prime minister from 1763 to 1765, had three sons and four sisters who maintained the family's upward trajectory.

The eldest son, also George, rose further by becoming Marquis of Buckingham in 1784. He followed the family tradition of public office, serving twice as lord lieutenant of Ireland. By marrying the heiress Mary Nugent he acquired estates in Essex, Cornwall and Ireland and lengthened his surname to Nugent-Temple-Grenville. He completed the project of turning Stowe, the main family seat, into a palace. The imposing classical frontage of the house, the sumptuous Egyptian Hall, Oval Saloon and Gothic Library, and the park with its lakes, bridges, monuments and decorative temples filled visitors with wonder. A keen collector, Lord Buckingham stocked his home with paintings, books and manuscripts. He needed a London residence to match, so he employed Sir John Soane to knock two Pall Mall houses together and create Buckingham House. Three storeys high, seven windows wide, and faced in Portland stone, it cost £11,000.

In London and at Stowe the marquis lived like a prince, and at Stowe in particular he entertained like one. Almost any pretext was seized for bouts of feasting and dancing that lasted for days, and one set of visitors pouring out of the house might see another set pouring in. Royalty was especially welcome. The King of Sweden stayed once, the Prince of Wales twice, and the exiled Louis XVIII of France twice. Lord Buckingham's hospitality to the French monarch went further, for he accommodated him at his Essex seat Gosfield Hall for eighteen months and gave substantial pecuniary assistance to members of his court. Lady Hester Stanhope, who knew the Grenvilles well, estimated that the marquis spent £25,000 a year keeping the French royalties, and at a time when few believed their kingdom would ever be restored to them.[2] And he was charitable closer to home, hosting parties for his tenants and giving dinners to hundreds of the local poor accompanied by rustic revels in the grounds.

Lord Buckingham governed his family's faction in parliament. Its chief ornaments were his brothers Thomas, who was President of the Board of Control and then First Lord of the Admiralty; and William, who after a spell as foreign secretary served as the second Grenville prime minister in 1806–1807 and was created Baron Grenville. Their sisters' marriages brought more families into the fold: Fortescues, Nevilles, Probys, and Williams Wynns. Other men acted as Grenville minions, some sitting for constituencies the marquis controlled. The Grenvillites were conservative Whigs, advocating full emancipation of Catholics, abolition of the slave trade, and moderate parliamentary reform, but opposing accommodation with France. Although less able than his brothers, Lord Buckingham expected them to defer to him, which they did. Indeed, such was his standing that he received a stream of communications from those at the head of political, diplomatic and military affairs and gave his counsel in stately replies.

Some found the marquis pompous. He showed a minute interest in his own dignity, taking umbrage if correspondents used the wrong form of address and threatening to resign his post in Ireland over minor questions of patronage. His grandeur was also on display at royal receptions at Stowe. However, with smaller parties of family and friends he was unpretentiously affable, and his merits were enhanced by the warm hospitality and benevolence of his wife. Much of the couple's charity was her initiative, and she took an active part in running a local school. Theirs was a successful marriage, and the marquis loved and venerated his wife. The one cloud over their happiness was her Catholicism, which he at first blithely assumed he could overcome and then, realising his error, feared as a political handicap in an era of no-popery agitation. She established an oratory in the house in which mass was said daily, but as a compromise she herself remained hidden behind a screen.[3]

Lord and Lady Buckingham were loving parents to their eldest son Richard, born on 20 March 1776, and to his siblings Mary and George, born in 1787 and 1789. Their error, in particular with Richard, styled Earl Temple, was to neglect all moral education. The marquis's belief that nothing was too good for a Grenville stopped him imposing any restraint on the whims of his heir, who grew up to be spoilt, proud and self-indulgent. There is little record of Temple's boyhood. During his father's time as Irish lord lieutenant he lived mainly in the viceregal apartments of Dublin Castle; otherwise he was at Stowe or in London. He was taught at home and in 1791, aged fifteen, admitted to Brasenose College, Oxford. In 1794 he received an MA, this being the usual award for noblemen, who paid higher fees but were spared academic rigours and gained their degree simply on completing two years of residence. He needed three years to fulfil this requirement because he hated Oxford and spent much of his time elsewhere.

This aversion is clear from his letters to William Henry Fremantle, a member of a Buckinghamshire family that warmed itself in the rays of the Grenville sun. Fremantle was ten years older than Temple and, thanks to the marquis, already held a minor government post. Temple's letters to him from Oxford show he liked eating, drinking and fencing lessons more than compulsory morning prayers, while reading and study are not mentioned. He began to complain about 'the stupidity and dullness of this detestable place' and groaned that his father would not let him leave it. One day in 1794 he had 'a devil of a quarrel with a Son of a Bitch of a *Fellow* of our College'. He enjoyed himself as best he could and had a venereal infection soon after turning seventeen. A year later he repeated the experience and found himself '*in for the Plate*', a reference to the mercury pills used to treat syphilis. After a few months he was well again: 'I cannot tell you how well my Father behaved when I told him of it.'

As striking as this precocious indulgence is the coarse cynicism of the letters, whether he was joshing Fremantle about his love life, asking for gossip about the Prince of Wales's mistress, or discussing a fellow student's affair with a lady's maid. This tone is present as early as 1793 in a passage on the secret marriage of Prince Augustus to Lady Augusta Murray: 'Consider what a sad dog a Prince of the Blood is who cannot by law *amuse* himself with any woman except a d—d German Princess with a nose as long as my arm and as ugly as the Devil.' His uncle, the future prime minister, is roughly treated in a letter of 1795 from Stowe: 'L^d & Lady Grenville have just left us. I wonder that Ld Grenville does not get that woman with child. She is just as thin & miserable as ever. I flatter myself that if she would accept my assistance, I might succeed better.' The same brutishness even pervades the principal topic of these letters, Lord Temple's drawn-out engagement to Lady Anna Eliza Brydges.

Her father the Duke of Chandos had more or less agreed to this union many years earlier, but his death and his wife's insanity left Lady Anna Eliza in the hands of guardians who feared the Grenvilles were inveigling an heiress into marriage. She was an only child, and would confer estates in Ireland, Middlesex, and Hampshire on her spouse. The young parties were eager to wed, and from the autumn of 1795 newspapers looked forward to their 'matrimonial coalition'. Finally the negotiations concluded, and since the betrothed were minors a bill had to go through the House of Lords to give a legal basis to the settlements. In April 1796, just after the bride's seventeenth birthday and before the groom's twentieth, they were married in London and then set out for Stowe. From Aylesbury the road was lined with cheering crowds. The objects of this loyalty were a fine-looking pair: the earl a tall, broad-shouldered man with open features; his countess a neat-looking, dark-eyed brunette.

In letters to Fremantle during the preceding years Lord Temple wrote of the means, involving several intermediaries, by which the couple corresponded and met. Anna Eliza loved him candidly, while his main feeling was impatience that something as above board as a semi-arranged marriage should be so difficult. He joked testily about a plan to give her elderly maid his miniature to wear 'in her bosom' so that she could request to look at it when she pleased: 'I can not say that I like being *planted* in such *barren soil*!' He reflected that the obstacles placed in the girl's way would only sharpen her desire for him and revealed that his father knew of his ruses to stay in contact with her. After the wedding his letters were triumphant. An account of the popular clamour during the newly-weds' progress to Stowe was followed by the 'good news' that the wine cellars at Avington, the Chandos seat in Hampshire, had not been touched since the duke's death: 'I promise myself some pleasure in opening them.'[4]

Having graduated from Oxford without academic examination and gained a rich wife through his family's machinations, the favoured child of fortune entered parliament after an uncontested election for Buckinghamshire, one of his father's seats, on coming of age in 1797. He took up the family profession with gusto, and eight years later his wife said politics was his abiding passion.[5] He took part in debates on taxation, press regulation, the union with Ireland, the status of Malta, and whale fishing off Greenland, and his contributions took their place in the long records of parliamentary proceedings that filled the newspapers. He corresponded with many figures inside and outside the family faction, writing well and sometimes wittily on men and measures. During his decade and a half in the House of Commons, he positioned himself at the conservative end of the Grenvillite spectrum, closer to William Pitt's Tories than Charles James Fox's Whigs.

Temple's public life is detailed in *Courts and Cabinets* (1853–1861), W. J. Smith's ten-volume edition of political correspondence of the Grenvilles in the eighteenth and nineteenth centuries. This shows his father and uncles pondering whether he should start in a minor office to show his zeal, or whether this was beneath him as the rising star of an august family.[6] In 1800 he was appointed a supernumerary on the Board of Commissioners for the Affairs of India. Lord Buckingham was pleased: 'I trust that he is fairly embarked in those habits of business which are necessary to the existence of a Grenville. In truth he is a very discerning young man, and if he continues to look to public business his talents will not disgrace him.'[7] A falling out with ministers led Temple to resign a year later, but when Lord Grenville became prime minister in 1806 he was made Joint Paymaster of the Forces and Vice-President of the Board of Trade. Grenville's hybrid ministry broke up after just a year and his nephew returned to the backbenches.

Temple's easy entry into political life did not endear him to fellow parliamentarians or the public. His clan's stranglehold on a clutch of constituencies as landlords and patrons, cajoling tiny electorates to vote for their placemen, stank in many people's nostrils. Worse were the emoluments the family had amassed, in particular the staggering fees of over £20,000 per annum that Lord Buckingham received for his sinecure post as Teller of the Exchequer. The Grenvilles' greed was a favourite theme of the press. In 1806 the *Courier* said that the family was 'gorged with places and pensions' and that Lord Buckingham could 'scarcely walk under the weight of his enormous sinecures'. Finally, the Catholic faith of his wife and the conversion of their daughter Mary in 1809 made people suspect the men of the family were closet papists, and it was said that Stowe's Gothic Library was the place 'where the Grenvilles performed their superstitions'.[8]

Above left: 1. 'A Peep at Christies; or, Tally-ho & his Nimeney-pimmeney Taking the Morning Lounge' (Elizabeth Farren and the Earl of Derby). Hand-coloured etching by James Gillray.

Above right: 2. Mary Robinson. Portrait in oil by Thomas Gainsborough. Wallace Collection, London.

Above left: 3. Sarah Siddons. Postcard after Thomas Gainsborough.

Above right: 4. Harriot Mellon as Volante in *The Honey Moon*. Engraving by Thomas Woolnoth after Sir William Beechey.

Above left: 5. Thomas
Coutts. Etching after
Sir William Beechey.

Above right: 6.
Interior of the Theatre
Royal, Drury Lane.
Hand-coloured
aquatint by Thomas
Rowlandson and
Augustus Charles
Pugin. Plate 32 of
Microcosm of London
(Bensley, 1808).

Left: 7. Harriot
Beauclerk, Duchess
of St Albans. Oil on
canvas by Sir William
Beechey. National
Portrait Gallery,
London.

8. 'A Sketch at St Albans, or Shaving the New Maid Dutchess!!!'. Caricature by Robert Cruikshank.

9. 'The Presentation of Dollalolla Accompanied by the Mighty Thumb'. Caricature by William Heath. National Portrait Gallery, London.

10. 'Longitude & Latitude of St Petersburgh'. Caricature by George Cruikshank.

Above left: 11. Princess Lieven. Engraving by William Bromley after Sir Thomas Lawrence.

Above right: 12. Prince Lieven. Copy in oil after Sir Thomas Lawrence. State Hermitage Museum, St Petersburg.

13. 'Frontispiece to the Illustrations to Almack's'. Caricature by Henry Heath.

Above left: 14. Charles Grey, 2nd Earl Grey. Oil on canvas after Sir Thomas Lawrence. National Portrait Gallery, London.

Above right: 15. Princess Lieven in middle life. Engraving after a portrait by John Lucas. Reproduced in *The Journal of Mrs Arbuthnot*, II, opp. p. 168.

16. The Duke of Buckingham. Oil on canvas by Sir William Beechey. Stowe School/SHPT.

Above left: 17. The Duke of Buckingham as a boy with his parents and a servant. Oil on canvas by Sir Joshua Reynolds. National Gallery of Ireland.

Above right: 18. 'The Fall of Icarus'. Etching by James Gillray. National Portrait Gallery, London.

Right: 19. The Duchess of Buckingham. Oil on canvas by Sir William Beechey. Stowe School/SHPT.

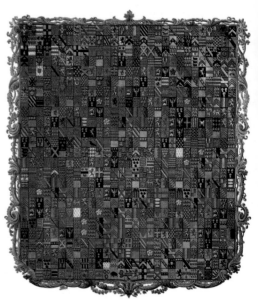

Above left: 20. The Duke of Buckingham. Artist unknown. Frontispiece to vol. 1 of Buckingham's *Private Diary*.

Above right: 21. Stowe Armorial by P. Sonard. Stowe School/SHPT.

22. Stowe House. Watercolour by John Buckler. Buckinghamshire County Museum, Aylesbury.

Right: 23. Colonel John and Lady Charlotte Campbell. Drawing by Henry Edridge. Reproduced in Constance, Lady Russell, *Three Generations of Fascinating Women*, opp. p. 187.

Below left: 24. 'Modern Elegance'. Etching by James Gillray.

Below right: 25. 'Ladies Dress, as it soon will be'. Etching by James Gillray.

MODERN-ELEGANCE.
A PORTRAIT.

Ladies Dress, as it soon will be.

Left: 26. Queen
Caroline. Oil on canvas
by James Lonsdale.
National Portrait
Gallery, London.

Below: 27. Inveraray
Castle. Drawn by John
Preston Neale and
engraved by Henry
Adlard.

Above left: 28. Sir Thomas Lawrence as a boy. Self-portrait engraved by Thomas Anthony Dean. National Portrait Gallery, London.

Above right: 29. Sally Siddons. Lithograph by Richard James Lane after Sir Thomas Lawrence.

Above left: 30. Sally Siddons by Sir Thomas Lawrence. Columbus Gallery of Fine Arts.

Above right: 31. Sir Thomas Lawrence. Self-portrait engraved by Richard James Lane. Scottish National Portrait Gallery.

Above left: 32. Sir Thomas Lawrence. Marble bust by Edward Hodges Baily. National Portrait Gallery, London. Photograph by Stephen C. Dickson.

Above right: 33. Sir Thomas Lawrence. Bronze medallion by George Gammon Adams after Edward Hodges Baily. For sale on eBay.

34. Private sitting room of Sir Thomas Lawrence in Russell Square. Published by Archibald Keightley. National Portrait Gallery, London.

35. Rosamond Croker. Oil on canvas by Sir Thomas Lawrence. Albright-Knox Art Gallery, New York.

36. Isabella Wolff by Sir Thomas Lawrence. Art Institute Chicago, Mr and Mrs W. W. Kimball Collection.

37. Queen Charlotte by Sir Thomas Lawrence, 1789. National Gallery, London.

38. Julia, Lady Peel by Sir Thomas Lawrence. The Frick Collection.

Above: 39. The Calmady children, Emma and Laura Anne, by Sir Thomas Lawrence. Metropolitan Museum of Art.

Left: 40. Charles William Lambton by Sir Thomas Lawrence. National Gallery, London.

Lord Temple's style made it even less likely he would be a popular tribune. He was a long-winded, bumbling orator, affecting a loftiness that ill became so young a man but punctuating it with fits of vexation in which his language turned violent. A friend of the Whig hostess Lady Bessborough thought a speech he gave in 1801 was 'arrogant, odious and absurd', and it earned him a rebuke from Fox. In 1802 he had a spat with Richard Brinsley Sheridan about the motives of the Grenvilles' public service, and his angry bluster about abuse directed at members of his family was turned to ridicule when the playwright-politician quoted back at him all the things he had said about others in the House. And in 1804 the artist Joseph Farington said Temple had been so badly shown up by Fox and Sheridan that his father had suffered a sleepless night after reading about it in the papers.[9]

The marquis did not, though, curb his son's sense of entitlement. In 1799, aged twenty-two, Temple wanted to be lord lieutenant of Hampshire on the strength of his wife's connection with the county. He was rebuffed, as he was the following year when he sought admission to the privy council. He waged a fruitless campaign to have the election of another MP, John Horne Tooke, overturned because he was an ordained clergyman, and in a crass breach of etiquette he called him 'the Reverend Gentleman' in the chamber. He intervened clumsily in the Hampshire elections of 1806, provoking caustic satire in the press. He vacillated on some of the questions of the day and lurched from one misjudgement to another, revealing all along the thinness of skin that was his father's worst failing. Nor was he a conscientious parliamentarian; despite what his wife said, his interest was a thing of fits and starts. He was also known for speaking dismissively of other members in private.

Those who disliked him savoured the report, corroborated later by his colleague Lord John Townshend, that on quitting his post in the pay office in 1807 he plundered it of official paper, pens and ink. This indecent acquisitiveness drew strong criticism in the press and some verses about his 'ninety Reams of Paper'. It was never forgotten. In 1809 the *Morning Post* joked that he might as well publish a speech he had made: 'It will cost him nothing in stationery, and the whole will be written with a Government pen.' In 1810 several papers printed an imaginary political will that bequeathed him a 'green covered cart, well adapted *for moving stationery* in wet weather'. In 1824 the *Leicester Chronicle* remembered that he had 'distinguished himself by his prudent foresight in regard to official pens, ink and paper'. Finally, the incident was mentioned in a poem recalled in the memoirs of the newspaperman William Jerdan in 1852–1853.[10]

The stationery theft made Temple a favourite of caricaturists, and so did his increasingly corpulent figure – Lady Hester Stanhope called him 'Leviathan', 'the Fat' or 'the Whale'.[11] From 1801 his paunch and bulging posterior were drawn time and again in connection with his political activities. For years after 1807 he was depicted making off with pens and paper, and the word 'foolscap' allowed artists to place a 'fool's cap' on his head. A balloon ascent from the gardens of Merton College, Oxford after Lord Grenville's investiture as chancellor gave James Gillray the idea of portraying him as an enormous gasbag. In these images he is one of a group, but one by Gillray portrays him as the subject of *The Fall of Icarus*. Flying away in the distance, illuminated by the sun, is Daedalus, his father Lord Buckingham, but the blubbery Icarus, his wings melting, falls to earth and is about to be impaled on a stake. His wings are made of quills spattered with sealing wax, and in the background stands a cart loaded with more items of stationery.

None of this graphic satire alludes to the topic Lord Temple spoke on most in parliament: the militia raised during the war with France as a home defence force. Temple argued for better officer pay and for the right to increase numerical strength at any time, not just in emergencies. This was an interest he inherited. Lord Buckingham commanded the Bucks Militia, later Royal Bucks Militia, as a function of his role as lord lieutenant of the county. He built barracks for the regiment, added a yeomanry contingent, and took it to Ireland during the rebellion of 1798. Buckingham met most of the cost of maintaining the force and now and again gave it dinners at Stowe. Temple went as one of his father's officers to Ireland, and in 1803 he took over the colonelcy of the regiment, travelling with it around the southern and eastern coasts of England. He took pains to increase its skill, and his letters on the subject bristle with enthusiasm.

The newspapers traced Temple's movements with his regiment and described other commanders reviewing it or him reviewing theirs. There were reports on the entertainments he gave his men at camps, with such pleasures as blind man's bluff, jumping in sacks, and grinning through a horse-collar, which one assumes means gurning; and on more refined parties for the officers and local gentry, with marquees, dances and dinners. The tone often conveys a pleasure in soldiering and soldierly conviviality that Temple felt himself. Indeed, a report of 1804 from Coxheath, Kent printed in the *York Herald*, with its first-person pronouns and inflated style, might have been his own composition:

We are all life, gaiety, and spirit here. On Monday Earl Temple gave an elegant ball and supper to the officers, among whom were Lord Southampton, Generals Finch, Hay &c. The ball presented a captivating display of beautiful women of rank and fashion. The military discipline is very strict, and the troops are constantly exercised in various manoeuvres, sham fights, reviews, &c. Amidst the hardships and fatigues of a camp, and preparations for battle, we are not unmindful of the refinements of peace. We at once study the art of war, and cultivate the favour of the graces.

Turning from political and military activities to the personal realm, we learn that on his marriage in 1796 Temple asked William Henry Fremantle to find a London house for him. It went without saying that the older man performed commissions for the heir to Grenville glory, whose letters to him give instructions about painting walls, installing furniture and buying horses. From the close of 1796 until 1804 the correspondence is lost, and after that it is almost wholly political. Newspapers supply some information about the Temples' early married life: they gave occasional parties for their own circle or for tenants and tradespeople at Avington, which they made their country residence; they moved from there to Stowe or to London, where they rented a succession of houses; Lord Temple went hunting with friends and Lady Temple appeared at the queen's drawing rooms. Their son and only child Richard was born in February 1797.

A more intimate view of their conjugal life emerges from the letters the countess wrote to her cousin Louisa Lloyd from 1804 to 1808. She refers to 'former happy days' and regrets 'more than ever that they are passed and gone'. Her husband restricts her movements or determines them without consulting her. They have '*serious* battles' when she wants to visit Mrs Lloyd and she thinks him 'quite *hard hearted*' for refusing. Rounding out this picture of a chilly marriage are the letters of Mrs Lloyd's mother Lady Louisa Harvey, who finds the countess eager for the company of female friends. One problem was Temple's unpredictability. Like other high livers of the age he had episodes of gout, which made him moody and depressed, but at other times he exhibited a manic energy that made him talk or sing for hours. Mrs Nugent, a relative by marriage, noted his insistent jocularity, and at one house party he was so noisy that the politician Lord Dudley was unable to write a letter.[12]

As in public, so in domestic settings he displayed great pride of caste. 'He endeavours to inspire his wife and son with the idea of the greatness of the Grenville family,' said Lady Hester Stanhope. Lord Buckingham was like this, but he had charm or at least bonhomie.

'Lord Temple is not so agreeable as His Father having great pride & a manner less pleasant,' Joseph Farington heard. Temple knew how to be warm and considerate and was so uniformly in his letters to his cousin Lady Mary Glynne, but many experienced his petulance and callous arrogance. In the diarist Elizabeth Fremantle's eyes, he could be friendly but also gross and vulgar. His upbringing was partly to blame. His uncle Thomas Grenville spoke of his 'very unfortunate education', which 'very much contributed to increase instead of correcting the faults which have hung upon his manner and behaviour'. Lord Dudley was blunter: 'I remember Lord Temple very many years ago,' he wrote in 1812. 'He was always an absurd, wrong-headed man.'[13]

The countess struck people as kind-hearted, merry in congenial company, but essentially serious-minded and a devout Anglican. She was quite often apart from her husband. In 1798, two years after their marriage, the diarist Melesina Trench found her living alone in Southampton: 'She is sensible, friendly, and pleasant.' Two years later Elizabeth Fremantle met her at Stowe: 'Lady Temple has very engaging gentle manners, and I like her excessively as she is perfectly unaffected.'[14] Later, in adversity, she proved herself to be a woman of spirit, but as a young wife she was all mildness. Perhaps to her husband's chagrin, she was not fashionable, and aside from appearances at court she seldom figured in society columns. When journalists mentioned her it was usually to commend her for donating to charity schools, giving food and clothes to the needy, and serving them dinners of roast beef, plum pudding and strong beer.

The earl was in the newspapers far more, and not just as an MP and militia colonel. A speech he gave at a county meeting; a carriage that was built for him; his stakes at the Glamorgan races; an altercation between his servant and a stranger; government jobs he might be given: these were among the facets of his life that were discussed. While his father lived, he was not a fully-fledged celebrity. He was, though, well enough known to be the subject of ribald jokes that readers were expected to grasp. In particular the *Morning Post*, yet to embark on its career of courtliness to the great, indulged in frequent punning, some now obscure, at his expense:

We must not wonder if fresh proofs of the oratorical talents of Earl Temple should *break out* every day, as his lordship possesses an inveterate *itch* for speaking.

A *bustard*, lately taken near Tilshead, in Wiltshire, has been purchased by Earl Temple for *thirty guineas*. His Lordship means to have it *stuffed* into a family likeness.

> Earl Temple *gallantly* sent a detachment of his Royal *Bucks*, to protect the promenading *belles* of Chelmsford, during the illuminations in that town on Tuesday last.
>
> The *venison* must be very *fat* in this country when we find Earl Temple a *representative* of *Bucks*.

Temple attained greater prominence when his parents died in late middle age. In 1812 the marchioness departed this life amid a chorus of praise for her piety and good works. The marquis fell into a deep despondency, and, unable to bear up against his own infirmities, followed her to the grave a year later. Temple became the second Marquis of Buckingham and master of an estate in a very flourishing condition. The first marquis, like his forebears, had attended closely to business and kept a sharp eye on accounts. He left balanced books and land amounting to about 39,000 acres yielding an income of well over £50,000. The tellership died with him, but the income generated from investments it had purchased did not. To this his son added the Chandos inheritance, now his in full owing to the recent death of his mother-in-law, amounting to another £20,000 or so. His total income fell short of the £100,000 or £110,000 friends and journalists excitedly spoke of, but he was extremely rich.

He also filled his father's positions as first man of the county, head of the family's faction in parliament, and master of its network of patronage. It was a tense moment for those, like the Fremantles, who lived in the Grenville orbit. A letter from William Henry Fremantle to his brother Thomas Francis shows that, despite being his constant correspondent, he liked the second marquis less than the first: 'I have no doubt he will continue a warm friend to our family, but you and I shall feel it greatly different, one cannot have the same affection and devotion to the one as to the other.' Before Grenville acolytes could ascertain what the passing of the baton meant for them, Lord Buckingham had a chance of military glory. Several times from 1808 he had offered himself and his militia for service abroad, but in vain. In 1813 it was said, wrongly, that he would be sent to Spain: 'He must get an Elephant, for no Horse can carry him. Think of a Quick charge, foot or Horseback, up the Pyrenees, with Ld. Buckingham to lead!!' joked Lady Bessborough.[15]

Then, in 1814, as Wellington's army entered France from Spain, the call finally came. At first it seemed his destination would be Holland, and in February the Royal Bucks Militia arrived in Plymouth, where their commander was promptly laid up with a fit of gout, or, said some reports, a sprained ankle. By the time he was on his feet again orders had changed and they embarked for Bordeaux in April, only to be wind-bound in the Cowes Roads. When the militia finally arrived the fighting was over, and in July they were shipped to Portsmouth. The memoirist Captain Gronow captures the hilarity this expedition caused. Describing Buckingham as 'enormously fat, and not unlike the pictures which are represented of Falstaff', he relates how his regiment got to Bordeaux 'a day after the fair' and compensated with pointless military parades twice a day. When off duty the men, incapably officered, drank heavily and got into scrapes. The marquis made a large purchase of Bordeaux wine, but when he opened the casks at Stowe it had turned to vinegar.[16]

In reality he went from Bordeaux to Paris, leaving his regiment to sail home and be given votes of thanks for their intended bravery in his absence. He got back to England a few weeks later, but from November 1815 until February 1816 he was in Paris again. The reason for these two visits was that he hoped the restored Louis XVIII, as a return for his late father's hospitality, would persuade the British government to appoint him ambassador to France. In the *Public Ledger*'s words,

> As to the Marquis of Buckingham's Embassy to France, it has been a matter of notoriety that Louis XVIII has been incessant in his application to the Prince Regent for some additional mark of distinction to a Noble family, to which of all others in England, his Majesty considered himself and his family most indebted.

While priming the French king to support him, Buckingham put out feelers to the British government. Nothing came of it, unsurprisingly to everyone except himself, and he had to make do with receiving parliament's thanks for the wartime services of his militia and then winding the force down. Happily for him, the yeomanry was allowed to continue as a mainly ornamental, semi-private army.[17]

After giving up his hopes of France the marquis busied himself with politics at home. His oratory in the upper house was no better than in the lower, but he was a substantial figure by virtue of his leadership of the Grenvillites, who since 1804 had been allied to the Whigs. The bedrock of his power was control of six, and from 1818 seven Commons seats, including St Mawes in Cornwall, Winchester in Hampshire and several in Buckinghamshire. Beyond this core were men in both chambers who cleaved to the Grenville interest because of family ties or shared ideology. The faction was not a distinct party, rather something more fluid. Moreover, historians have identified a split within it, opening up well before 1813, between a wing under

Lord Grenville that engaged earnestly with the big issues of the day, and a wing under the Stowe family that focused more on patronage and place-hunting.

This dichotomy simplifies a complex reality, but insofar as it is useful it also sheds light on a change that came over the faction after 1813. Partly because he did not esteem his nephew, Lord Grenville slowly withdrew from politics, leaving the marquis as sole leader. Some who had been close to Lord Grenville decided to abandon the group and become Whigs. The remainder, and their leader especially, saw less and less reason for an alliance with the Whig party, whose more advanced MPs held views that were distasteful to them. The Tories, led from 1812 by Lord Liverpool, were in government with a healthy majority and the regent's support, which made the prospect of office for those in opposition – Whigs, Radicals and Grenvillites – rather distant. Liverpool had snubbed Buckingham when he wanted the Paris embassy. On the other hand, he had made him lord lieutenant of Buckinghamshire on his father's death in 1813 rather than award the post to a member of his own party.

So the faction drifted into the Tory embrace, slowly at first, and then, after a definite schism with the Whigs in 1817, rather faster. However, Buckingham was not a plain dealer, and he calculated that he could make his group more desirable to Liverpool if he flirted with the ideas of reuniting with the Whigs or even, with the addition of other small groups, forming a third party. The intricate story of his twists and turns, his secretive approaches and withdrawals, reflects little credit on him, especially as most people saw that the conclusion of it all would be junction with the Tories. As early as 1815 the Whig Thomas Creevey wrote that Buckingham was 'trying hard for office'. In 1817 Lord Dudley said he was 'heartily sick of opposition' and that from a Whig standpoint the Grenvillites were beyond recall.[18] The press talked up the prospect too, but the Tories were hesitant, for a long time making no serious overtures to a man whose reputation was so dubious that allying with him was a less than joyous prospect.

As he manoeuvred, the marquis struggled to direct his faction, lacking the charisma and skill to inspire loyalty. His touchiness was notorious, and one by one his associates found themselves in his bad graces, either then reconciling with him or rupturing from him for good. A politically astute wife might have smoothed things over and created cohesion by hosting Grenvillite parties, but Lady Buckingham was not made for such a role. Some of the group's ablest and most public-spirited members peeled off, and those who remained under the banner looked an unprincipled set, willing to support ministers in exchange for power and emoluments. Only Lord Buckingham's cousin Charles Williams Wynn, the member for Montgomeryshire, a sober, diligent man who led the party in the Commons, had any standing. This made him unwilling to follow every zigzag in the path of his chief, who was often out of patience with him and called him 'very sulky & unmanageable'.[19]

Other aspects of his life brought the marquis less frustration and more pleasure than politics. The greatest pleasure was being master of Stowe, the princely house and park all his own. The town of Buckingham, three miles from the house and reached by its grounds, was little more than an adjunct of his great seat. Visiting in 1816, the politician Francis Horner said the house inspired 'something like the impressions, which Versailles, and Versailles alone in the same degree, make upon the eye'.[20] Lord Buckingham inherited Stowe more or less complete, though he did develop a suite of rooms adjacent to the Gothic Library and in the park created the Queen's Drive, the Copper Bottom Lake and the Japanese Garden, as well as enlarging the Octagon Lake. His main contribution was as a collector, stocking the house with artworks, plate, and furniture. Everything was of the finest quality, and finest of all was the 'Stowe service' of Worcester porcelain with hand-painted coats of arms decorated with gold against a salmon ground.

Many of Buckingham's acquisitions were reported in the press, especially of French, Italian and British art. Of great interest was his commission for the historical painter John Martin to produce 'The Destruction of Pompeii and Herculaneum', for which he paid 800 guineas on its completion in 1822. He bought Raphael Morghen's engravings, illustrated topographical histories and autograph letters, as well as books and manuscripts on a vast scale. His librarian Charles O'Conor wrote a catalogue of Stowe's manuscript collections in two volumes and a study of its chronicles of the early ecclesiastical history of Ireland in four volumes. Both were published at Buckingham's expense, and over many long years the contribution to scholarship represented by the work on the Irish chronicles won him plaudits in Ireland and England, not least as he gave presentation copies to several learned bodies.

Although the marquis bought too much, and at times paid too much, he was knowledgeable and cherished the artefacts he acquired. He was an amateur painter and a reader of ancient and modern literature who also wrote his own poetry and historical fiction.[21] His abiding passions, even above literature and art, were natural history and mineralogy. He paid £100, some said £110, for a newly discovered fossil skeleton of a plesiosaur, created a menagerie of stuffed birds at Stowe, and kept a rare breed of Spanish asses at Avington. He purchased a large collection of minerals, shells and fossils from Vienna and in 1824 sailed round the Highland lochs, Western Isles and Antrim coast with a team of geologists to survey rock formations and collect mineral specimens. The conservatory at Stowe he refitted as a museum for his specimens, and in later life he devoted several hours a day to his microscope. A commonplace book on his observations shows the extent of his scientific learning.[22]

Another source of delight and gratification, an even more costly one, was the Bucks yeomanry, which remained in being after 1815. Comprising nearly 700 men, it provided a splendid spectacle with frequent parades and trials of skill before crowds of admirers, while the training periods were a boon for shopkeepers in the chosen locations. The force was ready for use in civil disturbances, but its only real service in the fifteen years after the war was as guards during the coronation of George IV. Otherwise it was all martial display, the marquis in his scarlet uniform looking on as his men performed their evolutions. Press notices were a tonic too, like one in the *Windsor and Eton Express* in 1821:

> The First Regiment of the Buckinghamshire Yeomanry, which commenced their Annual Exercises at High Wycomb on Monday last, were on Saturday reviewed on Wycomb Rye, by the Marquis of Buckingham. The fine appearance of this corps, the completeness of their equipment, and their high state of discipline, called forth from the Noble Marquis the highest praise.

The lure of the sea grew with each passing year. He had owned a yacht since the end of the war, and in the 1820s he spent a lot of time on the water. Basing himself at a 'cottage' he built at Ryde in the Isle of Wight, he roamed far and wide, enjoying the tranquillity of life afloat and fortifying his health. He had a few mishaps, and of course the press reported them. When he sailed home from France in 1816 excise officials in Gosport boarded his vessel and seized a Sèvres china service. An awkward episode with the Royal Yacht Club, later Royal Yacht Squadron, was narrated by the *Age* in 1828. Buckingham withdrew his membership in a fit of pique, and when he applied to rejoin he was blackballed by a majority glad to be rid of him. However, he flew the club's burgee on entering the port of Le Havre, entitling him by courtesy of the French government to take in stores duty free and leave without paying harbour dues. On hearing of this the club determined on 'very strong proceedings' against him.

Finally, there were women. A man of the marquis's early habits and hard-boiled views was not cut out for a faithful spouse, and evidence of his philandering probably represents a small portion of it. One affair was with his wife's cousin Louisa Lloyd, causing the women's relationship to end in acrimony in 1816. Mrs Lloyd must have burnt incriminating letters he sent at the height of their liaison, but those of 1830–1831, with their erotically charged nostalgia, are revealing enough. He tells her he has a selfish interest in her coming to London, 'that is to say if you love me one quarter as much as in old times you told me you did'. In another letter he denies he ever cut himself off from her: 'You never had one who professed to love you who loved you better.' A third is in the same strain: 'I trust that we shall have many tête a tête meetings this winter and talk over old stories. But then you must be to me *what you were* [...] Promise to flirt with nobody but me. I have a large box at Drury Lane alternate nights.'[23]

Less satisfying from Buckingham's point of view was the episode with Louisa, Lady Hardy, the unhappily married wife of Sir Thomas Hardy, known to history as Nelson's Hardy. One version of events, which came to a head in 1816, is given in a letter from the Whig hostess Lady Holland to a friend:

> The town has been much occupied by a very strange affair which led to a duel between Ld. Buckingham and Sir Thos. Hardy. It is a mysterious business, but I sincerely hope quite over for ever. It was the charge of Ld. B. being the author of some very scandalous offensive anonymous letters to, and about, Ly. Hardy. You would naturally suppose that the character of a gentleman which Ld. B. has never forfeited would have been a sufficient guard to have repelled such a charge; but the Lady was angry. There are various conjectures about the writer of these letters; but, except just the angry parties, the world generally do justice to Lord B., from the impossibility of a man of character and in his station of life being capable of such a proceeding.

If Lady Holland was willing to give him the benefit of the doubt, Lady Hardy's biographer John Gore is not. In his account, which draws on a memorandum written by Lady Hardy, Buckingham fell in love with her and was so jealous of another man, Lord Abercorn, that he sent letters in a disguised hand to interested parties. Among the calumnies in these letters was that Sir Thomas Hardy was accepting money from Abercorn to turn a blind eye to his wife's adultery.[24]

What makes Gore's version ring false is that Buckingham was too cynical a sensualist to be 'furiously, insanely jealous' or send letters that 'reached the depths of infamy or the borderline of insanity'. Indeed, while all this was going on he wrote to his current flame Louisa Lloyd in a way that shows his real attitude to love affairs:

> There is a scandal going about that Lord Auckland is gone off with Lady Eliz. Fielding. I don't believe it – for what is he to get from eloping which he had not got before, except the pleasure of paying what-ever a jury may think Lady Eliz. F. worth? Were I foreman of said jury, I should say, five shillings, and rather dear.[25]

Nonetheless, Lady Hardy convinced her husband of her case and he insulted Buckingham in public, making a duel inevitable. Shots were exchanged without effect, and the marquis solemnly denied he had any part in the business. The press response was subdued: the duel and its origins were mentioned, but the story was not spun out or laced with broad humour. One reason for this was that Buckingham made it clear he would punish anyone who impugned him. When Lord Sefton, an admirer of Lady Hardy, put it about that he was her persecutor, he demanded a retraction and got it, as he informed Mrs Lloyd: 'This had ended the unpleasant business and I don't think it likely to be revived, as people will be shy now of advancing opinions which [they] see they must defend.'[26]

His affair with the actress Emma Murray from 1822 until 1827 was a more routine connection with a partner who knew the rules of the game. Two complications arose, however. The first was a £6,000 loan from Miss Murray to the marquis, who was temporarily embarrassed, in return for a quarterly allowance to be paid in perpetuity but which ended with his death. The second was a child, Eustace Clare Grenville Murray, born in 1823, who later wrote a novel in which his father is portrayed as the Duke of Courthope and Revel.[27] The affair was kept quiet during Buckingham's life, but afterwards his legitimate son was pestered by Mrs Murray Mills, as she had become, who wanted her allowance continued and a leg-up for her son. She had only moderate success, but luckily the foreign secretary and later prime minister Lord Palmerston, who had also enjoyed her favours and had a son by her, pushed young Eustace forward in the diplomatic line.

What the marchioness thought of her husband and his ways may be guessed. Newspaper notices attest to their spending ever more time apart and sometimes entertaining separately. In 1816, during the marquis's second stay in Paris, his wife told Thomas Grenville he had not written to her lately and she knew not when he might return. In the same year Lady Louisa Harvey wrote that she was no longer the old Lady Buckingham, and in 1821 that she lived much alone and felt low.[28] When her husband inherited Stowe she stayed devoted to Avington, her parents' seat, and was happier there as lady of the manor than amid the chilly grandeur of the Grenville palace or the whirl of London. Supporting worthy causes, giving alms to the poor and superintending dinners for them occupied some of her time, and her contentment therein was perhaps increased by reading press reports of her piety and goodness.

Her main anxiety was her son, styled Lord Temple from 1813. He was a sickly boy but grew into a handsome man with an easy charm and approachability that set him off from his father. After Eton he went to Oxford, where his great weakness, euphemistically termed a 'liking for low company', became apparent. In late 1816, when he was not yet twenty, he got engaged to the celebrated courtesan Harriette Wilson. Thomas Grenville rushed round to Buckingham House when he got wind of this and found it in turmoil, the marquis giving way to 'vehement and ungoverned feelings'. The news spread fast through the drawing rooms of London and found its way by letter to none other than Louisa Lloyd:

> Have you heard of the Breeze Lord Temple has sprung up, he has waltzed off with Harriet Wilson a famous lady of light character fully old enough to be his mother, and he has written to his father to say that unless he makes him an allowance of £5,000 a year and settles something on the Lady he will marry her, this is pretty good, I remember telling you he would break out violently some day. I never knew it turn out otherwise when a young man is kept too long to his mother's apron string; it will be a severe blow to Lord Buckingham.[29]

Miss Wilson was bought off and Temple sent on a Continental tour while the fuss died down. In Rome he fathered a daughter his family had to support, but otherwise appeared to grow sensible. In 1818 he entered parliament for Buckinghamshire and in 1819 he married a Scottish earl's daughter. This did not put an end to his whoring, however, or to sexual scandals surrounding him. Indeed, his relations with a certain Poll House, whom he maintained in Kensington, were the subject of a prurient publication some years later.[30]

Another major concern for the marquis was his claim to a dukedom. His father had solicited for the highest rank in the peerage insistently and felt mortified that George III did not grant it. The second marquis was even more fixated by this prize, and it was believed that Louis XVIII interposed with the regent on his behalf. If so, he had no better success than with his attempt to get him an embassy. Press reports from 1814 onwards of the imminent elevation and the French king's role in it only made the non-event more irksome. In 1820, following the regent's accession as king, Buckingham was created a Knight of the Garter. He was 'amazing proud of his star, I never saw one more so,' observed Lady Louisa Harvey.[31] But the rumour that this was intended to fob him off made him hungrier for his dukedom. George IV demurred, so there was only one thing to do: make receiving it a condition of supporting the government.

Speculation was rife from the 1817 schism with the Whigs that the Grenvillites were to join the government, and people wondered what their spoils would be. Would Buckingham be an ambassador at last, or perhaps first lord of the admiralty or lord lieutenant of Ireland? What would other faction members get? At this point Lord Liverpool could do without them, but two setbacks so hobbled him that gaining the marquis's eleven followers in the Commons became expedient. The first was the Peterloo Massacre of 1819 and the deep resentment caused by repressive measures in its wake. The second was the 1820 trial of Queen Caroline, whom the king wished to divorce, and whose cause was taken up opportunistically by the Whigs and angrily by the populace. The national mood was febrile and the government looked shaky. Buckingham stood squarely behind it, partly from alarm that the social order might be overturned, but partly to ingratiate himself with the king and his ministers.

His stance brought him into conflict with the common people of his county. 'I do believe Lord B.'s personal popularity in Aylesbury has for some time been, not gradually, but rapidly decreasing,' wrote his worried aunt Lady Williams Wynn in November 1820.[32] She was thinking of articles such as these in the *Public Ledger*:

On Saturday last the Marquis of Buckingham passed through Aylesbury on his road to Stowe. Though in his own carriage the people discovered him. An immense concourse collected round the carriage, whilst he was changing horses, and addressed to his Lordship the loudest reproaches on the conspicuous part he has thought it his duty to take against her Majesty during the late inquiry. The post-boys, when mounted, were dragged from their horses; and at last, with the greatest difficulty his Lordship was rescued from his perilous situation, and was permitted to proceed to Stowe amidst the most deafening groans.

Among other indignities offered to the Marquis of Buckingham on his passage through Aylesbury, as mentioned in our last, the Sovereign People amused themselves by throwing sheeps' heads, mud, &c. into his carriage, after which he was allowed to proceed, amidst the groanings and hissings of the multitude.

Buckingham's boast ten years before that he cared not if he was liked was now tested, and it would be tested further.

Newspapers and an ocean of published correspondence and diaries chart the negotiations between the government and the Grenville party in 1821. The substance of these was places, not policies, and Lord Buckingham was temperamentally unsuited to the protracted haggling the process required. Lady Louisa Harvey saw him in May and found him 'ill and fatter than ever I think, out of spirits, his Countenance altered, old and full of care'. Back and forth the letters between the main players went, until in mid-December Liverpool could tell the king the question had 'terminated in a manner that ought to be satisfactory to all parties'.[33] The marquis was created Duke of Buckingham and Chandos with the secondary title Marquis of Chandos for his son, Charles Williams Wynn became president of the India Board, William Henry Fremantle and another follower became commissioners of the same board, and two more adherents became Irish attorney general and minister to the Swiss Cantons.

A curious detail of Buckingham's preparations to coalesce with ministers reveals that he was not proof against bad publicity, at least in regard to his faction. This was his secret purchase in 1821 of the *Guardian* – not the *Manchester Guardian*, coincidentally launched the same year, but a short-lived London weekly. In a letter to Fremantle he enlarges on this transaction:

In consequence of communications with Charles Wynn, and feeling the importance of a connexion with the public press, arrangements have been for some time making, and are now concluded, by which the *Property* of the Guardian Weekly Paper is placed in *my* hands. The bearer of this is Mr White *the channel of communication* – He is an old friend of mine, was a Captn in our Regiment when we were in Ireland [...] Precautions have been taken by which it is *impossible* that the paper either now or hereafter can be traced to any body.

He goes on to say the newspaper will be given 'priority of Intelligence & ministerial communication', but that to prevent exposure of its purchaser any communication from himself or his closest acolytes to Mr White must be returned by the next post, and that even the editor does not know the new owner's identity.[34]

Most newspapers announced Buckingham's new title, of which the patent was granted in January 1822, without comment, but many had things to say about his faction going into government. The *Morning Chronicle* chided him for his tergiversations of the foregoing years, and the *Sheffield Independent* called his party 'a hungry set' with 'cormorant maws' who made sure to get many good things in return for their support. Private reactions to both developments were negative. Earl Grey felt 'a disgust which it is impossible to express' and Harriet Arbuthnot deemed the duke's elevation to be 'prostituting the honours of the peerage most shamefully'. Some made light of it. 'Everything has fallen in price except the Grenvilles' was a witticism that made the rounds.[35] Jokes about the duke's bulk and his greed dovetailed nicely as one seemed symbolic of the other. The Whig Lord Darnley wrote a poem about his double title:

> Two Dukes at once, and both in one!
> Where has our Sovereign found such Merit?
> Is the new Duke then greater grown
> Than old ones who the rank inherit?
> Unworthy of his high estate
> The Devil still must have his due
> For though he is any thing but *great*
> At least he's big enough for *Two*.[36]

Another Whig, the Duke of Bedford, referred in a speech at a county meeting to 'a great Borough Proprietor', formerly a marquis and now a duke, who, with his adherents, had been bought by the government. He should have expected a challenge and he received one. The two middle-aged men fought on a May morning in 1822: Bedford fired in the air, Buckingham missed, and their seconds agreed the affair was concluded.[37] Neutral observers felt a buzz of excitement, and the press enjoyed it too, with the *Sheffield Independent* printing a satirical poem and the *Morning Chronicle* remarking that an exchange of pistol shots did not lessen the truth of what had been said. Isaac Cruikshank and William Heath published caricatures entitled 'A Shot from Buckingham to Bedford' and 'The Bloodless Rencontre'. Almost alone in her sympathy for the challenger was Lady Williams Wynn, who hoped the duel would 'be productive of good effect in checking the outrageous black-guard Stile' of attacks on her family.[38]

Buckingham's step in the peerage and his faction's accession to power might emit a bad odour, but they took him to the apogee of his influence and allowed him to scoff at detractors. Nor could it be said that a man with a palatial seat, other fine residences and a huge rent roll lacked the wherewithal for a dukedom. What nobody yet knew was that waste and prodigality had made his position precarious. One problem was that his estate was badly managed by agents whose work was unsupervised and unaudited, a consequence of what Thomas Grenville called his 'fatal indolence'.[39] Parliamentary power-broking was also a burden. Contested elections cost thousands of pounds, and even in uncontested ones the expense of putting up hustings, paying election officials and giving dinners to electors ran into hundreds. Finally, equipment and revelries for the yeomanry set the duke back about a thousand pounds yearly.

Even so, he ought to have been able to live well within his income; instead he lived well beyond it. Unbridled gratification of his desires and a lofty conception of what became his rank led him to indulge himself without restraint. He kept households of servants and had the best of everything, be it wine, books, guns, carriages, clothes or jewellery. Of course he kept no accounts. Merchants' bills give an idea of his eye-watering expenditure, but the cost of other pleasures, such as his sex life and its unintended consequences, can only be guessed. He was a compulsive collector, and his outlay on paintings alone was so great that he often had to borrow from his banker Thomas Coutts. He employed Sir John Soane to redecorate Buckingham House and set up the Marquis of Chandos in a large way in London and Wotton, the old Grenville home in Buckinghamshire. When Wotton was destroyed by fire in 1820 the duke called in Soane to rebuild it. 'I had rather beg my bread than not do so,' he told Fremantle.[40]

For a long while he plugged gaps in various ways and kept his difficulties from public view. As well as getting loans from his banker and his mistress, he mortgaged properties and cut spending on their maintenance. When he needed stronger restoratives, he tried to turn land into cash. This was no easy matter. Generations of Grenvilles had settled and resettled large parts of the estate in such a way as to protect it from the depredations of a future spendthrift. The idea was to make it hard to sell land to pay off debts, and thus hard to raise loans against its value in the first place. Unfortunately for these careful dynasts, legal instruments were available to release portions of land from a settlement and, from time to time, even break the entail that should have ensured transmission to the next generation. Even as he sought to raise his family's prestige, Buckingham was destroying its financial basis.

Gosfield in Essex, which was not entailed and plainly surplus to requirements, could be sold without eyebrows being raised. Other sales and exchanges could be presented as a sensible consolidation of holdings. But the duke sold more than he bought, and much of what he bought was on mortgage. With his debts dispersed and interest on them growing briskly, he applied to the Pelican Insurance Office for a single loan of £120,000 to settle all his obligations. In a sign of how involved he had become, and of the waning rental income from his reduced and neglected estate, he was turned down, though other insurance companies lent him smaller sums. By the mid-twenties he could no longer hide his situation from his family, but nor could he change his habits, and in 1826 Lady Williams Wynn was appalled that despite 'his distress for money' he was parting with thousands of pounds for rare books and prints.[41]

More wanton still was his entertaining. Neither he nor his wife liked hosting London balls or country house parties. Instead the duke gave exhibitions of regal magnificence at Stowe to mark special occasions: his brother marrying in 1813, his son coming of age in 1818 and marrying in 1819, and his grandson being born in 1823 and christened in 1824. Events lasted for days, with fireworks, marquees, and oxen and sheep roasted whole. The park's ornamental temples were lit up and hordes of people fed in the banqueting room. In a rare flash of self-irony, the duke called the 1819 event a 'Grenvillade'.[42] Peers and royalty attended, but so did county notables, tenants and family hangers-on, creating a feudal character. The same character infused the annual public archery meetings, at which competitors were picturesquely attired in green. 'Their appearance reminded us of the descriptions given of the revels of knights and damsels of olden times,' wrote the *Morning Post* in 1826.

The press depicted Grenvillades in high-flown language, in a few cases before they had taken place, so that we may be sure someone was polishing the host's image. This image was not as a leader of high society or even of the political world, but as a *grand seigneur* at home. Other activities chronicled are of a piece with this: attending quarter sessions, chairing meetings of worthies to mark local and national events, feasting and parading with the Bucks yeomanry, or donating a stained-glass window to a church in Buckingham to commemorate his dukedom. Some thought he was overdoing it. His grandson's christening lasted a week and reportedly cost a staggering £15,000.

The *Windsor and Eton Express* was indignant: 'What my Lord! a military christening! drums and trumpets, and horse-haired helmets and coronation-warriors! Why, your Grace must have forgotten that you were living in an humble period of the nineteenth century.'

By playing the great patriarch Buckingham showed that his old disdain for popularity had given way to a hankering for respect, loyalty, maybe even affection. His charities in Buckinghamshire and Hampshire can be seen in the same light. They were smaller than his wife's, but they increased as the years went by. He was trustee to a new savings bank in Aylesbury, which paid interest on small deposits and thereby extended banking services to people previously without them. He supported Buckinghamshire's lace-makers, who struggled to sell their wares to the London market. In 1821 he gave the inmates of Aylesbury gaol a hearty dinner to celebrate George IV's coronation, and on his grandson's birth in 1823 he paid for the gaol's debtors to be freed. For all this he drank his mead of praise. Except for the *Bucks Chronicle*, which had a long-running feud with him, the newspapers, possibly prompted by himself or an agent, applauded his benevolent dealings with the lower orders.

Buckingham was a national figure as well as a county magnate, and from 1822, as a duke and leader of a government faction, he was a great man of the realm. This led to a surge in press attention, much of it reverent. He must have enjoyed the courtliness of the *Hampshire Chronicle*'s notice in 1824 that 'His Grace the Duke of Buckingham and Chandos has been pleased to appoint the Rev. George Deane, B.A. of St. Mary Hall, Oxford, to be one of his Grace's Domestic Chaplains.' No detail was too small to mention: a house engaged for him in Cheltenham, when he was expected there, the bells rung on his arrival, and the glass of water handed to him on a silver salver by the manager of the Old Royal Wells. During a journey he and the duchess made to Scotland in 1824 every move of the 'noble tourists' was described. This was too much for the *Morning Chronicle*, which, quoting some oily passages from the *Edinburgh Observer*, exclaimed:

From a paragraph before us it would appear [...] that his Grace is a greater man than we had imagined, and in truth, he seems to have been Buckinghamising it in the Western Isles in a most superb style. Had the King himself been the party, his motions could hardly have been more minutely dwelt on, or his actions set forth in loftier terms. A more nauseating piece of flummery than the following it has seldom been our fate to meet with – his Grace must be a glutton, indeed, if he relish it.

The duke's euphonious title had promotional value. His cook John Simpson's publisher used it to advertise Simpson's *Complete System of Cookery*. John Hewetson's *Noble Mansions of Hampshire* and John Henry Todd's *Historical Tablets and Medallions* came out under his patronage, as did a book of glees by the organist G. W. Chard. Notices of the public exhibition of John Martin's volcanic canvas gave the purchaser's name, and those of the ventriloquist Mr Flemmington stated that Buckingham had engaged him. He gave his approbation to Wycombe Sauce and his custom to a glass modeller of animals, and he was listed as a patron or trustee of insurance companies. What he got for these endorsements is unknown, but the desire to coin some easy money is obvious. It was not without risk, and when he was mentioned in the prospectus of the shady Gwennap Mining Company, which failed and left its shareholders out of pocket, the *Coventry Herald* blamed him for being 'content to let his name appear, upon condition of receiving a premium for the honour he conferred'.

His visual image was never good, and he was all too familiar from satirical prints, of which more were to come. He could have countered these with flattering pictures of his own commissioning, but his obesity made this no easy matter. Just after the turn of the century, when he was still fairly lithe, he and his wife sat to the leading portraitist Sir William Beechey: he is shown in a debonair pose in military uniform; she in a high-waisted dress holding her young son's hand. They are handsome pictures of a handsome couple, though probably even then no longer a happy one. Buckingham had his likeness taken only twice more. In 1815 George Sanders captured him in a Byronic pose with an open collar and exotic costume; this work was engraved for general sale by Robert Cooper. The second picture, made much later by an unknown artist, shows him in court attire wearing the Order of the Garter; it was engraved and used as the frontispiece to his diary of the late 1820s.

For all his Stowe junkets and other self-projection, Buckingham was not liked; people knew this great nobleman had a petty, ignoble nature. When his hard-pressed tenants petitioned for rent reductions he refused and let his stewards use harsh tactics. Among tradesmen and those engaged in land transactions with him he was notorious for requiring immediate payment but being slow to settle himself. In 1822 he told Buckingham shopkeepers, whose main business was supplying the great house, that unless they cut their prices by a third he would get his articles from London. His zeal against poachers on his properties and use of his local sway to have severe sentences imposed on them were also notorious. His sister Mary's husband Lord Arundell felt 'dislike and contempt for his fat brother-in-law', wrote the diarist Henry Edward Fox, 'of whose meanness he seems quite aware, tho', as is sometimes the case, it is wedded to the greatest and most expensive ostentation'.[43]

It was in politics that the duke most harmed himself in the eyes of the public. No sooner had he joined ministers than he began causing trouble, flirting with elements of the opposition and threatening to quit the administration three times in five months. He complained of being slighted and lost his temper if his patronage requests were not met. A reshuffle necessitated by Lord Castlereagh's suicide in 1822 led him to push hard for the Admiralty or Ireland, but Lord Liverpool, who knew he was unfit for high office, rebuffed him. The duke had driven a hard bargain for his faction's adhesion, and many wondered if it was too dearly bought. Within the cabinet Lords Harrowby and Eldon, who had opposed the arrangement, made their unhappiness clear. In particular the appointment of Charles Williams Wynn's brother Henry as envoy to Switzerland aroused ire as an unnecessary expense. After much heated discussion the post was abolished and he was transferred to the Court of Württemberg.

The duke blackened his name further by writing to other men with followings in parliament to suggest working together to increase their leverage. Creevey spoke of his 'base, intriguing spirit' and the Duke of Wellington called him 'a dirty blackguard' in conversation with Mrs Arbuthnot, who declared him to be 'utterly without talent or the respect of one human being'. His contributions in the Lords met with derision. The *Examiner* labelled him 'an orator of extreme pomposity' and the *Norwich Mercury* found the absurdity of his speeches 'really too much for the muscles of even a Stoic's face'. The Grenvillites as a group were no better regarded. 'There is not one amongst them worth a pin, & they are more grasping & avaricious than any set of men I ever met with,' wrote Mrs Arbuthnot.[44] The *Morning Advertiser* remarked sarcastically that they 'never shewed the least indisposition to give their services to their Country!'

As Buckingham's unpopularity grew, so did the tendency to ridicule his physique and misfortunes that befell him. In 1825 *Bell's Life in London* mused that the provisions of an act against cruelty to animals might be extended: 'Some tender-hearted Christian would go into fits and agonies at seeing his Grace the Duke of Buckingham, on the back of a horse, and would call for penalties for so grievous an oppression.' In the same year he was mocked for demanding Bank of England notes or gold on rent day and then being told by the Treasury that he must accept the notes of county banks as before. And in 1826 the *Worcester Journal* had another titbit: 'The Duke of Buckingham, in returning to town from Stow, on Monday evening, lost a large portmanteau, which was cut from his carriage, and which, amongst other valuable articles, contained the insignia of the Garter, including the costly and brilliant collar appended to the Order.' That neither the robbers were discovered nor the articles recovered only made the story better in subsequent retellings.

While Buckingham continued a thorn in the government's side, his relations with his followers were just as prickly. Exasperated by his guile, irritability and high-handedness, they fell out with him one by one. Some joined the Tories, others went their own way. Charles Williams Wynn, his first cousin and close associate, broke with him in 1825, partly because of a row about the constant letters he required from someone he saw as his representative in the cabinet. The worst blow in personal terms was the loss in 1827 of his right-hand man William Henry Fremantle, who later described him as 'never fixing on any one point, deceiving every part, & every friend he deals with, and having no scruples of writing right hand & left, imagining that People would not shew and compare his letters'.[45] Another headache was his brother Lord Nugent, whose advanced liberalism took him a long way from the Grenville line. Nugent offered to resign his Aylesbury seat, but out of family feeling the duke let him keep it.

As the foundations of his political influence crumbled, he suddenly saw a chance to erect a new edifice to his glory. In the spring of 1825 ministers looked likely to recall the governor-general of India Lord Amherst because of setbacks in the Anglo-Burmese war and a mutiny of Bengal sepoys. The duke realised he was the man to bring order to the subcontinent and canvassed for the position even while Amherst yet held it. Charles Williams Wynn was horrified, but as they were still allied at this time he baulked at impeding him. Buckingham misconstrued a civil response from the foreign secretary George Canning as an expression of support, and soon news of his imminent departure for India was in the press, even of the ship that was to carry him from Portsmouth. What happened next was very complex, but can be summed up as an intrigue to give the impression Wynn was endeavouring to get the duke appointed when he was doing no such thing; it failed because the double crosser was himself double-crossed. Amherst, for the moment, remained in post.

Buckingham was irate, of course, and the governor-generalship was the primary cause of his rupture with Wynn and Fremantle. The fact that press speculation about the appointment was laced with doubts about his capacity for it and jokes about his size must have soured his mood further. He cast about for allies to help him get to India, or perhaps France or Ireland, which some newspapers were still now reporting as his destination. He appealed directly about India to the king, who simply forwarded his letters to his premier with a covering note deprecating the 'very indelicate & improper communication'.[46] In February 1827 Liverpool had a serious stroke, and in the ensuing confusion Buckingham curried favour with those he thought might replace him while also plotting to form a new opposition force. When Canning became prime minister he took malicious pleasure in telling him bluntly he did not consider him the best person to govern India.

Many were puzzled to see a man in poor shape and used to every luxury so eager for the trials of a long sea journey and an unhealthy climate. In truth he wanted not just a prestigious post, but a means to bring order to his finances by drawing a large salary, shutting up Stowe, and ending his ruinous style of living at home. When his hope of high office was dashed he needed to achieve at least the second and third objectives and decided to go on a Grand Tour, leaving the duchess behind at Avington. Not that the preparations for his journey make it look like a way of saving money. He commissioned a 250-ton brig pierced for sixteen guns and designed so that a man of his size could move about in comfort. Reputed to have cost £16,000, the ship was named the *Anna Eliza* after the duchess and launched in front of 3,000 spectators in June 1827. It was to have a crew of forty-eight and carry a secretary, a chaplain, a doctor and a number of servants. In August, having said his goodbyes, Buckingham sailed for Gibraltar.

And now, as he sets forth, we have, for the first time, the duke's day-by-day record of his experiences. The *Private Diary* that relates his travels from the start almost to the end is highly finished, suggesting he meant to publish it, yet it contains frank references to private troubles and family discord he would have had to excise before doing so. At any rate it did not appear until 1862, long after his death. The itinerary it describes includes the usual Grand Tourist resorts. His first major stop was Sicily, which he explored thoroughly. Naples and its environs he also examined in detail, and then, after an excursion to Malta, it was on to Sardinia, Corsica and Genoa. From there the *Anna Eliza* sailed home loaded with minerals and fossils collected in various places, while the duke, after a stay in Turin, went south overland for a long sojourn in Rome. Then he headed north again through Tuscany to Venice and Milan, and the text ends abruptly with him roving through Switzerland.

If the journey and its two-year duration are conventional, the way he narrates it is a revelation. The man we have seen as egotistical, bombastic, devious and mean rises from these pages in a new form: a writer with great powers of observation, a humane interest in all conditions of people, a facility for colourful tableaux and anecdotes, a pleasant line in self-deprecation, and a fine prose style. He is curious about everything and lucidly conveys the topography, costume, governance and economic life of the places he visits. He carries out excavations, researches marine life, and surveys rock formations. He knows a good deal of architecture, archaeology, Classical and modern history, theology, art, music and meteorology, as well as botany and geology, and he imparts this knowledge in an engaging way, though some passages on minerals are too dense for the general reader. On other subjects he admits he is not able to form judgements, and he deplores the presumption and carping of other British travel writers.

There are uncomfortable moments of self-praise, with allusions to his large retinue and adroit handling of difficult situations; but these are minor blemishes. Otherwise the book is just the vivid miscellany a travelogue should be, informative and entertaining, moving rapidly from scene to scene and topic to topic, structured only by the author's personality and itinerary. Buckingham presents himself as what, to a certain extent and at certain times, he must have been: a man of great natural parts, the advantages of high birth, and some attractive personal traits; so it seems tragic that for most of his life and in most relationships these qualities were submerged by faults. His better side is discernible in his letters to Lady Mary Glynne and in some other cases where tact or sympathy were called for, but mostly it is hidden. He knew how to be likeable, even winsome, but for the most part he elected to be a disagreeable, indeed a bad man.

Much press coverage of his voyage simply chronicled his progress and people he met, with such odd particulars as the 'several fat oxen' sent to him from England for his Christmas fare in 1827. It was said he had suffered an apoplectic fit, made himself ill by inhaling sulphur from Mount Etna, or even died, but the *London Evening Standard* was 'happy to state that he is now restored to good health'. In February 1828 came the report that a naval vessel had escorted him from Sicily to Naples because he was afraid of pirates. The next months brought notices about the benefit to his health of travelling in Italy. In April 1829 the *Bucks Gazette* believed he was 'considered one of the best antiquarians now at Rome' and had lately discovered 'a very fine sarcophagus'. Society chatter was largely ill-natured. Even his aunt Lady Williams Wynn smirked when she had a letter from him that spoke of the invigorating effect of ascending Mount Vesuvius, 'which I believe, in point of fact nearly killed him'.[47]

A manuscript account of the last part of the journey, not printed in the *Private Diary*, charts his course round the Swiss cantons, down the Rhine, and west to Brussels. In November 1829 he sailed from Ostend to London and drove to Avington to join the duchess. He got a very cool reception. In Rome he had socialised with the family of Napoleon's brother Lucien Bonaparte, Prince of Canino, and he was with them on and off for the rest of his tour. He describes sightseeing in Rome with their daughter Mrs Wyse, 'a beautiful woman' living apart from her husband, and visits to her home there.[48] Newspapers observed them together in Switzerland and Germany and left readers to draw the obvious inference, while the *Brighton Herald* gave a broader hint by calling her the duke's 'bosom friend' and the *Morning Herald* joked suggestively about their attempt to climb Mont Blanc. Other titles dismissed the gossip, or affected to do so, but the travellers' arrival in London at the same time told its own story.

Mrs Wyse was something of a celebrity herself. Years later the *Examiner* remembered that her 'freaks and follies were at one time the general topic of conversation in London'. Born Letitia Bonaparte in 1804 and married at fifteen to Thomas Wyse of Waterford, she showed such impetuosity, scorn for etiquette and flirtatiousness that domestic harmony was out of the question. In early 1828 she left her husband and two sons for London, where her looks and bravura kept her in the public eye. She had an affair with a Tory MP and staged a suicide attempt when he tired of her. An army captain pulled her from the water in one of the London parks and took her to Rome in July. The nature of this man's link with Buckingham is unclear, but he was Mrs Wyse's ostensible chaperone for the period of her ducal connection. In December 1829 Irish papers reported her return to Waterford and unsuccessful attempt to gain access to her children. Soon afterwards she was in Bath, where the *Court Journal* found society divided as to whether or not to admit her.[49]

The duchess was horrified by the affair and its publicity and considered a permanent separation from her husband. He may have been chastened, and nothing suggests he saw Mrs Wyse after their return from the Continent. Their liaison stayed fresh in the minds of journalists for years, however. The *Satirist*, in particular, never tired of scurrilities about the duke and his paramour. In 1831 it stated that 'a very *wise* lady' had found an effective treatment for his gout; that she had dedicated a book to him about scaling Mont Blanc; that he had 'tasted every pleasure he could *de Vyse* (devise)'; and that she had spoken of his having a 'spasmodic attack' at Chamonix after taking off his flannel waistcoat. In 1832 it reported that a boat named after him had run aground 'at *Wyse-beach*'; that she had feelingly read him a passage from Shakespeare: 'Some are born great, some achieve greatness; Some have greatness *thrust upon them*!'; and that he was superstitious 'because he re-*lies* on a *Wyse* woman'.

It was not only the insult of his blatant inconstancy that made the duchess angry. She had taken the opportunity of his absence abroad to look into the duke's finances and was appalled at what she found, especially as wealth she had brought into the marriage had been squandered along with his own. Once she grasped how things stood she insisted on resettling her own estates to stop him selling them to pay off debts. With the help of the legal expert and MP Sir Edward Hyde East she got the legislation for this through parliament in 1828. At the same time she determined on the sale of lands away from the Buckinghamshire and Hampshire core, made cuts in her expenditure, and sold jewellery and other possessions. However, she refused to give up her charitable donations and poverty relief in her native county or her customary entertainments for local people at Avington.

Lord Chandos, too, was aghast at his father's disordered affairs, and especially that on succeeding him he would be liable for some of his debts. Even Wotton, his own home, carried a mortgage. He sought, like his mother, to curtail the duke's freedom in money matters. The two men kept up a united front in public and were seen together at county gatherings, but there was little sympathy and no trust between them. Buckingham also had an uneasy relationship with his brother Lord Nugent, who lived with his wife at Lilies, near Weedon in Buckinghamshire. He felt more fondness for sister Lady Arundell, and she for him, but her waxing piety made real closeness impossible. In 1826 Lady Williams Wynn found him 'feeling that there is not a creature in the World who loves Him, or cares what becomes of him'. In 1830 he said the same to Louisa Lloyd. He wished to revive their romance, but mainly he needed a friend: 'I want taking care of and it is a dismal thing being alone.'[50]

Tension among the Grenvilles was aggravated by politics, and here Buckingham found himself caught in the middle. On leaving for Italy he had declared a wish to forsake public life for good, but it was hard to let go, and when Canning died in August 1827 he offered to come home and serve under his successor Lord Goderich. This was not taken up, but while he was away newspapers were still keen to send him to Ireland as lord lieutenant or make him lord privy seal. They were equally interested in his stance on the long-running Catholic question, which was slowly building to a crisis when Wellington replaced Goderich as premier in January 1828. Buckingham upheld the Grenvillite position of favouring Catholic emancipation, but in doing so he pleased neither his doctrinaire Catholic sister, who thought he could somehow do more, nor his sternly anti-Catholic wife, who had raised their son with the same prejudices.

In 1825 the duke had held a meeting at his London house of sixty-five peers supportive of the Catholic cause, who signed a resolution in its favour. He spoke on the subject in the Lords and presented petitions from groups of citizens. Chandos began presenting contrary petitions and agitated in Buckinghamshire against Catholic claims. This enraged the duke, who from Italy sent an address on the subject to the county's freeholders that was much reprinted and won him votes of thanks in Ireland. In their home county, though, Chandos's views were more in tune with the general feeling. Locally and nationally, the spectacle of the duke and his heir falling out publicly was enjoyed to the full. This bone of contention was removed only by the passing of the Roman Catholic Relief Act in April 1829. 'God be praised that I have lived to see this day!' Buckingham wrote, though he bitterly felt his son's disloyalty.[51]

Advocacy of Catholic emancipation was the last gasp of the duke's liberalism in politics. Thereafter he was a thorough Tory, and in the Lords he backed Wellington's government on a range of subjects. Lord Ellenborough, the lord privy seal, found him quite effective and thought that in a debate on taxation he bested the Whig leader Grey, who hated him and called him 'the most unpopular man, perhaps, in England'. It was in his nature to want a reward for his support, and Wellington gave him one by making him lord steward of the household on William IV's accession in June 1830. Lady Williams Wynn was glad: 'Never was there such a creature more pleased than he is with his new situation, which he has found quite a specific for his Gout, his low spirits, & in short all his ills.'[52] As lord steward he was constantly in the papers, waving his white stave at court with gusto, but he had to relinquish it and the scarlet coat that went with it when Wellington's administration fell at the end of the year.

A new role came with the advent of Grey's Whig ministry and its policy of electoral reform. This threatened Buckingham's control over a handful of seats that he retained even after the collapse of the Grenville faction. Even worse, his rotten boroughs were held up as examples of abuses that required remedy. 'I wonder how he likes the boroughs of Buckingham and St Mawe's being bowled out,' wrote Creevey. 'He would never have been a duke without them, and can there be a better reason for their destruction?'[53] Faced with the powerful demand for reform, he shifted around, now opposing the whole idea, now admitting modest changes might be useful. Finally he put forward his own reform bill: a compromise between Grey's proposals and the status quo. A caricature by 'HB' named after Aesop's fable *The Mountain in Labour* shows him lying in bed, his mountainous form defined by the sheets, while a crowd of politicians gather round to see the mouse to which he has just given birth.

The plan's main handicap was its author. As the Whig jurist Denis Le Marchant put it, 'He is too false even for the moderate Tories. Perhaps there is no man whose life has been stained with more vices. He is also what vicious men are far from being invariably, very unamiable.'[54] It was assumed the duke was offering a sop to the angry multitude, enfranchising a few towns and consolidating a few boroughs the better to keep everything else the same. The press heaped sarcasm on the scheme, which the *Evening Mail* called 'a wretched patchwork' that Britons would see as 'a fraud upon their understandings, and a treachery to their rights'. He had to travel to and from London with the carriage blinds drawn down, and at Buckingham House the windows had to be shuttered. 'His Grace is occupying a position of painful eminence just now,' remarked the *Bucks Gazette*. His proposal remained in embryo, and when the Great Reform Act received royal assent in June 1832 it was forgotten.

By greatly extending the franchise the act ended parliamentary patronage and thus eliminated such factions as the Grenvillites. Instead, Tories and Whigs, or Conservatives and Liberals, dominated utterly; the two-party system was born. The duke continued to be vilified, for the new political reality prompted recollections of how bad things had been before. With the last vestiges of his power gone, he kept up his attendance in the Lords and spoke on taxation, church property and other topics. By now an ultra-Tory, he tried to rally those of the same ilk against the Whig government. But he was taken less and less seriously. *Bell's New Weekly Messenger* observed that 'his Grace of Buckingham's Reform Bill has been the source of a great deal of fun to the world' and that the *Examiner* had abused him 'like a pickpocket'. Journalists yet again recalled his theft of stationery, yet again made merry with his self-importance and obesity. In 1833 and 1834 his parliamentary contributions were routinely mocked.

He was further weakened by the political disunity of his family. With Chandos, the tussle about Catholic rights now behind them, he differed little. But he was poles apart from his brother Nugent, who threw his weight behind every progressive cause, including electoral reform. 'He has distinguished himself by his resolute, able, and effective advocacy of liberal principles, in opposition to all his friends,' as the *Perthshire Courier* put it. The duke railed against this treachery, but, characteristically, having vented his feelings he did nothing else. He must have felt relieved when Nugent was appointed lord high commissioner of the Ionian Islands in 1832. Just as awkward for Buckingham was the perception that his wife's staunch conservatism had pushed him towards the high Tory views he now espoused. The Grenvilles certainly were 'A Divided Family', to quote the title of an 1831 article about them in the *Reading Mercury*.

Further ignominy resulted from the duke's ever more obvious financial woes. The duchess's intervention and his patchy efforts to economise had only done so much. The Italian journey, meant to cut his expenses, had put him sadly in the way of temptation. The *Private Diary* details purchases of antiquities, gems, majolica, geological specimens and much else. Most of all he bought statues, as well as sitting for his own bust. His spree went on and on, and the *Windsor and Eton Express* knew that twenty-five tons of marbles had been shipped from Italy to Stowe in 1829. While he was away Buckingham House was renovated, and after his return its upkeep and the reopening of Stowe, together with election and yeomanry expenses and a profligate lifestyle, got him deeper into debt. By the spring of 1830 his estates carried twelve mortgages. To make matters worse, Chandos, vocal in criticising his father's spending, had himself been living beyond his means.

Chandos kept his difficulties a secret, but the press followed the decline in the duke's fortunes closely. Property sales and planned property sales were regularly mentioned. The failure in 1832 of the bank Duckett, Morland & Co., to which he owed over £10,000, was raked over, as was his sale of the *Anna Eliza* the following year, reputedly for £12,000. It was stated and then denied that he would let Buckingham House and reside wholly at Avington, the formula 'We are authorised to contradict' suggesting he had stepped in to scotch this rumour. He also gainsaid a notice that he would dispose of Avington and other parts of the Chandos estate to a London banker. But he did not challenge reports that the Zoological Society would purchase Buckingham House, which it did not; or that he would sell Stowe's Irish manuscripts, engravings collection, and etchings by Rembrandt, which he did. In 1833 the *Satirist* printed a little poem on the subject of his money troubles:

> The portly Duke, on saving bent,
> Reduces his establishment.
> If that's considered far too great,

For him to keep in ducal state;
He should begin, to spare some pelf,
With some reduction of himself.

Buckingham begged his wife to let him sell parts of the estate she controlled, but she refused. She had been irked by his decision to take up the reins of estate management again on his return home in 1829, and when she saw how bad things were with him and Chandos three years later, she was furious: 'I fear not the poverty and utter ruin now surrounding me but I do feel keenly the treatment I have received as coming from those bound to me by ties of affection and gratitude.' She insisted on placing their affairs in professional hands, and her husband was too cowed by her and too fearful of the consequences of his negligence to object. In August 1833 a trust was set up that would pay him £12,000 a year, from which he had to defray household expenses and wages. 'The embarrassments do indeed appear endless,' said one of the trustees, but with firm hands on the tiller things began to improve.[55] Thanks to the duchess, the humiliation of selling the contents of Stowe or even the house itself was averted.

It was hard work, for the fecklessness of her husband and son was ingrained. By raising funds at ruinous rates of interest Chandos got out of his depth, and when he turned to his mother in desperation she gave him her jewels and her good counsel but nothing more. Buckingham's will to make savings soon flagged: 'He must positively devour money!' a trustee exclaimed.[56] The threat that the trust would be wound up, exposing him to very chill winds, inspired him to renewed efforts. After more mischief from Chandos and interference from his father the trustees did indeed resign in mid-1835. The experience of being his own master was so stressful for the duke that he was only too pleased when a second trust was established in January 1836. This time there was no question of him meddling. The trustees had a large task disentangling his affairs, and for three years they stuck to it. At the end of that time they could look with satisfaction upon a diminished but stable estate.

Buckingham's fraught relations with his wife and son deteriorated further during the worst years of anxiety about money. He said that his heart had been broken by his son's misconduct and that his whole family had deserted him. Periods of estrangement were followed by reconciliations, but these were fragile. Domestic misery, combined with the failure of his parliamentary career, the chastening effect of financial constraint, the loss of control over his estate, and endless denigration from his contemporaries that the press both reflected and stimulated, finally broke his self-assurance. He withdrew from the political arena in the second half of 1834 and his attendance at county functions as lord lieutenant became irregular. His fits of depression grew blacker, and though not yet sixty his health was very poor: ever more frequent attacks of gout and severe asthma laid him low for long periods, and in 1836 he had an erysipelas infection.

Once he ceased to be a public figure the duke's illnesses were the main subject of usually brief mentions of him in the press. He was in a bad state and then recovering, in grave danger and then out of it. Beyond this, and occasional notices of his comings and goings, there was not much, and almost nothing of substance. Even the *Satirist*, which had been so tenacious, let him be. Now and again something hurtful appeared, like a piece in the *Examiner* in 1836 that imagined his chair giving way at a county dinner: 'No joiner's work could bear such a trial [...] and never had a chair juster cause for giving in.' But a fatal accident the same year was reported in several papers without adverse comment or humorous echo. Mr Broadway, the Stowe house steward, had devised an apparatus using a system of pulleys to convey the duke from one floor to another, and as he was testing it he was seized with giddiness on an upper floor and fell to his death.

In May 1836 the Duchess of Buckingham succumbed to a short illness. Voices were raised in unison to laud her humility, generosity, religion and strength of character. Latterly she had taken pity on her husband and nursed him during his ailments, and they were seldom apart. After her death he was very ill, and although he recovered he remained feeble. 'He never held up his head as before, but seemed to be waiting for his own call,' said an acquaintance.[57] He left his finances to the trustees and politics to his son, devoting himself to his microscope and his gardens at Stowe, which brought forth fruit that won prizes at horticultural shows. He maintained a disposition to charity that had grown during his wife's last years and must have been instilled by her. He distributed flannel, blankets and coals to the poor, gave dinners to estate labourers, helped fund a new infirmary at Aylesbury and the Hampshire county hospital, built and endowed a chapel in St Mawes, and donated to religious organisations.

Above all, he applied himself to the question of surplus labour and pauperism and the creation of new forms of employment that would provide livelihoods and contribute to the public good. His plan, or one he adopted and carried out on a small scale, was for 'cottage-allotments'. Landowners would let out an area to the parish for a modest rent so that the destitute could farm it for themselves. Some considered the measure paltry, and others deplored the use of parish funds for it, but praise was heard too. The *Yorkshire Gazette* believed the duke's 60-acre scheme at Avington had 'restored the condition of the labourers of those parishes to a state of comparative comfort and independence' and that poor rates had fallen sharply as a result. The *Bucks Herald* claimed the allotments had removed the need for poor rates entirely and their success would silence the objections made to them. Whether Buckingham had a hand in these articles is impossible to tell, but his philanthropy was real enough.

In August 1837 some papers stated that he had died at Stowe; others stated that he had not and that the rumour had been spread maliciously. In October he was taking daily airings in the grounds, but he had almost lost the use of his legs and his prospects were gloomy. In January 1838 guests at a Conservative dinner in Buckingham toasted him as a friend and neighbour known to all for 'many acts of benevolence and kindness'. In July he entertained barristers and judges on the Norfolk circuit at Stowe. In November he was said to be very weak, and on 18 January 1839 came the information that he had died the previous day, two months short of his sixty-third birthday. His son, daughter-in-law and grandson had been with him. Newspapers announced his demise respectfully, with accounts of his illness and brief biographies. They reported the funeral at Wotton, which was attended by over 400 tenants, and his burial in the family mausoleum there.

Only the *Morning Herald* offered a full obituary, which was then reprinted elsewhere. Surveying his life from a Tory standpoint, it lauded Buckingham's talent for public life, connoisseurship of art and literature, and generosity to the poor. In a long diatribe the *Oxford Chronicle* castigated his boroughmongering and the Grenvilles' greed for public office, but this tone, which might have prevailed if the duke had died earlier, was not taken up by others. He had receded from public view, his conduct had latterly been inoffensive, and thanks to the trustees he left a solvent estate. His son Chandos, the second Duke of Buckingham, would be more profligate than he, to the point that the contents of Stowe went under the hammer; and more brazen in his sexual immorality, to the point that his wife divorced him. He died penniless in a railway hotel. The family that had been born so high and reached its crest during the first duke's lifetime was brought low in two generations. Stowe is now a public school.

Like many celebrity lives, that of the first Duke of Buckingham and Chandos is a moral tale. Above all it demonstrates the effects of a bad upbringing, which trained him to use unworthy means to achieve his ends and gave him habits of unchecked self-indulgence. These defects caused a clever, sensitive man to be widely, deservedly disliked. The ingredients of a celebrity story are all there: greed, ambition, power, sex and money, shaped into an arcing narrative of rise and fall. Also classic is the fact that beside the feckless hero stands a long-suffering wife, hallowed by her virtue and dignity. The duke gave the world something to talk about for over three decades, but because his name was so tarnished his craving for military and political glory went unfulfilled. Indeed, for a man with so much laid into his cradle, he achieved remarkably little in any sphere. But there were gleams of something better, and a new warmth suffused his final years, so that we turn from him not with disgust but with regret for a life that might have been better lived.

4

The Elegant Novelist

Lady Charlotte Bury

Lady Charlotte Bury.
Stipple engraving by William Read.

At a dinner party the Secretary at War Sir Henry Hardinge gave one summer evening in 1828 the conversation turned to female beauty. John Wilson Croker, the first secretary to the Admiralty, said he had separately asked George IV and Sir Thomas Lawrence who they thought was the loveliest woman they had ever seen, and then he asked the other diners to guess which name the king and his official painter had both given. Two of them promptly produced it: Lady Charlotte Campbell. Croker recorded the exchange in his diary: 'I have never met any one, except the Duke of York, who had known her in their youth, who did not represent her as the most beautiful creature they had ever seen.' Our new acquaintance the Duke of Buckingham thought she possessed 'more real beauty than has ever existed since the days of the Venus de Medicis'. Other extravagant tributes abound.[1]

Could an artist do her justice? When John Hoppner painted her in 1796 he declared she had more antique beauty than any woman he had beheld. But his portrait was not well regarded: his fellow artist Richard Westall thought the head not well turned and the acerbic critic Anthony Pasquin said he had been unkind to her. Lawrence took up the challenge, and one evening at a ball the poet Thomas Moore found him studying her upturned eyes. 'Oh, if I could but catch that look!' he exclaimed. His portrait, shown at the Royal Academy in 1803, was unconvincing: the *Star* judged it very inferior to the original and the painter Henry Fuseli considered it his worst painting at the exhibition. Later a lesser artist, Charles Kirkpatrick Sharpe, tried to capture Lady Charlotte's likeness but admitted he had failed as badly as his predecessors.[2] 'Her beauty was that of a Goddess,' wrote the *Court Journal* in 1831, 'so much did it seem beyond all human imagination; for no pen could describe it, no pencil copy it! Every painter has failed, who attempted it.'

'The Flower of the House of Argyll', as she became known, was born Lady Charlotte Susan Maria Campbell on 28 January 1775. Her father was John Campbell, 5th Duke of Argyll and chief of Clan Campbell, who devoted his life to the army and rose to the rank of field marshal. Her mother was Elizabeth Gunning, one of the captivating Gunning sisters who were the admiration of London when they arrived there from Ireland in the early 1750s. The two girls prompted a spate of prints, poems and press articles and were ogled by crowds as they emerged from private houses and shops. Theatre audiences took their seats early to watch their entrance, and news that they were to visit the Vauxhall Gardens brought thousands to catch a glimpse of them. For the respectable but poor Gunnings all this show had a single aim, and it was soon achieved: Maria married the Earl of

Coventry and Elizabeth the Duke of Hamilton. When the duke died young his widow married the Duke of Argyll.

The couple had two sons, George and John, and two daughters, Augusta and Charlotte, who grew up amid the Gothic magnificence of Inveraray Castle, Argyllshire and at Argyll House, London. Charlotte's childhood experiences in both homes stocked her mind with happy memories. The duke was reserved in general company, perhaps a little stolid, and could seem curt, but he was a loving, fair-minded father. The duchess endeared herself to everyone with an easy charm and a warm, kindly nature that accolades to her beauty did nothing to spoil. Happy in their marriage, they spread happiness around them as indulgent parents, active benefactors on their Highland estate, and genial hosts there and in London. Visitors to Inveraray found Charlotte an intelligent, musical child, eager to converse with adults. The idyll of her early years ended with the death of her mother after a lingering illness in 1790. The duke never recovered his spirits in the fifteen years he outlived her, and a gloom spread over Inveraray.

During the duchess's decline the family spent several months in the warmer climate of Italy, and young Charlotte discovered a lifelong love of that country, its literature, architecture and art. She was herself discovered by the German artist Johann Heinrich Wilhelm Tischbein, who espied her near Naples as she fled from an oncoming carriage straight into the path of another and had to twist and dart aside again. The strenuous but fluid movements of the teenager's body appeared to Tischbein pure nature, the immediate expression of her mind, shorn of affectation and social convention. Back in England and Scotland too it was the naturalness and health of her looks rather than any show of feminine fragility that delighted contemporaries. She was '*fair* and FULL', as the Marchioness of Stafford put it.[3] Surprisingly, there is no more detailed verbal sketch of her than that of Lady Hester Stanhope: 'She had such a hand and arm, and such a leg! she had beautiful hair too, gold colour, and a finely-shaped nose, and fine complexion.'

She also walked well, recalled Lady Hester, neither striding nor mincing, but making perfect use of perfect limbs.[4] The glow of beauty was deepened by evident intelligence and a genial disposition. Lady Stafford, who thought her the prettiest girl she knew, was sure her mind and heart were good, too, and encouraged her son to court her. Horace Walpole specified that her understanding as well as her person were universally praised. Like her mother, she became a public spectacle, and Lady Hester and Croker saw theatre and opera audiences turning in a body to stare at her.[5] An elderly contributor to the *Glasgow Herald* in 1855 reminisced that she was once mobbed while walking in the streets of Glasgow and had to slip into a house and send for an escort. Naturally the newspapers made much of her, especially after her presentation at court aged seventeen, and her presence at balls and other assemblies was duly noted, often with details of which dances she performed and with which partner.

As her celebrity grew, she nurtured it further. Tischbein, in his effusive account, defined her physique and motion as embodying not just nature, but a perfection of nature that only classical art had ever captured. What he had hitherto admired in fleeing figures on bas-reliefs and floating dancers in the wall paintings at Herculaneum he now saw in flesh and blood. Lady Charlotte's statuesque form lent itself ideally to the antique simplicity of women's dress that was just then coming into vogue across Europe. She hastened to adopt the novelty, and no one wore high-waisted dresses of thin, clinging material, what became known as the Empire line or silhouette, with more panache. Whether or not she was, as the women's magazine *La Belle Assemblée* asserted, 'the first to introduce the style of Grecian costume to this country', she was in the vanguard and an object of imitation. In 1794 a friend of Lady Elizabeth Stanley described her as being 'dressed exactly like Lady Charlotte Campbell' with 'no waist', and in 1830 Lady Louisa Stuart spoke of a friend of her youth having copied Lady Charlotte's mode of dress.[6]

A survey of newspapers in the mid-1790s confirms the young beauty's status at the pinnacle of fashion. The *Chester Chronicle* claimed that she had rejected the artificiality of stays before anyone else, and that her elegant figure appeared to advantage without them. However, the writer continued, this natural look presented problems for those less well favoured, a caution echoed by others. The *Bury and Norwich Post* stated, 'Lady Charlotte Campbell is one of the most conspicuous leaders of the present fashion, which advances the *zone* from the waist to the shoulders!' And there was more trendsetting to note. The *Bath Chronicle* reported that she had displayed in Hyde Park a feather four feet higher than her bonnet, and the *Kentish Weekly Post* remarked that she had reintroduced high-heeled shoes as 'articles of fashionable dress'. Other titles simply commented in general on what she wore to this or that party, sometimes with a gracefully turned reference to her attractiveness.

Some reproved Lady Charlotte for using the Empire line to show off her body to an indecent degree. She did indeed favour the lightest of light, semi-transparent dresses, worn with no chemise underneath, though she was not alone in this. The *Chester Courant* remarked that in her no degree of exhibition was unflattering, but that 'there are in all women some things that it is better to veil from the vulgar gaze at least.' She had defenders too: Lady Stafford ascribed such criticism to envy in women and ill nature in men,[7] and the *Chester Chronicle* said it was surely better to display natural beauty, as she did, than artificial enhancements of it. To caricaturists the subject was a gift. Isaac Cruikshank's 'Too Much and Too Little, or Summer Cloathing' contrasts the minimal covering of a woman resembling Lady Charlotte with the stiff, bodiced dress of an Elizabethan. James Gillray's 'Ladies Dress, As It Soon Will Be' goes further, showing her in profile with her breasts exposed and a slit in her dress that reveals her posterior.[8]

Even more associated with Lady Charlotte Campbell was the fashion in 1793–1794 for the belly pad. The idea was to accentuate the high waist of the Empire style by creating a slight swell beneath it, in imitation of the shape of classical statues. This fad was satirised in every imaginable medium, and a stream of flippant verse poured forth. The epilogue of Frederick Reynolds's comedy *How to Grow Rich* of 1793 alluded to the pad, and the actor reciting it caused hilarity in the audience by producing one from under his coat. The drift of such humour was that the accessory made a woman look pregnant or helped her hide an unwanted pregnancy. For graphic artists, it was as good as the flimsy dresses that covered it. In 'Frailties of Fashion' Cruikshank shows Lady Charlotte in a group of recognisable figures, all sporting some kind of frontal projection, and in 'Modern Elegance' Gillray depicts her alone, again with the appearance of pregnancy, her hair escaping from a turban decorated with ostrich feathers.[9]

It was Lady Hester Stanhope's understanding that she brought the pad into vogue to hide a misstep of her own: 'At the time when she began to grow round, she bethought herself of introducing the fashion of padding the body behind and before; and, as she was so beautiful, she could make any fashion take: she continued to dress so for two years.' This is without corroboration, but it must reflect the gossip of the day. Lady Charlotte could laugh it off, however, and bask in the celebrity she had attained before even turning twenty. In true celebrity style she later told her friend Charles Kirkpatrick Sharpe that she 'would be rather spoken ill of than not talked of at all'. In any case everything in the newspapers was positive. They incessantly praised her looks and dress and chronicled her appearances at court. In the sartorial world she was a brand, and she naturally expected some return for endorsing those who clothed her, as another of Lady Hester's recollections makes clear:

The Miss Stewarts are mantua makers and milliners somewhere near Sloane Street. They were brought into notice by Lady

Charlotte Campbell and by me. Lady Charlotte would say 'Miss Stewart, make me a dress so and so: I want it for such and such a purpose'. Then she would wear it, and the next morning call on Miss Stewart and tell her that her dress had been very much admired – that Lady this, and the Duchess that, intended ordering one like it, and would then finish by 'There! Take mine back again, and hang it up as a shew-dress'; and in this way her things cost her nothing.[10]

At the height of this splendour she took the first of four steps that took her down the social scale over the course of her life. As the Duke of Argyll's daughter and a famous beauty she could have made a superb marriage. Instead, in June 1796, she wed her distant cousin John Campbell of Shawfield in Lanarkshire and Islay in the Inner Hebrides. He was a captain in the Scots Guards, four years older than she, tall and strong, 'a paragon of manly beauty' in the words of fellow soldier Archibald Montgomery Maxwell.[11] But 'handsome Jack Campbell', as he was known, was poor, and the circumstances of the couple would be narrow. The bride's friends regretted her choice, but it was plainly actuated by love and socially quite respectable. The problem for the Campbells was keeping up appearances. They could not afford to be much in London even though her father's town residence was available to them, and they lived mainly at Woodhall, John's Lanarkshire home, and in rented houses in Edinburgh.

Lady Hester Stanhope's remark that after her marriage Lady Charlotte 'all at once disappeared from the *beau monde*' overstates the case, but the role she would have had with a superior alliance was denied her.[12] She slid down from the summit of fashion, and mentions of her in the London press grew infrequent. She still shone at Inveraray, where during long sojourns she and her elder sister Lady Augusta Clavering sang and played for their father's guests or rode with them over the surrounding hills and glens. The castle was a stopping place for Highland tourists, among them the future Lords Melbourne and Palmerston, the painters J. M. W. Turner and Joseph Farington, the poet Thomas Campbell, and Matthew Gregory Lewis, known as 'Monk' Lewis after the Gothic novel that made him famous. House parties at Inveraray were lively affairs, and in 1802 Lewis, a regular visitor, wrote of a programme of theatricals, a weekly castle newspaper, and accommodation so full that guests left their bedrooms at the risk of finding them occupied on their return.[13]

Lady Charlotte's brightest light was cast on the Edinburgh literary scene. From early girlhood she had devoured poetry, prose and drama, and in 1797 her anonymous, privately printed *Poems on Several Occasions* appeared. She was always modest about this small volume, but all the more prone to admire the works of others, and this, together with her beauty and enlivening charm, perfectly fitted her for the role of salon hostess in the Athens of the North. Men of letters collected round her hearth, including 'Monk' Lewis, who was considered her chief literary adorer. In 1808 he dedicated his *Romantic Tales* to her with the following lines:

> While stranger-eyes, whene'er her form is seen,
> Own her of captive hearts unrivalled Queen;
> While stranger-ears, catching some passing strain,
> The music of her voice through life retain;
> Admired by all, with truth she still may boast,
> The few, who know her best, admire her most.

Another frequenter of her salon was Walter Scott, who addressed flattering verses to her on being given a copy of *Poems* and later headed a chapter of *The Heart of Midlothian* with some lines from the book. One day in 1798 she introduced him to Lewis, and Scott, still at the beginning of his stellar career, was glad to win the friendship and patronage of the popular purveyor of Gothic horror.

Lady Charlotte Campbell was one of two recognised queens of Edinburgh society, the other being the eccentric Duchess of Gordon. As well as receiving at home she attended private balls, but these were less frequent than in London because fewer great families had houses there. Instead, people gathered at places of public resort run on a commercial basis, and this gave her a chance to turn her renown to account by letting organisers use her name. She was a patroness of balls and concerts at the George Street Assembly Rooms and Corri's Rooms. Advertisements for these events gave ticket prices, and it seems no more was required for entry than the ability to pay. Just as frequent were notices of plays put on, supposedly at Lady Charlotte's desire, in various theatres. What arrangement lay behind the fiction of her patronising an entertainment or commanding a performance is impossible to fathom, and the same goes for Mr Mackintosh offering music lessons with reference to a strathspey he had named for her and other pretended acts of homage.

South of the border she was less talked of than prior to her marriage. She made a few forays into London society, with and without her husband, and newspapers named her among guests at elegant assemblies. It was as the subject of pictures that she was best known in England. Tischbein painted her soon after spotting her in Naples, showing her as a bacchante with a musical scroll on her lap and one hand resting on an oak branch. She also sat to other artists, the Italian Anna Tonelli, the Scot George Sanders and the Englishman Henry Edridge among them. The portraits by Hoppner, Lawrence, and Kirkpatrick Sharpe have been mentioned, and it was the one by Lawrence that excited most attention in the press. Some agreed with Fuseli that it was a comparative failure, and in particular that the languid pose was in poor taste, but the *Sun* praised the artist for infusing his model with 'animation and sensibility' and the *British Critic* commended him for uniting in her the goddess and the belle.

For the first three decades of her life we have little evidence of our heroine's thoughts and feelings and patchy information about the outward circumstances of her life. Her unpublished diary of 1805–1810 brings her closer to us. She and her husband had an unsettled life, moving between Woodhall, Edinburgh, Inveraray and Hartwell, a house they rented in Buckinghamshire, as well as visiting friends in many places. They stayed in Bath when John Campbell's gout needed attention, traipsed round Scotland with the Argyllshire militia, of which he became colonel on leaving the regular army, and covered every part of the Ayr Burghs constituency when he successfully stood for parliament there in 1807. Trips to London were the greatest treat for Lady Charlotte. 'I never felt so happy as I did to see London,' she wrote in 1806. 'Heaven Grant that We may be able to ensure a frequent repetition of this delight by procuring some thing that may put it in our power to do so. Alas! That vile Money.'[14]

Her vigour and love of new impressions adapted her well for a helter-skelter life of travel, be it occasioned by her husband's avocations and intermittent ill health or by the need to economise. On the other hand, she had acquired refined tastes as a duke's daughter and grew tired of life as a campaigning politician and militia commander's wife, with constant reiterations of drunken dinners and coarse speeches. During these peregrinations stays at Inveraray were a relief, but less of a pleasure over time. Hospitality at the castle had become threadbare and disorganised, partly because of the duke's slackening powers, but mainly because the staggering debts run up by his elder son George, Marquess of Lorne, brought him to the brink to ruin. George was an enigma: a strikingly handsome, talented, good-natured man with every advantage in life who was so apathetic that only the strongest stimulants of whoring, gambling and other dissipation could spark brief flickers of interest in him.

Lady Charlotte's other two siblings were no happier. Lord John Campbell was the opposite of his brother, a diligent, thoughtful man, plain in dress and manner. His wife was unfaithful and either forsook or was banished from their home, causing him such anguish that his health was impaired. Lady Augusta Campbell made a runaway match with Henry Mordaunt Clavering, a gambler and reprobate, and in her abject misery, alternately with and apart from him, it seemed that her mind might give way. In the summer of 1806, the Duke of Argyll died. Charlotte had been his favourite child, and his death after a massive stroke, and before she could reach him, was wrenching. George became the sixth duke, and although he took pains to make her feel welcome at Inveraray, her visits after her father's death no longer felt entirely comfortable, the more so as the decline in the family's and the castle's fortunes accelerated under his heedless stewardship.

What a contrast, Lady Charlotte mused in her diary, between her family's sorrows and the felicity she enjoyed with her husband. In 1805 she wrote that after eight years of marriage they had not spent a single night apart, and that she found a separation that exceeded a few hours hard to endure: 'Every thing without him is to me tasteless.' And, after her father's death: 'Oh the Joy of once more being with Him. – I was nearly dead with all I had gone through but felt a renovation of Life in being once more with Jack.' Both craved the buzz of social activity and were ever eager for fresh amusements. Both were fond of drama and music, and the latter in particular is a regular theme in the diary: 'How fortunate it is to Love Music and the sound of good Dancing Music inspires my feet with Motion and obliterates all other ideas for the Moment but the pleasurable Sensation.' Lady Sarah Spencer, Mary Berry and Matthew Gregory Lewis noted her skill and enthusiasm as a dancer, and Lewis and Thomas Moore extolled her singing.[15]

Her diary reveals two drawbacks to her domestic happiness. The first was bearing nine children in thirteen years. The inconvenience and discomfort of pregnancy and the searing pain of childbirth made her want to cry out with vexation, and more than once the return of her strength after a delivery was marred by post-natal depression. As her family grew, so did the resentment she felt at the deterioration of her looks. 'Alas! What an enormous Size I became *with the trade*,' she wrote to her newly married daughter Eliza many years later.[16] Even worse was the cloud of debt that hung over her. She sought 'any little party of gayety or Amusement that could turn My thoughts from what could not be help'd', but transient joys were soon checked by its recollection. It was 'a perpetual Mill Stone about my neck' and caused her and her husband 'dreadful distress'. And again: 'We can enjoy nothing the idea of our Debts presses upon us and weighs us down.'[17]

By setting the unpublished diary, the later published one, and her letters alongside the testimonies of contemporaries we can essay a sketch of Lady Charlotte's character. This is not easy, though, for it was composed of contradictory elements. Her love of socialising and dancing was part of a general zest for life. 'I felt all the Elasticity of the freshest Vigor,' she wrote after a ball – a typical effusion.[18] She was a keen walker and rider and exulted in fine scenery, bracing air and her own bodily health. Her high spirits expressed themselves in a boisterous sense of fun and a weakness for pranks, and she was always ready to laugh heartily at others' jokes. And yet all her life she was prone to melancholy and feelings of futility, prompting a desire to withdraw from the ado of the world and cultivate a rich inner life. With great regularity she wrote of time and opportunities wasted, of adverse circumstances, of sorrow oppressing her heart, and of the courage needed to bear it.

Some of this sadness sprang from a fear that she would never realise the ambition, largely hidden from others but burning bright within her, to achieve literary distinction. Writing verse was a habit, but a dejecting one: 'Sometimes I think My Poetry is Poetry at other times I am disgusted with it and more with myself for writing it but the fit, the delirium returns and I relapse into Rhyme as naturally as a Drunkard does into Wine.' She tried to hone her ability with serious study, noting down impressions of what she read, and she despised those who thought only of pleasures and creature comforts and refused to cultivate their minds. She knew her own gadabout life constrained her intellectual development, and kept resolving to spurn frivolous pursuits: 'A small & well chosen Society of clever Men and the Cultivation of My own Mind & Talents – their appreciation of these – this is all of Sweet that I expect.'[19] Endless childbearing and money worries also stood in the way of her development as a writer.

The early poetry collection shows that her muse was Romantic, indeed sentimental, and the way she lived her life indicates the same. Her cousin the sculptor Anne Damer saw her at sixteen 'carving *some* name on *some* tree and lolling on the arm of a confidante'. Her marriage a few years later to a handsome but impecunious and fairly obscure man was of a piece with this, as was her ability to be deeply moved by landscapes and the night sky: 'Whatever has been said in ridicule of Romance which is only a Caricature of Sentiment (and every thing may be Caricatured) I must always feel that the tenderest Holiest feelings are inspired by the Contemplation of the Moon.'

In her late thirties she told Mary Berry her inclinations were unaltered: 'I shall never be wiser or better. My heart is still at fifteen, and not worn out – the more's the pity, say you – and sometimes I think so too.' And when she was over forty another friend remarked that she was 'more eat up with sentiment than ever'.[20]

In line with this was the capacity for admiration that we have already mentioned. She was enchanted by landscapes and buildings, and most of all by writers, among them Mlle de Lespinasse and Mme de Sévigné. 'It is so necessary to me to admire that I am sure I would admire a Cabbage if there were no Roses,' she told a friend. But she was no less disposed to harsh judgements, and she could be catty too, as when she described the ex-Queen of Etruria as 'a woman of low, heavy form, which appears still more so, because her legs, if legs she has, are so short, that she is like a *walking torso*.' What she really hated was artificiality of manner, and even eminent contemporaries like the chemist Sir Humphry Davy were not spared when she detected this flaw: 'If every body would only be *natural!* but it is natural to some people to be affected.' She was, she said, never guilty of this herself: 'I never was made for any concealment; partly, through weakness, partly, through the sincerity of my nature.'[21]

The confidence Lady Charlotte reposed in the justness of her feelings and of her responses to individuals went side by side with diffidence about her grasp of more general, less personal subjects. She had a real Christian faith, regretted missing a Sunday service, cherished the miracles of revealed religion, and perceived the social value of the church, but she admitted she found it hard to evaluate the merits of different denominations. In politics she followed the Whig line of her family, lamenting the human cost of the war with France and hoping for peace rather than glorying in victories or railing against the Corsican tyrant, and later she articulated liberal opinions and sought the company of those who promoted them. Here too, though, she was modest about the compass and penetration of her mind. Perhaps she would have agreed with Anne Damer, who blamed her for frittering away her expensive education in a round of trivial, desultory pursuits. In a letter to Mary Berry she wrote, 'My Heart is composed of much better stuff than my Head.'[22]

This humility was engaging, especially since it was combined with a willingness to acknowledge the greater intellect of others. Also engaging was Lady Charlotte's apparent freedom from the conceit that might have been expected in someone of her rank and beauty. Tributes to her kindness, graceful manners and all-round likeability run thick in the period's memoirs. Walter Scott, whose integrity and powers of observation make his opinion worth heeding, thought highly of her. He fondly recalled convivial evenings she hosted in Edinburgh with simple meals, music and reciting. She was, he said, one of the women he esteemed most, one whose talents and disposition claimed more respect than her noble birth. He gave her a presentation copy of his *Minstrelsy of the Scottish Border* and, late in life, wrote a letter thanking her for her 'approbation bestowed most generously' on him as a young man, at a time when his friends were few and his prospects uncertain.[23]

In late 1807 Jack Campbell's intermittent ailments turned into a dangerous illness. He was not even forty years old. Lady Charlotte's diary, previously strewn with references to her love for him, is now a chronicle of his pain and her anxiety. Walter Scott, who was fond of them both, wrote that only she was able to soothe him and that she lived almost exclusively for him during this time. They journeyed round Scotland and England in quest of relief but found none. Jack spent his last two weeks in lodgings in George Street, Edinburgh, and in minute detail his wife describes the harrowing days prior to his death in March 1809. Only now do we learn what was killing him. The doctors told her his only chance lay in 'a complete & total Abstinence from all Strong Liquor', but she feared this was too drastic: 'I begged them to think what a violent mode of cure it was to take it away at once – they were decided – What could I do.'[24] Soon after this he died and the diary breaks off. Scott was not alone in assuming the Campbells were a happy couple, and the 1805–1810 diary, despite its revelation of alcoholism, ought to be conclusive proof that this was so.

It is therefore a shock to learn that the truth, which Lady Charlotte could not bring herself to record, was different. It is revealed in a letter the political thinker Germaine de Staël wrote in 1814, reporting what her British friend had told her: 'She married the man she loved; she had eight children. He died of inebriation and he beat her for almost fifteen years without her ever saying a word about it to anyone.' This is corroborated by a letter Lady Charlotte sent her daughter Eliza in 1818 that vividly portrays the misery of her marriage: the forced embraces, ill-treatment while pregnant, and subjection to low and debauched companions.[25] It is not surprising that the published diary and letters contain regular, if oblique, allusions to thorns and briars and the cruel fate she has endured, or that domestic abuse is one of the central themes of the novels she later wrote.

Nine months after her husband's death Lady Charlotte resumed her diary, and three months after that she had news to report: Caroline of Brunswick, Princess of Wales wished to appoint her as a lady of the bedchamber. In her despondent state the proposal at first agitated her disagreeably, but very quickly she roused herself to contemplate its advantages: an escape from the dreary solitude of widowhood; a salary to alleviate her poverty; and better prospects for her portionless daughters. Without asking anyone's advice she accepted the offer, but as soon as her friends got wind of it they tried to dissuade her from taking up the post, fearing, they said, for her good name. These fears were founded on the shady reputation of the princess, who had long been estranged from her husband and whose semi-official court was beset by rumours of sexual licence and plotting against the real court, specifically against the Prince of Wales, who became regent in 1811.

Lady Charlotte saw the challenge in heroic terms, thinking she might derive 'Lustre from the danger of the Pedestal on which the Statue is placed'. In any case she liked the princess and was flattered to have been thought of. Most of all, she was more than ready to jettison the by now ritualistic expressions of woe at Jack Campbell's death and plunge back into what she called the 'vortex of Folly and Dissipation'.[26] In April 1810 she left Inveraray for London, where she had an interview with Lady Charlotte Lindsay, another lady-in-waiting, who set out the terms of the appointment: she would have an apartment in Kensington Palace and a house at Blackheath, where the princess's own two residences were, and a salary of £500 a year. Some of her children could live with her, and her presence would only be required at certain times on certain days. Then she was taken to see the princess, who immediately put her at her ease. A new and eventful chapter in her life was beginning.

It was a pleasant life in some ways. There were dinners at which writers, scientists and politicians vied to amuse the princess. There were glamorous evenings out with a carriage provided and expenses met. But one can have too much of a good thing, and Lady Charlotte bemoaned her employer's ceaseless need to be entertained and the stamina that kept her, and of course her attendants, up until the small hours of the morning. Lady Charlotte had to produce hand-written invitations and play and sing for the princess's guests. Did she ever reflect, as she did so, that her family home had been a kind of court, centred more on herself than on her retiring father, while now she was a courtier herself, flitting round someone else's light? At least she regained some public visibility and attention from the press as she accompanied Caroline to the opera and exhibitions and on drives in Hyde Park. With unwitting poignancy, one notice described her as 'decorated with flowers, a little in the old style'. Her days as a fashion icon were long gone.

Foremost in the princess's mind, even as she sought distraction from them, were her constant tussles with her husband, who spied on her, spread unsavoury rumours about her, and restricted her access to their daughter. She schemed against him with leaders of the Whig opposition, and since her English was poor she asked Lady Charlotte to write her letters to them.[27] The courtier did as she was bidden and watched uneasily while the Whigs turned the slighted woman, who had popular support, into a political tool. Lady Charlotte was a true partisan of the princess, seeing in her a courageous victim of persecution. But being in her corner was frustrating, for Caroline was her own undoing. She was inconstant towards friends, needlessly provocative towards enemies, and prone to fits of frivolity and recklessness. She liked unsuitable companions best, and her clothes were at times staggeringly indecorous. Thus an intelligent woman capable of generosity and fine feeling harmed her own cause, and finally did so past redemption.

It was not in Lady Charlotte's nature to give unsolicited advice, and she knew the princess was too obstinate to take it. Instead she made soothing noises as Caroline bewailed her fate or explained her latest plan to master it, all the while sensing her compassion for her royal mistress ebb away. This shift in sentiment also grew out of a concern others had felt on her behalf and she now felt herself: that being a lady-in-waiting might compromise her. Partly from boredom, the princess imitated her husband's sexual self-indulgence. When she took two cottages in Paddington and placed Lady Charlotte with her children in one and a handsome Italian music teacher in the other, things grew awkward for a woman who, for her own and her daughters' sakes, had to be careful. The princess visited the maestro every day, and no one believed she only received singing lessons. Lady Charlotte's indirect role in the subterfuge was 'horridly degrading' to her, and she hated to see Caroline let herself down so badly.[28]

There were four ladies of the bedchamber operating a rota, so each had time for other pursuits. Lady Charlotte had her own social life, and not long after her appointment a rumour fluttered through society that the dandy Lord Petersham, known for his lisp and other affectations, had proposed to her. Her friends hoped it was untrue or she would refuse him, and at any rate no marriage took place. Despite her service with his wife, the regent invited her to a ball at Carlton House in 1811, and when she replied that she could not afford a new gown he had one made for her. She was no doubt resplendent in it, but her looks were slowly fading. Walter Scott found her 'still looking beautiful' in the same year, but weeks later the lawyer Lord Glenbervie called her 'a has-been'. In 1812 Thomas Campbell thought her 'lovely', and to Lady Clementina Drummond in about 1813 she was 'still beautiful'. In 1815, when she was forty, Archibald Montgomery Maxwell found her past her prime and portly, though with 'one of the loveliest faces that can be conceived'.[29]

In 1812 Lady Charlotte published *Self-Indulgence: A Tale of the Nineteenth Century*, in which a young aristocrat with a secret wife bigamously weds a wealthy merchant's daughter, with the surprising result that the two women forge a bond based on shared wrongs. This entry into the ranks of novelists may have been inspired by the example of Susan Ferrier, who was not yet published, but whose *Marriage* Lady Charlotte had read in manuscript in 1810. Ferrier's father had been land agent at Inveraray under the fifth duke, and the two women had a friendship that crossed the boundaries of class. Lady Charlotte admired Ferrier hugely and laughed so hard at the social satire in *Marriage* that her niece Charlotte Clavering thought she might have a fit. She also said fear of comparison with such gifts might discourage her from writing anything herself.[30] Nonetheless she pressed on with *Self-Indulgence*, but it sank like a stone and any hopes she may have had of augmenting her income were dashed.

After four years of attendance on royalty she was tired of it. Courts, she decided, showed human nature at its worst: 'Intrigues, jealousies, heart-burnings, lies, dissimulation, thrive in them as mushrooms in a hot-bed.' Indeed, this toxic atmosphere also affected her, diluting her native candour with a new element of cynicism that is first seen in letters of 1811 to Kirkpatrick Sharpe.[31] She had always been a gossip, but now this tendency increased, and to her frank criticism a new tincture of malice was added. It was time to break away, and she did so by using a real or pretended illness as a pretext to resign her post. The loss of her salary was a hardship, and reasons of economy as well as the love of travel implanted during her girlhood drove her abroad. In July 1814, soon after the peace with France, she crossed the Channel with some of her children. An invigorating stay in Paris was followed by a tour of Eastern France ending in Geneva, where she rented a house for several months.

Geneva at that time was a magnet for great minds of all nations, and Lady Charlotte's capacity for ungrudging wonder at the superior intellect of others was strongly stimulated, not least by the presence of Mme de Staël and the Swiss historian and economist Jean Charles de Sismondi. The former died three years later, but her friendship with the latter lasted three decades and confirmed her in the liberal views she had formed growing up at Inveraray. For the present, her mental pleasures were interrupted when the Princess of Wales, who had gained a large pension from the British government on condition that she leave the country, made a brief visit to Geneva. Lady Charlotte felt obliged to give her former mistress a ball, at which that lady appeared semi-naked and danced all night. In late 1814 the Campbell party took a meandering route to Nice, another resort of the international set but a disappointment to our heroine, who found it a claustrophobic place seething with petty quarrels and jealousies.

The stagnant life at Nice was given a jolt in March 1815 by the news that Napoleon had escaped from his exile on Elba and landed at Golfe-Juan, soon to begin his march on Paris. The British in France had to leave in a hurry, and Lady Charlotte and her family did so aboard the *Clorinde*, a small ship sent by the Princess of Wales from Genoa. After this rescue she could scarcely refuse to rejoin the princess's suite in Genoa and then Milan, but this meant once more submitting to her easy-going ways. The wit Samuel Rogers, also in Italy, later reproduced a specimen of these in his table-talk:

> I once travelled during a whole night in the same carriage with her and Lady Charlotte Campbell; when the shortness of her majesty's legs not allowing her to rest them on the seat opposite, she wheeled herself round and very coolly placed them on the lap of Lady Charlotte, who was sitting next to her.[32]

Worse than such slovenliness were Caroline's apparent compulsion to make a fool of herself in public and the thinly disguised carnality of her relations with Bartolomeo Bergami, her former courier. In May Lady Charlotte left her for good. She was the last British attendant to quit a service that no woman could now perform without staining her own reputation.

After seeing something of Rome she turned homeward. She took a house in London, established a literary salon, and befriended more men of mark. She gave sympathy and practical help to the Italian poet Ugo Foscolo, who was depressed and poor in his British exile and would never forget her kindness. Benjamin Constant came to her home, where he read to a small audience from the manuscript of his forthcoming novel *Adolphe*. She returned to Edinburgh and was in high demand there, and twice she was invited to the court of Queen Charlotte, who, like her son the regent, forgave her connection with the Princess of Wales. Meanwhile the young Princess Charlotte, mindful of her 'state of distress & her amiability', wished to take her into her own household, but nothing came of this scheme.[33] The distress was real, and she tried to live cheaply in Worthing and at Sydenham in Kent. Then, in July 1817, she and some of her daughters left for Italy again, this time for a stay of several years.

When they reached Florence, where they stayed longest, they used every contrivance known to the indigent upper classes to make their money last. This enabled them to socialise decently with the British community and accept invitations to the Tuscan court. Lady Charlotte was valued for herself but also for her troop of daughters, intelligent, well-read girls and good linguists with a plentiful measure of their mother's looks. 'How you *have* strewed the land with beauty!' Thomas Moore once exclaimed to her.[34] Eliza, the eldest, had married Sir William Gordon Cumming in 1815; Eleanora, the second, married the Earl of Uxbridge in 1819; and Beaujolois, the third, who wrote a journal of their Florentine residence, married Viscount Tullamore in 1821. Adelaide, Emma and Julia were still children. Her younger surviving son John was left at home, while Walter Frederick was on a grand tour with his tutor. Lady Charlotte had not been with her children constantly when they were small, and now she was more a good-natured companion to them than a figure of authority.

After their final parting Lady Charlotte still corresponded with the Princess of Wales, who, though hurt by her defection in Milan, remained fond of her former lady of the bedchamber. Her lifestyle grew more disreputable, and the sadness her old retainer felt on this score suggests that her attachment, too, was real. In 1820 the regent became king and the princess returned to England to take her place as queen, but his spies had gathered enough evidence of her misdeeds abroad for him to seek a divorce from parliament. Lady Charlotte, still in Italy at this time, was called as a witness for the defence and gladly made the journey to London to give the best account she could of the queen's conduct. After lengthy debates effectively amounting to a public trial, the Pains and Penalties Bill failed to complete its progress through the legislature. However, the following year the queen was physically barred from attending the coronation and died not long afterwards.

Before she played her minor role in these momentous events a major change took place in Lady Charlotte's private life. On leaving for Italy in 1817 she had been a widow eight years, and her diary shows that the weakness for male beauty that had led her to marry someone with nothing else to recommend him remained strong. She noted handsome men she met, and she referred to one as 'the flower of the flock' for looks among her acquaintance in Geneva.[35] Thus it is natural that the Rev. Edward John Bury, her son Walter's tutor, should have caught her eye on the occasions their itineraries brought them together. He was a young man of obscure but respectable family, who after taking a degree at Oxford had been appointed to the rectory of Litchfield, Hampshire, though he seems never to have officiated there in person. In 1817 the Duke of Argyll presented him at court just before his departure for the Continent, and given Lady Charlotte's financial straits it is likely the duke paid his salary.

Bury was a cultured man and a considerable amateur artist. In Beaujolois' journal he comes across as meek and studious, but others saw a flashiness of appearance and manner. To Walter Scott he was 'an egregious fop but a fine draughtsman' and 'a thorough paced coxcomb – with some accomplishments however'. Having expensive tastes and a lack of the wherewithal to satisfy them, he was probably glad of his post as a private tutor, which was undemanding, enlarged his income, and gave him a chance to travel. Unfortunately, becoming a paid member of a household took him beneath the social class into which he had been born. Lady Charlotte knew she would court disapproval by marrying him, but, as she told Eliza, the prospect was still sweet: 'Alas? I have never yet known happiness. I swear I never have.' They had similar interests, she said, and it was delightful to be prized for her mind: '[He has] a high consideration for my intellectual endowments and a pride in me as a Being of no common order.'[36]

In March 1818 Lady Charlotte took a second step downwards in society when she and Mr Bury were married at the house of the British minister in Florence. She was forty-three and, with Eliza's first child just born, a grandmother. The bridegroom was some fifteen years her junior. She had cast about for wedding guests among the city's British colony, and some had answered the call. Her letters to one of these, Elizabeth, Lady Fremantle, show deep gratitude for solidarity along with pain at forcing people to make an awkward choice. The British press reported the nuptials in a ceremonious tone laced with irony. For wags the middle-aged aristocrat marrying her son's tutor was irresistible. Lady Williams Wynn told a friend, 'I must tell you that she on her change of name was denominated Lady *Goose-berry*, which I think is certainly no mis-nomer.' But if she was a fool, no one should despise her, said the scientist Sir John Playfair:

After all, it is an action on her part more unwise than wrong, and I think ought not to be visited with the continuance of indignation and reproach. It brings her down a step below the *heroic* level to which her conduct and her beauty (for this last had its full share in fixing our opinions) had raised her in the estimation of the world, but she still remains at a height much above the common run of Men and Women even of her own rank.

Finally, Walter Scott, a little ungallantly, grieved over his 'old friend Lady Charlotte who has made a sad mess of it. Our Scottish proverb says there is no fool like an old fool.'[37]

Her harshest judges were her children. She implored Eliza, Lady Gordon Cumming, not to spurn her, but received only chilly acquiescence in return. Walter, who had begged her on his knees to think again, reacted with fury, cutting off her small allowance from the estate he had inherited from his father's family. Beaujolois was distraught and her Florentine journal came to a stuttering halt; two pages, presumably of emotional outpourings, were torn from it.[38] Walter fairly soon patched things up with his mother and stepfather, and his sisters accompanying her in Italy had to make the best of it, and of the additional blow to their pride when the Burys' daughter Bianca (Blanche) was born in July 1819. Eleanora's good marriage a month later and the courtship of Beaujolois and Lord Tullamore, who presently wed, were welcome distractions. Together the Burys and Campbells explored Tuscany and then settled in Rome, where Lady Charlotte held 'conversation parties' and Lorenzo Bartolini made a sculpture of her youngest daughters Emma and Julia.

In 1820 Lady Charlotte Bury and her family went to London for the queen's trial. Her attendance gave a fillip to her sagging celebrity, and she must have been pleased her good character was taken for granted even if she disliked being described as 'tall, fat' or 'rather fat'. She went to some high-society parties, without her husband, but a rebuff from an old friend showed that what her granddaughter Lady Russell called her 'unfortunate change of name' was not forgotten.[39] Sometimes she rubbed shoulders with the intelligentsia instead. She also returned to writing. *Conduct is Fate* (1822), a picaresque novel with a Swiss governess as its heroine, and *Alla Giornata* (1826), a romance set during the Crusades, were dilettantish efforts drawing on her knowledge of Italy. Neither got much attention from the press, and nor did *Suspirium Sanctorum, or Holy Breathings* (1826), prayers in verse for each day of the month, which Thackeray lampooned as 'Heavenly Chords; A Collection of Sacred Strains: Selected, Composed, and Edited, by the Lady Juliana Frances Flummery'.[40]

Lady Charlotte's remarriage was still a source of friction with her children, and it was the relationship with Eliza, who had reacted temperately at first, that frayed the most. Guided by her strait-laced husband, Eliza said she would only see her mother without Mr Bury.

Her elder siblings followed suit, and Lady Charlotte, roused to anger, refused to meet any of them who would not meet him too.[41] She did not regret her second exchange of vows. Five years after it she wrote:

> In my husband I am really bless'd. He has his faults, like us all, but as a husband has as few as possible – inexpressibly careful and tender of me – quite lover-like, never leaving me, and all his tastes and pursuits those which are most refined and most of a nature to keep him constantly at my side; indeed he has no wish ever to leave me and his child for a moment.[42]

Meanwhile her brother John had divorced his wife in 1808. Lady Charlotte nursed him when he was ill in London in 1816, and he made a happy second marriage in 1820. In 1810 her brother George, Duke of Argyll, had caused a stir by uniting himself with Caroline, Lady Paget, a divorced woman involved in a partner-swapping tangle. Lady Charlotte could not warm to the duchess and rarely visited Inveraray once she was established there. Her sister Augusta is not mentioned in her surviving correspondence, and we hear next to nothing about her younger son John, who married in 1824.

Happy as a wife and unhappy as a mother, Lady Charlotte had good and bad times in the early 1820s. But the black cloud of money troubles always glowered above her, the more so as she had an inactive spouse to maintain. She needed to turn breadwinner, and the means of doing so lay to hand. So far she had earned nothing from her writings; now she would be a commercial author. Her natural partner was Henry Colburn, the greatest puffer among publishers and the foremost purveyor of the Silver Fork novels that dominated the market for fiction from the 1820s until the 1840s. These novels depict the customs and trappings of high society in the streets and squares of Mayfair, large country houses and elegant watering places. Plots are driven by love, marriage and money, and casts of characters include idle young lords, bossy dowagers, spoilt daughters, possessive lovers, selfish uncles, selfless heiresses and unrefined *nouveaux riches*. It was a formulaic school of writing, and the individuality of its practitioners struggled to break though.

Colburn saw in Lady Charlotte not a unique talent to nurture, but someone who could meet his and his readers' requirements, and her being a duke's daughter and a former lady-in-waiting meant he could cry her up as a delineator of the best set. She, for her part, grasped the paradox central to the success of Silver Fork fiction: it titillated middle-class readers with peeps at the aristocratic world while gratifying them with the assurance that this world, unlike the worthy but rather dull one they inhabited, was dissolute, enervated and worthless. *Flirtation*, her first Colburn title, published in 1827, fits this bill. It exhibits two sisters: one cold, flaunting and artful; the other warm, modest and naïve. The former yields to the pleasures of flirtation and is punished by falling prey to a villain; the latter is rewarded for her devotion to others with a happy marriage to the ideal hero. The aim of the book, directly stated at intervals, is to show the corrupting effects on a woman's character of the temptation to flirt and of the desire to shine in fashionable society.

The Colburn machine was cranked up, and his puffs, masked as news items, appeared across the national and provincial press. Lady Charlotte's name was not on the title page, so he speculated that she was the author and then, as if anyone had doubted it, confirmed this wonderful fact. Her noble birth and connections, her piquant portrayal of high society, and her exposure of its vices were set forth countless times. Best of all, it seemed that the novel 'sketched from life two sisters, lately celebrated, in the *haut monde*, for their beauty, their accomplishments, the romantic singularity of their story, and the melancholy contrast of their destinies'. Who could they be? No one knew, and Colburn least of all. A complimentary letter from George IV to the author was a slice of good fortune that he exploited to the full. Finally, reviews, some of his own commissioning, were positive, and the service the work rendered by demonstrating the evil effects of flirtation was solemnly praised. The consequence of all this, very unfamiliar to Lady Charlotte, was three editions in a year.

Having started, she did not stop. The next decade saw a stream of novels, of which the titles indicate their genre: *The Exclusives, The Separation, The Disinherited, The Ensnared, The Devoted, The Divorced* and *Love*. At least some of these titles are likely to have been chosen by Colburn or by Richard Bentley, his rival turned partner who also published Lady Charlotte. Each book was advertised in the standard way, often with quotes from reviews, and further promoted with a selection of tried-and-tested manoeuvres: emphasis on the author's aristocratic credentials; praise for her depiction of social usages and all-round finesse; news, presented first as rumour and then as fact, that a story was based on real incidents and people; the judgement, apparently widely held, that the author's handling of her subject was morally instructive; and the joyful intelligence that the book was being extensively read and discussed. It is true that some critics not beholden to Colburn or Bentley thought well of Lady Charlotte's output. Others did not.

Her novels so resemble those of other Silver Forkists, Catherine Gore and Lady Blessington in particular, that a minute examination of style would be needed to tell them apart. Plots are impelled by creaky devices like chance encounters, misdirected letters and disclosed secrets. Characters are staples from the Silver Fork catalogue, many of them implausibly high-minded or evil. They are too wooden for their emotional self-communing or their moves on the chessboard of love to be even slightly engaging. Narratives move at a snail's pace or are stalled by drawn-out dialogues on general subjects that serve only to show the inanity of bored worldlings, often during set pieces at the opera, London dinners and country house parties. The author indulges in her own digressions, and it is interesting given her earlier trendsetting that some of these are on fashions in female dress. This padding makes her thin stories fill out Colburn's regulation three volumes, over 900 pages of print.

Lady Charlotte is also conventional in castigating the heartless artifice of high society and the craven snobbery of those who strive to join it. Not that she was untrue to herself on this score, for such attitudes were alien to her innate cordiality, and her critique often takes the form of frank, ingenuous characters colliding with the jaded cynicism of those around them. Nor was she really betraying her peer group, for although publishers' puffs dwelt on her elevated rank, inferior marriages and relative poverty had pushed her from the core of the class she belonged to by birth and given her an outsider's view. She readily adopted the Silver Fork line on the callous, amoral upper classes, and the school's highest-born author became their harshest judge. At the same time, she was intelligent enough to perceive that moralising about the idle elite was a sop for the consciences of readers who were being just as idle in letting their imaginations roam among the gilded saloons of the West End.

Had Lady Charlotte ever wished to stray from the beaten path, Colburn and Bentley would no doubt have ushered her back onto it. There are some minor features of her novels that look personal. She offloads her own verses and shows her learning with chapter epigraphs from great authors. She indulges in florid scene painting and the travelogue style of writing, something first essayed in the diary of 1805–1810. She shows flashes of humour, some in allusions to the physical aspect of love, and parades the amiable foibles and dialect of lower-class figures. And she is fond of general reflections, often distilled into maxims – this too an echo of the early diary:

> True politeness is a beautiful polish; nay more, it is a valuable lustre on worth and character; for it is the offspring of good feeling, and good feeling cannot bear to give pain.

There is always something in the manner and tone of one who is not downright and sincere which is easily understood by another who is likewise playing a part.[43]

But none of these features is unique to Lady Charlotte Bury; indeed, they are far from unusual among the novelists of the day.

Let us now turn from generalities to a specimen of her craft. The subject of *The Exclusives*, published by Colburn and Bentley in 1830, is indicated by its title, and the author states early on that her approach to it will be ethical. In particular she will reveal the baneful influence of gossip, inquisitiveness and boredom on fashionable life. A novel can do this better than a sermon, she goes on, for it depicts what it deplores, including its surface attractions.[44] In the opening chapter Lady Tilney, who is respected and feared as the despot of society, muses on how best to quash her younger rival the Duchess of Hermanton. With her acolytes she hatches a plan to heighten exclusivity by forming an inner group from which the insufficiently refined will be barred. Her opening move is a party on an evening already chosen for her own entertainment by a hostess whose light she wishes to dim. As Lady Tilney's guests circulate solemnly round her rooms, their only joy lies in knowing they belong to a new elect.

At this gathering we meet the handsome Lord Albert D'Esterre, a rising politician who is informally betrothed to his cousin Lady Adeline Seymour, hailed by another character as 'a world's wonder of beauty, and purity, and perfection'.[45] In the early chapters he is in London while she tends her sickly mother at their family seat in Wales, where she attracts the attention of the fortune hunter George Foley. Lady Adeline loves Lord Albert, as he does her, but Mr Foley, as a first step towards his goal, succeeds in becoming her trusted friend. Meanwhile in London the louche young widow Lady Hamlet Vernon decides to test her mettle by prising Lord Albert away from Lady Adeline. To this end she deploys bouts of illness, a show of literary sensitivity, feigned interest in his moral precepts, hints at her rival's supposed fondness for Mr Foley, and her own bewitching air. At the same time she and Mr Foley begin to correspond and plot together.

As Lady Hamlet Vernon fills Lord Albert's mind he also absorbs her insinuations about his beloved. When Lady Adeline finally arrives in London, eager to be reunited with him, she finds him chilly and constrained. One misapprehension begets another, some of them fostered by the two schemers. Lady Adeline faints after espying Lord Alfred in a box at the opera with Lady Hamlet Vernon, and when he rushes over, her aunt, offended by his recent behaviour, rejects his offer of assistance but accepts that of Mr Foley. Opportunities for explanations are missed or thwarted, and Lord Albert, assuming he has been thrown over, yields yet more to the pleasure of Lady Hamlet Vernon's company. This is observed by Lady Adeline, who imagines it is she who is rejected. A chance meeting makes Lord Albert realise he loves her as much as ever, but by this time the tangle of errors is impossible to unpick. She and her mother depart for Wales, and soon it is known that Mr Foley is visiting them there.

His betrothal to Lady Adeline now broken off, Lord Alfred dulls his pain by devoting himself to Lady Hamlet Vernon, and before long he proposes marriage and is accepted. The engagement does not last long, however, for a letter of hers to George Foley is mistakenly addressed to him and opens his eyes. The subject of this letter is the final failure of Mr Foley's pursuit of Lady Adeline, and in it the nature of their machinations is laid bare. Lord Alfred is horrified to discover Lady Hamlet Vernon's infamy and consumed with remorse about his faithless conduct and his misjudgement of Lady Adeline. After many pages of self-laceration he casts off the false siren, who squirms in disappointed passion and fury, and travels abroad to recover his equanimity. An unexpected meeting with Lady Adeline in Munich allows the love that has not died in the breast of either to be reignited. Soon they are back in England and married.

A second narrative strand features the cabinet minister Lord Glenmore and his naïve young wife. They wed under good auspices, but things go wrong when she befriends Lady Tenderden, a member of Lady Tilney's set, who tells her that to keep her husband's interest she should treat him coolly and permit the homage of other men. Sensing that her impulse to be always at her adored husband's side may seem ridiculous to him, she follows this advice and allows Leslie Winyard to hover round her, oblivious to his notoriety as a pitiless seducer. While the busy Lord Glenmore leaves the wife he loves alone for long periods, and actually encourages her to raise her social profile while he attends to affairs of state, Mr Winyard uses a shared interest in music and adroit responses to her moods to win her esteem. The more she indulges in high-society revels, the more their glamour, and the flattery she receives, become necessary to her, and she grows inured to her husband's frequent absences.

Lady Glenmore's peril increases when she and Lady Tenderden go abroad while Lord Glenmore remains tied to his desk. They are joined in Spa and Paris by Leslie Winyard, who acts the lover's part without being reproved. After Lady Glenmore's return, her husband chances upon the other man's portrait and letters among her effects.

The letters contain nothing positively incriminating but point to a warm attachment, and he demands to be told the truth. Distressed and remorseful, she explains how she has been groomed to act in a manner that was initially alien to her but became habitual. Her confession is, unwittingly, an indictment of Lord Glenmore's neglect, and as she speaks he begins to feel that some blame attaches to him for her waywardness. Her penitence and love call forth his own, and their bond is strengthened in being renewed. The next steps are Lord Glenmore's resignation from his all-consuming post and his wife's withdrawal from the maelstrom of fashionable life.

While this unfolds Lady Tilney continues her attempt to purify society and freeze out the Duchess of Hermanton. Her cronies shun an assembly given by the duchess and one of them omits some of the usual crowd from the guest list for a country house party. A fête of Lady Tilney's is similarly notable for those not invited, including, of course, the outcast duchess. In the end, the reigning queen of society neither succeeds nor fails in her project, but the insolence she shows condemns her in the eyes of every decent person. Nor are she and those around her secure in their ascendancy, for fashion is a protean thing beyond the control of any individual or group. Together, Lady Tilney's coterie and the two main plot strands illustrate how living in the highest circles corrodes the sense of right and wrong. The final paragraph execrates the 'selfishness, heartlessness, and cold over-reaching' of those circles and proclaims 'the moral lesson intended to be covered by this general view of EXCLUSIVE SOCIETY'.[46]

An intriguing aspect of this novel, penned by a celebrity writer, is how it represents celebrity. Publishers of Lady Charlotte's other works could claim that certain characters were based on real people. *The Exclusives* goes further: it is a *roman à clef*, its main figures being portraits of politicians, dandies and society hostesses. The parlour game of identifying these continued until a key was printed to settle the question. The fictionalised personages, the author, the publisher and the press benefited from the publicity, a case of the apparatus of celebrity bringing fame, profit or both to all who partake in it. For celebrities even an unflattering image was welcome, as a dialogue in the author's first Silver Fork title *Flirtation* suggests. Speaking of a new novel that dresses real people in fictional garb, a character says they will be frightened to see themselves in print. '"Frightened!" said Mr. Lepel [...] "delighted you mean; the generality of people live only upon being talked *of*, or *at*, no matter which, *or how*."'[47]

The Exclusives takes the theme of the nexus of fame and the media further. Lady Tilney says she is glad press freedom makes the private lives of well-known people a public matter. Lady Baskerville, on the other hand, finds it 'quite abominable that those vulgar editors of newspapers should be allowed to comment upon what we do'. Lady Tilney counters: 'Allow me to assure you that we are much more known – much more distinguished – much more *répandus* by being all named occasionally, never mind how or in what manner, in the public papers.' Nobody thinks ill of an adversely noticed person for long anyway, she remarks. The only line she wishes to draw is between those who merit column inches by being in vogue and outsiders who puff themselves: 'There are always a set of would-be fashionables, who pay for the putting in of such paragraphs about themselves, *et l'on sait parfaitement à quoi s'en tenir* respecting them.' Her approach is that of a practised, self-aware celebrity who wants to live and thrive in the public eye.[48]

Another interesting focus of Lady Charlotte's fiction is women's domestic lives. Her private remarks create no expectation of proto-feminist views in her writing. In one letter she asserts that women are hemmed in by their ignorance and prejudice, and in another that no one believes more firmly in wifely duties than she.[49] This is mirrored in the novels by repeated statements that a wife must defer to her husband, that her only ambition should be for him, and that her sphere is household management. Yet simply by depicting women's vulnerability she exposes injustice, and her realism is arguably more eloquent than decrials or calls for change would be. For example *The Divorced* (1837), the first book to which she put her name, shows double standards in regard to female and male divorcees. Its sympathetic portrayal of the financially and socially blighted life of the protagonist, who yielded to a temptation that ended her first marriage, implicitly censures the harsh moral code.

More radical is Lady Charlotte's treatment of domestic abuse, a subject near to her heart and rarely discussed in or out of literature at this time. It first appears in *Conduct is Fate*, in which the heroine elopes with a fortune hunter who grows neglectful and then violent. In *The Ensnared* a woman leaves her husband for a lover, who tires of her and becomes abusive. In *Love* an aristocrat beats his wife for years while carrying on affairs. And in *The Manoeuvring Mother* a young wife suffers physical cruelty and dies in misery. The few reactions to this topic were negative. William Blackwood, who published *Conduct is Fate*, found it distasteful and thought British readers were 'not accustomed to a husband knocking down his wife, nor yet to some other traits of Continental manners'. And Thackeray, in a review of

Love, scoffed at the idea of well-born men kicking their wives out of bed and flogging them. His mocking tone reflects little credit on him.[50]

Other than in their handling of celebrity and of spousal abuse, Lady Charlotte's novels were, as has been said, very conventional. The need for money was the mainspring of her authorship and she worked in a hurry. 'Writing to coin money is slavery to body and mind,' she told Kirkpatrick Sharpe. 'I am that slave.'[51] She did her best and had things she wanted to say, but all was trimmed to fit the demands of publishers and readers. Calibrating the real opinions of reviewers is made difficult by not knowing exactly which pens were in the pay of her publishers, which were hostile to them (as some were), and which were neutral. She certainly had some disinterested praise. In 1837 *John Bull*, definitely not a Colburn or Bentley organ, called her 'one of our most delightful fiction-mongers'. She was in the front rank of the Silver Fork School, and according to newspapers Colburn gave her £1,000 for *Flirtation*, though later the visiting American journalist Nathaniel Parker Willis claimed she got a modest £200 per book.[52]

To augment her income she engaged in other literary work. She wrote *The Lady's Own Cookery Book* and edited *A Marriage in High Life* by Caroline, Lady Scott and *Memoirs of a Peeress* by Catherine Gore. She was a prolific contributor to annuals – finely illustrated and bound collections of poems, short stories and articles, usually with a popular writer as editor. They were not high-brow, but because their publishers paid well they drew on the best talents. Lady Charlotte published small pieces of prose and verse in the *Journal of the Heart*, *The English Annual*, *Heath's Book of Beauty*, *The Keepsake* and *The Christmas Box*, and she edited the first title more than once. As a Colburn writer she naturally appeared in his *New Monthly Magazine*. This spread her renown, not least as issues she was associated with often contained an engraving of her, as did John Burke's *Portrait Gallery of Distinguished Females* of 1833.

These texts and images were noticed in the press, which also reprinted parts of periodical reviews, excerpted passages from her novels, and carried advertisements for cheap editions of her works. An issue of the *Ladies' Pocket Magazine and Gem of Fashion* was dedicated to her, as were Barry King's serenade 'Awake Thee Rosalie' and one of John Weippert's 'Lothian Quadrilles'. She appeared as a character in *Mephistophiles in England*, a political novel by Robert Folkestone Williams, and Walter Scott's lines on receiving her verse juvenilia found their way into newspaper columns. Now and again her earlier glories were recalled, and in 1827 many papers printed an effusion of the writer Sir Henry Bate Dudley:

Look what a shape!
Limbs fondly fashioned in the wanton mould
Of Nature – warm in love's sly witcheries;
And scorning all the drapery of Art.
A spider's loom now weaves her thin attire;
Through which the roguish airs and tell-tale winds
Do frolic as they list.

And in 1838 a writer in the *Monthly Repository* reminisced that she had once 'made her appearance at a masquerade in the character of Venus, and presented an appearance so very like Venus, both as to beauty and to looseness of attire, as to scandalise the town'.[53]

From the early 1830s Lady Charlotte cut a figure in the world of letters only. A woman who wrote for a living, turned her rank to commercial advantage, ran down the aristocracy in print, and was not above publishing a cookbook could have little credit in the *beau monde*. For the third time she had gone down a rung on the social ladder, and she was now rarely mentioned in fashionable movements columns. More often, as other sources show, she was in the company of writers, painters, reviewers and newspaper editors. At a literary party of 1830 she and Maria Edgeworth were the 'two Lionesses', according to the latter.[54] Although come down in the world, she was still fully respectable as well as renowned in her field, and she was welcome at the homely court of William IV and Queen Adelaide. She attended the queen's drawing rooms and other royal occasions and was invited to see her by private appointment.

Eyewitnesses give an idea of her person and manner in her first decade as a successful novelist. In 1827 Prince Pückler-Muskau found she was still recognisable as the woman in Hoppner's portrait, and, echoing Foscolo, he said she was one of the most likeable women he had met in England and he would not forget her kindness to him. In 1829 the poet Anne Grant thought her 'certainly much changed in appearance, though her charming manners, all ease and simplicity, are unchanged'. Maria Edgeworth, a year later, left a more detailed impression:

She must have been a very fine perhaps beautiful woman with a fair complexion and bright color but on a very large bold scale and now the remains are melancholy not interesting. She dresses too young and is not well made-up – her own gray hair coming here and there into view between the false – too evidently false masses of brown. Her own hair is dragged up some way so that it gave me a pain at my temples to look at her. Her mouth once beautiful is now all fallen in and she is like a much worn antique bust.

In a kinder vein, the same writer observed that 'her voice and conversation are both agreeable – unaffected – free from authorship pretension or pretension of any sort.' Lastly, Thomas Moore in 1833 found her so altered from what she had been that he did not know her until she spoke to him and invited him to call on her at her modest lodgings over a grocer's shop.[55]

When she moved to this habitation Lady Charlotte was a widow again, for after a long illness Edward John Bury had died in June 1832, aged forty-two. This time she did not have to whip up feelings of grief to prove her romantic sensibility. Many people had been dubious about Mr Bury, and most assumed he was sponging on her, but she thought him the best of husbands. Some notices of his death mentioned that he had been working on illustrations for a book she was writing about Italy. Completing *The Three Great Sanctuaries of Tuscany* must have been a solace to her, and it opens with a loving tribute to him. Reviewers commended her historical essays and poems on the monasteries of Vallombrosa, Camaldoli and Laverna and responded to his pencil drawings with delight. 'A treat rarely to be found on canvass or on paper', wrote the *Morning Post*, while the *Quarterly Review* thought his 'exquisite engravings' proved that 'the world has lost a truly great artist.' Some years earlier, Sir Thomas Lawrence had seen Bury's work and called him 'a man of genius'.[56]

Meanwhile, bonds with the children of her first marriage had healed after the rupture created by her second. Walter restored her allowance and named the new settlement of Port Charlotte after her on his island of Islay. She could also be glad that despite having no portions her younger Campbell daughters all found husbands. There was sorrow too. In 1828 her daughter Eleanora, Lady Uxbridge, died aged thirty; in 1830 her younger son John followed her; and in 1831 her sister Augusta's tormented life ended. Her daughter Beaujolois, Lady Tullamore had a fast reputation, though she just about held on to her respectability. A note she appended to a letter received from her mother in 1832 indicates a lack of trust between them.[57] Lady Charlotte remained close to her brother John, and it was at his home in Dunbartonshire that Mr Bury spent his last days. In the case of George the coolness between her and his wife kept them apart, though brother and sister were never on bad terms themselves.

Money was still an acute problem, and because Lady Charlotte was always hard up she sold copyrights to her works straight off and earned no royalties if they did well or from later reissues. In 1831, while her husband was still alive, she sent a begging letter to Lord Brougham, now lord chancellor in the Grey government. It gives her history and refutes the notion that Mr Bury's extravagance was to blame for her plight. 'I end as I began by imploring You Dear Lord Brougham to do something for us. I am in the greatest distress.' Then came reports that she was selling some curios, and a series of humble, rather forlorn letters to Mrs Wyndham Lewis of 1832–1833 suggest that the wealthy political wife was discreetly supporting her. She dedicated *The Disinherited; and The Ensnared* to the botanist Aylmer Bourke Lambert in 1834 to thank him for having afforded her 'asylum at a time of distress and destitution'. And in a letter of 1838 to her daughter Eliza she called herself a 'poor beggar'.[58]

This is the context of the great controversy of our heroine's life, which caused her fourth and biggest step down the social scale. We have seen that she kept a diary of her life as a courtier, and this, with all its indiscretions, she now placed before the public as *Diary Illustrative of the Times of George the Fourth, Interspersed with Original Letters from the Late Queen Caroline and from Various Other Distinguished Persons*. Her granddaughter Lady Russell tried to wash away this stain on her honour by claiming that Mr Bury revised the manuscript and had it published without her knowledge.[59] However, since that reverend gentleman was long dead when the book appeared in 1838–1839 this can be discounted. The truth is that Lady Charlotte, in desperate straits, offered it to Colburn. It was said he gave her £1,000, and if so he made an excellent bargain. He puffed away as usual, but for once his canny techniques were not required. With its shocking revelations about the royal family and other powerful figures, this was a book that sold itself.

The bulk of its four volumes comprises Lady Charlotte's diary and letters she got from friends. Her name is absent from the title pages, but, either because she was aghast at what she was doing or because Colburn thought obfuscation might sharpen the work's appeal, further steps were taken to hide her from view. The keeper of the diary and recipient of the letters is not identified, and doctoring of the text produces a diarist-cum-author, presented as male, who mentions her in the third person – neutrally or positively, but always dispassionately. He is with her when she ships from Nice to Genoa to join Princess Caroline, who receives them both. Her name appears in some of the letters as a third party and at one point she is a speaking character. Numerous footnotes by an editor elucidating or quibbling with the text, a disquisition on the legal case against the princess, essays on notabilities of the regency and reign of George IV and other extraneous items are clearly not Lady Charlotte's work.

Much of this addition and alteration can be laid to the account of the novelist and literary hack John Galt, who is acknowledged as editor in the last two volumes. Not that his and unknown others' input really screened the author, for only she, with her experiences and acquaintances, could have written the diary or received the letters. Jarring elements such as confused dating, discontinuities, passages obviously interpolated later, and inconsistent practice in naming and suppressing names suggest the book was hurriedly cobbled together, but perhaps give it an air of authenticity. Lady Charlotte's hand is seen in mawkish verses strewn amid the prose, voyeuristic glimpses of high society, moral censure of that society, and trite philosophising, all of which recall her novels; in gossip about her friends and sketches of people she met at home and abroad; and in polished slabs of descriptive text, possibly imported from an Italian travelogue she had written but not published.

At the centre of the book is Princess Caroline, and here Lady Charlotte had a balancing act to perform. To appear as a trustworthy witness, she had to make plain her connection with the princess's court while distancing herself from its laxity. Authorial respectability mattered personally, in the event of her anonymity being breached, but also to the perceived truth-value of the *Diary*. Her strategy was to criticise the princess freely: her shallowness, unseemly familiarity, recklessness and so on. She let her damn herself as well by printing some of her silly, spiteful letters. Her facial expressions and physique are not spared, and nor are amusing Teutonisms like 'Mine Gott! Dat is de dullest person Gott Almighty ever did born!' Most damaging are allusions to her sexual licence. Yet Lady Charlotte is a friend too, showing her as a gracious, soft-hearted woman who was persecuted by her husband and exploited by politicians: 'Poor Princess! she was an ill-treated woman, but a very wrong-headed one.'[60]

The Prince of Wales comes off worse. He had, says the author, 'a vindictiveness in his character which makes it quite odious'. She gives her employer's sordid account of his behaviour on their wedding night as well as details of his mistresses and intrigues and the skulduggery of his hangers-on. Many were struck by the scene in which the princess makes a wax effigy of her husband adorned with horns and then pierces it through and through with pins before throwing it in the fire.[61] More serious was the revelation of flaws in Princess Charlotte's character and her hatred for her grandmother and namesake, which ran counter to the hagiographical tone that dominated after her death in childbirth in 1817. All in all, courts are represented as nests of insincerity, exploitation and loathing. Finally, to add spice to the scandal, the letters in the book, all printed without their writers' leave, bristle with salacious and disobliging comments about persons still living, as do the pages of Lady Charlotte's diary.

The book was a sensation, and several editions came out in a short space of time. 'For the last month nothing has been thought of or talked of but the *Diary*,' wrote the novelist Lady Morgan. The letter-writer Lady Louisa Molyneux also found it the universal topic, 'more, it appears, from its atrocity than from any merit it has'.[62] It succeeded by promising and delivering scandal, but had its sale been determined by critics it would have been meagre indeed. Periodicals, led by the *Quarterly Review* and the *Edinburgh Review*, were severe, as were newspapers. They berated the author for denigrating the woman who had paid her a salary, betraying her correspondents, and belittling many others. *Bell's Weekly Messenger* pleaded that the book contained 'harsh and unnecessary gossiping' but no actual slander, and the *Champion* and the *Dublin Evening Packet* thought the author was an amusing chronicler although she had certainly misbehaved.

People enjoyed the fuss even as they slashed away at the person who had caused it. The juiciest extracts were printed in one newspaper after another, and the *Comic Annual* produced epigrams, of which one is printed in the *Courier*:

> THE LAST WISH
> When I resign this world so briary
> To have across the Styx my ferrying,
> O, may I die without a Diary!
> And be interr'd without a Bury-ing!

Thackeray, who could not let Lady Charlotte alone, had his fun in *Fraser's Magazine* by adopting the servile, simple-minded persona of Charles Yellowplush, who could not believe that a nobly born author would act dishonourably, write for money or betray her benefactor. For others it was too serious for jest. The political diarist Charles Greville spoke for many in calling the book 'catchpenny trash' and fearing it might herald a slew of similar offerings, though surely nothing worse, 'for nobody could by possibility compile or compose anything more vile and despicable.'[63]

No one was taken in by the mystification about the author, who was identified by name in reviews. Even Colburn, who might have felt honour-bound to uphold her anonymity, allowed his pet periodical the *Literary Gazette* to hint and then confirm that the book was hers. Those she had singed squealed loudly or put on a show of offended dignity. Here is Charles Kirkpatrick Sharpe on seeing his epistolary froth in print:

> I cannot express my vexation about the book you mention. [...] When I wrote the silly, impertinent letters in question, between twenty and thirty years ago, I knew that I was writing to the Duke of Argyle's daughter, and thought myself safe by all the common rules of good-breeding and morality. But I find I was extremely deceived.

The judgements of others struck an ominous note for the miscreant. Lady Louisa Molyneux said the book contained 'so many bad stories ill told, and so many personal remarks on living people, that I cannot imagine anybody ever speaking to her again'. Lord Grey agreed: 'She ought to be excluded from society.'[64] She had probably hoped that by not acknowledging the work and keeping a low profile for a while she could weather the storm. Now she saw she could not.

In her anxiety Lady Charlotte took the futile step of actively disavowing authorship. She had her solicitor draw up a statement to this effect, which was printed or reported in many newspapers. An open letter from a son of John Galt accused her of taking advantage of his death in April 1839, before volumes three and four went on sale, to claim that he was the culprit:

> Lady Charlotte has been, and is still, indefatigable in endeavouring to attribute to him only the entire odium of collecting the papers and writing the connecting narrative. She hopes to be again received in courtly society by thus throwing the scandal on the dead – for the tomb tells no tales.

She even dissimulated in a letter to her daughter Eliza: 'Everyone who says that abominable book is mine I consider to be My Enemy – it is unwarrantable to affix My name to an Anonymous work.'[65] It was to no avail, and another round of announcements in the press declared the question of her authorship to be settled.

The only real defender of the *Diary* in print was, ironically, John Galt in his posthumous preface to the third volume. He asserted that no critic had found errors of fact in the book and that, far from traducing Caroline, it judged her fairly and in some ways vindicated her. The charge of indecency was ludicrous, he went on, when equally indiscreet memoirs were rolling off the presses all the time. Finally, the *Diary* was a rich mine of information on its period and would 'undoubtedly remain a standard work for historians to refer to', a prediction that has been borne out. These arguments would not have moved those keen to express outrage on their own or others' behalf. Nor, probably, would these reflections in an article by Nathaniel Parker Willis for the American periodical *The Corsair*:

> This lady has, as they say in London, 'got herself into a precious mess with her "Life and Times of George the Fourth."' One or two of her friends, I was told, made an effort to receive her, but it was found that her company was *malsain*, and she is now cut altogether. I was expressing a regret, at a dinner party, that she should have been so unwise, when a lady of some celebrity present objected to the phrase. 'Why unwise?' she said; 'Lady Charlotte was starving in the midst of these 500 friends, who would not have lent her a guinea to save her life. She had the opportunity of choosing between these friends and a thousand pounds. Why would she hesitate?'[66]

She put a brave face on her ostracism. 'Many of my soi-disant Old Friends have cut me but I have made Many New Ones – and they do quite as well,' she told Eliza.[67] Press reports that 'a most Illustrious Personage', in other words Queen Victoria, had cautioned her to stay away from court made her ignominy complete. However, as foreign visitors noted, British society had a short attention span and its disfavour was often brief. In any case, fair-minded folk would have sensed that Lady Charlotte was good at heart and concurred with her self-appraisal in a letter to Sismondi: 'Thus much I can say with truth, I never was the first to change either in Friendship or in Love, and I can add (thank God) whatever unfortunate circumstances may have led to the supposition of the contrary that I never really wish to do any living creature harm.'[68] So the ban was lifted. She attended a queen's drawing room in 1840, and in the same year the papers named her among 'a sprinkling of the higher classes' at the opera and the 'distinguished fashionables' at the theatre.

For the next two years she resumed the grind of novel-writing, producing *The History of a Flirt*, *Family Records* and

The Manoeuvring Mother. In 1844 came *The Wilfulness of Woman*, but after this a long silence. She was almost seventy, and her popularity was in decline along with that of the Silver Fork School. Promotion and reviewing of her titles tailed off, and her migration from publisher to publisher suggests a struggle to get good terms from any. The financial woes that had dogged her whole adult life became public knowledge when creditors turned on her in force in 1841 and her inability to satisfy them led to a proclamation of outlawry. Efforts to reach a settlement inspired punsters: 'An offer of *five shillings* in the pound has been made to the creditors of Lady Charlotte Bury. A *crown* for a *coronet* is liberal indeed!' More humiliation ensued, with an upholsterer going to law against her and an auction of the letters published in the *Diary*. She thus 'turned the last penny' out of them, as one newspaper put it.

For the remainder of her life she mostly lived in rented London houses. In 1840 she visited Inveraray, now home of her brother John, who had succeeded the childless George as Duke of Argyll the year before. She had fond childhood memories of the place and a soft spot for Highland scenery, but little real love for Scotland. She deprecated the 'Coarseness of Scotch Society' and spoke of her 'distaste for the Manners and Habits & Sounds' of Edinburgh, and she was happier in London, 'the only place in Britain worth living in'.[69] She had next to no British national feeling either, despite some patriotic posturing in her novels – another part of the Silver Fork ethos to which she adhered. The country she liked best was Italy, and she kept going there almost to the end of her life. This we learn from press notices and from letters to Sismondi, which show her as a woman buffeted by fate, resigned and fairly uncomplaining, where possible cheerful, and always interested in her surroundings and other people.

The daughter and mother of large families, Lady Charlotte had few intimates in old age. More of her children predeceased her: in 1842 Eliza, after bearing her thirteenth child; in 1848 Beaujolois, a victim of tuberculosis; in 1855 Walter, who had lived in France since his bankruptcy of eight years before; and in 1858 Julia, who had married twice. Only Emma, Mrs William Russell and Adelaide, Lady Arthur Lennox from her first marriage and Blanche from her second outlived her. Her brother John died in 1847. In the 1850s she published two novels, *The Roses* and *The Lady of Fashion*, but they passed almost unnoticed. There was little press about her personally aside from a few banal reports of her movements. In 1855 the *Glasgow Herald* mused even more banally on the merciless march of time: 'The beautiful and fascinating belle, whose name resounded throughout every corner of our island in her early days, is now the old, faded, and decrepid Lady Bury, bending under the load of fourscore years and nearly forgotten by the world.'

On the other hand, the essayist Elizabeth, Lady Eastlake found her still beautiful in 1850. And Susan Ferrier, who had broken with her after the *Diary*, was won over at a meeting of 1851: 'I had a long visit yesterday from Lady C., as soft and caressing as ever, so that I begin to feel the old *glamour* coming over me.' [70] A later glimpse is dismal. Blanche Bury married a wealthy older man, David Lyon, but he left her, citing her use of opiates, and reports of their court battles in 1859 portray Lady Charlotte as a muddled, anxious dependent of her daughter. Finally, she grew 'childish from great age', as Mrs Lyon put it. Where she then went is unclear, but according to Lady Russell her surviving Campbell daughters, friends and relations filled the close of her life with warmth. She received them in a rich satin gown, chinchilla-trimmed mantle and gauze mobcap, sitting very upright in her chair 'with that wonderful manner which was so characteristic of her, a mixture of queenly dignity and gracious urbanity'.[71] This is almost certainly rose-tinted, but let us accept it as a parting view.

Lady Charlotte Bury died aged eighty-six on 31 March 1861. A few paragraphs in the newspapers, printed and reprinted without attribution, reminded readers who she was:

> Lady Charlotte Bury was well known in the paths of literature from her numerous novels and literary contributions some years back.
>
> In her youth Lady Charlotte was remarkable for her personal beauty, and throughout life for the charm of her manners and for her literary talents.
>
> Lady Charlotte Bury, the author of some once fashionable novels, &c., of a very flimsy material, has departed this life. Her literary reputation departed long ago.

More than her loveliness, her dress or her fiction, it was the *Diary*, her mark of shame, that was recalled in these notices. Her greatest renown was born of the exigencies of penury. These, she must have felt, were the remorseless conductor of her life, accompanying and then dictating its downward path. It was a life of frustrated hopes, and words Walter Scott wrote in 1809 only grew more pertinent as time went by: 'I can never think on her without deep emotion, with talents, rank, beauty, accomplishments, above all with the best of human hearts how much she has had to suffer in her passage through this valley of Sorrow.'[72]

* * *

Of the celebrities we have considered so far, only Lady Charlotte Bury recorded a desire for lasting fame and the pain of disappointed ambition. One day, while in the Princess of Wales's service, she accompanied her to the British Museum:

> I was interested in walking through the magnificent library, and in looking at the statues; yet whenever I view these collections my mind is depressed. I devoured with greedy eyes the outside of the volumes, and wished – oh! How vainly – that their contents were stored in my brain. A whole life of learned labour would not suffice for that; what chance have I then, in the middle of my days, of accomplishing such a wish? – Then those beautiful statues, which, even in their mutilated state, testify the glorious conceptions of the minds that formed them! Yes, they breathe the spirit of the departed genius, and will continue to do so, to ages yet unborn; but I – I shall leave nothing to excite one emulative sigh when I am gone! I shall die, and nothing will tell of my existence! But happier far are those who have never indulged a wish for fame. If a few who have loved us in life mourn us when dead, that is the only tribute to our memories which is, in fact, worth seeking for. Down, then, proud thought, of living in after ages! be that which you are destined to be – fulfil the course which is pointed out by Providence, and be content.[73]

Even early readers of this passage in the *Diary* might have found the yearning for the status of 'departed genius' to 'ages yet unborn' an antiquated sentiment. Another type of recognition was at hand, easier to gain and offering more immediate gratifications. However, the ageing process, which embalms the truly famous while they yet live, can be cruel to those who take the shorter route to celebrity and then outlive the interest they have aroused. They might wish they had settled for the fulfilment of immediate duties and fixed their hopes on living after death in the affectionate memories of a few.

5

The Fashionable Artist

Sir Thomas Lawrence

Self-portrait, 1788, by Sir Thomas Lawrence. Denver Art Museum.

On 24 July 1804 Joseph Farington recorded in his diary an arresting remark relayed to him by his fellow artist George Dance:

> Dance mentioned to me that the late Lord Camden had observed to Him that in England everything was open to talents & industry, & the consequence was 'that in half a century the Community might be sd. to be turned upside down,' that is that the rich became poor & the poor rich.[1]

In no field did the former lord chancellor's vision of social mobility come nearer the truth than in art. Dance was the son of an architect and Farington of a rector, but many of their colleagues had humbler origins. Richard Parkes Bonington's father was a lace-maker, David Cox's a blacksmith, J. M. W. Turner's a barber, and John Opie's and Francis Chantrey's were carpenters. And in the years in which they flourished, the most successful painter was an innkeeper's son.

Thomas Lawrence was born on 13 April 1769, and at that time his father, also Thomas, was supervisor of the excise in Bristol. He was a man of obscure origins whose handsome person and facility for writing romantic verse had won him, by the expedient of elopement, a bride above his station. She was Lucy Read, daughter of a pluralist clergyman of Tenbury, Worcestershire. Unfortunately Mr Lawrence lacked the head for business to succeed as a revenue collector or in his subsequent role of landlord of the White Lion, also in Bristol. As an innkeeper he gave his attention to interior decoration, reciting poetry and inserting addresses about his establishment to 'the nobility, gentry, and others' in local newspapers rather than to the mundane but remunerative aspects of his work. In contrast with his noisy self-confidence was the resigned dignity of his wife. She spent their Bristol years bearing children, of whom the future President of the Royal Academy was the fourteenth.

In 1773 Mr Lawrence failed at the White Lion. He used the *Bath Chronicle* to inform the usual three classes of humanity that he had acquired the Black Bear in Devizes, Wiltshire, 'where he humbly intreats a Continuance of their Countenance and Support, assuring them that no Endeavours of his shall be wanting to accommodate and oblige them in a Manner most becoming'. Only five of the couple's offspring lived long enough to make the move to Devizes, and as the years rolled by amid the bustle of a coaching inn it grew apparent that the youngest was a boy of exceptional ability. Under his father's tuition little Tom became a precocious declaimer of Milton and Shakespeare, and in sketching likenesses, which he taught himself, he showed a skill almost miraculous. Mrs Nalder, who superintended the bar at the Black Bear, recalled decades afterwards that he had produced an excellent likeness of her when he was four years old.

People who have known brilliant achievers as children are apt to infuse their early memories of them with a sense of retrospective predestination, so that later renown seems determined by inborn qualities that are discernible at a tender age. Mrs Nalder, speaking of the first efforts of Tom's pencil, is a case in point:

> These portraits, I think I may venture to affirm, were the foundation on which the painter's fame was raised, as from this time numbers of persons became anxious to have their likenesses taken by a child in petticoats, and the reputation which he thereby acquired, was the cause of his talents being at length directed solely to that occupation which nature had so distinctly pointed out for him.

Thus the celebrity narrative opens. One of those who added to it was the novelist Frances Burney, who while staying at the Black Bear was shown the 'most lovely boy', the 'wonder of his family', and knew not whether to admire him or his uninstructed ability more. Another was the Rev. Dr Henry Kent, a local worthy who heard that a young lad had made a caricature of him, but on seeing it, instead of being angry, was so astonished at the performance that he bought him his first box of colours and some books. There are many such accounts, and many claims to priority in discovering him.[2]

He was his parents' idol, and his father took to presenting him to guests at the inn and offering to have him recite poetry or draw their portraits. Some thought the landlord should restrict himself to describing his rooms and giving the bill of fare, and this was the view of the future attorney general Lord Kenyon and his wife, who arrived one day tired and peevish from their journey. Lady Kenyon later recalled that they were on the point of sending their host about his business when the five-year-old boy rushed in and won their hearts. Even when he said he would take her likeness in profile because her face was not straight they could not help laughing. This story is given in the biography D. E. Williams published after the artist's death as one of the many instances when those disposed to resent the father's importunity were 'enraptured' by the son's 'beauty, infantile grace, and genius'.[3]

Tom's gifts, then, were accompanied by comeliness and innate refinement. He was self-possessed beyond his years, making him 'a perfect man in miniature' according to the actor John Bernard, who knew him when he was nine.[4] Adults felt a desire to help him however they could. One left him a legacy, another wanted to send him to be educated in Italy, a third invited him with his father to London to see and copy artworks, and a fourth, the Earl of Warwick's sister, hoped to adopt him. Some tales of the child prodigy and his enlightened well-wishers are of a later date, coloured by the renown of the mature artist, but image-building was already underway, and Mr Lawrence was content to see a cluster of anecdotes form around his son. Indeed, while his paternal pride and hope that Tom would one day be a great man could bring him close to tears, he was also entertaining less sentimental ideas about the immediate future.

These ideas gained urgency when the inept publican had to give up the Black Bear in 1780 and declare bankruptcy. Rather than exert himself further for his family on his own account he used his turn for promotion to set up as an impresario of genius. After touring with the eleven-year-old artist to Oxford, Salisbury and Weymouth, the family settled in fashionable Bath. The showman revived his practice of verbose press advertising, but word of mouth sufficed to ensure that everyone knew of Master Lawrence and wanted to employ him. He had exchanged his pencil for crayons and could produce three or four heads, busts or half-lengths in a week. His prices rose, and after two years his family could move from lodgings to a house near the Assembly Rooms. His patrons included the aristocratic and otherwise notable people who lived in or visited Bath, among them Georgiana, Duchess of Devonshire, of whom he completed a delicate, expressive portrait in 1782, when he was thirteen.

Young Lawrence found avuncular friends in the physician William Falconer and the philosopher's daughter Mary Hartley, who brought him into contact with Bath's cultured circles and supplied the total want of schooling after the age of eight that resulted from his father's exploitation. Similarly, the elder Lawrence's belief that any regular artistic training would spoil his son's style was discreetly countered by some of the town's resident artists, and by those like Miss Hartley who were versed in the graphic arts. Thus he received advice, studied others' methods, and had access to collections of books and pictures. He experienced the thrill of contemplating and copying Old Masters and dreamed of receiving instruction in the higher reaches of art so that he could do more than produce pot-boiling portraits. But a second offer from a wealthy man to cover the cost of a sojourn in Rome had to be turned down, for he was his family's sole support.

It was not all work and self-improvement. Lawrence enjoyed athletic pursuits like boxing, fencing and coursing, and he was a fine billiards player. In the drawing rooms of his patrons he was welcome for his intelligence, enthusiasm and perfect manners, and because he was a joy to behold. 'He was remarkably handsome as a boy,' wrote Sarah Thackeray forty-five years later. 'He wore his collar thrown back, and his hair, which was beautiful, was so abundant, that its rich dark curls almost obscured his face when he stooped to draw.'[5] His spouting of Shakespeare had implanted a love of the theatre, and in some moods he thought of a career on the stage. In a much-retold anecdote his horrified father, determined to stifle this notion, plotted with two actors to give him a hard task at an audition and no help in accomplishing it, and then tell him solemnly that he did not possess the advantages required to prosper in the profession.

This little scheme relied for its effect on Lawrence's devotion to his family, which emerges from many stories of these years. All his life he loved his close relations without reserve and felt responsible for their welfare. The best way to serve them was marked out when the Society of Arts in 1784 gave him a prize for his copy of Raphael's final work *The Transfiguration*. He was fifteen, and had executed the crayon drawing two years before. He ached to go to London and benefit from formal instruction, but his father hesitated to exchange his lucrative career in Bath for the uncertain glories of an assault on the metropolis. Meanwhile his siblings completed their education and went their various ways: Andrew studied at Oxford University and became a clergyman; William obtained an army commission and was sent abroad; Lucy taught before marrying a Birmingham solicitor named John Meredith; and Anne was a paid companion and then married a Warwickshire rector named Richard Rouse Bloxam.

At some point two Bath artists showed Lawrence how to set a palette and paint in oils, and soon he was proficient in the medium. The town had given him all it could, and in 1787 loans and securities from patrons keen to see him develop further at last induced his father to take him to London and install him in lodgings in what is now Leicester Square. The aspiring painter divided his time between presenting letters of introduction to those who could smooth his path and studying the works of foreign and native artists, some of whom he also met. The most important new acquaintance was Sir Joshua Reynolds, the doyen of the British art world. Their first interview seemed to go badly when Reynolds pointed out defects in the self-portrait in oil Lawrence had brought along, but he then addressed him kindly: 'It is clear you have been looking at the old masters; but my advice to you is, to study nature; apply your talents to nature.'[6]

No document attests to this Olympian pronouncement or to the invitation that apparently followed it to call whenever he pleased, but it is part of the legend of Lawrence's life, gaining poignancy from the fact that he came to be seen by many as Reynolds's successor. The next step towards that status was to acquire the technical mastery only an art school could provide, and to this end he enrolled as a student at the Royal Academy in September 1787. Letters he wrote to his mother and Mary Hartley in this phase of his life give his voice for the first time. The warmth and exuberance of boyhood are displaced by the sobriety of a youth who feels the responsibility his talent imposes on him. He is affectionate but slightly reserved, with a stately courtesy that would become his hallmark. In speaking of his progress he is self-assured without arrogance, and he evaluates other painters in earnest, measured tones.[7] The transition from wonder child to mature artist was underway.

He was not long a student, for, as ever, he needed to devote his energies to earning fees. His parents had given up their house in Bath and followed him to London, where they set up a separate establishment but gave him his dinner. To maintain two households Lawrence knuckled down and soon replicated his success in Bath on a larger scale. His name was bruited about in the best circles, and the best people came to his studio. Seven of his crayon drawings were accepted for the Royal Academy's annual exhibition of 1787, as in the next year were five crayons and his first commission in oil. In 1789 he exhibited thirteen items in different mediums and had favourable press reviews. Work streamed in and he was spoken of as the coming man in the art world. His contemporary Martin Archer Shee noted in that year that 'Lawrence, of all the artists, stands foremost, and deservedly carries away the greatest share of praise.'[8]

Of his personal life little is known. From Leicester Square he moved to Jermyn Street and then Old Bond Street. To mark the onset of manhood he powdered his hair and tied it at the neck, and he began to take care over his dress. With his winsome looks and personality he was readily admitted to the homes of new sitters, and his former Bath client the Duchess of Devonshire introduced him to the Whig society of which she was a leader. He knew acceptance of this kind enhanced his prospects, for fine people liked to be painted by a gentleman and in a crowded field every advantage told. If he did very well, his life might be sweet indeed. In terms of demand portraits far outstripped other genres, and since they were usually commissioned they did not need to be sold. The curiosity to see them was such that the Royal Academy, reliant on entry fees, gave them pride of place in its exhibitions, a form of free advertising for their creators.

A fly in the ointment was Lawrence senior, who, not content to live off his son's earnings, embarrassed him with clumsy promotional initiatives. He used the *World* to sing his praises, asking rhetorically what Gainsborough and Reynolds had been at his age and asserting that the 'future *Sir Joshua*' was already reaping his just rewards. He used his progeny's art as bait for a venture of his own, puffing his contributions to the 1788 Academy and then grandly stating that drawings he had produced aged thirteen and fourteen would be exhibited next door to Academy's Somerset House premises. This was followed by a conventional advertisement in the same resonant style, in which it was explained that these drawings would take their place alongside automaton figures moved by clockwork, a diamond beetle, specimens of needlework, a collection of shells and an artificial waterfall.[9] It is to the artist's eternal credit that he never voiced frustration with his impossible parent.

Any fears these antics might check Lawrence's upward course were dispelled by a command in 1789 to paint Queen Charlotte. The result was regal yet natural, lifelike but with an elegance the consort rarely exuded. Next came a commission to portray the actress Elizabeth Farren, and his vision of her beguiling face and willowy form in a pastoral scene remains one of his best-known pictures. Both works went to the Academy of 1790, and his heart must have leapt when he read the reviews. He also had lessons in how difficult sitters could be. The queen was in a bad mood, sullen and inattentive, and she refused to put on some trinkets he wished to include. Miss Farren asked for alterations to make her figure fuller and her back straighter, while her admirer Lord Derby haggled over the price. Lawrence responded with a suavity based on self-confidence and got his way: the queen is shown wearing bracelets; the actress acquired no extra bulk; and the peer paid the full price for his picture.

The praise of critics for these efforts was pitched high, and the claim in the *World* that Van Dyck would have been proud of Queen Charlotte's portrait was not far above the rest. According to tradition, Sir Joshua Reynolds, whose portrait of the singer Elizabeth Billington hung next to Lawrence's of Miss Farren, turned to him at a private view and said, 'In you, sir, the world will expect to see accomplished what I have failed to achieve.'[10] Following the exhibition George III wished Lawrence to be made an associate of the Royal Academy, but the proposal was felt to encroach upon that body's autonomy and for this reason rejected. The kerfuffle inspired a verse lampoon from the satirist John Wolcot, known as Peter Pindar, entitled 'The Rights of Kings'. Appearing therein as 'Master Lawrence' because of his youth, the source of the discord could rejoice that he had attained the status of public figure at the age of twenty-two.

With the example of Reynolds before him, our hero knew that painting people who were talked about would make him talked about. Among this group was Amy Lyon, otherwise known as Emma Hart and soon to be Emma, Lady Hamilton. She had yet to gain notoriety as Lord Nelson's mistress but was celebrated as the muse of George Romney, whose popular likenesses made Lawrence even more eager to paint her himself. A commission to do so came from the Marquess of Abercorn, but Lawrence had to pull other strings and wait anxiously before he gained access to the diplomat Sir William Hamilton and secured his permission to commence sittings. Spurred on by his belief that he could do the young beauty better justice than Romney, he set to work, portraying her in classical costume as an allegorical character from John Milton's poem *Il Penseroso*. In the 1792 Academy this work was exhibit no. 1, placed above the entrance to the Great Room at Somerset House.

This privilege showed that the academicians' defiance of 1790 had not been meant as a snub to Lawrence, and in 1791 they made him an associate of their own accord. In 1792 Reynolds died and the history painter Benjamin West was elected to succeed him. Another post left vacant at Sir Joshua's death was that of Painter in Ordinary to His Majesty, which was instantly awarded to Lawrence. Reynolds had further been Painter to the Dilettanti Society, an association of noblemen who had seen Italy and sought to promote the arts in Great Britain. They waived their rule that only men who had crossed the Alps were admissible so that Lawrence could be appointed. Finally, in 1794, aged twenty-five, he became a full academician. For an artist who had received little instruction at home and none abroad, who had passed his formative years exploiting raw talent to earn money with mundane work, this was a signal achievement.

Lawrence's ascent excited uncharitable feelings in some fellow portraitists, but such was the force of his irruption on the scene that only two counted as real competitors, both older men with children. Sir William Beechey, an unflashy hard worker liked by the king, did not treat him with any outward animosity, but John Hoppner, who enjoyed the Prince of Wales's patronage but had lost out to Lawrence at the 1794 election, missed no opportunity to run him down. Farington's diary reveals that comparing the three rivals was a regular hobby among artists, and if Lawrence had the best of it on balance he was not the universal favourite. The king joined the debate one year, declaring that Hoppner and Beechey had excelled themselves and Lawrence lost ground. In some years Hoppner in particular also had more garlands from the press. Tellingly, though, Lawrence's fees always equalled or surpassed those of the others.

He reflected on his rapid rise in a letter of 1796 to his Bath friend Sophia Lee. What he had achieved, he said, fulfilled his wishes and exceeded his expectations: 'To hear the voice of praise, nor feel it ignorance or flattery, is sweet and soothing.' His claims were acknowledged by 'the circle of taste' and by his rivals. He would not get carried away, however: 'Believe not that I am inflated with a triumph which, however great when compared with contemporary merit, did never yet satisfy the soul that thirsted for fame.' Such fame was an achievement of a different order, born of an 'ardency in man' that was 'evidence of Deity itself'. When he asked himself 'What shall I do to be for ever known?' his answer was mournful: 'I feel myself a sluggard in the race.'[11] The acclamation of contemporaries was his; would he also leave an enduring monument? Only time would tell.

Lawrence's 'circle of taste' included Miss Lee herself and her sister Harriet, who lived together writing novels and plays in London and Bath. It further included opulent patrons of the arts such as Lord Abercorn, for whom he painted Lady Hamilton, and Lord Mountjoy, later Earl of Blessington, with whom he was so familiar that he advised him on his second marriage.[12] More important still were the intermarried families of Angerstein, Lock and Boucherett, all belonging to the cultivated merchant class. The elderly patriarchs William Lock and John Julius Angerstein were art collectors who took a liking to Lawrence as a man and painter, commissioned numerous portraits from him, and generally did whatever they could for him. Their kin treated him almost as one of their own during his long stays in their homes in Surrey, Kent and Lincolnshire.

A more agreeable guest for a London entertainment or a country house party would be hard to find. His conversation was sensible, sometimes acute or amusing, and he danced and sang well. His scanty education had left him without the smattering of Latin most men round the table would have had, but few were better read in the literature of their own language. He wrote well-turned light verses, not a unique skill but indicating sensitivity to language and pleasure in its use. His demeanour was assured but tactful and unobtrusive, and he was a good listener. He had shown refinement while yet a child, as we have said, so this trait was natural, but in its developed form it was the fruit of an acting ability nurtured from the same tender age. He observed urbanity and reproduced it. To this he added a graceful figure and carriage and a face so handsome that the painter William Hoare said he would choose him as his model for Christ.[13]

Those who beheld him in these settings must have found it curious that this superbly accomplished man was the son of a West Country innkeeper. But there was nothing of the social climber in Lawrence, and if he adopted the forms of his superiors he was never tempted into snobbish concealment of his origins. Indeed, in later years he took a wicked delight in alluding to their father's former occupation in the presence of his siblings, who were happier to dwell on their mother's genteel relations. His utter loyalty to his father is surprising in the circumstances, but he never forgot that he had been the old man's favourite, his pride and joy. Farington recorded in 1793 that he paid him no less than £300 a year from his income.[14] There are hints, but no proof, that Lawrence senior indulged in unwise speculations and incurred liabilities his son had to meet. The artist also got into the habit of making regular cash gifts to other members of his family.

This generosity, warranted or not, should have been affordable. Lawrence charged forty guineas for a three-quarters portrait, eighty for a half-length, and 160 for a full-length.[15] He was busy despite these high fees, and even the war with France from 1793, which greatly affected some painters, did not dampen the appetite for his work. The problem was that money ran through his fingers. His Bond Street lodgings cost £200 a year, and in 1794 he took a lease for a large house in Piccadilly at £250 a year excluding tax and then laid out £500 to decorate it. This and his father's impositions explain why, despite a substantial income, he was already in financial trouble. Late in life he bemoaned the errors of these first London years: 'The truth is, I began life wrongly. I spent more money than I earned and accumulated debts for which I have been paying heavy interest.'[16] For now he was fortunate that William Lock and John Julius Angerstein gave him discreet assistance.

Lawrence's filial piety faced one test more. During the Academy of 1795 a notice in the *Oracle* pointed out that he was younger than his rivals, claimed his submissions were the best, and lamented that they had been poorly hung. His father's hand in this was unmistakable, and the idea that people might think he had sanctioned it made him shudder. He sent a disavowal to the editor of the paper to save himself, as he said, 'from the interpretation of being a vain and contemptible coxcomb'. In May 1797 his mother died, a kind but indistinct figure who had passed her existence in her husband's shadow. The widower went to live with his daughter Anne in Rugby, where he died five months afterwards. He must have had some compelling qualities, for a few weeks earlier Lawrence had written of the deep love his sons and daughters felt for him. Only the final sentence, with utmost gentleness, admits a reservation: 'To be the entire happiness of his children, is perhaps the lot of no parent.'[17]

When his father died Lawrence was twenty-eight years old and something of an enigma. He generally passed for a steady character, but he had a hectic social life and *La Belle Assemblée* stated later that he was at this time 'much devoted to what are termed the pleasures of the town'. However this may be, it does not seem his affections were engaged, although he had to deny rumours about himself and the miniaturist Anna Foldstone. The facetious airing of these in the *Morning Herald* showed that a degree of celebrity was already his:

> A coalition of palettes, colours and brushes is talked of between Lawrence the portrait painter and Miss Foldstone the pretty enamellist. The affections of this female artist, though delicately pencilled in miniature, are expected soon to be matured at whole length; as from Lawrence's design, though but a hasty sketch, it is evident he intends to place Hymen in the foreground.[18]

As an object of romantic interest Lawrence extended the appeal of good looks and artistic renown with the gift of sympathy, of making the person speaking to him feel she was at the centre of his thoughts. It has been said of him that he was fascinated by emotional vibrancy in women and fanned it with flirtatious talk. With no wish to be cruel, he toyed with feelings, including his own, and indulged in nervous infatuations. Evidence for this view is thin, especially since paying inane compliments to young women was a basic form of courtesy in those days. It may be that Lawrence took it too far, as an anonymous female acquaintance quoted by Williams suggests:

> He could not write a common answer to a dinner invitation without its assuming the tone of a billet-doux; the very commonest conversation was held in that soft, low whisper, and with that tone of deference and interest, which are so unusual, and so calculated to please. I am myself persuaded, that he never intentionally gave pain. He was not a male coquette; he had no *plan* of conquest.[19]

This purposeless pattern of conduct was broken by a bizarre episode that could have done great harm to Lawrence's career. The germ of the aberration was his enthusiasm for the theatre, from which grew a lifelong devotion to the Kemble dynasty of actors. The greatest of the Kembles was Sarah Siddons, whom he first met in Devizes when he was six and she twenty. In Bath the boy artist made portrait drawings of the town's favourite actress, and she filled him with a wonder he later expressed in a poem. The acquaintance grew in London, deepened by friendships between her daughters and his sisters. When his parents died he moved from his Piccadilly house to theirs in Greek Street, separated only by the gardens of Soho Square from the Siddons home in Great Marlborough Street. Well before this he attended evening parties there, enjoying the company of a woman he admired in the most exalted terms.

It was perhaps natural that his admiration should mutate into love for one of her grown daughters: Sally, born in 1775; or Maria, born in 1779. Lawrence fixed on Sally and they were courting by early 1796. It was a good match, for both were sensitive and affectionate, literary and musical in their tastes, and domestic in their inclinations. Mrs Siddons, however, worried about Lawrence's tangled finances and feared he might tire of a sickly wife, for Sally, like Maria too, had a weak chest. In fact his large income, properly managed, would have ensured their comfort, and his family feeling made him the last man to neglect an ailing wife. But other spectres clung to the mind of the great tragedian. Her regard for him, once maternal, had undergone a change. It is a difficult subject to fathom, but her behaviour over the next years points to subconscious emotions convulsing her. For now, she told the lovers to keep their courtship a secret, even from her ineffectual husband, and gave them no hope of a happy union.

Thus frustrated in his intentions, Lawrence grew agitated, though his pride obliged him to maintain a cool dignity and kept him from confiding in friends. His turmoil grew until it triggered a perverse revolution in his mind: he became convinced he had chosen the wrong sister. Maria, fiery and self-absorbed, and long jealous of Sally for having a dazzling lover, took advantage of a malady that laid her elder sister up in 1797 to captivate him. He was so infatuated that he proposed marriage, and she used an illness of her own to persuade her distracted mother that unless she had her way she might go into a fatal decline. Sally was distressed, but love for her sister and a strain of self-abnegation in her character made her bear her predicament without protest. Mr Siddons, at last brought into the picture, consented to an engagement that was made public in the spring of 1798. By this point, though, Lawrence had spent enough time with the spoilt, vain, shallow Maria to realise he had made a ghastly error and fall back in love with Sally.

As this drama unfolded its cast swelled to include friends of Sarah Siddons and her daughters as well as Lawrence's sisters and a friend of theirs, who together wrote enough letters to fill Oswald G. Knapp's book *An Artist's Love Story* a century later. In June 1798 Maria entered the last phase of tuberculosis and was nursed in Clifton by her mother's friend Penelope Pennington while her mother fulfilled contractual obligations in the Midlands. Sally had forgiven Lawrence and come to a renewed understanding with him, but they reckoned without Maria, who was incensed at his reversion. While her parents staggered about in the storm buffeting their family, Maria resolved that, if it was her last act, she would stop Lawrence marrying Sally. She spoke of her repugnance for him and her certainty that he would make Sally wretched. Just before she died in October she extracted a solemn promise from her that she would never be his wife.

Well before her end Lawrence knew he had an enemy in Maria, and when Sally at her behest wavered and then withdrew from him he suffered torments of guilt, frustration and rage. His usually calm, benevolent personality was unrecognisable in his alternating moods of dejection and vehemence. He used emotional blackmail against Mrs Pennington and Mrs Siddons, including threats of suicide. 'He has TERRIFIED me into my *toleration* of his love for Sally by the horrible desperation of his conduct,' the latter told the former. When Mrs Pennington informed him of Maria's dying injunction and Sally's compliance he became hysterical. 'It is only my Hand that shakes, not my Mind,' he replied. 'I have play'd deeply for her, and you think she will still escape me. I'll tell you a Secret. *It is possible she may. Mark the End.*' He then menaced her with consequences if she told anyone of the deathbed scene: 'I will pursue your name with execration.'[20]

Instantly sensing that he had gone too far, he rowed back, but Mrs Pennington was not to be mollified. Mrs Siddons, on the other hand, felt as tenderly for him as ever. Before Maria's death she had mused on his 'many excellencies and lofty genius' even as he wrought havoc on her family. Just days afterwards she tried to ensure that no gossip seeped into the public domain that could 'ruin that poor young man's future prospects'. She opposed his union with Sally for the same reasons as before, hidden jealousy in all likelihood among them. In any case Sally felt bound by her promise and rebuffed his attempts at contact. As his equilibrium returned, Sally, who loved him still, felt more and more disconsolate, while Sarah, who urged her to be firm, had no scruples about resuming friendly relations with him. For his part, Lawrence was glad to have the woman he called 'my beloved Mrs Siddons' back in his life.[21] Thus the tension fizzled away, and in 1803 Sally succumbed to the same disease as her sister.

Mrs Siddons had reason to fear gossip, on her own account as well as Lawrence's. Shortly after Maria died Mrs Pennington warned her that news of the love triangle had spread: 'Everybody's eyes will be on you and dear Sally, and your conduct respecting this connexion closely watch'd and commented upon.' The story placed its male protagonist in a dubious light, but it was broadcast in too limited and distorted a form to damage him much. More pain was inflicted a few years later by tittle-tattle about him and Mrs Siddons herself. In 1804 Farington read 'much wicked allusion' to them in newspapers and found people inclined to believe it. This harassment, he surmised, was an attempt to destroy the careers of actress and artist alike.[22] It may also have been extortion. Mr Siddons offered a reward for the names of the calumniators, but even this step, with its implied threat of a duel, did not silence them entirely.

The rumour mill ground out other romances for Lawrence, but none with any clear basis in truth. After Sally Siddons's death he seems to have loved a Miss Upton, sister to an Irish peer, but she only toyed with him, drawing from him some angry verses about 'the cold Coquette'. A letter of his suggests another unrequited attachment a little later. On the other hand, an acquaintance said he was 'oftener wooed than wooing', and Williams, who quotes her, asserts that in affairs of love he 'had need of the fortitude of St. Anthony, for he was often tempted, and was more sinned against than sinning'. What are we to make of this? The thread that runs through it and connects it with the impression mentioned above of his flirtatious manner with women, is a kind of half-heartedness, a lack of will to bring things to the point with any. 'His love lay most in talking,' the biographer of artists Allan Cunningham reported an anonymous lady as saying.[23] Lawrence neither married nor had a mistress in the accepted sense.

If we review the Siddons imbroglio in the light of this it appears oddly insubstantial. The longer we plough through the sea of letters, the more the turbulence they express comes to seem literary, a series of fine sentiments and protestations. Passion, agony, anger, betrayal and guilt are described and analysed in language that is ornate, even abstract. Only in the build-up to the crisis and the crisis itself is there any raw emotion; otherwise the love story, though certainly no sham, appears rather bloodless. It is hard not to notice that it resembles an opera plot and that its characters are histrionic but rather inactive. In the end the heroines die of disease, not despair, and the hero works diligently throughout, maintains the esteem of his clients, and carries on his social life in and out of London as usual. Could it be that he had a sort of spiritual love for women but little or no physical desire?

A few scholars have briefly stated the possibility that Lawrence was homosexual, but it is worth listing the indications of what, if true, would be a major factor in his management of his public image. The painter Benjamin Robert Haydon supposed he would not unlace a woman's stays even if she let him: 'Women were too easy in his presence to be flattering to any man.' Of another artist he wrote, 'The women treat him as if he was harmless – as they did Lawrence.' In a third passage the perspective passes to the Countess of Blessington: 'She spoke of Lawrence rather with contempt & said she was certain no woman ever loved him.' Among other artists, Martin Archer Shee called him 'rather effeminate in his manner' and James Northcote, using a well-understood euphemism, labelled him 'a sort of man-milliner painter'. After these oblique remarks it is a jolt to read in Charles Greville's diary that he was 'probably a bugger'.[24]

A secret life would solve a mystery that has baffled historians: Lawrence's endless pecuniary troubles. It is true that he opened his purse for his siblings, budding artists and needy friends. He also began collecting Old Master drawings, which were not cheap, though not remotely as costly as they became. He kept no accounts and was averse to thinking about money, which he blamed on not having been brought up to prudential habits. His tradesmen, sensing this, imposed upon him somewhat. Even so, it is odd that a man who in his mature years enjoyed the income of a landed aristocrat and neither entertained at home nor had children should repeatedly be within an ace of imprisonment for debt merely because he was generous and disorganised. He knew people found it a puzzle, and in letters he denied he was extravagant and specifically rejected two accusations: that he gambled, and that he had 'secret sources of ruin from vulgar licentiousness'.[25] His biographers have taken him at his word.

The charge that he was a gamester pursued Lawrence through life, and his banker Thomas Coutts received anonymous warnings on this head. His *Morning Chronicle* obituary stated that he had frequented public billiards tables, but he claimed never to play for money. As for cards, he said he kept to small stakes and did not know the rules of hazard, the game preferred by exponents of deep play. Yet he was a founder member of Watier's Club, a notorious gambling house where huge sums were won and lost, which may have a bearing on the matter. A gambling addiction, like an unavowable sex life, would explain his debts. In the second case blackmail was a possibility. He once asked a friend for a large loan 'to enable me to keep my word with a coarse man, whom I have appointed to-morrow at three o'clock to receive it'.[26] This sounds less like a tradesman who had given him credit, or a bailiff, who would not give notice of his visit, than an extortionist with incriminating information.

The point is that dangerous rumours were abroad of clandestine activity in Lawrence's private hours, and these, together with the Siddons episode and stories of heartless flirting, made the last years of the century the most problematic for his reputation as a man. He needed to take control of himself and of the narrative of his life. Essential to this was mastering his debts, which made him vulnerable by creating a cycle of dependency on patrons to give him emergency loans and on tradesmen to supply his personal and professional needs on credit. He had made a start by ridding himself of his ruinous Piccadilly establishment, but his circumstances remained parlous, and in 1801 Farington noted that they were 'so notoriously bad as to be a common talk'.[27] Six years later, when his debts stood at over £20,000, Coutts suggested that he use the expedient of personal bankruptcy to begin afresh.

Lawrence was too proud to accept this humiliation, and before it was even suggested he had resolved to honour his debts by labouring hard in his studio. In 1798, the climax of the love triangle, he sent six paintings to the Academy; in 1799 he sent another six, including an acclaimed portrait of Elizabeth Jennings, who later married into the Lock family; and in 1800 he exhibited seven, among them a portrait of John Philpot Curran in which he overcame the politician's famous ugliness by capturing his animation when conversing. The Academy of 1801 had six Lawrences, that of 1802 had nine, and one of the five in 1803 was a portrait of the former Lord Chancellor Baron Thurlow that critics hailed as a masterpiece. The *British Press* wrote:

> Of portrait, the *Thurlow*, by Lawrence, for stern characteristic, energy, comprehension, and equality of execution, leads the van; and it is, perhaps, a question whether a better portrait in every essential requisite, has ever been produced by the masters of any school on this or that side of the Alps.

And so it went on through the French invasion scare of 1803–1805 and thereafter. Coutts, who ceded control of Lawrence's affairs to Sir Francis Baring in 1807, remained friendly and in the next year commissioned portraits of his three daughters.

Another defence against malevolent gossip was the serenity of Lawrence's public persona. Overstrained as he appeared at times to the Siddons circle, everyone else found him a composed and pleasant companion. His swelling fame did not abate his unassuming geniality, and he was one of those people who fit in everywhere without seeming to belong to a particular set. He joined in private theatricals at Lord Abercorn's seat The Priory, Stanmore, Middlesex in 1803, apparently with great aplomb, but he took care not to associate himself with the lax worldliness of the marquess and his friends. Indeed, he vowed to his sister Anne that he would take this pleasure in moderation and would stick steadily to his work. When he trod The Priory's boards again in 1805 he refused to play an immoral character and persisted in this even at the risk of being considered difficult. He had his way and won further plaudits for his acting.

He still had his talent for making others like him, and his most valuable friend, who helped with his finances, art and image, was Joseph Farington. Born in 1747, Farington was a mediocre artist but a mover and shaker in the art world, a man who loved power but used it well, and his watchful care over Lawrence shows him at his best. He arranged commissions for him, advised him on how to run his studio efficiently, calculated his income and outgoings, drew up schemes of retrenchment, and went several times to Coutts & Co. to discuss proposals to stabilise his finances. With a painter's eye he spotted defects in his works in progress and made general criticisms with the freedom of a paternal adviser, which only made Lawrence ask for more. Farington also smoothed away friction between his friend and clients or other artists and told him how to belie whisperings about his relations with Mrs Siddons.

As the the nineteenth century and Lawrence's fourth decade began, he must have known that his would be a solitary life devoted to art. This suited him well enough, for his ambition burned bright, but to reach his potential he would need to make wise choices. He lived under the long reign of the hierarchy of genres, which placed history painting – encompassing historical, religious, mythological and certain literary themes – at the apex. This was followed, in order, by portraiture, scenes of everyday life, landscape art, animal painting and still life. History stood highest because its sublime subjects called for idealism and originality of composition in the artist. The Royal Academy acknowledged this primacy, though for commercial reasons it covered the walls of Somerset House with portraits. There was some overlap between the first and second genres, not least since capturing significant expression was common to both, and Sir Joshua Reynolds had hovered over this liminal zone with great effect.

History painting always fascinated Lawrence. As a boy he tried his hand at scriptural subjects, and at sixteen he produced a large canvas of Christ bearing the Cross. Even as he made rapid strides as a portraitist in London he told Sophia Lee in 1796 that he was taking the second path but his limbs were strong enough for the first.[28] He had already transcended pure portraiture in 1792 with his allegorical depiction of Lady Hamilton. He took a loftier flight in 1797 with *Satan Summoning his Legions*, likewise a subject from Milton. His model was the boxer 'Gentleman' John Jackson, but the face was that of his good friend John Philip Kemble, the brother of Sarah Siddons. He never again completed a purely imaginative work, but the following year he began a series showing Kemble in roles from Shakespeare and other dramatists, what are known as his half-history portraits.

The surreal quality of some of these pictures, with fixed stares and well-muscled bodies in contorted, theatrical postures, is at some remove from the sedate world of Lawrence's bread and butter. Ever afterwards he considered *Satan* his finest work; others thought differently and it never sold. Even an untrained eye can discern that this is a branch of art to which his talents were not adapted. When it was first shown the unease of critics was palpable. Anthony Pasquin, belligerent at this time but not yet a professional defamer, savaged it:

> The figure of Satan is colossal and very ill-drawn; the body is so disproportioned to the extremities, that it appears all legs and arms, and might at a distance be mistaken for a sign of the spread eagle. The colouring has as little analogy to truth as the contour, for it is so ordered, that it conveys an idea of a mad German sugar-baker dancing naked in a conflagration of his own treacle.

Haydon expressed the same contempt, while Allan Cunningham and James Northcote said Lawrence was devoid of imaginative power.[29] The Kemble pictures were more appreciated, but far less so than his most popular conventional portraits.

History painting was Lawrence's siren song. Farington knew it, and in 1804 he urged him to strive for such excellence in portraiture as to put him indisputably at the head of that department, and only then, with fame and fortune assured, to embark on a new course. Lawrence kept to his task, but the next year told his friend again he wished to free up time for historical pictures. Some days he felt sick of painting faces. To Mrs Boucherett he complained in 1801 of being 'harnessed and shackled into this dry mill-horse business', and in 1811 he wrote to Farington that he was 'heavily Depress'd in Spirit from the strong impression of the past dreadful waste of time and improvidence of my Life and Talent'.[30] The spectacle of a great artist forced away from his highest vocation into profitable labour would be a sad one were it not evident that his gift was for that labour and that in brighter moods it afforded him much satisfaction.

In 1810 the early decease of John Hoppner created a watershed for Lawrence by taking the only portraitist who could vie with him from the scene. As long as Hoppner had lived, so had the sport of pitting them against each other. Beechey's reputation was in decline, and John Opie, highly respected but only moderately popular, had died in 1807. In the second rank were William Owen, Thomas Phillips and John Jackson, and, with no outstanding history painter, Lawrence was supreme. He greeted this reality with trepidation: 'The death of Hoppner leaves me, it is true, without a rival, and this has been acknowledged to me by the ablest of my present competitors; but I already find one small misfortune attending it, viz. that I have no sharer in the watchful jealousy, I will not say, hatred, that follows the situation.' In fact, his smooth, unpretentious manner made it easy for colleagues to accept his status. John Constable, after visiting the Academy of 1811, told Farington that Lawrence 'stood unrivalled in the opinion of all'. Farington himself found 'such a sense of His power in the art prevailing in the minds' of academicians that he told him it was time to raise his prices to 300 guineas for a whole length and the other sizes in proportion.[31]

Lawrence did raise his prices, which made him more exclusive and, exclusivity being a good brand image, more sought after. The rich and famous crowded his studio, and the days when he had to seek access to a star were long past. He increased his fees several more times during his career; each time it was reported in the press and added to his public estimation. Like Reynolds before him, he was a broker of celebrity and a celebrity himself. He could make an unknown girl a coveted beauty by painting her and then meet her as a fellow denizen in the world of fashion. Newspapers noticed his social movements, and the diarist Harriet Wynne was excited in 1805 to find that 'Mr Lawrence the famous painter and the handsomest man in London was of our party.'[32] His amateur acting drew a lot of comment and prompted a perhaps unwittingly perceptive reflection in the *Sun*:

Mr Lawrence, the Artist, is the Gentleman who has distinguished himself so much in the theatrical amusements at Stanmore. He is so successful in his *representations* of *character* on *canvass*, that it is not surprizing to find that he displays equal *expression* on the stage.

The connection between acting and conveying expression in portraits is a subject to which we shall return.

A less welcome celebrity outing came as a sequel to a portrait he painted of Caroline, Princess of Wales in the winter of 1800–1801. She lived apart from her husband in Blackheath, and for convenience he slept at her home while the work was in hand. At the time this passed without comment, but the 'Delicate Investigation' of 1806 into the princess's morals heard from a former page that they had been intimate. Lawrence signed an affidavit vindicating his conduct, which the commissioners accepted, and as they worked in secret nothing came out in the press. In 1813 flaring hostility between the Prince and Princess of Wales caused details of the investigation to be leaked: Lawrence's affidavit, servants' testimony and the princess's evidence were all printed. Adultery with her was, in theory, treasonable, and the matter might have been serious. Instead it faded, and a satirical print years later with the painter's image among those of her supposed lovers, shown as stains on her dress, did him no harm.[33]

Scandal never again imperilled the artistic crown that critical opinion had placed on Lawrence's head. The basis of his ascendancy was skill with his pencil, an inborn talent honed since early boyhood and enriched by close study of the drawings of Rubens, Michelangelo, Caracci and others in his possession. By general consent he was a peerless limner of faces and hands, above Gainsborough and Reynolds and well above his own contemporaries. He never gave up drawing for its own sake, working in pencil, chalk and pastel with great speed to produce results that combined poetry with precision. Those he liked best he had engraved, mostly to be given to friends. When he painted in oils he always drew on the canvas before taking up his palette, and Lady Elizabeth Leveson-Gower, who saw his preliminary drawing of her, thought it 'almost a sin' to lay colour over something so perfect.[34]

Along with astonishing accuracy, the hallmarks of Lawrence's oil portraits are vitality and glamour. Because he painted thickly his canvases have a luxurious feel, with a sensuous delight in rendering silks, satins, furs and other textures. He ably combined colour with the play of light and shadow, and in particular picked out reflections of light on hair, facial features and draperies. Most striking of all are his eyes, with highlights to give extra sparkle, and Fuseli's exclamation that Lawrence painted eyes better than Titian has often been quoted. Others, however, thought they gleamed too much. More generally, those who liked repose in paintings considered his glossy style meretricious. The virtuoso effects of light and shade, sometimes with several sources of illumination, displeased a number of fellow artists and other commentators, who applied words like 'tinselly', 'metallic' and 'glittering' to his work.

Lawrence's figures are less assured than his faces and hands. Limbs might have odd lengths and angles, and there are mistakes in foreshortening. This reflects his lack of formal training in anatomy, without which the human body's proportions and the play of muscles cannot convincingly be depicted. Most of his subjects are in stately interiors, but those placed outdoors gave him a chance to display his finesse in painting trees, greensward and skies. The gossamer beauty of the scenery in Elizabeth Farren's picture staked his claim to these accomplishments, and had he wished he might have left a fine corpus of landscape painting. Other works have indeterminate backgrounds, some of which look like billowing smoke. He was reproached with dashing on colour to fill the rest of the canvas once face and figure were complete, but his defenders said this was done deliberately to fix the viewer's attention on the sitter.

A few newspaper reviewers made technical points, but most just commended a picture's taste, grace, sweetness or brilliance, perhaps with the claim that better things had rarely been seen. Comparisons with Van Dyck were frequent. Negative remarks tended to focus on a particular work that had fallen short of Lawrence's standard. The private verdicts of painters were also largely positive. It is to their credit that Shee, West, Dance, Owen and many more battened down envy and applauded him. Some found faults: Charles Robert Leslie thought him a poor colourist; Haydon found his flesh bloodless and his figures monotonously idealised; and William Blake felt he had bartered his birthright as an artist for mere social success. But even detractors tended to admit his technical mastery. Fuseli, who also disapproved of fashionable portrait-painting, said he did it better than anyone in Europe and repeated the parallel with Van Dyck.

There was some debate as to whether Lawrence's male or female portraits should be preferred. The latter made the bigger splash, and his picture of Elizabeth Jennings alarmed artists at the Academy of 1799. Beechey wished he had kept all but one of his own pictures back, Opie and Northcote were astounded, and West said it made the other ladies exhibited 'look like dowdies'. But some felt Lawrence made women too enticing, turning them into coquettes. In his early years the elderly Reynolds found them 'deficient in the meek and modest composure which belongs to the loftier order of female expression'.

They only got sexier. With parted lips, lustrous eyes and showy dress, they invited desire, and Haydon waspishly suggested it was this that made fashionable ladies covet a Lawrence portrait.[35] Many made the contrast with Reynolds's more demure treatments and regretted that these belonged to the past.

Such viewers turned with relief to Lawrence's men. A critic in 1803 censured 'gaudy dissoluteness of taste' in his women but hailed the dignified likeness of Lord Thurlow.[36] The portraits of John Julius Angerstein and other patriarchs were liked for their severe grandeur. This is, though, a contrast of young women with old men. His young men were as eager to captivate as his women, with raffish looks, Byronic swagger and smouldering eyes – posing dandies, said some, and with an unsettling effeminacy. A better polarity than male–female is old–young. In tackling subjects with no claims to youth or beauty Lawrence was more alive to individuality, and he said as much while working on a portrait of Pope Pius VII:

> The face [...] is not finished; for the Pope being an old man, his countenance has a great deal of detail in it; and a good and cheerful nature, with a clear intellect, gives it variety of expression. He is a very fine subject, and it is probable that the picture will be one of the best that I have painted.

Sir Walter Scott, whose Lawrence portrait was also much admired, made the same point: 'I believe the hard features of old Dons like myself are more within the compass of the Artist's skill than the lovely face and delicate complection of females.'[37] Cardinal Consalvi, Elizabeth Carter, Warren Hastings, Queen Charlotte and Lady Robert Manners are examples of Lawrence's sensitive treatment of elderly subjects. Finally, to posit another axis, while his high-society portraits were flamboyant, he also painted merchants, lawyers, men of letters and scientists in sober tones with every bit as much care.

A regular theme in appraisals of Lawrence was that he sought to overcome his defects, notably the over-brightness to which he was inclined, and improved over time. This was the view of Haydon and of the art patron Sir George Beaumont. 'Mr Lawrence is commendably getting out of that glitter of manner which has distinguished his pictures for some years,' the *Star* noted in 1803. The *Public Ledger* commented in 1811 that he painted 'with more vigour and truth than formerly' and that he had left off a tendency to excessive varnishing. He was not a good judge of his own works, expressing strange and vacillating views on some of them, and he knew he stood in need of the honest opinions of discerning friends. He therefore encouraged them to identify failings in his output. When Henry Fuseli joked that his flesh looked like glass he said he felt the force of the comment and sought to benefit from it.

He never stopped learning, and faced with an adverse response he tended to put vanity aside in the hope of finding a useful lesson. This showed good sense and modesty, and these were themselves the best guarantee that his prowess would increase. Even Anthony Pasquin's diatribes of the 1790s met with a mild response from him, and he wished to see one that had passed him by because he 'found much benefit from the severest criticism'. Really venomous censure did annoy him, especially if motivated by political animosity to a sitter, and in one case he wrote to an editor in protest. He also defended his practice if he thought it had been misunderstood. For example, he denied his sketchy backgrounds gave an unfinished look to a canvas, for 'the appearance of facility is not undesirable, where the essential details of a work have received obvious care and attention.'[38]

Lawrence was known for his industry, and there are statements about this from him and others: that he worked six days a week and was too fatigued to go out in the evenings; that he painted from seven o'clock one morning through the night to the end of the next evening without cease; that he might admit four sitters a day, paint by gaslight, or bolt his meals. By his own account he had to fight against a constitutional languor in order to work hard and stick to a routine. He also said that despite temperate habits his health was not robust and he was subject to minor ailments. No wonder he sighed as he toiled, or that Farington 'urged Him to consider the bad effects of over application'.[39] But his need for money forced him to rise early each morning and resume his task. A lesser artist might have cut corners, but those familiar with Lawrence's methods agreed he took infinite pains over every commission.

His urbanity and kindness put his clients at their ease when they sat to him. It was said he flattered them in speech and then in paint. According to Haydon he was happy to 'perfume' them and be their 'slavey', while Northcote quipped that 'Lawrence makes coxcombs of his sitters and his sitters make a coxcomb of Lawrence.'[40] But these are the barbs of less successful artists, and his correspondence shows he was politely insistent in matters of costume and pose. Once sittings were over, paintings might languish in his studio for considerably longer than his clients expected. One reason for this was that he found it difficult to decide a work was as good as it possibly could be. Time after time he applied the final touches with a feeling of exhilaration at what he had done, only to begin making changes the next day. Completing paintings was desirable, he told Farington, but aiming at perfection was more so.

There was another, less reputable reason for dilatoriness. Since Lawrence took half-fees in advance each new commission brought an injection of cash, and the straits he was always in led him to start more than he could finish. Customers chivvied him with polite reasoning, offended lordliness, pointed irony or frank vexation. The Marchioness of Stafford called his system 'a sad illiberal way of going on'. Others saw the funny side: when Harriet Arbuthnot received her portrait a decade after her first sitting she joked that people might ask if she had ever really looked like that; the poet Thomas Campbell said his portrait would show 'how I shall look when I grow young again in heaven'; and the Whig MP Joseph Jekyll said a man of mature years must find an executor to complete his sittings and he meant to find a handsome one to do it for him. They and others learned that for all his courtesy Lawrence was in charge, and they would get their pictures when he was ready. Sadly, some never did.[41]

Engravings added to his income. Publishers paid hundreds of pounds to make prints of a popular Lawrence, and in 1822 Hurst, Robinson & Co. agreed to pay him £6,000 over two years in exchange for the right to reproduce his works during that time. Here, too, he displayed an unseemly greed in some people's minds by expecting owners of his paintings to let them be engraved for his, not their profit, claiming a copyright that had no legal force for visual images. On the other hand, he tried to ensure that engravers were decently paid by publishers, treated them considerately, and did his best to get employment for those just starting out. The frequency of newspaper advertisements for his prints indicates the level of interest in them, and the engravers Peltro William Tomkins and Thomas Goff Lupton marketed themselves by publishing his praise of them in the papers.

Though avid for money, Lawrence amply demonstrated that he loved art for its own sake. He gave every assistance he could to those in the foothills of the profession. He bought works by living artists and turned his house into a museum of painting and sculpture. He collected over a thousand Old Master drawings and cherished them as an aesthetic scholar and as a practising artist. His joy when he saw a great artwork unfamiliar to him is plain from his letters and Farington's diary. All his life he felt deep reverence for Reynolds, 'our great master' as he called him.[42] He could not warm to the work of all his peers, but his praise was uttered in public and his criticism in private. He was a sound judge of merit, past and present, and could value styles that were unlike his own. He treasured the drawings of Fuseli and Blake he had purchased, and he subscribed to one painting by Haydon and helped him sell another. None of these men was willing or able to do like justice to him.

For an artist of his repute Lawrence kept a low profile in the Royal Academy, avoiding the dissension and intrigue that were the stuff of life to Farington. Only if he felt something dishonourable was afoot did he speak out, for instance against cabals to end West's presidency. A pessimistic bent to his character made him continue to assume he faced more envy and hostility than he really did. Aside from the bond with Farington he was a loner in the art world, blandly pleasant to all but seeking neither friends nor disciples. In his studio he liked to do everything himself, declining the suggestion that he let other hands finish his portraits, and while he did have a few pupils and assistants over the years, he struggled to occupy them. Nor had he any gift for teaching, and even with goodwill on both sides these relationships were unsatisfactory. For this reason he never founded a school, though there were first-rate talents who imitated him, notably George Henry Harlow and Thomas Sully.

His looks changed with time, but Lawrence remained a fine figure of a man. Allan Cunningham described him thus:

> Lawrence was five feet nine inches high, with handsome limbs, a body finely proportioned, and a countenance open and noble. His head was bald, but so finely shaped, that the want of hair was a beauty. There was a winning sweetness in his smile; his voice was gentle and musical; and when he spoke, he moved his hand and head in accordance with the sentiments he uttered.

He had large, lustrous eyes, Cunningham went on, full of fire even as his attitude remained placid, and a dry sense of humour. At the height of his fame he was still more a listener than a speaker, though what he said showed the sharpness of his mind. The travel writer Charles MacFarlane was taken with 'the perfection of his manners' and the 'ease and natural elegance of his deportment'. He had a liveliness and grace that MacFarlane thought must have taken pains to achieve, though no pains were apparent. The American visitor Harriet Douglas called him 'that truly elegant man'.[43]

It was pleasing to be treated as someone special by so distinguished a person, although the dose was rather strong. In Scott's view, Lawrence was 'a little too fair spoken otherwise very pleasant'. Haydon granted his elegance but thought him more deferential than was truly well bred.

Moore wished he could like him but agreed with the wit Henry Luttrell that he was oily. The poet Samuel Rogers called him 'simpering' and the novelist John Galt 'a very saponaceous character'. Courtliness did not detract from his dignity, however; quite the reverse. Some who wished for a closer connection with him were chilled by it, as Charles Robert Leslie observed. Here is Cunningham again: 'There was a defensiveness about his manners to the world; a sort of holding back, a fastidious modesty, a too high polish, which equalised his bearing to all, and perhaps wore the air of being somewhat artificial.'[44]

This bred resentment, and Lady Charlotte Bury and the diarist Thomas Creevey were not alone in finding Lawrence snooty and insincere. The artist Henry Thompson said his coldness had alienated academicians whom he had never positively offended in word or deed. One possible explanation for this conduct was his excessive suspicion of jealousy on their part. Cunningham makes another point when he says that circumspection naturally displaces candour among those who mingle in the upper reaches of society.[45] And there is something else: the celebrity's mechanism for preserving a private space, an inner being, and for keeping false friends and opportunists at bay. Lawrence's idol Sarah Siddons did the same thing, with more grandeur but the same reserve and unapproachability, qualities that surprised those who had only known her for the passion of her stage performances and him for the exuberance of his canvases.

This suave, guarded Lawrence was met with at Royal Academy functions and West End entertainments. He attended dinners given by Sir George Beaumont or the literary sisters Mary and Agnes Berry, where poets, painters and scientists mingled. He held his own amidst the cut and thrust of the Whig intelligentsia at Holland House or the witty jousts under the roof of the worldly clergyman Sydney Smith. But there was another Lawrence. He could be found unwinding after a day's toil with a few friends in his own home or, more often, in one of theirs. Here, in his inner circle, he was genial and spontaneous, all courtliness gone. He told amusing stories or took up the questions of the day, including political ones, though he was never a partisan. If he was tired, as so often, he might sit quietly for a while before joining in the talk, and sometimes he read aloud passages from his favourite novelists, Walter Scott and Jane Austen.

It was mainly with intimate friends that Lawrence indulged his love of the theatre. He was gripped by great dramas and laughed heartily at the farces that served as afterpieces, and to Farington he gave his views of actors and plays, old and new. Naturally he joined in the craze for the boy actor William Betty, whom he declared to be inferior only to the divine Sarah Siddons. He attended her last night as Lady Macbeth in 1812 and John Philip Kemble's as Coriolanus in 1817. Though they saw each other infrequently, his feelings for Mrs Siddons remained strong, and he broke down in tears on hearing of her wish that he and her brother Charles should be her pallbearers, a solemn privilege he never exercised because she outlived him. At the very end of his life he eagerly followed the stage debut of her niece Fanny Kemble, Charles's daughter, sending her long appraisals of her performances, in which he saw the Kemble magic live again.

The close friends with whom Lawrence went to a playhouse or sat by a homely fire were a cultured, upright, firmly middle-class set far from the limelight. Alongside Farington and the Lock-Angerstein-Boucherett constellation it included the architect Robert Smirke, the antiquarian Samuel Lysons, the artist William Hamilton and his wife, and the Lee sisters. Very near his heart was Elizabeth Croft, sister of a prominent surgeon, whose home was a haven of warmth to him. She took a wide interest in his life, gave practical advice, and helped run his household. Most intense was the romantically tinged attachment to Isabella Wolff, the estranged wife of the Danish consul. Cynics assumed they were lovers, but unless their correspondence was an elaborate hoax they were not. She was clever, sensitive, beautiful and pious, and Lawrence truly venerated her. He expressed this homage in one of the most exquisite portraits he ever painted.

His fairly small knot of friends were all people whose character and principles gave Lawrence what he called 'a most solid Comfort and Delight'. He was not shy of saying what they meant to him. He told Miss Croft he could confide his joy and sorrow to her, 'and heighten the one or alleviate the other, by communicating them to worth like yours, and to a friendship so generous and feeling'. Bachelorhood made him value these ties the more, as did success, which could have made the opening of heart to heart difficult: 'I am blest in the notice and Affection of dear and most valuable Friends,' he wrote to Farington, 'whose Regard for me in prosperity is a still surer Test of disinterested attachment, than in times of less cheerful aspect.'[46] Envy is one the trials of celebrity, so he felt a deep gratitude to the women and men whose tender feelings towards him were not weakened or made impure by the felicity of public favour.

His friends saw in Lawrence the kindness and loyalty his siblings had always known. They saw a man without arrogance, convinced that as an artist he still had scope to improve, aware of the attainments and merits of others, and, perhaps inoculated by his father's puffing, utterly averse to boastfulness. To those with fewer claims on him he was affable and liberal, helping where he could and showing delicacy where he could not. His behaviour to those whose place in society made them unable either to advance or harm his interests was exemplary. If a servant fell ill he went far beyond the conventional decencies to render assistance. Whenever Mrs Nalder, the former barmaid at the Black Bear, visited London in his years of glory he welcomed her to his home. Further examples abound, as they do also of his ability to forgive, which made up for his over-sensitivity to slights, and a steady truthfulness in his dealings with others.

His letters to friends and family bring us as close to him as we can get. The love of language displayed in his acting and poetry recital is manifest in the poise of his writing style. Even the inimical Haydon, after reading his letters in the Williams biography, pronounced them delightful, and the reviewer in the *Literary Gazette* agreed.[47] The personal matter is enlivened by impish humour and touches of self-deprecation, though some anecdotes are a little laboured. Passages on more general topics are thoughtful and wide-ranging. Lawrence is full of political news, some picked up from sitters, and fascinated by the wheeling and dealing of statesmen. Anything to do with arts and letters engrosses him, and he discourses on these subjects with balance and refinement, if no great originality. He writes a good deal about what other people have said and done, yet not in a gossipy and certainly not in a malicious way.

A feature probably absent from Lawrence's personal demeanour but sometimes present in his letters is high-mindedness. Tendentious musing and frequent use of abstractions like integrity, principle and honour take him close to pomposity, just as his moral rigour takes him close to prudery. He had, for example, a horror of indecency in dress, and Elizabeth Croft recalled him coming from the theatre one evening incensed at having seen a woman there in a gown that revealed her bare back down to her girdle. To the same friend he wrote in praise of women who forswore such provocation: 'Husbands and lovers are greatly indebted to this feeling of judicious modesty, and beauty itself is so much the gainer by it, that the contrary practice ought to be confined (if it must exist at all) to ugliness and vice.'[48] His regard for women who were virtuous and pure-minded was unmistakeably sincere.

This brings us again to the question of Lawrence's sexuality. Abstemious in his habits, an aesthete rather than a pleasure-seeker, he seems to have shied away from the physical aspect of love. His emotions were strong but cerebral, sublimated into worship of a feminine ideal, while real women he adored from a safe distance.

In the letter to Sophia Lee already quoted he wrote of his 'disdain for low enjoyments' and 'relish for whatever is grand, however above me'.[49] If a woman he had venerated cheapened herself in his eyes he could be bitter, as revealed in the 'cold Coquette' poem, a study of a flirt, and in verses he sent in a letter to Lord Mountjoy:

> On Waltzing
> What? The Girl I adore by another embrac'd!
> What? The balm of her breath shall another man taste.
> What? Prest in the whirl by another bold knee.
> What? Panting re[c]lin'd on another than *me*!
> Sir, She's Yours – You have brush'd from the Grape its soft blue
> From the Rose-bud You've shaken its tremulous Dew –
> What you've *touch'd, you may take*. – Pretty Waltzer adieu!

This is usually attributed to the antiquary Sir Harry Englefield, and a print of two waltzers was published with it and his name underneath. The sentiment expressed was criticised as precious in the press, but Lawrence, who names no author, speaks of lines 'which I think not bad – certainly not the worse, for being on my own side or view of the subject'.[50] We may surmise that he loved women, not men, but that impossibly lofty notions and disgust with carnality repressed his appetites. This may not be the last word on the subject, but without more evidence it is probably the safest way to leave it.

Early in 1814 Lawrence left his house in Greek Street, which he and his visitors had long felt was inadequate to his requirements, and moved to 65 Russell Square, Bloomsbury, where he lived and worked for the rest of his life. Its capacious show room, filled with pictures and casts from antique statuary, and its painting room, with crimson wallpaper and a big mirror behind where he sat at his easel, became familiar to hundreds of well-known people. Shortly afterwards the armistice with France enabled him to make his first Channel crossing and study the treasures of the Louvre before they were restored to the countries from which Napoleon had taken them. He felt inspired by what he called 'the noblest assemblage of the efforts of human genius that was ever presented to the world'.[51] This can only have renewed his periodic yearning to escape from the narrow groove of portraiture into the most elevated branch of art.

Lawrence knew that he was living in a heroic epoch, and that his country's victories by land and sea would ring down the ages. It dawned on him that he might be an artist with a historical dimension without quitting the field in which his best talents lay. An early essay in this direction was a portrait of William Pitt the Younger, the prime minister who had carried the nation through the darkest hours of the war. This, remarkably, was executed from a post-mortem cast after Pitt's death in 1806. Critics saw at once that it was something special, for it faithfully represented the premier's appearance while giving it the dignity and elevation of mind that were discernible in his speech and action, but not in his undistinguished features. 'It is a portrait in the epic style of painting, and worthy of going down to posterity,' one critic wrote.[52] Now Lawrence would use the skills he had brought to this picture to rise to the highest tier of his achievement.

The impetus was a summons from the prince regent to portray the crowned heads, commanders and statesmen who came to London in the summer of 1814 to celebrate the Allied triumph. Lawrence hurried home from Paris to begin his task. Working in his Russell Square studio and in St James's Palace, he painted Prince Blücher, the Duke of Wellington, Hetman Platov of the Don Cossacks, Prince Metternich and the regent himself. The project was public knowledge and aroused considerable excitement. Unfortunately, a busy schedule of ceremonies for the illustrious visitors restricted his access to them, and when they dispersed many of their likenesses had not been begun. To complete the gallery, Lawrence would need to go abroad, and so as to ensure the best possible reception at European courts his sovereign knighted him in April 1815. Various practical difficulties, the Hundred Days among them, delayed his departure.

Meanwhile his fame grew and grew. The Academy of 1815, in which he exhibited the royal commissions he had finished so far, was a high point in his career. He appeared with 'annihilating splendour', said the *Oxford Herald*, while the *Sun* believed his portraits would be the centre of attention, 'not only from the exalted rank of most of the subjects, but from the talents and celebrity of the Artist'. He raised his prices again, to 500 guineas for a full-length, becoming even more exclusive and thus even more in vogue among those with deep enough pockets. In 1816 he was one of two painters consulted by a select committee of the House of Commons on the expediency of the state acquiring the Elgin Marbles, the other being West. He spoke warmly in favour, unlike some of the sculptors who gave evidence, and his testimony was reported in detail. He probably had no small part in the decision to set £35,000 aside for the purchase.

Lawrence's stock had never been higher, but worries crowded upon him. He quarrelled with the Royal Academy about the hanging of his pictures and he was sadly overworked, labouring evening after evening by lamplight. Despite big repayments of liabilities he was in grave financial trouble, and in 1815 Angerstein, like Coutts before him, recommended bankruptcy. Again Lawrence baulked, and with Farington's help he averted the disgrace of public exposure but kept himself in thraldom. His beloved family brought him joy and comfort, but also sorrow. His sister Lucy, Mrs Meredith, died of tuberculosis in 1813. Next year he was proud to be able to pull strings to secure a full-pay majority for his brother William, but he died in 1818. His sister Anne's marriage to Richard Rouse Bloxam gave him three nieces and six nephews, all precious to him, but 1818 brought more pain with the death of his niece Susan, aged just sixteen.

The same year arrangements were at last put in place for him to conclude his series for the regent. He was to attend the Congress of Aachen, where he would find the dignitaries who had been in London in 1814 and receive his standard fees plus £1,000 for expenses and his time. He was apprehensive, but Farington wrote to fire his ambition and advise him how to make the most of his mission. It began with an element of farce provided by the British government, which for some reason thought Aachen had no quarters suitable for him to work in and so had a prefabricated structure of three rooms made. Lawrence arrived in early October but owing to difficulties in transporting his suite he found other accommodation that confirmed its superfluity. Indeed, the painting room the city's magistrates gave him was the best he had ever had. Newspapers relished the mishap, and the *Morning Post* and *British Press* published poems about it.

Lawrence made hay in Aachen. He set to work on the Prussian king, the Austrian emperor, the Russian tsar and the ministers Prince Hardenberg, Count Nesselrode and the Duc de Richelieu. Each loved his portrait, and when the empress dowager of Russia saw the one of her son she screamed with delight. The artist was petted immensely and had a harvest of gracious messages, tokens of esteem and acts of royal condescension. From Aachen he proceeded to Vienna, where he stayed five months and portrayed notabilities and leaders of the Austrian *beau monde*. The rule excluding those without noble ancestry from the highest circles was waived for him, and his social life was glittering: 'Comfortable Dinners and the Theatre – Splendid Dinners and High Society – Reviews and Court Fetes', as he summed it up.[53] He must, though there is no knowing when or how, have acquired the ability to converse in French.

From Vienna the regent sent him to Rome to paint Pius VII and his wily diplomat Cardinal Consalvi. He was a little reluctant, feeling he ought to get back to Russell Square and earn fees not even a royal commission could match. Travel had made him aware of his waning bodily strength, and he missed his friends. He could not disappoint the regent, though, so on he went to Italy, the paradise of artists, not as a long-haired student of eighteen, but as a bald, harassed man of fifty. He enjoyed it every bit as much as he should. Nine months in Rome and shorter periods in Naples, Florence, Bologna and Parma were a delight. In the Vatican he was accorded every attention, and his large portraits of the pope and cardinal and a smaller one of the sculptor Antonio Canova were hailed as masterpieces. In long letters home he described the artworks he had seen, which gave him the highest aesthetic pleasures he had ever experienced.

Lawrence's reception throughout his tour was nothing short of dazzling. This reflected enthusiasm for his art, which placed him to many minds at the head of European portraitists, as well as his status as the regent's painter at a time of great national prestige. He also made the best impression personally, and grandees unused to seeing such qualities outside their own class marvelled at his dignity and social aplomb. Henry Thompson heard that among the Viennese court and nobility 'his *manners* were admired equally if not more than his Art.' Metternich grew fond of him and wrote to him after his return to England, and an Austrian princess thought that apart from Lord Castlereagh he was 'the most graceful, elegant, polished gentleman' from abroad to have visited Vienna in a long while. When David Wilkie was in the city eight years later, he found people still 'full of the circumstances' of his visit.[54]

It was the same in Italy. A letter sent to the *Collector* from Rome stated that Lawrence had made 'a sensation beyond description'. The writer went on, 'He was regarded as a superior being, and a wonder, as indeed he was here. His elegant manners made him so many friends, and these and his talents procured him so many distinctions, that he could scarcely prevail upon himself to quit the place.'[55] Gratified as he was, he never let such things intoxicate him and he never grew presumptuous. His level head is evident in the matter-of-fact narration of his splendid progress through Europe in letters to his friends. He took candid pleasure in responses to his art and in the high times his hosts gave him, but he did so without conceit. Nor was he tempted into dissipation, he said, and he was careful about his diet, sleep and exercise. His thoughts were often with those he had left behind, and he was impatient for their news.

The uncommon appeal of Lawrence's personality, and the way it made people want to serve him, emerges again from his relations with Lord Stewart, from 1822 Marquess of Londonderry. Stewart has gone down in history as a flashy sybarite of moderate ability and very aristocratic notions. But to Lawrence, who painted a vibrant portrait of him in a hussar's uniform in 1812, he was zealously devoted. As military commissioner of the Allied armies he hosted him during his stay of 1814 in Paris and during a second visit he made there in 1815 and did all he could to entertain him. He was an intermediary in his contacts with the regent the same year and subsequently hatched schemes for him to paint other monarchs. It was at his suggestion that Lawrence was knighted, he was constantly at his side in Aachen, he was his host as British ambassador in Vienna, and he managed his relations with the regent until his return home. No wonder Lawrence called him his '*intimate and loved friend*'.[56]

On returning to England from his grand tour in March 1820, our hero embarked on the last and brightest phase of his career. Ten days before his arrival West had died, and without ado academicians elected Lawrence to succeed him as their president. The regent, now king, was in raptures with the works he had brought home and gave him a gold chain bearing a medal with his likeness and the words 'From His Majesty King George IV to the President of the Royal Academy'. He had the new title Principal Painter in Ordinary to His Majesty, gifts from foreign sovereigns to fill a cabinet, and diplomas from numerous art academies abroad. 'You have now a *spring tide*,' Farington crowed, 'a command of everything that can be had in this world.'[57] Lawrence enjoyed his laurels, but he showed not a shred of self-importance, rather the absolute sobriety that no caressing from the great and the good could ever shake.

He was now a member of the Establishment. At the coronation in July 1821 he walked in the procession alongside Sir Humphry Davy, President of the Royal Society. He took the chair at functions of the Royal Academy with perfectly polished civility, and one day Scott was a gently amused observer of his style: 'Sir Thomas Lawrence did this very well and compliments flew about like sugar plums at an Italian carnival. I had my share and pleaded them immunities of a sinecure for declining to answer.'[58] Lawrence's public addresses as president, if less substantial than the aesthetic discourses of Reynolds, were gracious and eloquent. His emollience made the brotherhood of artists less fractious, and when discord did arise he restored harmony and conciliated the offended parties. His relations with the court and the government were excellent.

Few artists have ever used a position of influence more effectually to assist fellow labourers in the field. He helped William Etty make the most of his travels in Italy, gave Thomas Uwins commissions that enabled him to sojourn there, and employed William Bewick to copy figures from Michelangelo's Sistine Chapel ceiling. Turner, Wilkie and Bonington felt his benevolence too. It was a disposition of long standing, but now with larger scope, and his cash gifts, purchase of early works, helpful criticism and recommendations are documented in grateful tributes. 'There are many who owe their reputation to his fostering aid,' Uwins wrote, 'and others who without him could never have been able to make their first step in life with courage and stability.'[59] Verses in the *Morning Post* in 1830 were well deserved:

> In genius vigorous, yet refined,
> Noble in art, yet more in mind –
> Sweet-temper'd, gifted Lawrence, great,
> In singleness of heart innate;
> Pleas'd others genius to commend,
> And kind a ready hand to lend
> To merit, when it wants a friend.

He was generous with time and money to charities for impoverished artists. He made donations to cultural institutes, and loaned pictures he had painted or bought to provincial exhibitions.

His official duties were onerous, but he gave fully of himself. He played a major part in the founding of the British Academy of Arts in Rome in 1821 and the Royal Hibernian Academy in Dublin in 1823. After Angerstein's death in the latter year he was instrumental in ensuring his collection went to the state to form the nucleus of the National Gallery. Such items of business swelled his correspondence, with a sea of official communications and enquiries and requests from people he hardly knew. He attended to it all punctiliously and with a delicate consideration that belongs to the age, but above all to himself. Finally, his new status made him more society's darling than ever. He spent many evenings in the West End of town, and a glance at the papers shows if a 'splendid assembly', 'grand entertainment' or 'party of distinction' took place he was likely to be there.

Indeed the press, which had tracked his foreign tour in polite notices, now gave him unremitting coverage: honours he gained at home and abroad; dinners and prize-giving ceremonies he presided at; subscriptions he instigated and supported; other philanthropy and toasts drunk to him at civic dinners; appreciations of past and present British painters in his speeches; the prospect, never realised, of a public exhibition of the king's commissions and the question of where they should finally be hung; and, most of all, engravings of his works for sale. Poetasters found their way into the columns of the

Morning Post: John Taylor with a jubilation on Lawrence's return to his native soil in 1820 and E. L. C. with an effort of 1825 that hailed his destiny, "Mid Statesmen, Heroes, Kings, to bear the palm away!' He was apostrophised as 'the greatest portrait painter in existence', 'our English Rubens' or, most commonly, 'the English Titian'.

An attribute of true fame, as opposed to celebrity, is that those who attain it become objects of patriotic pride. Lawrence began to arouse such feelings during his foreign tour. He was a cultural ambassador of sorts, and he knew his reception in European capitals was honorific to his country as well as himself. Other Britons knew it too. 'It is pleasant on the Continent,' he wrote to Andrew Lawrence from Naples, 'to be greeted by one's Countrymen, who all seem'd to consider my presence, or rather my Works, as general advantage to the Character of England in what relates to the progress of the Arts.' In 1823 William Etty informed him with delight of the boost he had given to the reputation of British art in Italy.[60] During his presidency journalists proclaimed his supremacy or boasted that foreign artists were avid students of his style, and speakers on formal occasions referred to him as a national treasure.

Lawrence was glad to see the advances of British art recognised in countries with longer traditions of excellence, and in a lecture he spoke with satisfaction of 'the rising School of England', the fruit, he said, of the efforts of Reynolds and West.[61] But he never sounded the note of jingoism, least of all on his own account, and in commending Napoleon's support for the arts he differed from those who thought no good ever came of him. George IV, meanwhile, wanted to expand his gallery of the Corsican tyrant's vanquishers to include, without much justification, Charles X and the dauphin. The French king, who had just admitted Lawrence to the Legion of Honour, readily acceded to this idea and invited him to Paris in 1825. In person he found him as charming as every sovereign had done, took every care to make his stay agreeable, and gave him a superb service of Sèvres china. These distinctions prompted fresh trumpetings in the British press.

George IV also kept Lawrence busy portraying him in various poses and costumes, and it is fair to say he never embellished a sitter more. The transformation caused hilarity, and the essayist William Hazlitt said he had turned a man in his fifties into 'a well-fleshed Adonis of thirty-three'. The king, who loved dressing up and pretending to be young, was thrilled. He invited the president to court, confided in him with his usual indiscretion, and went out of his way to show his attachment to the man he called 'the most finished gentleman in my dominions'.[62] Lawrence's royal service was not mere opportunism;

his letters reveal that he was deeply loyal, hating to hear his master criticised. No British painter before or since has had such a close relationship with the monarch. Sadly, neither saw the gallery of Allied victors in its final home, for the Waterloo Chamber at Windsor Castle was not created until both were in their graves.

The portraits of the king – their commissioning, composition and exhibition – gained huge press attention, most of it positive and some rather servile. Prints were advertised in the stilted language deemed appropriate to the subject and sold well. Lawrence continued to shine at the yearly Academies, with critics thinking him not only far too strong for competitors but getting stronger. 'You will be glad to know, that I have never painted better,' he told Anne Bloxam in 1825. He featured in exhibitions of drawings, while engravings of his works in all media were coveted by editors of the annuals that mushroomed in this decade. He began to send pictures to the Paris Salon, where advocates of Romantic over Classical tenets in painting acclaimed him. One of his French admirers was Eugène Delacroix, who wrote an article in his praise in the *Revue de Paris*. He was, the painter Charles Eastlake wrote in 1826, 'an ornament to his country in every way'.[63]

It is hard to name works worthy of particular mention: perhaps the portrait of Julia Peel, wife of the home secretary Robert Peel, who outshines her opulent apparel and jewellery; or that of the admiralty secretary John Wilson Croker's daughter Rosamond, which was so bewitching that men stood in a half-circle at Somerset House to gaze at it. Children, too, captivated the public. Lawrence's earlier likeness of Sarah Moulton, known as 'Pinkie', had established him as a portrayer of infant beauty. His image of Charles Calmady's daughters caused great excitement in 1824, and this was exceeded in 1825 on the appearance of the portrait of Charles William Lambton, the 'Red Boy', his masterpiece in this category. A reviewer called it 'one of the most exquisite representations of interesting childhood' and Williams held it to be 'one of the most beautiful paintings of a child, ever produced by art'.[64] These were among Lawrence's most reproduced canvases.

He resolved not to bask in praise or relax his efforts in the absence of a serious rival, but to be his own taskmaster and strive to improve. And whatever could be said against him for taking too many half-fees in advance, no one could accuse him of rushing to dispatch a canvas to get the remaining amount. Back in 1811 Farington had told him he was more like someone 'who disregarded the time employed, than like one who thought of getting money', and as the years went by he took ever greater pains. The apparent facility in some of his works was deceptive, for it was achieved only by intense, sustained effort. As he wrote to Isabella Wolff, '[I] am as much the slave of the picture I am painting, as if it had a living, personal existence, and chained me to it.' He never relaxed the habit of hard work and long hours he had acquired as a boy in Bath. 'I shall live and die in harness,' he wrote to a friend in 1829, and so he did.[65]

In this, the crowning decade of Lawrence's career, his highest merit came into focus: an ability to find beauty in the reality before him without distorting that reality, to represent and transfigure nature at the same time. Some accused him of prettifying, justly so in the case of his George IV portraits. But, with this exception, pleasing clients was secondary to a romantic desire to idealise. According to the *Cardiff and Merthyr Guardian* in 1833, 'Sir Thomas Lawrence, when accused of flattery, used to say that he never gave to the countenance an expression excelling that which at some fortunate moment had played upon the features which he pourtrayed.' Viewers were taken aback by this combination of truth and beauty. Of his Canova portrait Thomas Moore said, '[It] has all the beau ideal of the countenance, yet still possessing a strong likeness.' Even Haydon, albeit grudgingly, conceded that in 'purifying' his sitters no one could equal him.[66]

An article in *La Belle Assemblée* of 1830 allows us to dig a little deeper into this. Lawrence possessed, it asserts, far beyond any other artist, 'the grand important secret of preserving a living breathing, characteristic resemblance of the original, at the same time that, in all points, he improved and heightened the general effect', and this produced 'an animated and glowing resemblance'. In other words, he elevated his sitters by capturing their individuality. The Victorian biographer of the anti-slavery campaigner William Wilberforce takes this point further with reference to an incomplete portrait of him: 'The head was wrought up to a high degree of finish, and is an instance of the success with which Lawrence often caught the finest expression of his subject without any sacrifice of its identity. The intellectual power and winning sweetness of the veteran statesman and philanthropist are happily blended in this portrait.'[67]

Lawrence exalts his subject not by some abstract refinement of facial features, but by conveying character as expressed through them. The way he made people feel they interested him deeply was not just for show. They really did, and with rare acuity he felt his way into their minds – as an actor might, and of course he was a good actor. The transmission of mind to canvas impressed observers even more than the enhanced beauty that attended it. Davies Gilbert, President of the Royal Society, the empress dowager of Russia, Thomas Uwins,

Harriet Arbuthnot and a reviewer of the Williams biography were among those who described this quality of his work.[68]

Lawrence was fulfilled, but he was exhausted, not least as he had no secretary to help him with his mountain of correspondence. 'My time is more perpetually and fatiguingly occupied than it ever yet was at any period of my life,' he sighed a few months into his presidency.[69] Gradually he withdrew from social engagements he had felt obliged to fulfil so as to represent the dignity of the Royal Academy. Instead, he often worked in the evenings, and his life grew more solitary. He suffered two severe blows in 1821 with the deaths of his brother Andrew and of Joseph Farington, whose newspaper obituary, laying stress on his generosity as an adviser, Lawrence may have written. John Philip Kemble died in 1823, the year he also lost John Julius Angerstein, and in 1824 it was the turn of Sophia Lee. Good friends remained, and he gained new ones in his patrons Peel and Croker, but his eminence had a lonely, careworn aspect.

As he grew accustomed to life at the pinnacle of his profession, reiterations of success and recognition began to pall. He often felt unwell and older than his years, his body worn out despite the care he had taken of it. To friends he wrote of ceaseless toil, of weariness, of life having lost its savour. He never stopped wanting to paint, but exertions at his easel alternated with lassitude. His melancholy, fleetingly eclipsed by moments of artistic satisfaction or the solace of companionship, was in part a mystery, emanating from some secret sadness. He was still beset by rumours of risky gambling and low connections, though these circulated only in society, not in the press. 'It is said that he regularly loses at the billiard table all of the enormous sums his art earns him,' wrote Prince Pückler-Muskau. Croker said he was kept poor by generosity to women, and that he knew who two or three of them were.[70]

Poor he certainly was, but he did not desist from giving money in public and private charity or from acquiring Old Master drawings, or indeed from helping his surviving sister Anne and her children, four of whom he put through Oxford. Without Farington's restraining hand, his finances became chaotic. It is odd that although his troubles pressed sorely upon him he never sought to curtail unnecessary expenditure. Rather, he made desperate appeals to Croker and Peel to save him from immediate ruin. Samuel Rogers and the Earl of Dudley, who knew him less well but had soft hearts and great wealth, made emergency loans that were not repaid. He was never actually arrested for a debt, though he came perilously close to it, and thus he evaded the shame his father had endured of having his insolvency blared out in the newspapers. The scandal for a man in his position would of course have been infinitely worse.

An occasional bad review was the worst that appeared in the press. Lawrence was the nation's foremost artist, a dignitary who honoured others and was honoured by them. Aside from a few innocuous, rather impersonal little anecdotes and puns, there is little sense of him as a man. During the Siddons and Princess of Wales scandals, and generally in his younger days, he had been a celebrity, with interest focused on his life as well as his work. Now he had risen higher and stood on the plinth of true fame. In 1826 he had a mention in fiction, with the Marquess of Carabas in Disraeli's *Vivian Grey* remarking of his own portrait, 'It was one of Sir Thomas's happiest efforts.'[71] Frank Howard's engravings to illustrate Shakespeare's *As You Like It* were dedicated to him in 1827, as was a painting manual by John Burnet the following year. In 1829 the freedom of his native city of Bristol was conferred upon him.

The period after Lawrence's last visit to Paris was busier than ever. Among other things he painted fifteen senior British politicians for Robert Peel, a domestic supplement to George IV's gallery. He was, Peel told him, labouring 'for your future fame by completing a series of Portraits for me (many of which will be the paintings of real History)'.[72] It has often been said that his powers did not decline in these final years, but nor should they have, for he was only in late middle age. He was still without a challenger, still pitting his efforts against himself. In 1829 he increased his prices again, this time to 700 guineas for a full-length. In this and the previous year his output was particularly rich, reflecting a more intense concentration than ever. If critics ever felt tempted to dispraise him or say he was getting monotonous just to change their tune they did not do so, and the only monotony was in the vocabulary of their panegyrics.

Lawrence's social life, besides quiet evenings with good friends, had dwindled to almost nothing, and his correspondence, too, he pared right down. He still went to court but rarely left London, one of his last journeys being in 1827 to Wynyard in County Durham, the seat of Lord Londonderry, formerly Lord Stewart. He was in constant contact with the widowed Isabella Wolff, but for reasons of economy she had retired to Herefordshire, where he made two brief visits. The friend he saw most, 'my sister, for such I consider you', was Elizabeth Croft, who after he died wrote touching reminiscences of him. He also spent time with their common friend and his near neighbour Archibald Keightley, a young solicitor. On one of his rare evenings in general company 'a lady of discernment' studied him:

I thought I never saw any body look so pale, to be in health – yet so very handsome. When we could catch him without the animation that lights him when speaking, he looks like a marble statue, with the lips and eyes only tinted. I cannot think but that he applies much too closely for his health, and indeed that he cannot be quite well, whatever he may say. His gaze made me melancholy when sitting opposite him in the evening: to my idea, there never was so much sweetness, and benignity, and gentleness expressed in any countenance, where also so much genius and brilliant animation, and such forcible and searching inquiry, are depicted.[73]

In the spring of 1829 Isabella Wolff died, and Lawrence was so stricken that for a while he laid down his brushes and saw no one. Theirs had been an intellectual union with a tenderness amounting to love on both sides. Many thought she was his mistress, but if so she would hardly have moved from London to a remote spot near the Welsh border. To her he wrote his most wide-ranging, entertaining letters, but on her death it was above all her moral and religious principles that he exalted. These he had imbibed, and no other bereavement drew from him such direct avowals of Christian faith. He now sensed that his own end might be near. It was noticed that he was pallid and drowsy and walked feebly, and he complained of fatigue, pains in his body, and hotness about the forehead. Before old age could impair his ability to paint, a period he positively hoped for as a merciful rest from his labours, his heart gave out.

Doubtless a life of overwork and anxiety contributed largely to his demise. In his last months he felt severe trepidation about his debts, which drew bailiffs to his door, and about an illness of his sister. He had more unfinished canvases than ever. 'His disease, a spasmodic affection of the heart, was unquestionably accelerated by the perplexed condition of his affairs!' stated the *Court Journal* after his death.[74] He hoped to spend Christmas 1829 with Anne in Rugby, but the press of work kept him in London. At the turn of the year he fell ill, but doctors suspected a stomach complaint and gave him medicine for this. He went on painting in short bursts, but as his pain worsened friends grew alarmed and he was bled. On 7 January 1830 Mr Keightley was reading him an article about the sculptor John Flaxman when he felt his grip on life loosen and asked his friends to leave the room. Minutes later, he died in his manservant's arms.

Although he had been unwell for months, the president's death at the age of sixty startled almost everyone. The sense of loss, and of his irreplaceability, was piercing. Diaries and letters record a grief that testifies to his worth, and it was whispered angrily that bleeding had caused a fatal depletion of his strength. The press registered the same shock and sorrow, and the same uncertainty about how he had died, with differing reports and corrections about his heart and bowels. In the first days, paragraphs of prose and numerous turgid threnodies praised his personal qualities and magisterial work. The *Courier* recalled 'the incontestable and almost unenvied supremacy accorded throughout Europe' to him, and *Bell's Weekly Messenger* spoke of the nation in mourning after 'the extinction of so splendid a light among its chiefest ornaments'. Then came obituaries, the most reprinted being a celebration of his life in the *Literary Gazette*.

The elaborate funeral, conducted over two days, attracted great public attention. Lawrence's body was conveyed to Somerset House to lie in state and then to St Paul's Cathedral, where it was interred in the crypt. His executor Archibald Keightley had no small task because of the disarray of his friend's accounts. Lawrence had ardently hoped to leave his Old Master drawings to the nation, but the government refused to pay for them and the collection was broken up. Moreover, the proceeds of this, together with the sale of his unfinished works, barely met the claims of creditors, and his nieces and nephews, the intended beneficiaries of his will, got nothing. Instead they were paid the net receipts of the British Institution's retrospective exhibition of May 1830, to which the king lent thirty-one pictures. The artist was also well represented in that year's Academy, and critics burst into applause at his portrait of the foreign secretary Lord Aberdeen.

The newspapers gave accounts of his funeral procession, published his will, acclaimed his posthumous exhibitions, printed tributes from notable figures at home and abroad, and described the medal and the portrait engravings that were soon made. Amid this commemoration of the great man, the human being came back into view as diverse recollections were unearthed: his charm and precocity as a boy in Devizes and Bath; his interaction with Reynolds, with whom his achievement and public service were compared; his generosity to struggling artists; and so on through his life. The other side of the coin was turned up, too. Old conjecture about gambling and money troubles was rehashed and linked to his pocketing of half-fees for works he had only a distant prospect of completing. He was, said the *Chester Chronicle*, 'supposed to have left behind him more works unfinished than any artist either of ancient or modern times'.

Almost without exception journalists skated round the Siddons love triangle, but the *Literary Gazette* obituary, though laudatory, gave offence by alluding to his dejection after the death of 'Mrs W.', whom it called 'his dearest connection'. This could only be taken to mean an illicit liaison, and other titles picked up the scent and named the lady. 'When this hateful calumny met my eyes in the "Literary Gazette" I spurned it with all the indignation it merited,' wrote Lawrence's friend Amelia Angerstein née Lock.[75] She was not alone, and the magazine issued a retraction and stated that 'nothing inconsistent with the strictest morality and decorum' had occurred. Another well-aired story was that when a bond for £5,000 came into the hands of Coutts & Co. the artist went to the bank, prostrated himself before the Duchess of St Albans, under whose stewardship it was conducted, and was told by her to think no more of the matter.

Private evaluations of Lawrence were confided in journals and letters, often to be published later. A second wave of public responses was prompted in 1831 by *The Life and Correspondence of Sir Thomas Lawrence* by D. E. Williams. Unknown except as the author of this work, Williams was keen to share his admiration of Lawrence, but he earned little for himself with the confused structure, eccentric views, extraneous detail and diffuse style of his two volumes. Puffing from the publishers Colburn and Bentley could not persuade people it was a good book, though later scholars have found it invaluable as a repository of Lawrence's correspondence. Its tendency to exculpate him in the Siddons affair provoked some negative reactions not to the benefit of his memory. The living statue, who for years prior to his death had seemed to the public an institution of national cultural life, was a man again, warts and all.

And what of his artistic reputation? He himself did not expect many fresh laurels from posterity. To Andrew Lawrence he wrote in 1820, 'I can never expect that the labors of my Pencil will have so great an interest at any future time as they now have, nor their Superiority be so generally acknowledg'd.'[76] So it was; he had been a fashionable painter, and fashions change. His association with George IV, of which he was so proud, was held against him. For Victorians the bright, rich colours of his palette and the sultry looks of his women tainted him with the flashiness and sensualism of the Regency, a view supported by persistent rumours of gambling and other irregularities in his private life. The same austere judges found portraits of men that betrayed his theatrical instinct and taste for grandeur to be preening and stagey. For much of the nineteenth and twentieth centuries he was accused of insincerity, flattery, vulgarity and sentimentality.

If critics had looked at his portraits of aged subjects rather than the superficially more appealing ones of the younger generation, this perception would not have taken hold. It is also hard to reconcile with his earnest devotion to art and profound knowledge of it, or with his tireless efforts to promote it. As a public man he could hardly have done more for art in Britain, and on this account alone he deserves to stand alongside the political, military, religious, literary and theatrical figures whose features he perpetuated. And, whatever Victorians felt, there is no obloquy now in being associated with the Regency, which appears a heroic age full of zest, optimism and creativity, of brilliant advances in all areas of human achievement. Lawrence takes his place in the forefront of this world. In the words of Thomas Campbell, he was 'a man fit for a Golden Age'.[77]

At Lawrence's death many assumed his work would meet the ultimate test of fame; others thought his reputation would decay fast. Each opinion has seemed right at different times since then. Today, being strongly identified with his period does not seem to limit him; rather he transcends that period as a pictorial historian, a creator of portraits that give us our image of it. Nor is this just a record of important people's faces, for he conveyed their natures and the force of their personalities. And he caught them in moments of beauty or inspiration, blending likeness with an aesthetic ideal that he and they shared but he alone had the imagination to capture. He showed them as they wanted to he seen, and his era as it wanted to be seen. In this he was truly a history painter: a cultural ambassador of his country while he lived, a cultural ambassador of his age to us now.

Notes

CONTEXT

1 Celebrity Culture

1. Mole, *Byron*, p. 3.
2. Boone and Vickers, p. 904.
3. Turner, p. 119.
4. Rojek, p. 52. Rojek ascribes the growth of celebrity culture partly to the need for comfort in what he calls 'the world of the stranger' (p. 74).
5. Braudy, p. 9.
6. On this apparatus see Mole, *Byron*, pp. xi, 1–3.

2 The Birth of Celebrity Culture

1. See Eisner, p. 3; Braudy, pp. 6, 549; Cashmore, p. 7; Turner, pp. 10–13; Mole, *Byron*, pp. 6–7.
2. Proponents of this view include Baker, p. 7; Boone and Vickers, p. 906; Inglis, pp. 3, 6, 8; Lilti, pp. 7, 12; McPherson, p. 9; Mole, *Byron*, p. xi; Tillyard, p. 61. The early eighteenth century is proposed by Jenner, pp. 100–05, 127.
3. The earliest example I have found is in the *Dublin Morning Register* of 21 February 1831: 'All the celebrities of the Carlist faction had a rendezvous, and collected money for the wounded of the ex-Royal Guard.' Another is in the 1835 diary of the novelist Sydney, Lady Morgan, II, 394: 'Dinner at Mr Dilke's – sat near Allan Cunningham – immense fun – Willis, the American poet, and other celebrities.' But while these instances show 'celebrity' used to designate a person, the conceptual distinction between fame and celebrity came later.
4. Figures given in Mason, p. 14.
5. Rush, pp. 107–08.

6. Quoted in Higgins, p. 46.
7. Greville, II, 273.
8. An attempt by the prince regent's crony Colonel John McMahon to bully and bribe an editor favourable to the prince's estranged wife Caroline of Brunswick is narrated in Creevey, *Papers*, pp. 178–79.
9. H. Hunt, I, 543–44. Henry Dundas, Viscount Melville was a Tory politician.
10. Quoted in McCreery, *Satirical Gaze*, p. 16.
11. Quoted in Mole, *Byron*, p. xii.
12. Egan, pp. 48, 192.
13. Albemarle, I, 347.
14. Meryon, *Memoirs*, I, 280–81.
15. Newman, p. 90; Pascoe, p. 245.
16. J. Grant, 1st series, I, 17.
17. Lach-Szyrma, p. 277; Cowell, p. 46.
18. Pascoe finds that newspaper notices about Ann Hatton so closely mimic the 'aggrieved, aspirational, grasping' tone of her letters that 'we must conclude either that Hatton wrote both or that those who wrote on her behalf did so with a keen sense of her preferred public presentation' (pp. 255–56).
19. Meryon, *Memoirs*, III, 158–59.
20. Fletcher, p. 231; Pückler-Muskau, *Dead Man*, p. 71; Rush, p. 126.
21. Munby, pp. 8, 12 (autographs). I. Kelly, *Brummell*, pp. 191–208; I. Kelly, *Cooking*, pp. 188–89 ('the first celebrity chef' is taken from this work's subtitle).
22. Tillyard, p. 61; 'Famous for being famous' is a distortion of Daniel Boorstin's quip that a celebrity is 'a person who is known for his well-knownness' (p. 57).

3 Byron and Other Poets
1. Bulwer-Lytton, p. 294.
2. Jewsbury, pp. 2–3.
3. For an account of Burney's secret hunger for fame see Brock, pp. 110–28.
4. Seymour, pp. 246–47.
5. Campbell quoted in Mason, p. 45; Jerdan, III, 173.
6. See Brock, p. 9 and Higgins, pp. 60, 163 (note 7).
7. Egan, pp. 29–30.
8. Foster, pp. 364, 376; H. Holland, p. 206. The scholarship on Lord Byron and his celebrity is extensive and I have drawn on it gratefully, especially the studies of Tom Mole and Clara Tuite and the collection of essays edited by Frances Wilson.

9. Scott, *Letters*, III, 98; Dudley, *Llandaff*, pp. 207–08.

10. *Lara*, canto 1, verse 17, lines 289–302.

11. Lady Morgan, II, 200 (Lamb); Greville, I, 368; Scott, *Journal*, p. 9; Stowe, p. 51.

12. On portraits of Byron see Mole, *Byron*, pp. 79–83 and F. Wilson, *Byromania*, p. 124.

13. Lovell, *Blessington*, p. 220; Haydon, *Diary*, II, 485.

14. On Byron's female fans see Throsby's article.

15. *Don Juan*, Dedication and canto 7, verse 18, lines 141–42; Page, p. 134.

16. Jack, p. 69; Lovell, *Medwin*, pp. 168–69, 206, 214.

17. Stowe, p. 51 (Milbanke); Kilgour, p. 25 (Curran); Lovell, *Blessington*, p. 85; Thackeray quoted in Mason, p. 65.

18. On the Murray-Dallas collaboration and Murray's advertising see Mason, pp. 74–80. The term 'Byromania' was coined by Annabella Milbanke in 1812.

19. Greville, I, 368.

20. On visual images of Byron see Mole, *Byron*, ch. 5.

21. Lockhart, 'Lord Byron', p. 136; H. Holland, pp. 206–07.

22. Eisner, p. 12 (Wilson); J. L. Hunt, p. 223.

23. Quoted in Eisner, p. 3.

24. Lady Morgan, II, 341.

25. See Mason, p. 123.

26. See Mason, pp. 2–3. In this and the next paragraph I draw heavily on this study.

27. Quoted in Goldsmith, p. 812.

28. Quoted in Eisner, p. 158.

29. Jewsbury, pp. 53–59.

30. On Byron and Keats, with quote, see Eisner, pp. 10, 58; Moore, V, 1789.

31. See Andrew Bennett's monograph on this subject.

32. H. C. Robinson, I, 246. Byron, by contrast, said, 'I never persecute the public. I always bow to its verdict, which is generally just': Lovell, *Medwin*, pp. 159–60.

33. H. C. Robinson, I, 245; Watts, I, 240; Haydon, *Correspondence and Table-Talk*, II, 24; Wordsworth quoted in Bennett, p. 49. See also H. C. Robinson, I, 339.

34. On Wordsworth's view of biography see North, pp. 39–43.

35. As Leo Braudy wryly observes, 'Often enough, the announcement of exclusive belief in the judgment of the future was made loudly in the present' (p. 425).

36. Broughton, I, 100; Bennett, p. 189.

37. Murray, p. 72.

4 *Actors and Actresses*
 1. J. Grant, 1st series, I, 23.
 2. J. L. Hunt, p. 154.
 3. Elizabeth, Duchess of Devonshire gives an eyewitness account of the frantic enthusiasm for Betty: Foster, pp. 191–92. See also Adolphus, II, 127; Boaden, *Mrs Jordan*, II, 167–70.
 4. Haydon, *Correspondence and Table-Talk*, II, 297–98.
 5. These points are made with modern comparisons by Kahan, pp. 155–56.
 6. The educational philanthropist Hannah More told Garrick he had gained 'a fame which has had no parallel, and will have no end': *Letters*, p. 54.
 7. Adolphus, II, 341.
 8. That Garrick profiled himself like a celebrity but without the full celebrity apparatus to back him up is shown by Mole, *Byron*, pp. 9–10.
 9. Boaden, *Mrs Siddons*, p. 2.
10. Quoted in Wanko, 'Patron or Patronised?', p. 217.
11. In Boaden's neat formulation, actresses 'changed the sex of their patrons, and were frequently received in the best society': *Mrs Siddons*, p. 3.
12. On portraits of actresses see the collection of essays edited by Robyn Asleson.
13. Thomson, II, 151–52.
14. Adolphus, I, 389.
15. M. Robinson, p. 99.
16. Brock, p. 78 (Egan); M. Robinson, pp. 90, 113.
17. M. Robinson, p. 117; McCreery, '*Bon Ton*', p. 221.
18. M. Robinson, p. 113.
19. Boaden, *Mrs Siddons*, p. 179.
20. Comparing Gainsborough's portraits of Siddons and of Georgiana, Duchess of Devonshire, Heather McPherson (p. 88) finds that the former 'exudes elegant aloofness and majesty' while the latter looks 'flashily seductive', so that a viewer unaware of their identities might mistake the actress for the duchess.
21. Boaden's unauthorised biography appeared in 1827, four years before Siddons died.
22. McPherson, p. 179; Dyce, p. 135.
23. Gillies, I, 319; Farington, I, 280; Burney quoted in Bloxam, pp. 73–74.
24. Braudy, p. 27; H. C. Robinson, I, 209, 251.
25. Moore, III, 1146 (reporting Rogers); Kemble, III, 12.

PORTRAITS

1 The Parvenue Duchess

1. R. Richardson, p. 81.
2. Baron-Wilson, I, iv, 339.
3. Baron-Wilson, I, 196–98. Coleridge (II, 236–37) casts doubt on this story.
4. According to Adolphus, II, 50.
5. Pearce, pp. 96–97 (Anne Mathews); Baron-Wilson, I, 203.
6. Baron-Wilson, I, 176; Oxberry, III, 106.
7. Quoted in Baron-Wilson, I, 272. See also pp. 276–77.
8. Lennox, II, 38; Boaden, *Mrs Jordan*, I, 277; Oxberry, III, 104.
9. Oxberry, III, 104.
10. *Gentleman's Magazine*, 8:2 (1837), p. 420; Pearce, p. 130 (Abington).
11. Baron-Wilson, I, 304.
12. An anecdote of her generosity in these years is related by Angelo, p. 388.
13. Baron-Wilson, I, 149–50; 326.
14. Mathews, *Memoirs*, II, 66–67; Haydon, *Autobiography*, p. 358; Oxberry, III, 91, 100–02, 105; Mathews, *Tea-Table Talk*, I, 75.
15. Baron-Wilson, I, 223–25.
16. Baron-Wilson, I, 274.
17. For the view that the friendship was not sexual see Haydon, *Autobiography*, p. 357; Mathews, *Tea-Table Talk*, I, 80, 83; Oxberry, III, 99–100; Farington, IV, 195.
18. These are printed in Coleridge, II, 249–60, 288–310. Her replies are lost.
19. Bruce, p. 348.
20. Coleridge, II, 341, 365, 366.
21. Coleridge, II, 345; J. T. Smith, p. 386.
22. Haydon, *Autobiography*, p. 358.
23. Meryon, *Additional Memoirs*, pp. 148, 155–56: Glenbervie, II, 304, 310–11.
24. Creevey, *Papers*, p. 345.
25. Gronow, I, 170; Mathews, *Tea-Table Talk*, I, 88–89.
26. Perkin, p. 142.
27. Perkin, pp. 145, 202.
28. Harrowby MSS, 3rd series, vol. LX, folios 203–04: letter of 4 January 1824.
29. Harrowby MSS, 3rd series, vol. LX, folios 336–37: letter of 30 October 1824 to Lord Dudley Coutts Stuart; vol. LXI, folios 1–2: letter of 4 January 1825 to the same.
30. Baron-Wilson, I, xi.

31. This was also published with another, equally long title, of which the first words are *A Tale of the Last Century*.
32. Like the *Secret Memoirs*, this appeared in various versions.
33. Baron-Wilson, II, 58, 245.
34. Baron-Wilson, I, vii.
35. Oxberry, III, 100–01; see also Baron-Wilson, II, 176–78, 257–58.
36. Creevey, *Papers*, p. 344; Redding, III, 217; Anon., *Gentleman's Magazine*, 8:2 (1837), p. 420.
37. Baron-Wilson, II, 257.
38. Egan, pp. 251–53; Westmacott, I, 308–13; II, 297–98; Disraeli, pp. 55, 59–60, 61, 62, 70, 74–77, 81, 98.
39. Baron-Wilson, I, 189–91.
40. Quoted in Perkin, p. 153.
41. Lieven, *Private Letters*, p. 271; Pückler-Muskau, 'Erinnerungsbilder', II, 43 (my translation); Fox, p. 361; Harrowby MSS, 3rd series, vol. LXII, folios 39–40, 106–07 (letters).
42. Airlie, *Lady Palmerston*, I, 121.
43. Scott, *Journal*, pp. 13–14, 217.
44. Lady Holland, *Letters*, p. 65.
45. Broughton, III, 203; H. C. Robinson, II, 112.
46. *Gentleman's Magazine*, 21:1 (1828), p. 72.
47. Lady Morgan, II, 238; Stirling, I, 185–86 (Cheltenham anecdote); Pückler-Muskau, *Dead Man*, p. 306.
48. Mathews, *Tea-Table Talk*, I, 86–87.
49. Baron-Wilson, II, 229; Pückler-Muskau, 'Erinnerungsbilder', II, 43 (my translation).
50. Baron-Wilson, II, 249–53.
51. Baron-Wilson, II, 217.
52. MacFarlane, pp. 48–49.
53. Boaden, *Mrs Jordan*, I, 278; Mathews, *Tea-Table Talk*, I, 85, 90–91; Baron-Wilson, I, 5–6; *Gentleman's Magazine*, 8:2 (1837), p. 421; Oxberry, III, 101–02.
54. Gilchrist, *Etty*, I, 362.
55. Baron-Wilson, II, 245–46, 259, 320–21.
56. Suffolk Record Office: Hervey Family Archives 941/5/11/5/24: letter of 12 November 1828 to the Marquess of Bristol; Anon., Review of 'Epistle to Harriet, Duchess of St Albans', in *Literary Gazette*, 616 (8 November 1828), p. 712.
57. Baron-Wilson, I, 7–10, 17, 19–21; II, 58–60.
58. See Oxberry, II, 105.
59. Exceptions are Thomas Creevey (*Life and Times*, p. 266) and Charles Macready (I, 406). Henry Edward Fox had mixed feelings (pp. 364–65).

60. Kemble, III, 5.
61. H. Arbuthnot, I, 408; II, 306; J. Gore, p. 146; Lady Holland, *Letters*, pp. 106, 116.
62. Creevey, *Papers*, p. 559; 'The Queen Dowager', *Hull Packet*, 31 May 1839.
63. R. Richardson, p. 81 (letter to Scott); Sala, I, 28.

2 The Tsar's Intriguer

1. Thackeray, *Vanity Fair*, pp. 364–65.
2. Lieven, *Private Letters*, p. 15; Daudet, pp. 23–24.
3. Daudet, pp. 76–77 (my translation).
4. Cromwell, p. 37.
5. Lieven, *Letters/Residence*, p. 3; Shelley, II, 139; Lieven, *Letters/Residence*, p. 3; Allardyce, II, 75.
6. Frampton, pp. 159–60; Lieven, *Letters/Residence*, pp. 3, 18, 31, 32, 34.
7. Calvert, p. 205; Princess Charlotte, p. 90; Sir G. Jackson, II, 139; Nesselrode quoted in Lieven, *Diary and Sketches*, p. 31.
8. Countess Granville, II, 86; Rush, p. 62.
9. Calvert, p. 196; Frampton, p. 159.
10. Wellington, p. 302.
11. Blakiston, p. 53; Countess Granville, I, 56 (my translation), 221; Wellington, pp. 49–50.
12. Countess Granville, I, 176–77; Neumann, I, 34.
13. Lieven, *Private Letters*, pp. 74–75; Neumann, I, 36–37.
14. Lieven, *Diary and Sketches*, pp. 34–37.
15. Lieven, *Letters/Residence*, pp. 22, 26.
16. H. Holland, p. 185.
17. 'High mightinesses' is taken from the dedication to Marianne Spencer Stanhope's novel *Almack's*; Gronow, I, 32. An example of Countess Lieven's high-handedness as a patroness is given in Creevey, *Life and Times*, p. 181.
18. Lieven, *Letters/Residence*, p. 19.
19. Countess Granville, II, 13.
20. Bury, *Diary*, III, 323; Boigne, II, 181 (my translation).
21. Princess Charlotte, p. 227.
22. C. Arbuthnot, p. 13.
23. Cromwell, p. 80.
24. Countess Granville, I, 210; Palmerston, p. 115; Lieven, *Private Letters*, p. 180.
25. Lieven, *Letters/Residence*, p. 47; Lieven, *Private Letters*, p. 261.
26. Countess Granville, I, 200; II, 38–39.
27. Countess Granville, II, 46; Raikes, I, 142; Boigne, II, 181 (my translation); H. Arbuthnot, II, 54.

28. H. Arbuthnot, II, 53–54; Lieven, *Private Letters*, p. 20. On this 'rivalry' see Boigne, II, 179–80.
29. Lieven, *Letters/Residence*, p. 66; Lieven, *Private Letters*, p. 128.
30. Greville, I, 324; Londonderry, pp. 99–100.
31. Lieven, *Private Letters*, p. 169.
32. Lieven, *Private Letters*, pp. 294–95.
33. Naville, I, 49 (my translation).
34. Quoted in Lieven, *Diary and Sketches*, p. 72.
35. H. Arbuthnot, II, 31, 37–38, 65.
36. Lieven, *Diary and Sketches*, p. 89.
37. Lieven, *Diary and Sketches*, p. 198.
38. Lieven, *Private Letters*, p. 291; Creevey, *Papers*, p. 651; Lieven, *Private Letters*, p. 265.
39. Lieven, *Private Letters*, pp. 244–45.
40. Cromwell, p. 3 (Nesselrode); Sneyd, p. 8 (unnamed statesman).
41. Sudley, p. 13.
42. Lieven, *Private Letters*, p. 370; Sudley, p. 39.
43. H. Arbuthnot, II, 54, 79; Blakiston, p. 294.
44. Cromwell, pp. 80 (Metternich), 90 (Tsar Alexander I); Sneyd, p. 6; H. Arbuthnot, II, 165; Boigne, II, 181 (my translation); Malmesbury, p. 386; Lady Holland, *Letters*, pp. 126, 157.
45. Lieven, *Private Letters*, p. 179; Le Strange, II, 226; Lieven, *Private Letters*, pp. 145, 294.
46. H. Arbuthnot, II, 168.
47. Greville, I, 262.
48. Shelley, II, 174 (Arbuthnot); Le Strange, I, 385.
49. Malmesbury, pp. 374–75.
50. Charmley, p. 175.
51. Le Strange, I, 329–30, 335; Countess Granville, II, 44; Greville, I, 324; H. Arbuthnot, II, 312–13 (she wrote '*basse flagornerie*'); Sudley, p. 302.
52. Ellenborough, II, 27–28; Greville, I, 312.
53. H. Arbuthnot, II, 312, 339; Le Strange, I, 398, 418.
54. Le Strange, I, 416; H. Arbuthnot, II, 339.
55. Le Strange, II, 289.
56. Sudley, pp. 21, 24.
57. Quoted in Lieven, *Letters/Residence*, p. ix.
58. H. Arbuthnot, II, 376 (William IV); Sudley, p. 118
59. Le Strange, I, 474; Raikes, I, 142; Pückler Archive, Varnhagen-Sammlung, boxes 163–64; letters of 22 November 1826, 20 February & 5 November 1827 from Hermann von Pückler-Muskau to his ex-wife Lucie (my translations).

60. Creevey, *Papers*, p. 604; Dino, II, 72–73.
61. Lieven, *Letters/Holland*, p. 1 (my translation). It has gone unnoticed that Lady Holland's introductory essay is almost exactly the same as Ralph Sneyd's article, also in French, in the *Miscellanies of the Philobiblon Society* over eighty years earlier. However, where Lady Holland has 'a celebrity', Sneyd has 'celebrated'.
62. Pückler-Muskau, 'Erinnerungsbilder', I, 35–36.
63. Shelley, II, 139. In English prose: 'A tragedy queen's air of boredom and disdain, an artificial dignity, embroideries and sulkiness, and trimmings enough for four – meet the ambassadress from a barbarian land.'
64. Greville, II, 262; Talleyrand, III, 406 (my translation).
65. Quoted in Cromwell, p. 133.
66. Le Strange, II, 181–83; Lady Holland, *Letters*, pp. 117–18.
67. Moore, IV, 1532.
68. Palmerston, p. 202.
69. Le Strange, I, 160; H. Arbuthnot, II, 168, 193, 195; Wellington quoted in Charmley, p. 179; Le Strange, I, 379; II, 87–88.
70. Le Strange, II, 221.
71. For a long criticism of her behaviour in society see Bury, *Diary*, III, 369–70.
72. Gallatin, pp. 262–63; Pückler-Muskau, 'Erinnerungsbilder', I, 35–36.
73. Lieven, *Letters/Residence*, pp. 365–66.
74. Cromwell, p. 156; Greville, II, 350–51, 430.
75. Blakiston, p. 301; Greville, III, 39; Lady Holland, *Letters*, p. 148.
76. Dino, II, 72–73, 112–13; Lady Holland, *Letters*, p. 147.
77. Blakiston, p. 313. See also p. 301.
78. Sudley, p. 81.
79. Sudley, p. 173; Greville, VII, 263; Countess Granville, II, 238, 243.
80. Daudet, pp. 390, 391 (my translations).
81. Malmesbury, p. 386; Talleyrand, III, 405 (my translation); Greville, VII, 258; Raikes, I, 142; Lieven, *Letters/Holland*, p. 5; Cromwell, p. 237 (Hübner).

3 The Last Grandee

1. See newspaper reports and Bowman, *Real 'Persuasion'*, pp. 45–47.
2. Bruce, p. 279.
3. In 1855 the Catholic journal *The Rambler* published Lady Mary Arundell née Grenville's account of how her mother won the right to practise her faith.

4. Lord Temple's letters to W. H. Fremantle from 1792 to 1796 are in the Centre for Buckinghamshire Studies, D FR/46/8. The letter about Prince Augustus is in Aspinall, *Prince of Wales*, II, 339.

5. Essex Record Office, Lloyd Family Papers, D/DGu Z1: letter of 1805 to Louisa Lloyd.

6. See W. J. Smith, *George the Third*, III, 74–78. The correspondence is ostensibly edited by the 2nd Duke of Buckingham; see J. Beckett, pp. 262, 269 (note 52).

7. Melville, *Wellesley Papers*, I, 132.

8. The *Courier* quoted in Sack, *Grenvillites*, p. 38; Horner, II, 339.

9. Earl Granville, I, 310 (Lady Bessborough); Farington, II, 276.

10. Sack, *Grenvillites*, p. 170 (verses); Jerdan, II, 328–29.

11. Meryon, *Additional Memoirs*, pp. 6, 142, 157; Cleveland, p. 245.

12. Essex Record Office, Lloyd Family Papers, D/Dgu Z1: letters of 1804–1808 from Lady Temple to Louisa Lloyd; D/Dgu Z2: letters of 1805–1807 from Lady Louisa Harvey to the same; Nugent, p. 328; Dudley, 'Ivy', p. 27.

13. Meryon, *Additional Memoirs*, p. 74; Farington, II, 276; A. Fremantle, III, 126, 194, 242 ('cross et vulgaire' on p. 194 must be a misreading for 'gros et vulgaire'); J. Beckett, p. 100 (Thomas Grenville); Dudley, 'Ivy', p. 170.

14. Trench, pp. 26–27; A. Fremantle, III, 25–26.

15. Parry, p. 128 (W. H. Fremantle's letter); Earl Granville, II, 493.

16. Gronow, II, 217–19.

17. Besides newspapers, the letters of W. H. Fremantle's nephew John, an officer in the Coldstream Guards, give information about Buckingham's movements from 1814 to 1816: J. Fremantle, pp. 178, 179, 220–21, 223, 226, 228.

18. Creevey, *Papers*, pp. 215–17; Dudley, *Llandaff*, pp. 168, 171.

19. Centre for Buckinghamshire Studies, D FR/46/11: letter of 4 February 1821 to W. H. Fremantle.

20. Horner, II, 338.

21. *Legend of the House of Yonne and A Sicilian Tale* was published privately in 1830. *A Tale of the Civil Wars* is unpublished. Specimens of Buckingham's poetry are printed at the close of the third volume of his *Diary*.

22. See J. Beckett, p. 125 (note 98).

23. Essex Record Office, Lloyd Family Papers, D/Dgu Z1: letters of 29 October, 3 November & 20 November 1830.

24. Creevey, *Papers*, p. 256; J. Gore, pp. 48–51.

25. Essex Record Office, Lloyd Family Papers, D/Dgu Z1: letter of 1 September 1816.

26. Essex Record Office, Lloyd Family Papers, D/Dgu Z1: letter of 1 September 1816. On the Lady Hardy affair see also J. Beckett, pp. 104–05.
27. E. C. G. Murray, *Young Brown; or, The Law of Inheritance*, 3 vols (London: Smith, Elder, 1874). On Buckingham and Emma Murray see Berridge, pp. 4–7, 11–12; J. Beckett, pp. 105–06; Bourne, pp. 204–05.
28. Centre for Buckinghamshire Studies, D 54/15: letter of 21 January 1816 from the Marchioness of Buckingham to Thomas Grenville; Essex Record Office, Lloyd Family Papers, D/Dgu Z2: letters of 10 May 1816 and of 1821 from Lady Louisa Harvey to Louisa Lloyd.
29. J. Beckett, p. 113 (Thomas Grenville); Essex Record Office, Lloyd Family Papers, D/Dgu Z6: letter of 2 January 1817 from Sir Felton Hervey-Bathurst.
30. *A Curious and Interesting Narrative of Poll House and the Marquis of C******, (Late Lord T----)*, published by J. L. Marks and reprinted with an introduction in Peakman, V, 359–404. Peakman must be mistaken in thinking the booklet appeared in 1820 since Temple did not become Marquis of Chandos, and nor was there any notion such a title would exist, until 1822.
31. Essex Record Office, Lloyd Family Papers, D/Dgu Z2: letter of 1 July 1820 to Louisa Lloyd.
32. Leighton, p. 254.
33. Essex Record Office, Lloyd Family Papers, D/Dgu Z2: letter of 4 May 1821 to Louisa Lloyd; Aspinall, *George IV*, II, 482 (Liverpool).
34. Centre for Buckinghamshire Studies, D FR/46/11: letter of 17 November 1821. See also the autobiography of the *Guardian*'s editor C. Knight, I, 258–79.
35. Sack, *Grenvillites*, p. 193 (Grey); H. Arbuthnot, I, 130; Dudley, *Llandaff*, p. 301.
36. Sack, *Grenvillites*, p. 194.
37. The duel is well documented: Centre for Buckinghamshire Studies, D FR/46/10: letter of 25 April 1822 from the Duke of Buckingham to W. H. Fremantle; D FR/46/12: letter of 6 May 1822 from the same to the same; D FR/48/3: notes and correspondence relating to the duel. See also W. J. Smith, *George IV*, I, 320–22; Leighton, pp. 281–90.
38. Leighton, p. 290.
39. J. Beckett, p. 134. The information in this chapter about Buckingham's estates and general finances is almost all drawn from this study.

40. Centre for Buckinghamshire Studies, D FR/46/11: letter of 30 October 1820.
41. Leighton, p. 343.
42. Gladstone Library, Glynne-Gladstone MSS: letter of 7 March 1819 to Lady Mary Glynne.
43. Fox, pp. 309–10.
44. Creevey, *Papers*, p. 411; H. Arbuthnot, I, 133, 193–94, 398–99.
45. Sack, *Grenvillites*, pp. 216–17.
46. Aspinall, *Prince of Wales*, VIII, 453.
47. Leighton, pp. 367–68.
48. Buckingham, III, 99–100, 110, 139, 142.
49. On Letitia Wyse see Bonaparte-Wyse, pp. 20–23; Bowman, *Fortune Hunter*, pp. 153–56.
50. Leighton, p. 345; Essex Record Office, Lloyd Family Papers, D/DGu Z1: letters of 29 October & 20 November 1830.
51. Buckingham, III, 87, 104, 232.
52. Aspinall, *Three Diaries*, pp. 52, 161; Le Strange, II, 9; Leighton, p. 379.
53. Creevey, *Papers*, p. 563.
54. Aspinall, *Three Diaries*, p. 223.
55. J. Beckett, pp. 158, 167.
56. J. Beckett, p. 171.
57. J. Beckett, p. 181.

4 *The Elegant Novelist*
1. Croker, I, 428; Essex Record Office, Lloyd Family Papers, D/DGu Z1: letter of 13 November 1831 to Louisa Lloyd.
2. Farington, I, 141; II, 95; Moore, IV, 1570; Bury, *Diary*, I, 100; Allardyce, II, 441.
3. Rauser, 'Living Statues', p. 463; Earl Granville, I, 22.
4. Meryon, *Memoirs*, III, 81, 185.
5. Earl Granville, I, 65, 76; Russell, p. 184; Meryon, *Memoirs*, III, 185; Melville, *Regency Ladies*, p. 111.
6. *La Belle Assemblée* of 1826 quoted in Rauser, 'Living Statues', p. 480; Sermoneta, p. 106; Stuart, II, 221.
7. Earl Granville, I, 79.
8. M. D. George, VII, 303, 307.
9. Reynolds, II, 162–63; M. D. George, VII, 61, 218–19.
10. Allardyce, II, 505; Meryon, *Additional Memoirs*, pp. 224, 233.
11. Maxwell, I, 109.
12. Meryon, *Memoirs*, III, 81.
13. Airlie, *In Whig Society*, pp. 64–67.

14. British Library, Microfilm 497: entry for 24 May 1806.
15. British Library, Microfilm 497: entries for 22 September 1805, 23 December 1806 & 4 June 1807; Lyttelton, p. 4; Berry, II, 343; Macdonald, p. 169; Russell, pp. 184–85.
16. National Library of Scotland, Dep. 175/164/1: enclosure in letter of 28 August 1816 from Eleanora Campbell to Eliza, Lady Gordon Cumming.
17. British Library, Microfilm 497: entries for 16 May & 23 December 1806, 22 January & 2 October 1807.
18. British Library, Microfilm 497: entry for 26 January 1806.
19. British Library, Microfilm 497: entry for 18 June 1805; National Library of Scotland, Dep. 175/164/1: letter of 2 July 1817 to Eliza, Lady Gordon Cumming.
20. Melville, *Berry Papers*, p. 50; British Library, Microfilm 497: entry for 4 June 1807; Melville, *Berry Papers*, p. 308; Doyle, p. 132.
21. Prucher, p. 94; Bury, *Diary*, I, 88–89, 200; II, 240–41.
22. Webb, p. 145; Melville, *Berry Papers*, p. 295.
23. Scott, *Letters*, I, 130, 132, 137, 183, 327–29; XI, 465.
24. Scott, *Letters*, II, 232–33; British Library, Microfilm 497: entry for 27 March 1809.
25. Staël, p. 255 (my translation); National Library of Scotland, Dep. 175/164/1: letter of 10 February 1817 to Eliza, Lady Gordon Cumming.
26. British Library, Microfilm 497: entries for 1 April & 21 April 1810.
27. Some letters Lady Charlotte penned to Henry Brougham and Samuel Whitbread are in the Brougham Archive held by University College London.
28. Bury, *Diary*, I, 300.
29. Scott, *Letters*, II, 432; Glenbervie, II, 131; Beattie, II, 213; Davies, I, 67; Maxwell, II, 102, 108.
30. Doyle, pp. 105–06, 112.
31. Bury, *Diary*, I, 1–2; Allardyce, I, 443–45, 450–53.
32. Dyce, p. 217.
33. Princess Charlotte, p. 233.
34. Moore, IV, 1570.
35. Bury, *Diary*, II, 65.
36. Scott, *Journal*, pp. 566, 572; National Library of Scotland, Dep. 175/164/1: letter of 10 February 1817 to Eliza, Lady Gordon Cumming.
37. Centre for Buckinghamshire Studies, D FR/42/14: letters of 17 March 1818 & undated to Elizabeth, Lady Fremantle; Leighton, pp. 217–18; Melville, *Berry Papers*, pp. 394–95; Scott, *Letters*, VI, 29.

38. Campbell, pp. 134–37.
39. Bury, *Diary*, III, 312; Russell, p. 198.
40. Thackeray, *Heads of the People*, I, 77.
41. National Library of Scotland, Dep. 175/164/1: letters of 26 November 1821, 28 June 1822 & one undated; Dep. 175/161/2: letters of 26 November 1821, 20 June 1822 & several undated.
42. Russell, p. 199.
43. Bury, *Flirtation*, p. 324; Bury, *Disinherited and Ensnared*, p. 294.
44. Bury, *Exclusives*, I, 33–34.
45. Bury, *Exclusives*, I, 173.
46. Bury, *Exclusives*, III, 334.
47. Bury, *Flirtation*, pp. 251–52.
48. Bury, *Exclusives*, II, 23–25.
49. Prucher, p. 98; National Library of Scotland, Dep. 175/164/1: letter of 30 August 1816 to Eliza, Lady Gordon Cumming.
50. Doyle, p. 156; *The Times*, 11 January 1838.
51. Allardyce, II, 497.
52. 'Pencillings by the Way', *New-York Mirror*, 18 April 1835.
53. Printed in *Bell's New Weekly Messenger*, 11 February 1838.
54. Edgeworth, p. 449.
55. Pückler-Muskau, 'Erinnerungsbilder', I, 64; J. P. Grant, III, 155; Edgeworth, pp. 448–49; Moore, IV, 1570.
56. Review of William Beckford's *Italy; With Sketches of Spain and Portugal* in the *Quarterly Review*, 51 (1834), pp. 426–56 (p. 440); Lawrence's letter is printed in the *Cardiff Times*, 4 February 1862.
57. National Library of Scotland, Dep. 175/164/1: letter of 10 May 1832 to Beaujolois, Lady Tullamore and note.
58. University College London, Brougham Archive: letter of 10 October 1831 to Lord Brougham; Bodleian Library, Dep. Hughenden 188/2, folios 288–304: letters to Mary Anne Wyndham Lewis; National Library of Scotland, Dep. 175/164/1: letter of 4 March 1838 to Eliza, Lady Gordon Cumming.
59. Russell, p. 201.
60. Bury, *Diary*, I, 39, 264.
61. Bury, *Diary*, I, 306; II, 238.
62. Lady Morgan, II, 431; Creevey, *Papers*, p. 675.
63. Thackeray, *Yellowplush Papers*, pp. 57–73; Greville, IV, 13.
64. Allardyce, I, 35; Creevey, *Papers*, p. 675; Le Strange, III, 256–57.
65. A. S. Galt's letter in *Fraser's Magazine* reprinted in the *Globe*, 31 December 1840; National Library of Scotland, Dep. 175/164/1: letter of 4 March 1838.
66. Reprinted in the *Leeds Times*, 28 September 1839.

67. National Library of Scotland, Dep. 175/164/1: letter of 4 March 1838.
68. Prucher, p. 102.
69. National Library of Scotland, Dep. 175/164/1: letters of 29 June & 30 August 1816 to Eliza, Lady Gordon Cumming.
70. Eastlake, I, 256; Doyle, p. 323.
71. Russell, pp. 202–03.
72. Scott, *Letters*, II, 232.
73. Bury, *Diary*, I, 49–50.

5 *The Fashionable Artist*
 1. Farington, II, 270.
 2. T. B. Smith, pp. 194–95 (Nalder); pp. 198–99 (Kent); Hill, p. 209 (Burney).
 3. Williams, I, 40–41, 51.
 4. Bernard, II, 81.
 5. Williams, I, 86.
 6. Williams, I, 98.
 7. Williams, I, 82–84; Warner, II, 469–77.
 8. Shee, I, 115.
 9. The material from the *World*, with the supposition about its author, is discussed in Lucy Peltz's text in Albinson, Funnell and Peltz, pp. 87–88. For the advertisement see Goldring, p. 76.
10. The authority for this is Whitley, II, 129.
11. Williams, I, 178–79.
12. Royal Academy of Arts Archive, Autographs vol. 3: letter of early 1818 from Lawrence to the Earl of Blessington.
13. *La Belle Assemblée*, 11:62 (February 1830), p. 54.
14. Farington, I, 8.
15. These terms are confusing because the first refers to the size of the head.
16. Williams, I, 131.
17. Lawrence's disavowal quoted in Goldring, p. 94; Williams, I, 186.
18. *La Belle Assemblée*, 11:62 (February 1830), p. 54; the *Morning Herald* quoted in Goldring, p. 100.
19. Williams, II, 97.
20. Knapp, pp. 80, 138.
21. Knapp, pp. 87, 124, 140.
22. Knapp, p. 166; Farington, II, 254; III, 25–26.
23. Williams, I, 313, 389–91; II, 91–92, 101–02; Cunningham, VI, 217.

24. Haydon, *Diary*, III, 533; Haydon, *Correspondence and Table-Talk*, II, 192; Haydon, *Diary*, IV, 137; Shee, I, 116; Fletcher, p. 147; Greville, I, 363. 'Bugger' is in cypher in Greville's manuscript.
25. Williams, II, 41.
26. Croker, II, 89. For Lawrence's membership of Watier's Club see Farington, III, 299–300.
27. Farington, I, 304.
28. Williams, I, 178.
29. Williams, I, 171 (Pasquin); Haydon, *Diary*, III, 533; Cunningham, VI, 182; Fletcher, p. 149.
30. Williams, I, 221–22; Layard, p. 84.
31. Williams, I, 304; Farington, VI, 263, 265.
32. A. Fremantle, III, 165.
33. M. D. George, X, 234.
34. Gower, pp. 37–38.
35. Farington, I, 268 (portraitists' alarm); Cunningham, VI, 169 (Reynolds's reported speech); Haydon, *Diary*, III, 411.
36. Williams, I, 243.
37. Williams, II, 159; Scott, *Journal*, p. 236.
38. Goldring, p. 106; Williams, II, 483.
39. Farington, VII, 74.
40. Haydon, *Correspondence and Table-Talk*, I, 141; Haydon, *Diary*, IV, 71; Goldring, p. 229 (Northcote).
41. Earl Granville, II, 66; H. Arbuthnot, II, 47; Beattie, II, 222; Moore, III, 1238 (Jekyll). Lawrence's letters of 1820–28 to Lord Gower, later 2nd Duke of Sutherland, show consideration for a sitter's needs, apologies for delay and a refusal to be hurried: Staffordshire Record Office, D593/P/22/1/18.
42. Huntington Library, LR 178: letter of 16 April 1824 to Sir Edward Hawke Locker.
43. Cunningham, VI, 261–62; MacFarlane, pp. 146–47; Davidson, p. 101.
44. Scott, *Journal*, p. 358; Haydon, *Diary*, III, 412; Moore, III, 973; Farington, II, 246 (Rogers); Galt, II, 271; Leslie, I, 71; Cunningham, VI, 262–63.
45. Bury, *Diary*, III, 345–48; Creevey, *Life and Times*, p. 247; Farington, IV, 49 (Thompson); Cunningham, VI, 165–66.
46. Layard, p. 87; Williams, I, 359; Layard, p. 143.
47. Haydon, *Diary*, III, 533; *Literary Gazette*, 747 (14 May 1831), p. 307.
48. Williams, II, 135.
49. Williams, II, 41.

50. Huntington Library, HM 11237: undated letter to Viscount Mountjoy. Lawrence painted Englefield's portrait, and a friendly letter of 10 August 1812 he received from him is in the Royal Academy of Arts Archive, Autographs vol. 2.
51. Williams, I, 338.
52. Quoted in Goldring, p. 212.
53. Layard, p. 142.
54. Farington, VIII, 236 (Thompson); MacFarlane, p. 146 (princess); Layard, p. 205 (Wilkie).
55. Quoted in Williams, II, 227.
56. Williams, II, 292.
57. Layard, p. 154.
58. Scott, *Journal*, p. 468.
59. Uwins, II, 114. Lawrence's kindness to Wilkie, for whom he gained permission to engrave a work of his in the king's collection, emerges in unpublished letters of 1820–1822 and undated in the National Library of Scotland, MSS 9385–86.
60. Layard, pp. 151 (Lawrence), 182 (Etty).
61. Williams, I, 423.
62. Hazlitt quoted in Goldring, p. 255; Williams, I, 373 (George IV).
63. Williams, II, 368–69 (Lawrence); Uwins, II, 297 (Eastlake).
64. Williams, II, 363, 366.
65. Farington, VI, 263–64; Williams, II, 52, 519.
66. Moore, I, 254; Haydon, *Diary*, III, 278, 498, 530.
67. *La Belle Assemblée*, 11:62 (February 1830), p. 56; Harford, p. 256.
68. Gilbert's speech reported in the *Courier*, 30 November 1830; Layard, pp. 140–41 (empress dowager); Uwins, I, 44; H. Arbuthnot, I, 120–21; *Edinburgh Review*, 54/108 (1831), pp. 468–69.
69. Layard, p. 155.
70. Pückler-Muskau, *Dead Man*, p. 211; Croker, II, 81.
71. Disraeli, p. 31.
72. Albinson, Funnell and Peltz, p. 21.
73. Layard, p. 256; Williams, II, 340–41.
74. Quoted in the *Cumberland Pacquet*, 26 January 1830.
75. Williams, II, 47.
76. Layard, p. 156.
77. Beattie, II, 200.

Select Bibliography

Unless stated otherwise place of publication is London.

Manuscript Sources
Bodleian Library, Oxford
Papers of Benjamin Disraeli: Letters of Lady Charlotte Bury to Mary
Anne Wyndham Lewis

British Library, London
Lady Charlotte Bury's diary of 1805–1810

Centre for Buckinghamshire Studies, Aylesbury
Fremantle MSS; Other papers relating to the Grenville family; Letter
of Lady Charlotte Bury to Elizabeth, Lady Fremantle

Essex Record Office, Chelmsford
Papers of the Lloyd family of Rolls Park, Chigwell

Gladstone Library, Hawarden
Glynne-Gladstone MSS: Letters from the Duke and Duchess of
Buckingham to Lady Mary Glynne

Huntington Library, San Marino
Letters of Sir Thomas Lawrence in various collections

National Library of Scotland, Edinburgh
Letters from Sir Thomas Lawrence to Sir David Wilkie and others;
Letters of Lady Charlotte Bury and her family

Pückler Archive, Branitz
Prince Pückler-Muskau's 'Erinnerungsbilder' (scrap books) and letters
to Lucie von Pückler-Muskau

Royal Academy of Arts Archive, London
Sir Thomas Lawrence, PRA, Letters and Papers

Sandon Hall, Staffordshire
Harrowby MSS: Letters from and to the Duke and Duchess of
St Albans; Letter of Princess Lieven to the Countess of Harrowby

Staffordshire Record Office, Stafford
Letters from Sir Thomas Lawrence to Lord Gower

Suffolk Record Office, Bury St Edmunds
Hervey Family Archives: Letter from the Duchess of St Albans to the
Marquess of Bristol

University College London
Brougham Archive: Letters of Lady Charlotte Campbell to Lord
Brougham and Samuel Whitbread

Primary Printed Sources
Anon., *The Secret Memoirs of Harriet Pumpkin* (Cahuac, 1825)
Anon., *Epistle to Harriet, Duchess of St Albans; or, The First Lash of
Nemesis* (Ilberry, 1828)
Anon., *Fine Acting; or, A Sketch of the Life of Miss H. M- of Drury
Lane Theatre, and of T. Coutts, Esq., Banker* (1815)
Anon., *The Golden Nuptials, An Epithalamium on the Marriage of T.
C—tts, Esq. and Miss H. M—ll—n* (1815)
Anon., *Authentic Memoirs of the Lives of Mr and Mrs Coutts* (Fairburn,
1819)
Anon., *Life of the Late Thomas Coutts, Esq., Banker in the Strand*
(Fairburn, 1822)
Anon., *Biographical and Historical Addenda to the Life of Thomas
Coutts* (Fairburn, 1822)
Anon., *Strictures on a Slanderous and Indecent Book* (Homerton:
Turner, n.d.)
Adolphus, J., *Memoirs of John Bannister, Comedian*, 2 vols (Bentley,
1839)
Airlie, M., Countess of, *In Whig Society 1775–1818* (Hodder and
Stoughton, 1921)

Airlie, M., Countess of, *Lady Palmerston and Her Times*, 2 vols (Hodder and Stoughton, 1922)

Albemarle, Earl of, *Fifty Years of My Life*, 2 vols (Macmillan, 1876)

Allardyce, A., ed., *Letters from and to Charles Kirkpatrick Sharpe, Esq.*, 2 vols (Edinburgh: Blackwood, 1888)

Angelo, H., *Angelo's Pic Nic; or, Table Talk* (Ebers, 1834)

Anglesey, Marquess of, *One-Leg: The Life and Letters of Henry William Paget, First Marquess of Anglesey, K.G. 1768–1854* (Leo Cooper, 1966)

Arbuthnot, C., *Correspondence*, ed. by A. Aspinall (Royal Historical Society, 1941)

Arbuthnot, H., *Journal 1820–1832*, ed. by F. Bamford and the Duke of Wellington, 2 vols (Macmillan, 1950)

Argyll, Duke of, *Intimate Society Letters of the Eighteenth Century*, 2 vols (Stanley Paul, 1910)

Arundell, M., Lady, 'A Conversion under the old Penal Laws', *The Rambler*, 3:13 (January 1855), pp. 44–59; 3:14 (February 1855), pp. 117–26

Aspinall, A., ed., *The Formation of Canning's Ministry* (Camden Society, 1937)

Aspinall, A., ed., *The Letters of King George IV 1812–30*, 3 vols (Cambridge: Cambridge University Press, 1938)

Aspinall, A., ed., *Three Early Nineteenth Century Diaries* (Williams and Norgate, 1952)

Aspinall, A., ed., *The Later Correspondence of George III*, 5 vols (Cambridge: Cambridge University Press, 1962)

Aspinall, A., ed., *The Correspondence of George, Prince of Wales, 1770–1812*, 8 vols (Cassell, 1963–71)

Barante, Baron de, *Souvenirs*, ed. by C. de Barante, 8 vols (Paris: Calmann Lévy, 1890–1901)

Baron-Wilson, M. C., *Memoirs of Harriot, Duchess of St Albans*, 2 vols (Colburn, 1840)

Bates, W., *The Maclise Portrait-Gallery of 'Illustrious Literary Characters'* (Chatto & Windus, 1883)

Beattie, W., *Life and Letters of Thomas Campbell*, 3 vols (Moxon, 1849)

Berkeley, G. F., *My Life and Recollections*, 4 vols (Hurst and Blackett, 1865–66)

Bernard, J., *Retrospections of the Stage*, 2 vols (Colburn and Bentley, 1830)

Berry, M., *Extracts of the Journals and Correspondence of Miss Berry, from the Year 1783 to 1852*, ed. by Lady T. Lewis, 3 vols (Longmans, Green, 1865)

Betham, E., ed., *A House of Letters* (Jarrolds, 1905)

Blakiston, G., *Lord William Russell and His Wife 1815–1846* (Murray, 1972)

Boaden, J., *The Life of Mrs Jordan*, 2 vols (Edward Bull, 1831)

Boaden, J., *Memoirs of Mrs Siddons, Interspersed with Anecdotes of Authors and Actors* (Gibbings, 1893)

Boigne, Comtesse de, *Mémoires*, ed. by C. Nicollaud, 4 vols (Paris: Plon, 1907–08)

Broughton, Lord, *Recollections of a Long Life*, ed. by Lady Dorchester, 6 vols (Murray, 1909–11)

Bruce, I., ed., *The Nun of Lebanon: The Love Affair of Lady Hester Stanhope and Michael Bruce* (Collins, 1951)

Buckingham and Chandos, R., Duke of, *Private Diary*, 3 vols (Hurst and Blackett, 1862)

Bulwer-Lytton, E. G., *England and the English*, ed. by S. Meacham (Chicago: University of Chicago Press, 1970)

Burke, J., *Portrait Gallery of Distinguished Females*, 2 vols (Bull, 1833)

Bury, Lady C., *Flirtation* (Paris: Baudry, 1836)

Bury, Lady C., *The Exclusives*, 3 vols (Colburn & Bentley, 1830)

Bury, Lady C., *The Three Great Sanctuaries of Tuscany, Valombrosa, Camaldoli, Laverna* (Murray, 1833)

Bury, Lady C., *The Disinherited; and The Ensnared* (Paris: Baudry, 1837)

Bury, Lady C., *The Divorced*, 2 vols (Colburn, 1837)

Bury, Lady C., *Diary Illustrative of the Times of George the Fourth*, 4 vols (Colburn, 1838–39)

Bury, Lady C., *Family Records; or, The Two Sisters*, 3 vols (Saunders & Otley, 1841)

Byrne, J. C., *Gossip of the Century: Personal and Traditional Memories – Social Literary Artistic etc.*, 2 vols (New York: Macmillan, 1892)

Calvert, F., *An Irish Beauty of the Regency*, ed. by A. E. Blake (John Lane, 1911)

Campbell, H. C. B., *A Journey to Florence*, ed. by G. R. de Beer (Bles, 1952)

Carlyle, T., *On Heroes, Hero-Worship, and the Heroic in History*, ed. by C. Niemeyer (Lincoln, NE: University of Nebraska Press, 1966)

Castle, E., ed., *The Jerningham Letters (1780–1843)*, 2 vols (Bentley, 1896)

Charlotte, Princess, *Letters 1811–1817*, ed. by A. Aspinall (Home and van Thal, 1949)

Chateaubriand, Vicomte de, *Mémoires d'outre tombe*, ed. by J.-C. Berchet, 4 vols (Paris: Borda, 1989–98)

Colchester, C. Abbot, Lord, *Diary and Correspondence*, ed. by C., Lord Colchester, 3 vols (Murray, 1861)

Collins, W. W., *Memoirs of the Life of William Collins*, 2 vols in 1 (Wakefield: EP Publishing, 1978)

Cowell, J., *Thirty Years Passed Among the Players in England and America* (New York: Harper, 1844)

Cowley, Lord, *Diary and Correspondence 1790–1846*, ed. by F. A. Wellesley (Hutchinson, n.d.)

Creevey, T., *The Creevey Papers*, ed. by Sir H. Maxwell (Murray, 1912)

Creevey, T., *Creevey's Life and Times*, ed. by J. Gore (Murray, 1934)

Croker, J. W., *The Croker Papers*, ed. by L. J. Jennings, 3 vols (Murray, 1885)

Cunningham, A., *Lives of the Most Eminent British Painters*, 6 vols (Murray, 1829–33)

Czartoryski, Prince, *Memoirs*, ed. by A. Gielgud, 2 vols (Remington, 1888)

Davidson, A., *Miss Douglas of New York* (New York: Viking, 1953)

Davies, Lady C., *Recollections of Society in France and England*, 2 vols (Hurst and Blackett, 1873)

Deans, C., *Memoirs of the Life of Mrs Charlotte Deans*, ed. by F. Marshall (Kendal: Titus Wilson, 1984)

Dibdin, T., *Reminiscences*, 2 vols (New York: AMS Press, 1970)

Dino, Duchesse de, *Mémoires*, ed. by C. Muller, 7 vols (Clermont-Ferrand: Paleo, 2003–04)

Disbrowe, C. A. A., *Old Days in Diplomacy: Recollections of a Closed Century* (Jarrold, 1903)

Disraeli, B., *Vivian Grey* (New York: Century, 1906)

Donaldson, W., *Recollections of an Actor* (Maxwell, 1865)

Doyle, J. A., ed., *Memoir and Correspondence of Susan Ferrier, 1782–1854* (Eveleigh Nash & Grayson, 1929)

Dudley, Earl of, *Letters to the Bishop of Llandaff* (Murray, 1840)

Dudley, Earl of, *Letters to 'Ivy'*, ed. by S. H. Romilly (Longmans, Green, 1905)

Dundonald, Earl of, *Answer to the Mis-statements contained in the Life of the late T. Coutts* (Limburd, 1822)

Dyce, A., *Recollections of the Table-Talk of Samuel Rogers*, ed. by M. Bishop (Richards, 1952)

Eastlake, E., Lady, *Journals and Correspondence*, ed. by C. E. Smith, 2 vols (Murray, 1895)

Edgeworth, M., *Letters from England, 1813–1844*, ed. by C. Colvin (Oxford: Clarendon Press, 1971)

Egan, P., *Tom & Jerry: Life in London* (Chatto and Windus, 1903)

Elers, G., *Memoirs (1777–1842)*, ed. by Lord Monson and G. L. Gower (Heinemann, 1903)

Ellenborough, Earl of, *A Political Diary 1828–1830*, 2 vols (Bentley, 1881)

Farington, J., *The Farington Diary*, ed. by J. Greig, 8 vols (Hutchinson, 1922–28)

Fletcher, E., ed., *Conversations of James Northcote R. A. with James Ward on Art and Artists* (Methuen, 1901)

Foster, V., *Two Duchesses: Georgiana, Duchess of Devonshire, Elizabeth, Duchess of Devonshire – Family Correspondence* (Blackie, 1898)

Fox, H. E., *Journal*, ed. by the Earl of Ilchester (Thornton Butterworth, 1923)

Frampton, M., *Journal 1779–1846*, ed. by H. G. Mundy (Low, Marston, Searle & Rivington, 1886)

Fremantle, A., ed., *The Wynne Diaries 1798–1820*, 3 vols (Oxford University Press, 1940)

Fremantle, J., *Wellington's Voice: The Candid Letters of Lieutenant John Fremantle, Coldstream Guards 1808–1837*, ed. by Gareth Glover (Frontline, 2012)

Gallatin, J., *A Great Peace Maker: The Diary of James Gallatin*, ed. by Count Gallatin (Heinemann, 1914)

Galt, J., *Autobiography*, 2 vols (Cochrane and McCrone, 1833)

Gilchrist, A., *Life of William Blake*, ed. by R. Todd (Dent, 1942)

Gilchrist, A., *Life of William Etty, R.A.*, 2 vols in 1 (Wakefield: EP Publishing, 1978)

Gillies, R. P., *Memoirs of a Literary Veteran*, 3 vols (Bentley, 1851)

Glenbervie, Baron, *Diaries*, ed. by F. Bickley, 2 vols (Constable, 1928)

Gore, C. G. F., *Sketches of English Character*, 2 vols (Stroud: Nonsuch, 2005)

Graham, J. J., ed., *Memoir of General Graham* (Edinburgh: Clark, 1862)

Grant, J., *The Great Metropolis*, 1st series, 2 vols [1836] (New York: Saunders and Otley, 1837); 2nd series, 2 vols [1837] (Philadelphia: Carey & Hart, 1838)

Grant, J. P., *Memoir and Correspondence of Mrs Grant of Laggan*, 3 vols (Longman, Brown, Green, and Longmans, 1844)

Granville, Earl, *Private Correspondence, 1781–1821*, ed. by C., Countess Granville, 2 vols (Murray, 1916)

Granville, Countess, *Letters 1810–1845*, ed. by F. L. Gower, 2 vols (Longmans, Green, 1894)

Greville, C., *Memoirs, 1814–1860*, ed. by L. Strachey and R. Fulford, 8 vols (Macmillan, 1938)

Gronow, R. H., *The Reminiscences and Recollections of Captain Gronow*, 2 vols (Nunney: Surtees Society, 1984–85)

Grosvenor, C. and Lord Stuart of Wortley, *The First Lady Wharncliffe and Her Family (1779–1856)*, 2 vols (Heinemann, 1927)

Guest, Lady C., *Extracts from Her Journal 1833–1852*, ed. by the Earl of Bessborough (Murray, 1950)

Hanoteau, J., ed., *Lettres du Prince de Metternich à la Comtesse de Lieven 1818–19* (Paris: Plon, 1909)

Haydon, B. R., *Correspondence and Table-Talk*, ed. by F. W. Haydon, 2 vols (Chatto and Windus, 1876)

Haydon, B. R., *Autobiography*, ed. by E. Blunden (Oxford: Oxford University Press, 1927)

Haydon, B. R., *Diary*, ed. by W. B. Pope, 5 vols (Cambridge, MA: Harvard University Press, 1960–63)

Hazlitt, W., *Conversations of James Northcote*, ed. by F. Swinnerton (Hutchinson, 1952)

Hill, C., *The House in St Martin's Street, Being Chronicles of the Burney Family* (John Lane, 1907)

Hobhouse, H., *Diary (1820–1827)*, ed. by A. Aspinall (Home & van Thal, 1947)

Holland, Lady, *Journal 1791–1811*, ed. by the Earl of Ilchester, 2 vols (Longmans, Green, 1908)

Holland, Lady, *Letters to Her Son, 1821–1845*, ed. by the Earl of Ilchester (Murray, 1946)

Holland, Lord, *Further Memoirs of the Whig Party 1807–1821*, ed. by Lord Stavordale (New York: Dutton, 1905)

Holland, Lord, *The Holland House Diaries 1831–1840*, ed. by A. D. Kriegel (Routledge and Kegan Paul, 1977)

Holland, Sir H., *Recollections of Past Life* (Longmans, Green, 1872)

Horner, L., ed., *Memoirs and Correspondence of Francis Horner, MP*, 2 vols (Murray, 1843)

Hunt, H., *Memoirs*, 3 vols (Dolby, 1820–22)

Hunt, J. L., *Autobiography*, ed. by J. E. Morpurgo (Cresset, 1949)

Jackson, Sir G., *The Bath Archives: Diaries and Letters*, ed. by Lady Jackson, 2 vols (Bentley, 1873)

Jerdan, W., *Autobiography*, 4 vols (Hall, 1852–53)

Jewsbury, M. J., *Occasional Papers*, ed. by E. Gillet (Oxford University Press, 1932)

Kelly, M., *Reminiscences*, ed. by R. Fiske (Oxford University Press, 1975)

Kemble, F. A., *Record of a Girlhood*, 3 vols (New York: Holt, 1879)

Kilgour, A., *Anecdotes of Lord Byron* (Knight and Lacey, 1825)

Knapp, O. G., ed., *An Artist's Love Story* (George Allen, 1904)

Knight, C., *Passages of a Working Life During Half a Century*, 3 vols (Shannon: Irish University Press, 1971)

Knight, E. C., *Autobiography*, ed. by R. Fulford (Kimber, 1960)

Knighton, Lady, ed., *Memoirs of Sir William Knighton*, 2 vols (Bentley, 1838)

Lach-Szyrma, K., *London Observed: A Polish Philosopher at Large, 1820–24*, trans. by M. Machnice and A. Kiersztejn, ed. by M. K. McLeod (Oxford: Signal, 2009)

Landseer, T., ed., *Life and Letters of William Bewick*, 2 vols in 1 (Wakefield: EP Publishing, 1978)

Layard, G. S., ed., *Sir Thomas Lawrence's Letter-Bag* (George Allen, 1906)

Leconfield, Lady and J. Gore, eds, *Three Howard Sisters: Selections from the Writings of Lady Caroline Lascelles, Lady Dover and Countess Gower 1825 to 1833* (Murray, 1955)

Leighton, R., ed., *Correspondence of Charlotte Grenville, Lady Williams Wynn and Her Three Sons* (Murray, 1920)

Lennox, Lord W. P., *Fifty Years' Biographical Reminiscences*, 2 vols (Hurst and Blackett, 1863)

Leslie, C. R., *Autobiographical Recollections*, ed. by T. Taylor, 2 vols in 1 (Wakefield: EP Publishing, 1978)

Le Strange, G., trans. and ed., *Correspondence of Princess Lieven and Earl Grey*, 3 vols (Bentley, 1890)

Lewis, M. G., *Romantic Tales*, 4 vols (Longman, Hurst, Rees, and Orme, 1808)

Lieven, Princess, *Letters of Dorothea, Princess Lieven during her Residence in London, 1812–1834*, ed. by L. G. Robinson (Longmans, Green, 1902)

Lieven, Princess, *The Unpublished Diary and Political Sketches of Princess Lieven*, ed. by H. Temperley (Cape, 1925)

Lieven, Princess, *The Private Letters of Princess Lieven to Prince Metternich 1820–26*, ed. by P. Quennell (Murray, 1937)

Lieven, Princess, *Letters of Princess Lieven to Lady Holland 1847–1857*, ed. by E. A. Smith (Oxford: Roxburghe Club, 1956)

Lockhart, J. G., 'Lord Byron', *Blackwood's Edinburgh Magazine*, 17:97 (February 1825), pp. 131–51

Lovell, E. J., ed., *Medwin's 'Conversations of Lord Byron'* (Princeton: Princeton University Press, 1966)

Lovell, E. J., ed., *Lady Blessington's 'Conversations of Lord Byron'* (Princeton: Princeton University Press, 1969)

Lyttelton, Lady, *Correspondence 1787–1870*, ed. by Mrs H. Wyndham (Murray, 1912)

MacFarlane, C., *Reminiscences of a Literary Life*, ed. by J. F. Tattersall (Murray, 1917)

Mackintosh, R. J., ed., *Memoirs of the Life of the Right Honourable Sir James Mackintosh*, 2 vols (Moxon, 1835)

Macready, W. C., *Diaries 1833–1851*, ed. by W. Toynbee, 2 vols (Chapman and Hall, 1912)

Madden, R. R., *The Literary Life and Correspondence of the Countess of Blessington*, 3 vols (Newby, 1855)

Malmesbury, Earl of, *Memoirs of an Ex-Minister* (Longmans, Green, 1885)

Martineau, H., 'Literary Lionism', *London and Westminster Review*, 32 (1839), pp. 263–80

Mathews, A., *Memoirs of Charles Mathews, Comedian*, 4 vols (Bentley, 1838–39)

Mathews, A., *Tea-table Talk, Ennobled Actresses, and Other Miscellanies*, 2 vols (Cautley & Newby, 1857)

Maxwell, A. M., *My Adventures*, 2 vols (Colburn, 1845)

Mayne, J., *Journal During a Tour on the Continent Upon Its Reopening After the Fall of Napoleon, 1814*, ed. by J. M. Colles (John Lane, 1909)

Melville, L., ed., *The Berry Papers* (Bodley Head, 1914)

Melville, L., ed., *The Wellesley Papers*, 2 vols (Herbert Jenkins, 1914)

Meryon, C. L., *Memoirs of the Lady Hester Stanhope*, 3 vols (Colburn, 1845)

Meryon, C. L., *The Additional Memoirs of Lady Hester Stanhope: An Unpublished Historical Account for the Years 1819–1820*, ed. by M. Guscin (Brighton: Sussex Academic Press, 2017)

Minto, Countess of, *The Life and Letters of Sir Gilbert Elliot, First Earl of Minto*, 3 vols (Longmans, Green, 1874)

Montgomery, R., *The Age Reviewed: A Satire* (Wright, 1828)

Montgomery, R., *The Puffiad: A Satire* (Maunder, 1828)

Moore, T., *Journal*, ed. by W. S. Dowden et al., 6 vols (Newark: University of Delaware Press, 1983–91)

More, H., *Letters*, ed. by R. B. Johnson (John Lane, 1925)

Morgan, Lady, *Autobiography, Diaries and Correspondence*, ed. by G. Jewsbury, 2 vols (Allen, 1862)

Murray, J., *Letters to Lord Byron*, ed. by A. Nicholson (Liverpool: Liverpool University Press, 2007)

Naville, J., ed., *Lettres de François Guizot et de la Princesse de Lieven*, 2 vols (Paris: Mercure de France, 1963)

Neumann, P. von, *Diary 1819–1850*, trans. and ed. by E. B. Chancellor, 2 vols (Allan, 1928)

Newman, J. H., *Discourses Addressed to Mixed Congregations*, ed. by J. Tolhurst (Leominster: Notre Dame, 2002)

Nicholas, Grand Duke, ed., *Scenes of Russian Court Life*, trans. by H. Havelock (Jarrolds, 1917), pp. 265–91

Nugent, M., Lady, *Journal*, ed. by F. Cundall (West India Committee, 1934)

Oman, C., *The Gascoyne Heiress: The Life and Diaries of Frances Mary Gascoyne-Cecil 1802–1839* (Hodder and Stoughton, 1968)

Oxberry, W., *Dramatic Biography, and Histrionic Anecdotes*, 5 vols (Virtue, 1825–26)

Page, N., ed., *Byron: Interviews and Recollections* (Basingstoke: Macmillan, 1985)

Palmerston, Lady, *Letters*, ed. by T. Lever (Murray, 1957)

Passavant, J. D., *Tour of a German Artist in England*, 2 vols (Saunders and Otley, 1836)

Peakman, J., ed., *Whore Biographies 1700–1825*, 8 vols (Pickering & Chatto, 2006–07)

Phipps, E., *Memoirs of the Political and Literary Life of Robert Plumer Ward, Esq.*, 2 vols (Murray, 1850)

Priestley, E., Lady, 'An Artist's Love Story', *Nineteenth Century and After* (April 1905), pp. 642–54

Pückler-Muskau, H. von, *Letters of a Dead Man*, trans. and ed. by L. B. Parshall (Washington, DC: Dumbarton Oaks, 2016)

Raikes, T., *Portion of the Journal Kept by Thomas Raikes, Esq.*, 2 vols (Longman, Brown, Green, Longmans & Roberts, 1858)

Raymond, G., *Memoirs of Robert William Elliston*, 2 vols in 1 (New York: Blom, 1969)

Redding, C., *Fifty Years' Recollections, Literary and Personal*, 3 vols (Skeet, 1858)

Reid, S. J., *Life and Letters of the First Earl of Durham 1792–1840*, 2 vols (Longmans, Green, 1906)

Reynolds, F., *Life and Times*, 2 vols in 1 (New York: Blom, 1969)

Richardson, E. M., *Next Door Neighbours (at 9 and 10 Grafton Street, W.,)* (Hutchinson, 1926)

Robinson, H. C., *Diary, Reminiscences and Correspondence*, ed. by T. Sadler, 2 vols in 1 (New York: Hurd and Houghton, 1877)

Robinson, M., *Perdita: The Memoirs of Mary Robinson (1758–1800)*, ed. by M. J. Levy (Peter Owen, 1994)

Romilly, J. and F. Romilly, eds, *Memoirs of the Life of Sir Samuel Romilly, With a Selection from His Correspondence*, 3 vols (Shannon: Irish University Press, 1971)

Romilly, S. H., ed., *Romilly-Edgeworth Letters 1813–18* (Murray, 1936)

Rush, R., *A Residence at the Court of London* (Century, 1987)

Sala, G. A., *Life and Adventures*, 2 vols (Cassell, 1895)

Scott, Sir W., *Letters*, ed. by H. J. C. Grierson et al., 12 vols (Constable, 1932–37)

Scott, Sir W., *Journal*, ed. by W. E. K. Anderson (Oxford University Press, 1972)

Sermoneta, Duchess of, *The Locks of Norbury* (Murray, 1940)

Seymour, Lady, ed., *The 'Pope' of Holland House: Selections from the Correspondence of John Whishaw and His Friends, 1813–1840* (Unwin, 1906)

Shee, M. A., *The Life of Sir Martin Archer Shee*, 2 vols (Longman, Green, Longman, and Roberts, 1860)

Shelley, F., Lady, *Diary 1787–1817*, ed. by R. Edgcumbe, 2 vols (Murray, 1912–13)

Sismondi, J. C. L. de, *Lettres inédites*, ed. by S. Taillandier (Paris: Michel Lévy, 1863)

Smith, T. B., 'Early Life of Sir Thomas Lawrence, P. R. A.', *Wiltshire Archaeological and Natural History Magazine*, 9:24 (1866), pp. 194–205

Smith, W. J. [Duke of Buckingham and Chandos], *Memoirs of the Court and Cabinets of George the Third*, 4 vols (Hurst and Blackett, 1853)

Smith, W. J. [Duke of Buckingham and Chandos], *Memoirs of the Court of England During the Regency 1811–1820*, 2 vols (Hurst and Blackett, 1856)

Smith, W. J. [Duke of Buckingham and Chandos], *Memoirs of the Court of George IV, 1820–1830*, 2 vols (Hurst and Blackett, 1859)

Smith, W. J. [Duke of Buckingham and Chandos], *Memoirs of the Courts and Cabinets of William IV and Victoria*, 2 vols (Hurst and Blackett, 1861)

Sneyd, R., 'Notice of the Late Princess Lieven', *Miscellanies of the Philobiblon Society*, 13:4 (1871–72)

Staël, G. de, *Lettres de Madame de Staël à Madame Récamier*, ed. by E. Beau de Loménie (Paris: Domat, 1952)

Stanhope, M. S., *Almack's*, 3 vols (Saunders and Otley, 1827)

Stirling, E., *Old Drury Lane: Fifty Years' Recollections*, 2 vols (Chatto and Windus, 1881)

Stuart, Lady L., *Letters of Lady Louisa Stuart to Miss Louisa Clinton*, ed. by J. A. Home, 2 vols (Edinburgh: Douglas, 1901–03)

Sudley, Lord, trans. and ed., *The Lieven-Palmerston Correspondence 1828–1856* (Murray, 1943)

Talleyrand, C. M. de, *Mémoires*, ed. by the duc de Broglie, 8 vols (Paris: Calmann Lévy, 1891)

Thackeray, W. M., *Vanity Fair: A Novel Without a Hero* (Guild, 1980)

Thackeray, W. M., *The Yellowplush Papers* (New York: Appleton, 1853)

Thackeray, W. M., *Heads of the People, or, Portraits of the English*, 2 vols (Bohn, 1864)

Thomson, K., *Recollections of Literary Characters and Celebrated Places*, 2 vols in 1 (New York: AMS, 1975)

Trench, M., *The Remains of Mrs Richard Trench*, ed. by R. C. Trench (Parker, Son, and Bourn, 1862)

Uwins, S., *A Memoir of Thomas Uwins*, 2 vols in 1 (Wakefield: EP Publishing, 1978)

Warner, R., *Literary Recollections*, 2 vols (Longman, Rees, Orme, Brown, and Green, 1830)

Watts, A. A., *Alaric Watts: A Narrative of His Life*, 2 vols (Bentley, 1884)

Wellington, Duke of, ed., *Wellington and His Friends* (Macmillan, 1965)

Westmacott, C. M. [Bernard Blackmantle], *The English Spy*, 2 vols (Methuen, 1907)

White, C., *Almack's Revisited*, 3 vols (Saunders and Otley, 1828)

Whitley, W. T., *Artists and their Friends in England*, 2 vols (Medici Society, 1928)

Williams, D. E., *The Life and Correspondence of Sir Thomas Lawrence, KT*, 2 vols (Colburn and Bentley, 1831)

Wyndham, P., *Strictures on an Imposter and Old Actress, formerly Bet the Pot-Girl, alias the Banker's Sham Widow, with Particulars of her Appearance at the Bar of Bow-Street, of the Child Manufactory at Highgate, and Madam's Sleeping at the Horns at Kennington* (Turner, 1822)

Secondary Printed Sources

Adamson, D. and P. B. Dewar, *The House of Nell Gwyn: The Fortunes of the Beauclerk Family 1670–1974* (Kimber, 1974)

Adburgham, A., *Silver Fork Society: Fashionable Life and Literature from 1814 to 1840* (Constable, 1983)

Albinson, A. C., P. Funnell and L. Peltz, eds, *Thomas Lawrence: Regency Power and Brilliance* (New Haven: Yale University Press, 2010)

Altick, R. D., *The English Common Reader: A Social History of the Mass Reading Public, 1800–1900* (Chicago: University of Chicago Press, 1957)

Ambrose, T., *The King and the Vice Queen: George IV's Last Scandalous Affair* (Stroud: Sutton, 2005)

Asleson, R., ed., *Notorious Muse: The Actress in British Art and Culture* (New Haven: Yale University Press, 2003)

Baker, T. N., *Sentiment and Celebrity: Nathaniel Parker Willis and the Trials of Literary Fame* (New York: Oxford University Press, 1999)

Barbour, J., 'Silver Fork Novel', in *An Oxford Companion to the*

Romantic Age: British Culture, 1776–1832, ed. by I. McCalman (Oxford: Oxford University Press, 1999), pp. 705–06

Barry, E., 'From Epitaph to Obituary: Death and Celebrity in Eighteenth-Century British Culture', *International Journal of Cultural Studies*, 11:3 (2008), pp. 259–75

Beckett, I. F. W., *Call to Arms: The Story of the Bucks' Citizen Soldiers from Their Origins to Date* (Buckingham: Barracuda, 1985)

Beckett, J., *The Rise and Fall of the Grenvilles, Dukes of Buckingham and Chandos, 1710 to 1921* (Manchester: Manchester University Press, 1994)

Bennett, A., *Romantic Poets and the Culture of Posterity* (Cambridge: Cambridge University Press, 1999)

Berridge, G. R., *A Diplomatic Whistleblower in the Victorian Era: The Life and Writings of E. C. Grenville-Murray* (published online, 2013)

Bevington, M., *Stowe House* (Holberton, 2002)

Bieri, J., *Percy Bysshe Shelley: A Biography – Exile of Unfulfilled Reknown, 1816–1822* (Newark: University of Delaware Press, 2005)

Bloxam, S., *Walpole's Queen of Comedy: Elizabeth Farren, Countess of Derby* (Ashford: n.p., 1988)

Bonaparte-Wyse, O., *The Issue of Bonapare-Wyse: Waterford's Imperial Relations* (Waterford: Waterford Museum of Treasures, 2004)

Boone, J. A., and N. J. Vickers, 'Celebrity Rites', in *Celebrity, Fame, Notoriety*, special issue of *Publications of the Modern Language Association*, 126:4 (October 2011), pp. 900–11

Boorstin, D., *The Image: A Guide to Pseudo-Events in America* (New York: Athenaeum, 1973)

Bourne, K., *Palmerston: The Early Years, 1784–1841* (Allen Lane, 1982)

Bowman, P. J., *The Fortune Hunter: A German Prince in Regency England* (Oxford: Signal, 2010)

Bowman, P. J., *The Real 'Persuasion': Portrait of a Real-Life Jane Austen Heroine* (Stroud: Amberley, 2017)

Braudy, L., *The Frenzy of Renown: Fame and Its History* (New York: Vintage, 1986)

Brock, C., *The Feminization of Fame, 1750–1830* (Basingstoke: Palgrave Macmillan, 2006)

Brown, S., P. Clements and I. Grundy, eds, 'Lady Charlotte Bury: Life', screen within *Orlando: Women's Writing in the British Isles from the Beginnings to the Present*, Cambridge University Press online

Byrne, P., *Perdita: The Literary, Theatrical, Scandalous Life of Mary Robinson* (New York: Random House, 2004)

Cashmore, E., *Celebrity/Culture* (Routledge, 2014)

Charmley, J., *The Princess and the Politicians: Sex, Intrigue and Diplomacy, 1812–40* (Viking, 2005)

Clarke, T., *The Countess: The Scandalous Life of Frances Villiers, Countess of Jersey* (Stroud: Amberley, 2016)

Cleveland, Duchess of, *The Life and Letters of Lady Hester Stanhope* (Murray, 1914)

Coleridge, E. H., *The Life of Thomas Coutts, Banker*, 2 vols (John Lane, 1920)

Copeland, E., *The Silver Fork Novel: Fashionable Fiction in the Age of Reform* (Cambridge: Cambridge University Press, 2012)

Cowen, T., *What Price Fame?* (Cambridge, MA: Harvard University Press, 2000)

Craske, M., *Art in Europe 1700–1830* (Oxford: Oxford University Press, 1997)

Cromwell, J. L., *Dorothea Lieven: A Russian Princess in London and Paris, 1785–1857* (Jefferson, NC: McFarland, 2006)

Cruse, A., *The Englishman and His Books in the Early Nineteenth Century* (New York: Blom, 1968)

Dames, N., 'Brushes with Fame: Thackeray and the Work of Celebrity', *Nineteenth-Century Literature*, 56:1 (2001), pp. 23–51

Darracott, J., *England's Constable: The Life and Letters of John Constable* (Folio Society, 1985)

Davis, R. W., 'Buckingham 1832–1846: A Study of a "Pocket Borough"', *Huntington Library Quarterly*, 34:2 (February 1971), pp. 159–81

Davis, R. W., *Political Change and Continuity 1760–1885: A Buckinghamshire Study* (Newton Abbot: David and Charles, 1972)

Daudet, E., *Une Vie d'ambassadrice au siècle dernier: La Princesse de Lieven* (Paris: Plon-Nouritt, 1903)

Donald, D., *The Age of Caricature: Satirical Prints in the Reign of George III* (New Haven: Yale University Press, 1996)

Donoghue, F., *The Fame Machine: Book Reviewing and Eighteenth-Century Literary Careers* (Stanford, CA: Stanford University Press, 1996)

Edwards, R. and L. G. G. Ramsey, eds, *The Regency Period 1810–1830* (The Connoisseur, 1958)

Eisner, E., *Nineteenth-Century Poetry and Literary Celebrity* (New York: Palgrave Macmillan, 2009)

Elfenbein, A., *Byron and the Victorians* (Cambridge: Cambridge University Press, 1995)

Engel, L., *Fashioning Celebrity: 18th-Century British Actresses and Strategies for Image-Making* (Columbus: Ohio State University Press, 2011)

Erickson, L., *The Economy of Literary Form: English Literature and the Industrialization of Publishing, 1800–1850* (Baltimore, MD: Johns Hopkins University Press, 1996)

Fisher, J. L., '"In the Present Famine of Anything Substantial": *Fraser's Portraits* and the Construction of Literary Celebrity', *Victorian Periodicals Review*, 39 (2006), pp. 97–135

Fitzgerald, G. P., 'Princess Lieven and Her Friendships', *Temple Bar*, 119:473 (April 1990), pp. 517–28

Foulkes, N., *Dancing into Battle: A Social History of the Battle of Waterloo* (Weidenfeld & Nicolson, 2006)

Fraser, F., *The Unruly Queen: The Life of Queen Caroline* (Macmillan, 1996)

Fraser, F., *Princesses: The Six Daughters of George III* (Murray, 2004)

Fulford, R., *Royal Dukes: The Father and Uncles of Queen Victoria* (Collins, 1973)

George, L., 'Byron, Brummell and the Fashionable Figure', *Byron Journal*, 24 (1996), pp. 33–41

George, M. D., *Catalogue of Prints and Drawings in the British Museum: Division 1, Political and Personal Satires*, vols 5–11 (Oxford: Oxford University Press, 1949–1952)

Gibbs, R., *Worthies of Buckinghamshire and Men of Note in that County* (Aylesbury: Gibbs, 1888)

Goldring, D., *Regency Portrait Painter: The Life of Sir Thomas Lawrence* (Macdonald, 1951)

Goldsmith, J. N., 'The Promiscuity of Print: John Clare's "Don Juan" and the Culture of Romantic Celebrity', *Studies in English Literature*, 46:4 (Autumn 2006), pp. 803–32

Gore, J., *Nelson's Hardy and His Wife (1769–1877)* (Murray, 1935)

Gower, Lord R. S., *Sir Thomas Lawrence* (Goupil, 1900)

Graver, B. E., 'Wordworth, St. Francis, and Lady Charlotte Bury', *Philological Quarterly*, 65 (Summer 1986), pp. 371–80

Gray, J., 'Lady Charlotte Bury', in *Dictionary of Literary Biography: British Romantic Novelists 1789–1832*, ed. by B. K. Mudge (Detroit: Gale, 1992), pp. 55–68

Greaves, M., *Regency Patron: Sir George Beaumont* (Methuen, 1966)

Harford, J., *Recollections of William Wilberforce, Esq. MP* (Longman, Green, Longman, Roberts & Green, 1865)

Healey, E., *Lady Unknown: The Life of Angela Burdett-Coutts* (Sidgwick & Jackson, 1978)

Healey, E., *Coutts & Co 1692–1992: The Portrait of a Private Bank* (Hodder & Stoughton, 1992)

Hibbert, C., *George IV: Regent and King 1811–1830* (Newton Abbot: Readers Union, 1975)

Higgins, D., *Romantic Genius and the Literary Magazine: Biography, Celebrity, Politics* (Routledge, 2005)

Holmes, R., *Thomas Lawrence Portraits* (National Portrait Gallery, 2010)

Hughes, W., 'Silver Fork Writers and Readers: Social Contexts of a Bestseller', *Novel: A Forum on Fiction*, 25:3 (1992), pp. 328–47

Humpherys, A., 'Breaking Apart: The Early Victorian Divorce Novel', in *Victorian Women Writers and the Woman Question*, ed. by N. D. Thompson (Cambridge: Cambridge University Press, 1999), pp. 42–59

Hyde, H. M., *Princess Lieven* (Harrap, 1938)

Inglis, F., *A Short History of Celebrity* (Princeton, NJ: Princeton University Press, 2010)

Jack, I., *The Poet and His Audience* (Cambridge: Cambridge University Press, 1984)

Jackson, H. J., *Those Who Write for Immortality: Romantic Reputations and the Dream of Literary Fame* (New Haven: Yale University Press, 2015)

Jenner, G., *Dead Famous: An Unexpected History of Celebrity from Bronze Age to Silver Screen* (Weidenfeld & Nicolson, 2020)

Jerman, B. R., *The Young Disraeli* (Princeton, NJ: Princeton University Press, 1960)

Jordan, J. O. and R. L. Patten, eds, *Literature in the Marketplace: Nineteenth-Century British Publishing and Reading Practices* (Cambridge: Cambridge University Press, 1995)

Jupp, P. J., *Lord Grenville 1759–1834* (Oxford: Clarendon, 1985)

Jupp, P. J. 'The Roles of Royal and Aristocratic Women in British Politics, c. 1782–1832', in *Chattel, Servant or Citizen: Women's Status in Church, State and Society*, ed. by M. O'Dowd and S. Wichert (Belfast: Institute for Irish Studies, 1995), pp. 103–13

Kahan, J., *Bettymania and the Birth of Celebrity Culture* (Bethlehem: Lehigh University Press, 2010)

Kelly, I., *Cooking for Kings: The Life of Antonin Carême, the First Celebrity Chef* (Short Books, 2003)

Kelly, I., *Beau Brummell: The Ultimate Dandy* (Hodder and Stoughton, 2005)

Keppel, S., *The Sovereign Lady: A Life of Elizabeth Vassall, Third Lady Holland, With Her Family* (Hamish Hamilton, 1974)

Klancher, J. P., *The Making of English Reading Audiences, 1790–1832* (Madison, WI: University of Wisconsin Press, 1987)

Knowles, R., *What Regency Women Did For Us* (Barnsley: Pen & Sword, 2017)

Lees-Milne, J., *The Bachelor Duke: William Spencer Cavendish 6th Duke of Devonshire 1790–1858* (Murray, 1991)

Levey, M., *Sir Thomas Lawrence* (New Haven: Yale University Press, 2005)

Lilti, A., *The Invention of Celebrity*, trans. by L. Jeffress (Cambridge: Polity, 2017)

Lindsay, I. G. and M. Cosh, *Inveraray and the Dukes of Argyll* (Edinburgh: Edinburgh University Press, 1973)

Londonderry, Marchioness of, *Frances Anne: The Life and Times of Frances Anne Marchioness of Londonderry and Her Husband Charles Third Marquess of Londonderry* (Macmillan, 1958)

Luckhurst, M. and J. Moody, eds, *Theatre and Celebrity in Britain, 1660–2000* (Basingstoke: Palgrave Macmillan, 2005)

Luttrell, B., *The Prim Romantic: A Biography of Ellis Cornelia Knight 1758–1837* (Chatto & Windus, 1965)

McCreery, C., 'Keeping Up with the *Bon Ton*: The *Tête-à-Tête* Series in the *Town and Country Magazine*', in *Gender in Eighteenth-Century England: Roles, Representations and Responsibilities*, ed. by H. Barker and E. Chalus (Longman, 1997), pp. 207–29

McCreery, C., *The Satirical Gaze: Prints of Women in Late Eighteenth-Century England* (Oxford: Clarendon, 2004)

Macdonald, D. L., *Monk Lewis: A Critical Biography* (Toronto: University of Toronto Press, 2000)

McKendrick, N., 'Josiah Wedgwood and the Commercialization of the Potteries', in N. McKendrick, J. Brewer and J. H. Plumb, eds, *The Birth of a Consumer Society* (Bloomington: Indiana University Press, 1992)

McPherson, H., *Art and Celebrity in the Age of Reynolds and Siddons* (University Park, PA: Penn State University Press, 2017)

Mandler, P., 'From Almack's to Willis's: Aristocratic Women and Politics, 1815–1867', in *Women, Privilege, and Power: British Politics, 1750 to the Present*, ed. by A. Vickery (Stanford: Stanford University Press, 2001), pp. 152–67, 354–58

Mansel, P., *Louis XVIII* (Blond and Briggs, 1981)

Manvell, R., *Sarah Siddons: Portrait of an Actress* (Heinemann, 1970)

Marshall, P. D., *Celebrity and Power: Fame in Contemporary Culture* (Minneapolis: University of Minnesota Press, 1997)

Mason, N., *Literary Advertising and the Shaping of British Romanticism* (Baltimore: Johns Hopkins University Press, 2013)

Matoff, S., *Marguerite, Countess of Blessington: The Turbulent Life of a Salonnière and Author* (Newark: University of Delaware Press, 2016)

Mayne, E. C., *A Regency Chapter: Lady Bessborough and Her Friendships* (Macmillan, 1939)

Melville, L., *Regency Ladies* (Hutchinson, 1926)

Mole, T., *Byron's Romantic Celebrity: Industrial Culture and the Hermeneutic of Intimacy* (Basingstoke: Palgrave Macmillan, 2007)

Mole, T., ed., *Romanticism and Celebrity Culture, 1750–1850* (Cambridge: Cambridge University Press, 2009)

Morgan, M., *Manners, Morals and Class in England, 1774–1858* (Palgrave Macmillan, 1994)

Munby, A. N. L., *The Cult of the Autograph Letter in England* (Athlone, 1962)

North, J., *The Domestication of Genius: Biography and the Romantic Poet* (Oxford: Oxford University Press, 2009)

Pakenham, E., *Soldier, Sailor: An Intimate Portrait of an Irish Family* (Weidenfeld & Nicolson, 2007)

Parissien, S., *George IV: The Grand Entertainment* (Murray, 2001)

Parry, A., ed., *The Admirals Fremantle 1788–1920* (Chatto & Windus, 1971)

Pascoe, J., 'Ann Hatton's Celebrity Pursuits', in Mole, *Romanticism*, pp. 245–63

Patterson, C. B., *Angela Burdett-Coutts and the Victorians* (Murray, 1953)

Patterson, M. W., *Sir Francis Burdett and His Times (1770–1844)*, 2 vols (Macmillan, 1931)

Pearce, C. E., *The Jolly Duchess: Harriot Mellon, Afterwards Mrs Coutts and the Duchess of St Albans* (Stanley Paul, 1915)

Perkin, J., *The Merry Duchess* (Athena, 2002)

Pilbeam, P., *Madame Tussaud and the History of Waxworks* (Hambledon and London, 2003)

Postle, M., ed., *Joshua Reynolds: The Creation of Celebrity* (Tate, 2005)

Prucher, A., *Figure Europee del Primo '800 nel 'Diary' di Lady Charlotte Bury* (Florence: Olschki, 1961)

Rauser, A., 'Living Statues and Neoclassical Dress in Late Eighteenth-Century Naples', *Art History*, 38:2 (2015), pp. 462–87

Rauser, A., 'Vitalist Statues and the Belly Pad of 1793', *Journal18*, 3 (25 March 2017)

Reid, J. C., *Bucks and Bruisers: Pierce Egan and Regency England* (Routledge and Kegan Paul, 1971)

Ribeiro, A., *The Art of Dress: Fashion in England and France, 1750–1820* (New Haven: Yale University Press, 1995)

Richardson, R., *Coutts & Co., Bankers* (Stock, 1902)

Roach, J., *It* (Ann Arbor: University of Michigan Press, 2007)

Roberts, G., *The Angel and the Cad: Love, Loss and Scandal in Regency England* (Macmillan, 2015)

Roberts, R. E., *Samuel Rogers and His Circle* (Methuen, 1910)

Rojek, C., *Celebrity* (Reaktion, 2001)

Rosa, M. W., *The Silver-Fork School: Novels of Fashion Preceding 'Vanity Fair'* (Port Washington: Kennikat, 1964)

Ross, M., 'Scandalous Reading: The Political Uses of Scandal in and around Regency Britain', *Wordsworth Circle*, 27:2 (1996), pp. 103–12

Russell, C., Lady, *Three Generations of Fascinating Women* (Longmans, Green, 1904)

Sack, J. J., 'The Decline of the Grenvillite Faction under the First Duke of Buckingham and Chandos, 1817–1829', *Journal of British Studies*, 15:1 (Autumn 1975), pp. 112–34

Sack, J. J., *The Grenvillites* (Chicago: University of Illinois Press, 1979)

Sanders, L., *The Holland House Circle* (New York: Blom, 1969)

Schickel, R., *Intimate Strangers: The Culture of Celebrity* (Chicago: Dee, 2000)

Smith, E. A., *Wellington and the Arbuthnots: A Triangular Friendship* (Stroud: Sutton, 1994)

Smith, J. T., *Nollekens and His Times*, ed. by Edmund Goss (Bentley, 1895)

Solkin, D. H., ed., *Art on the Line: The Royal Academy Exhibitions at Somerset House, 1780–1836* (New Haven: Yale University Press, 2001)

Spring, D., 'Lord Chandos and the Farmers, 1818–46', *Huntington Library Quarterly*, 33:3 (May 1970), pp. 257–81

Stevenson, L., *The Wild Irish Girl: The Life of Sydney Owenson, Lady Morgan (1776–1859)* (Chapman & Hall, 1936)

Stowe, H. B., *Lady Byron Vindicated: A History of the Byron Controversy from Its Beginning in 1816 to the Present Time* (Sampson Low, Son, and Marston, 1870)

Strachan, J., *Advertising and Satirical Culture in the Romantic Period* (Cambridge: Cambridge University Press, 2007)

Sutherland, J., 'Henry Colburn: Publisher', *Publishing History*, 19 (1986), pp. 59–84

Throsby, C., 'Flirting with Fame: Byron's Anonymous Female Fans', *Byron Journal*, 32 (2004), pp. 115–23

Tillyard, S., '"Paths of Glory": Fame and the Public in Eighteenth-Century London', in Postle, *Joshua Reynolds*, pp. 61–69

Timbs, J., *Anecdote Lives of William Hogarth, Sir Joshua Reynolds,*

Thomas Gainsborough, Henry Fuseli, Sir Thomas Lawrence and J. M. W. Turner (Bentley, 1887)

Tomalin, C., *Mrs Jordan's Profession: The Story of a Great Actress and a Future King* (Viking, 1994)

Tuite, C., *Lord Byron and Scandalous Celebrity* (Cambridge: Cambridge University Press, 2015)

Turner, G., *Understanding Celebrity* (Sage, 2014)

Vincent, E. R., *Ugo Foscolo: An Italian in Regency England* (Cambridge: Cambridge University Press, 1953)

Wagner, T., 'Silver-Fork Legacies: Sensationalizing Fashionable Fiction', *Women's Writing*, 16:2 (2009), pp. 301–22

Wake, J., *Sisters of Fortune: Marianne, Bess, Louisa and Emily Caton 1788–1874* (Chatto & Windus, 2010)

Wanko, C., *Roles of Authority: Thespian Biography and Celebrity in Eighteenth-Century Britain* (Lubbock, TX: Texas Tech University Press, 2003)

Wanko, C., 'Patron or patronised?: "Fans" and the Eighteenth-Century English Stage' in Mole, *Romanticism*, pp. 209–26

Ward, J. A., 'Byron and the Discourse of Celebrity', *Prism(s): Essays in Romanticism*, 12 (2004), pp. 57–68

Wardroper, J., *Wicked Ernest: The Truth about the Man who was Almost Britain's King* (Shelfmark, 2002)

Webb, R., *Mrs D: The Life of Anne Damer (1748–1828)* (Studley: Brewin, 2013)

West, S., 'Thomas Lawrence's "Half-History" Portraits and the Politics of Theatre', *Art History*, 14:2 (1990), pp. 225–49

Wilson, C. A., 'Almack's and the Silver-Fork Novel', *Women's Writing*, 16:2 (2009), pp. 237–52

Wilson, C. A., *Fashioning the Silver Fork Novel* (Pickering & Chatto, 2012)

Wilson, F., ed., *Byromania: Portraits of the Artist in Nineteenth- and Twentieth-Century Culture* (Macmillan, 1999)

Wilson, F., *The Courtesan's Revenge: Harriette Wilson, the Woman who Blackmailed the King* (Faber and Faber, 2003)

Wilson Knight, G., *The Dynasty of Stowe* (Fortune, 1945)

Worrall, D., *Celebrity, Performance, Reception: British Georgian Theatre as Social Assemblage* (Cambridge: Cambridge University Press, 2013)

Zamoyska, P., *Arch Intriguer: A Biography of Dorothea de Lieven* (Heinemann, 1957)

Ziegler, P., *The Duchess of Dino* (Collins, 1986)

Index